Atlas Of The Nervous System

Including An Epitome Of The Anatomy, Pathology, And Treatment

Christfried Jakob
Edward D. Fisher

Alpha Editions

This Edition Published in 2021

ISBN: 9789354443237

Design and Setting By
Alpha Editions
www.alphaedis.com
Email – info@alphaedis.com

As per information held with us this book is in Public Domain.
This book is a reproduction of an important historical work. Alpha Editions
uses the best technology to reproduce historical work in the same manner
it was first published to preserve its original nature. Any marks or number
seen are left intentionally to preserve its true form.

EDITOR'S PREFACE.

THE translation of Dr. Jakob's "Atlas of the Nervous System and its Diseases" should prove of great value to the physician. The book is virtually divided into the Anatomy, the Pathology, and a Description of the Diseases of the Nervous System.

The plates illustrate this division most completely; and especially is this so in regard to the pathology. The exact site and character of the lesion are shown in a way which can not fail to impress itself on the memory of the reader.

I know of no work in which so much is compressed within so small a space. The book is comprehensive and practical.

EDWARD D. FISHER.

MARCH, 1901.

PREFACE.

DURING his term as assistant in the medical clinic of this city, Dr. Jakob devoted a great deal of time to the study of the normal and pathologic anatomy of the nervous system. As he is the owner of an extensive collection of histologic sections, prepared by himself according to the best methods of investigation, he is in a position to compile the present atlas for the most part from his own preparations. I am sure that any impartial critic will agree with me that the illustrations accomplish all that can be expected of illustrations. They present the actual conditions in the plainest and most intelligible manner possible, and illustrate very fully the numerous and important discoveries which have been made in the study of the nervous system. The student and the practising physician who is not thoroughly familiar with this branch of medical science can, with the help of this atlas, obtain a clear idea of the present state of neurology with comparatively little trouble. There is perhaps not another department of medicine in which the intimate connection between clinical pathology and normal and pathologic anatomy is so manifest and so constant as in neuropathology. The consistent treatment of the relations between the facts of normal anatomy and pathology, together with the fullness and attention to detail shown in the illustrations,—which, although not schematic, yet give a comprehensive view of the things they portray,—can not fail to be of the highest didactic value.

The author has devoted himself with untiring industry to the task of achieving a work of real and lasting value, and I heartily trust it may meet with the success which it deserves.

DR. STRÜMPELL.

AUTHOR'S PREFACE.

In the present volume I have endeavored to free an important branch of medicine—one that is admittedly regarded by the majority of students and practitioners in every department of our science as the least attractive, and which is, therefore, the least familiar—from the odium which unfortunately clings to it, by presenting the peculiarities of its normal and pathologic anatomy in an intelligible form.

It has been my object to help the student to understand the clinical pictures he sees in the clinics, and their underlying pathologic processes, and to enable the practising physician, who is naturally less familiar with the modern development of neurology, to grasp the significance of the more important recent discoveries.

I have, accordingly, made the fullest possible use of pictorial representation, and have kept all unnecessary details, especially those relating to the histology, in the background in the preparation of the explanatory text.

The illustrations in the main present the actual conditions rather than a diagrammatic version of them. Although the stained preparations were found to be indispensable, a number of fresh, unstained specimens were also utilized. It is to be remembered, however, that even the most faithful reproduction, such as that afforded by a photograph, can not take the place of actual dissection and examination of the fresh brain.

The reproduction of the specimens in lithographs and wood-cuts was done by competent workers under my constant supervision. The atlas is founded on the collection of specimens which I was able to gather during the years that I acted as assistant in the medical clinic in Erlangen.

To my former chief, Dr. von Strümpell, I am deeply indebted for his kindness in placing all the necessary material at my disposition, and for his amiable assistance in the elucidation of difficult questions, and I wish to seize this opportunity of once more expressing my sincerest thanks.

A word more in regard to the study of the plates: As the space devoted to the text was necessarily limited, it was, of course, impossible to give a minute description of the wealth of facts presented for study by the illustrations, and the descriptions, therefore, contain only the essential points. I do not, however, regard this altogether as a disadvantage, for I believe it will prove the means of supplying the necessary impetus to careful, independent study of the plates, and thus lead the student to form an independent opinion, which is the highest pleasure we enjoy in the pursuit of our science. I believe the material contained in the plates to be sufficient for this purpose.

CHRISTFR. JAKOB.

PREFACE TO THE SECOND EDITION.

THE illustrations, as well as the text of the present edition, have been carefully revised. The plates have been remodeled under my constant supervision, and new ones have been added, which have turned out so successfully that the atlas is now of decided value in scientific work. The number of pathologic specimens was also increased. The text, in view of the purpose for which it is intended, did not seem to call for many alterations; some passages have, however, been expanded, and the whole has been subjected to a general revision.

My thanks are due to the editor for his liberality in giving me all the assistance to make the volume as perfect as possible.

Since the publication of the first edition, translations into English, French, Russian, and Italian have appeared, and have received very favorable notices.

CHR. JAKOB.

BUÊNOS AIRES,
    Ospicio de las Mercedes.

LIST OF PLATES.

I. MORPHOLOGY OF THE CENTRAL NERVOUS SYSTEM.

PLATE
1. Brain *in situ*, seen from above after removal of the calvarium.
2. Right hemisphere after removal of the meninges.
3. Outer surface of right hemisphere.
4. Mesial surface of left hemisphere.
5. Base of the brain.
6. Horizontal section of the hemispheres immediately above the corpus callosum.
7. Schema of the ventricular system.
8. Horizontal section through the brain after the third ventricle has been exposed.
9. Horizontal section through the basal ganglia.
10. Brain-stem and rhomboid fossa seen from above.
11. Four coronal sections through the brain of a dog.
12. Coronal section through the brain-stem of man.
13. Coronal sections through the brain-stem. Parallel transverse sections through the medulla oblongata and spinal cord.
14. Sections of the spinal cord *in situ*.

II. DEVELOPMENT AND STRUCTURE OF THE NERVOUS SYSTEM.

15. Embryonal area.
16. Development of the brain.
17. Arrangement of the neurons.
18. Glia cells and ganglion cells.
19. The cerebral cortex.
20. A cerebral and a cerebellar convolution.
21. Cerebral convolutions.
22. Motor and sensory nuclei of cranial nerves.
23. Lateral view of medulla oblongata.
24. Nuclei of the motor peripheral neurons.
25. Fig. 1.—Transverse section through white substance of spinal cord.
    Fig. 2.—Section through a spinal ganglion.
    Fig. 3.—Cross-section of a peripheral nerve.
26. Figs. 1, 2.—Diagrammatic representation of the position of the cervical and lumbar enlargements.
    Fig. 3.—The central canal and adjoining structures.

12 LIST OF PLATES.

III. TOPOGRAPHIC ANATOMY OF THE NERVOUS SYSTEM.

PLATE
27. Distribution of the cranial and spinal nerves.
28. Fig. 1.—Frontal section through genu of corpus callosum and anterior segment of frontal lobe.
  Fig. 2.—Frontal section through head of caudate nucleus.
29. Fig. 1.—Frontal section through middle of septum lucidum.
  Fig. 2.—Section through anterior commissure.
30. Fig. 1.—Frontal section behind anterior commissure.
  Fig. 2.—Section through knee of inner capsule.
31. Fig. 1.—Section through middle of third ventricle.
  Fig. 2.—Section through central convolutions.
32. Fig. 1.—Section through pulvinar thalami.
  Fig. 2.—Section through parietal lobe.
33. Fig. 1.—Section through occipital lobe.
  Fig. 2.—Sagittal section through brain-stem.
  Fig. 3.—Sagittal section through brain-stem and corpus callosum.
34. Fig. 1.—Horizontal section immediately above the corpus callosum.
  Fig. 2.—Horizontal section through the center of the corpus callosum.
  Fig. 3.—Horizontal section immediately below figure 2.
35. Fig. 1.—Horizontal section through middle of optic thalamus.
  Figs. 2, 3.—Sections through base of optic thalamus.
36. Horizontal sections through subthalamic region and corpora quadrigemina.
37. Fig. 1.—Vertical section through anterior corpora quadrigemina and pulvinar.
  Fig. 2.—Section between anterior and posterior corpora quadrigemina.
38. Fig. 1.—Section through posterior corpora quadrigemina.
  Fig. 2.—Section through middle of pons.
39. Fig. 1.—Section through posterior extremity of pons.
  Fig. 2.—Section through nuclei of auditory nerve.
40. Fig. 1.—Section through right optic thalamus at level of middle commissure.
  Fig. 2.—Section through anterior corpora quadrigemina on left side.
41. Fig. 1.—Section through tegmentum behind posterior corpora quadrigemina.
  Fig. 2.—Section through nuclei of trigeminus.
42. Fig. 1.—Section through right tegmental region at level of nucleus cf facial nerve.
  Fig. 2.—Section through ventral nucleus of auditory nerve on left side.
43. Fig. 1.—Section through cerebellum and medulla oblongata.
  Fig. 2.—Section through medulla oblongata at level of glossopharyngeo-vagus nucleus.
44. Fig. 1.—Section through medulla at level of nuclei of tenth and twelfth nerves.
  Fig. 2.—Section through calamus scriptorius in medulla.
45. Fig. 1.—Section through nuclei in posterior columns.
  Fig. 2.—Section through medulla below the olives.
46. Fig. 1.—Section immediately above decussation of pyramids.
  Fig. 2.—Section through decussation of pyramids.
47. Fig. 1.—Section through spinal cord immediately below decussation of pyramids.
  Fig. 2.—Section through spinal cord at level of fourth cervical nerve.
48. Fig. 1.—Section through cervical enlargement at level of seventh cervical nerve.

LIST OF PLATES.

PLATE
Figs. 2, 3.—Sections through thoracic portion of spinal cord.
49. Fig. 1.—Section through thoracic portion of spinal cord.
Fig. 2.—Section through upper portion of lumbar cord.
Fig. 3.—Section through lower portion of lumbar cord.
50. Fig. 1.—Section through middle sacral portion of cord.
Fig. 2.—Section through cauda equina and conus medullaris.
Fig. 3.—Section through posterior root and spinal ganglion from lumbar portion of cord.
51. Fig. 1.—Transverse section through sciatic nerve at its point of exit.
Fig. 2.—Longitudinal section of a nerve bundle from sciatic nerve.
Fig. 3.—Transverse section of a nerve bundle from sciatic nerve.
Fig. 4.—Transverse section of a normal optic nerve and sheath.
52. The gray matter of the spinal cord.
53. Process of medullation in the fetal brain.
54. Schema of the most important nerve tracts from a clinical point of view.
55. Figs. 1, 2.—Formation of tegmentum and crusta from tracts of cerebral hemispheres.
Fig. 3.—Schema of optic nerve and oculomotor tract with their connections.
56. Fig. 1.—General view of the projection paths.
Fig. 2.—Schema of position of sensory nerve tracts.
57. Schema showing course of fibers in spinal cord.

IV. GENERAL PATHOLOGIC ANATOMY OF THE NERVOUS SYSTEM.

58. Fig. 1.—Section through cerebral cortex and meninges in epidemic cerebrospinal meningitis.
Fig. 2.—Cerebral cortex in tubercular meningitis.
59. Fig. 1.—Aneurysm immediately above corpora quadrigemina.
Fig. 2.—Caries of a vertebra.
Fig. 3.—Tumor on inner surface of dura.
60. Fig. 1.—Brain abscess.
Fig. 2.—Tubercle in the pons.
61. Fig. 1.—Chronic hydrocephalus.
Fig. 2.—Acute hemorrhagic encephalitis.
62. Fig. 1.—Subcortical cerebral focus after hemorrhage. Secondary degeneration.
Fig. 2.—Embolic softening. Secondary degeneration.
63. A to F.—Products of degeneration of nerve-cells and fibers.
Fig. 1.—Specimen of acute myelitis.
Fig. 2.—Specimen of acute neuritis.
Fig. 3.—Specimen of chronic sclerosis.
Fig. 4.—Specimen of chronic myelitis.
64. Diseases of the muscle-fibers.
65. Fig. 1.—Porencephalus, left hemisphere.
Fig. 2.—Hemorrhagic focus in crus cerebri.
66. Fig. 1.—Section through anterior corpora quadrigemina.
Fig. 2.—Section through medulla oblongata in a subject of hereditary tuberculosis.
Fig. 3.—Chronic progressive ophthalmoplegia.
67.
68. } Secondary degenerations of the crusta.

LIST OF PLATES.

PLATE
69. Secondary degenerations of the pons.
70. Secondary degenerations in the medulla oblongata.
71. Descending degeneration of pyramidal tract in spinal cord after a focal lesion of cerebrum.
72. Descending degeneration in spinal cord in diseases of the cord.
73. Ascending degeneration of spinal cord.
74. Ascending degeneration in cervical portion of cord and medulla oblongata.

V. SPECIAL PATHOLOGY OF THE SPINAL CORD AND OF THE PERIPHERAL NERVES.

75. Various forms of myelitis.
76. Syringomyelia.
77. Multiple cerebrospinal sclerosis.
78. Fig. 1.—Section through medulla oblongata in chronic bulbar paralysis.
    Fig. 2.—Section through lower cervical cord in amyotrophic lateral sclerosis.
    Fig. 3.—Section through anterior horn of cervical cord in spinal muscular atrophy.
79. Tabes dorsalis (thoracic and lumbar portions).
80. Tabes dorsalis (cervical region).
81. Spastic spinal paralysis.
82. Combined system diseases.
83. Degenerations of the peripheral nerves.
84. Multiple neuritis.

CONTENTS.

PART I.

Morphology of the Nervous System.
(PLATES 1 to 14.)

	PAGE
GENERAL ANATOMY:	
Membranes	1
Lobes and convolutions of the cerebral hemispheres	3
Interior of the hemispheres. Ventricular system	6
Optic thalamus and third ventricle	9
Corpora quadrigemina	12
Cerebellum and fourth ventricle	13
Pons and medulla oblongata	14
Spinal cord	15
Cranial nerves	17
Spinal nerves	18
Sympathetic system	19
Blood-vessels. Nerves	20

PART II.

Development and Structure of the Nervous System. Ontogenesis and Histology of the Nervous System.
(PLATES 15 to 53.)

THE PRINCIPAL CONNECTING FIBERS:	
Development of the medullary canal	22
Development of the brain	22
Spongioblasts and neuroblasts	25
Motor and sensory roots	26
Medullation	27
Histology of neuroglia, ganglion cells, axis-cylinders, and nerve-fibers	27
Neuron	28
Commissural fibers	30
Association fibers	30
Projection fibers	32

PART III.

Anatomy and Physiology of the More Important Nervous Pathways.

(PLATES 54 to 57.)

	PAGE
1. THE MOTOR PATHWAY:	
General description...	40
Motor cranial nerves...	43
Motor spinal nerves..	47
2. THE SENSORY PATHWAY:	
General description...	49
Spinal portion...	51
Cerebral portion...	53
Sensory cranial nerves and nerves of special sensation...........	59
3. THE REFLEX PATHS AND REFLEX ACTION............................	64
4. THE VOLITIONAL PATHWAYS.......................................	66
Function of the cortex. Association processes...................	67
The act of speech..	69
5. COORDINATION-PATHWAYS AND THEIR FUNCTION......................	73

PART IV.

General Pathology and Treatment of Diseases of the Nervous System.

(PLATES 58 to 72.)

1. The causes of diseases of the nervous system...................	75
2. Pathologic alterations in nervous diseases.....................	78
3. Symptomatology and topical diagnosis of nervous diseases.......	81
I. SYMPTOMS OF FOCAL DISEASES....................................	84
A. *Cerebral*...	84
Convolutions..	85
White matter..	87
Brain-stem (Optic thalamus, corpora quadrigemina)...........	88
Pons, medulla...	89
Cerebellum..	90
Base of the brain...	91
B. *Spinal*...	92
Unilateral lesions..	92
Cervical enlargement..	93
Thoracic region...	94
Lumbar enlargement..	94
Sacral region...	94
Cauda equina..	95
C. *In Lesions of the Peripheral Nerves*........................	95
Plexus paralysis..	96
Lesions of the cranial nerves...............................	96

CONTENTS.

	PAGE
Lesions of the more important spinal nerves	100
Disease of the sympathetic	103
II. SYMPTOMS OF SYSTEM DISEASES	103
4. General considerations on methods of examination and diagnosis	106
History and general condition of the patient	106
I. *Examination of the Motor Sphere*	106
1. Inspection and mensuration	106
2. Motor irritative symptoms	107
3. Motor power	107
4. Power of coordination	108
5. Electrodiagnosis	108
II. *Examination of the Sensory Sphere*	113
1. Subjective symptoms	113
2. Cutaneous sensation (tactile sense, temperature sense, etc.)	113
3. Deep sensation	116
4. Special senses	117
Sense of sight	117
Sense of hearing and of smell	118
Sense of taste	119
III. *Examination of the Reflexes*	119
General remarks	119
Cutaneous and tendon reflexes	120
Pupillary reflex	121
IV. *Examination of the Functions of Bladder and Rectum*	122
V. *Examination of Trophic and Vasomotor Disturbances*	123
VI. *Examination of the Psychic Functions*	124
Speech and writing	124
Memory	127
Psychic disturbances	128
Diagnosis and prognosis	128
5. General remarks on the treatment of nervous diseases	129
Prophylaxis	130
Curative treatment	130
Abstention cures	130
Syphilis, malaria	131
Surgical treatment	131
Symptomatic treatment	133
Psychic treatment	133
Physical (hygienic) treatment	134
Medicinal treatment	135

PART V.

Special Pathology and Treatment.

(PLATES 58 to 84.)

I. DISEASES OF THE MEMBRANES AND BLOOD-VESSELS OF THE BRAIN:	
1. Internal hemorrhagic pachymeningitis	136
2. Acute leptomeningitis	138
3. Tubercular meningitis (Plate 58)	138

CONTENTS.

	PAGE
4. Syphilitic or gummatous meningitis and brain syphilis	139
5. Thrombosis of the sinuses	140
6. Diseases of the arteries	141

II. DISEASES OF THE BRAIN SUBSTANCE:
  A. *Organic Diseases:*
    Circulatory disturbances and their consequences 141
      (*a*) Anemia and hyperemia 141
      (*b*) Cerebral hemorrhage 142
      (*c*) Brain embolism and thrombosis 145
      (*d*) Aneurysm 146
      (*e*) Arteriosclerosis 147
    Inflammatory diseases of the brain substance 147
      (*a*) Brain abscess 147
      (*b*) Acute encephalitis (Plate 60). Cerebral paralysis of children 148
    Brain-tumor (Plate 60) 149
    Internal hydrocephalus 151
    Paralytic dementia 152
    Ophthalmoplegia 154
    Bulbar paralysis 155
    Diseases of the cerebellum 156
  B. *Cerebral Diseases of Unknown Character and Localization (Cerebral Neuroses):*
    Neurasthenia 157
    Hypochondria 158
    Hysteria 158
    Traumatic neuroses 162
    Hemicrania and migraine 162
    Cephalalgia 163
    True epilepsy 163
    Eclampsia infantum 164
    Chorea minor (Sydenham's chorea) 165
    Chronic hereditary chorea (Huntingdon's chorea) 166
    Paralysis agitans 166
    Myotonia congenita 166
    Idiopathic tremor 166

III. DISEASES OF THE SPINAL CORD:
  A. *Diseases Caused by Focal Lesions Involving a Cross-section of the Cord:*
    Diseases of the spinal meninges 167
    Hypertrophic cervical pachymeningitis 167
    Syphilitic spinal meningomyelitis 168
    Compression myelitis (Plate 59) 169
    Acute and chronic myelitis (Plate 75) 172
    Syringomyelia (Plate 76) 174
    Hemorrhages in the central canal 175
    Multiple cerebrospinal sclerosis (Plate 77) 175
  B. *System Diseases:*
    Spastic spinal paralysis (Plate 81) 176
    Amyotrophic lateral sclerosis (Plate 78) 177
    Progressive spinal muscular atrophy (Plate 78) 177
    Neurotic muscular atrophy (Plate 83) 178
    Progressive muscular dystrophy (Plate 64) 179

	PAGE
Anterior poliomyelitis (Fig. 28)	180
Acute	181
Chronic	182
Tabes dorsalis (Plates 79 and 80)	182
Hereditary ataxia	185

IV. DISEASES OF THE PERIPHERAL NERVES:
  A. *Diseases of Single Nerves:*
    Etiology 186
    Diseases of the motor nerves 187
      Isolated palsies 187
      Isolated spasms (occupation neuroses) 188
    Diseases of the sensory nerves 189
      Neuralgias 190
  B. *Multiple Neuritis* 191
    Alcoholic, diphtheric, saturnine, etc. 192
    Infectious multiple neuritis (Plate 84) 193
    Infectious polymyositis 193

OTHER DISEASES OF THE NERVOUS SYSTEM THE NATURE AND SEAT OF WHICH ARE UNKNOWN:
  Basedow's disease 194
  Myxedema 195
  Acromegaly (Plate 83) 195
  Tetany 195
  Tetanus 196

PART VI.

General Remarks on Autopsy Technic and the Microscopic Examination of the Nervous System 197

Bibliography 202
List of abbreviations 203
Index 207

I.

MORPHOLOGY

OF THE

CENTRAL NERVOUS SYSTEM.

(Part I. of Text.)

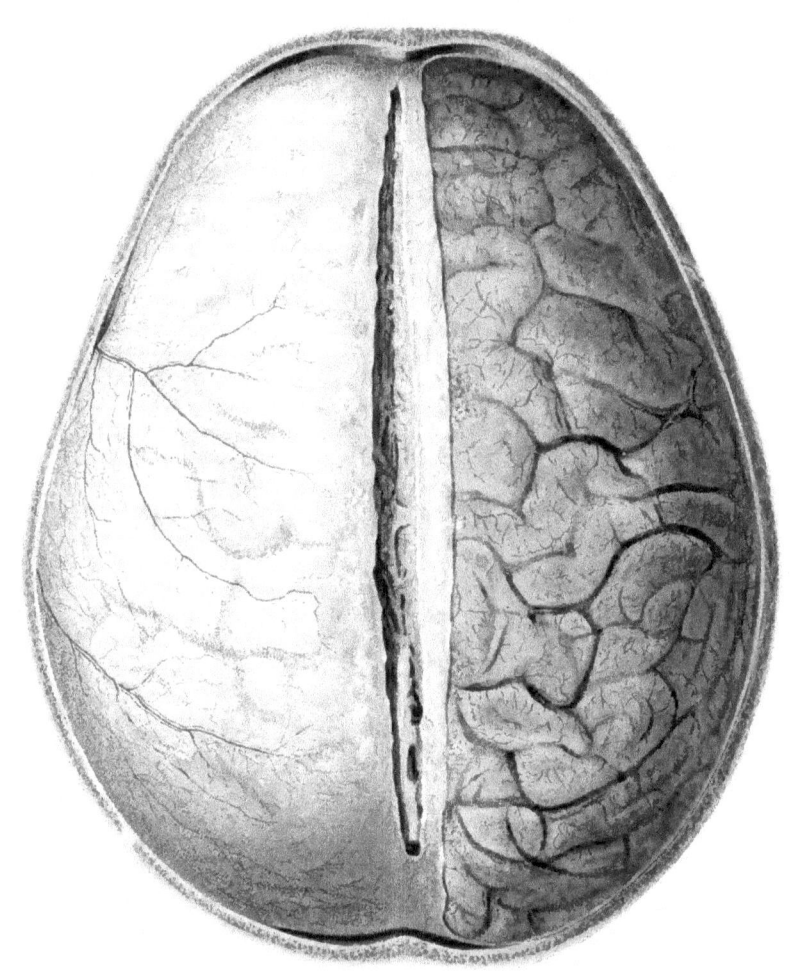

Tab. I.

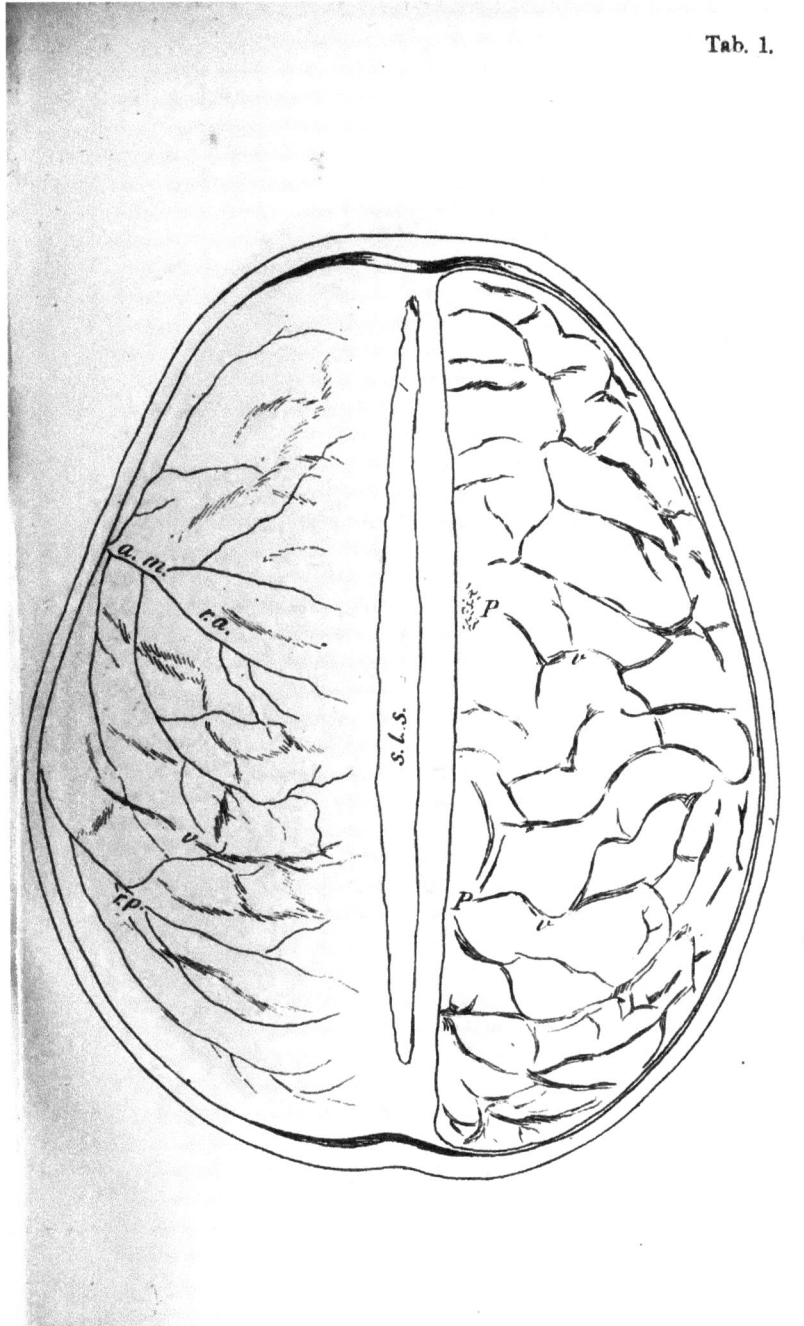

Tab. 1.

PLATE 1.

Brain in situ, Seen from Above after Removal of the Calvarium.

After the calvarium has been removed the brain is seen covered by the dura mater (left half of the plate). The engorged veins (v) in the pia-arachnoid are seen through the aponeurotic, glistening membrane, which appears tightly stretched. On the surface of the dura, lodged in bony grooves of the vitreous table, are the branches of the middle meningeal artery, $a.\ m.$ (ram. ant., $r.\ a;$ ram. post., $r.\ p$). The superior longitudinal sinus ($s.\ l.\ s$) is laid open.

On the right side the dura has been removed with scissors, and the convolutions on the convexity, covered by the pia-arachnoid, are exposed. The veins, which are always engorged (especially in the posterior portions), on account of the position of the body before the autopsy, empty into the longitudinal sinuses. On either side of the median line are the Pacchionian bodies (P), consisting of connective-tissue proliferations from the arachnoid, and covered with the arachnoidean endothelium; they are often abnormally developed, and produce marked depressions on the bones of the skull.

PLATE 2.
Right Hemisphere after Removal of the Meninges.

After the meninges have been removed with the forceps the convolutions (gyri) and fissures (sulci) of the hemispheres are exposed.

Frontal lobe: Superior, middle, and inferior convolutions; superior and inferior frontal fissures.

Central convolutions: Anterior and posterior central convolutions, divided by the principal fissure, or sulcus centralis of Rolando, which runs from above and behind, downward and forward. The junction of the frontal with the anterior central convolution is called the foot of the convolution (*pfs*, foot of the superior, *pfm*, foot of the middle, *pfi*, foot of the inferior frontal convolution).

Parietal lobe: Superior parietal lobule (subject to many variations), separated by the interparietal fissure (*ip*) from the inferior parietal lobule, the anterior segment of which is called the supramarginal gyrus, the posterior, the angular gyrus (*pli courbé*). The junction between the supramarginal gyrus and the posterior central convolution is similarly called the foot of the inferior parietal lobule.

Occipital lobe: Superior and middle occipital convolutions.

Abbreviations.—*P. F*, frontal pole; *P. O*, occipital pole; *pct*, postcentral fissure; *poc*, parieto-occipital fissure; *prci*, inferior precentral fissure; *prcs*, superior precentral fissure.

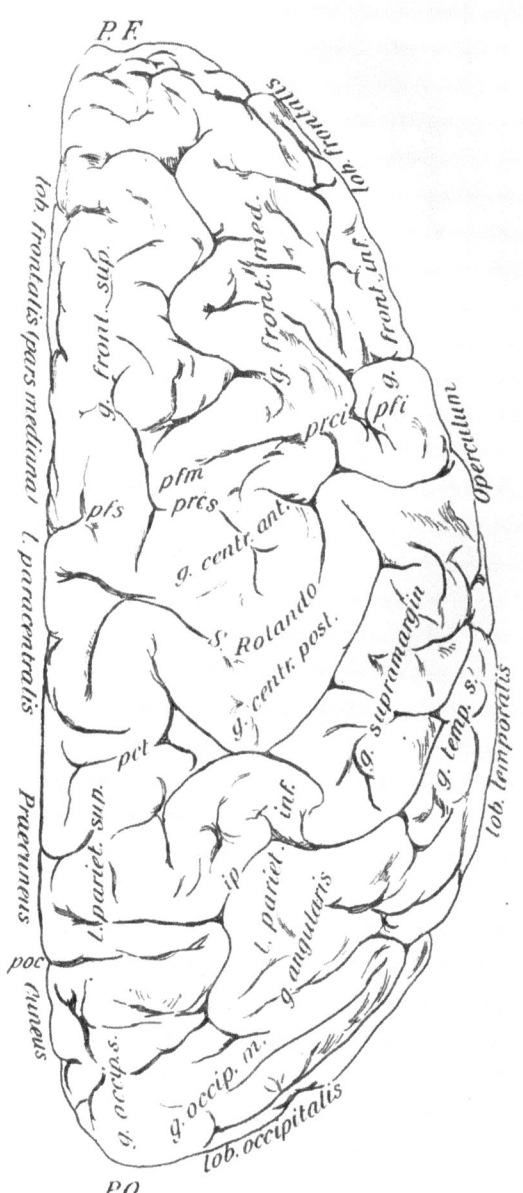

Tab. 2.

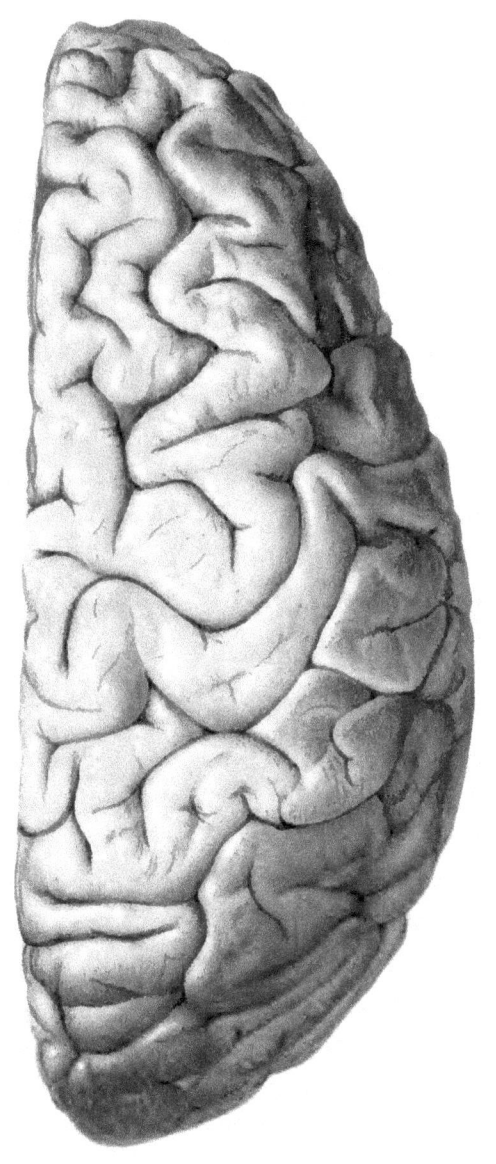

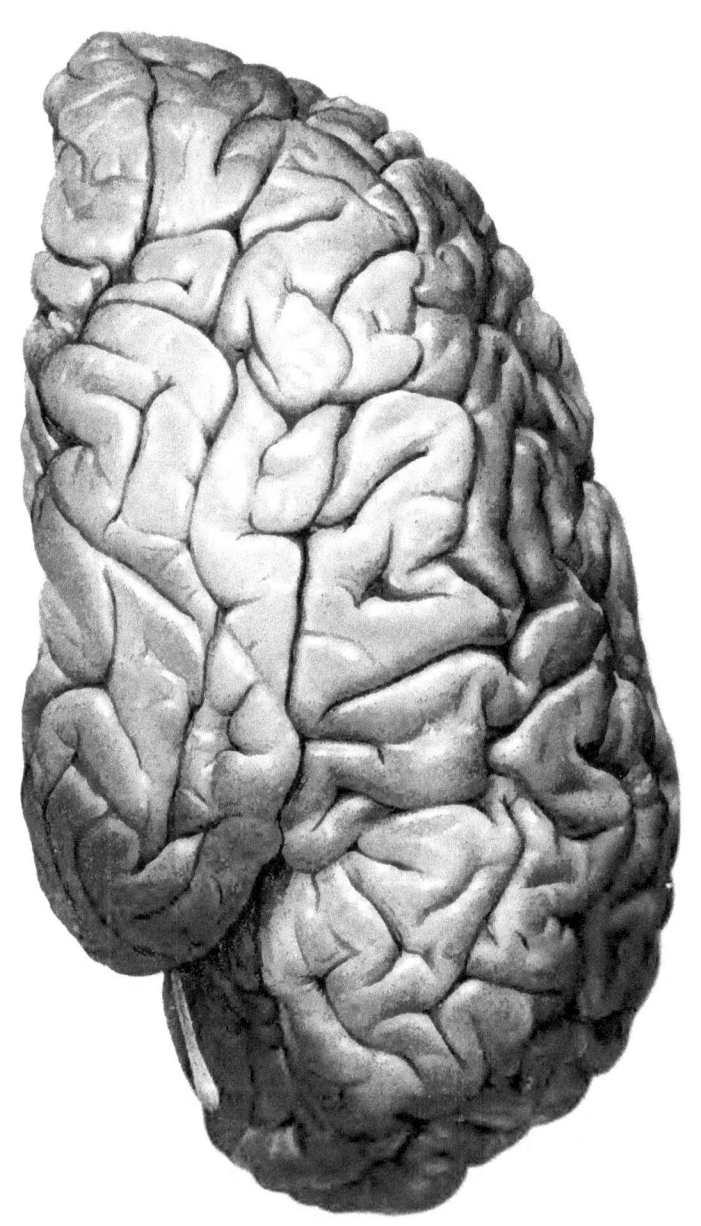

Tab. 3.

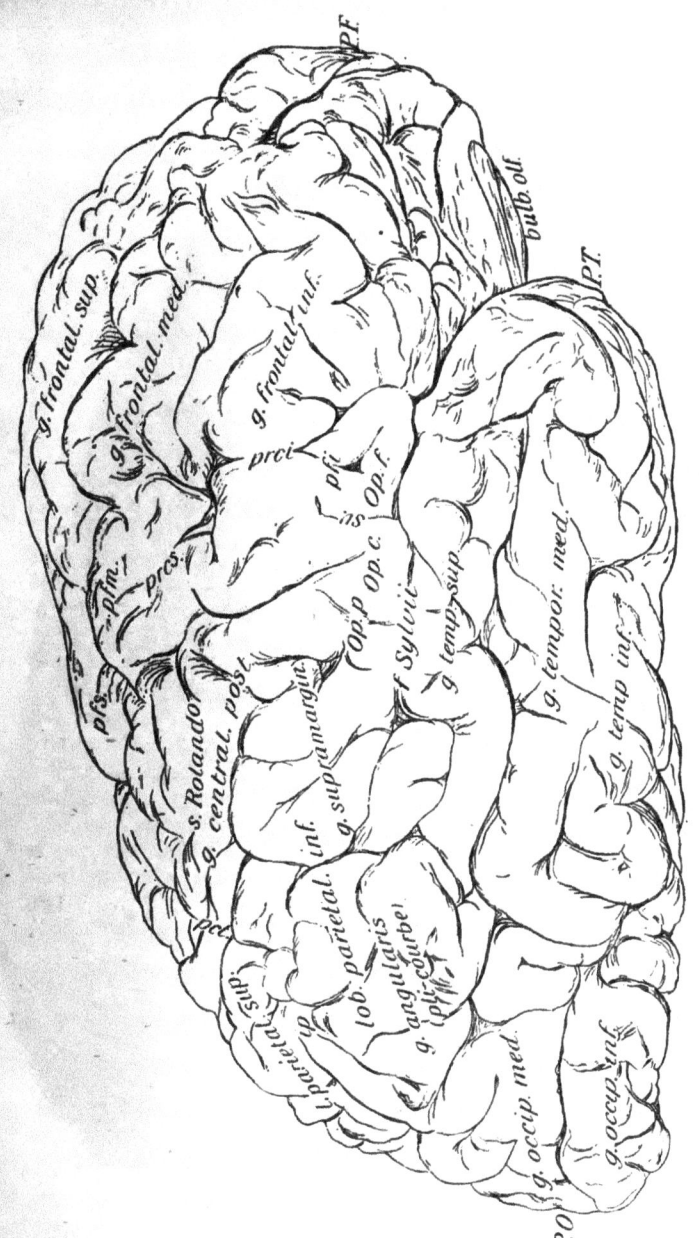

PLATE 3.
Outer Surface of Right Hemisphere.

The convexity of the hemisphere presents, in addition to the lobes described on plate 2, the temporal lobe, which is divided from the central convolutions and from the frontal lobe by the fissure of Sylvius. The temporal lobe contains three convolutions—the superior, middle, and inferior temporal convolutions. The figure shows also the inferior occipital convolution.

At the bottom of the fissure (or fossa) of Sylvius lies the island of Reil, covered by a group of convolutions collectively termed the operculum. The latter is divided into the frontal ($Op. f$), central ($Op. c$), and parietal ($Op. p$) operculum.

The olfactory bulb is lodged in a groove on the orbital surface of the frontal lobe.

Abbreviations.—*ip*, interparietal fissure; *pfs*, *pfm*, *pfi*, foot of superior, middle, and inferior frontal convolutions; *prcs*, *prci*, superior and inferior precentral fissure; *pct*, postcentral fissure; *sv*, ascending limb of the fissure of Sylvius; *P.F*, *P.T*, *P.O*, frontal, temporal, occipital pole.

PLATE 4.

Mesial Surface of the Left Hemisphere.

Outer group of convolutions: Superior frontal convolution, paracentral lobule, containing the terminal extremity of the fissures of Rolando (*s. Rol*), precuneus (parieto-occipital fissure), cuneus (calcarine fissure), lingula, and occipito-temporal convolution.

Inner or marginal group of convolutions: Gyrus fornicatus, bounded above by the callosomarginal fissure (*f.c.m*), gyrus hippocampi, and uncus.

Beneath the upper marginal convolution is the corpus callosum with its genu, rostrum (*r*), and splenium (*splen*); under the corpus callosum the fornix, and beneath this, the free mesial surface of the optic thalamus (*thalamus o*), which projects into the third ventricle (*v. iii*). After the septum lucidum, which is placed anteriorly between the fornix and corpus callosum, has been removed, the caudate nucleus (*n. caud*) is seen on the floor of the lateral ventricle.

Abbreviations.—*P. F, P. O, P. T,* frontal, occipital, and temporal pole; *a,* anterior commissure; *A. S,* aqueduct of Sylvius; *c,* corpus albicans; *Ch,* chiasm; *c. g,* corpus quadrigeminum; *g,* ganglion habenulæ; *H,* pineal gland; *i,* infundibulum; *is,* isthmus of gyrus fornicatus; *l,* lamina embryonalis ; *M,* foramen of Monro ; *m,* middle commissure; *Ped,* crusta (pes); *pla,* anterior, *plp,* posterior fold of gyrus fornicatus; *pa, pp,* anterior and posterior connecting gyri (plicæ) between the gyrus fornicatus and the precuneus; *t,* tænia thalami; *tc,* tuber cinereum; *teg,* tegmentum; *bulb. olf,* olfactory bulb; *tr. o,* olfactory tract; *tub. o,* olfactory tubercle; *N,* optic nerve; *gts, gtm, gti,* superior, middle, and inferior temporal convolutions.

Tab. 4.

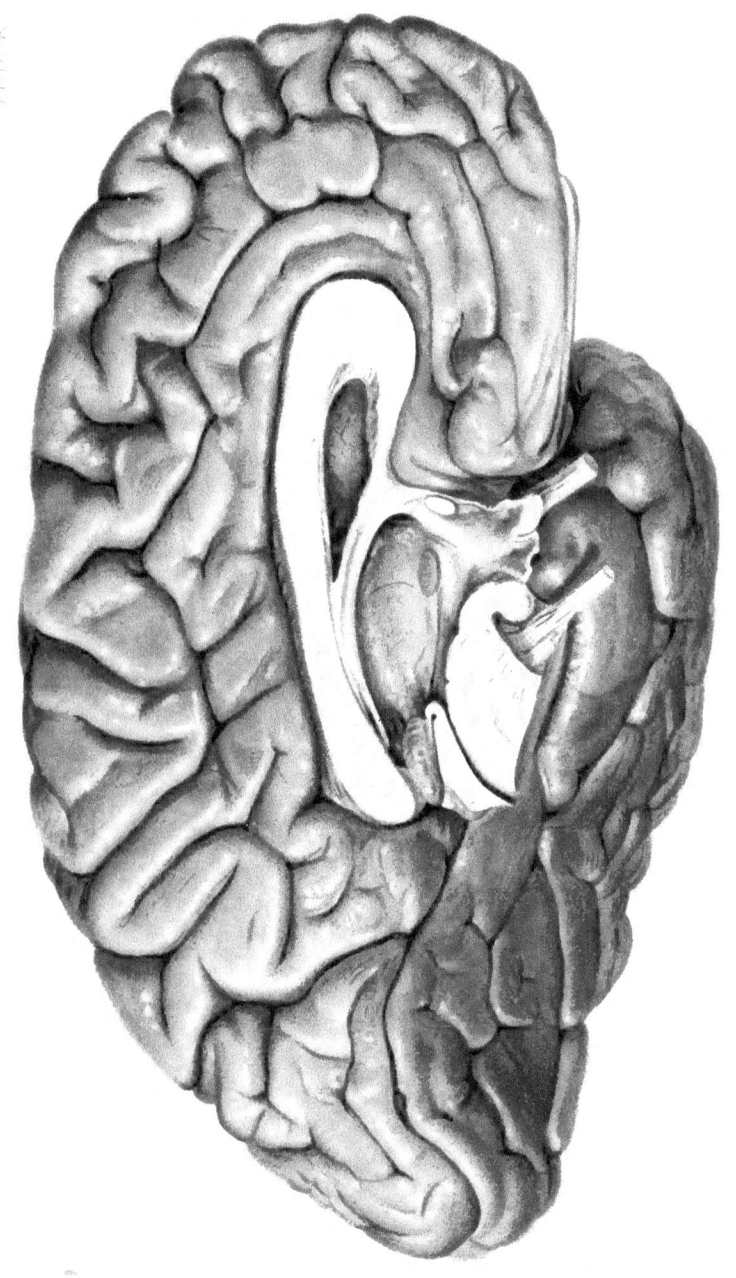

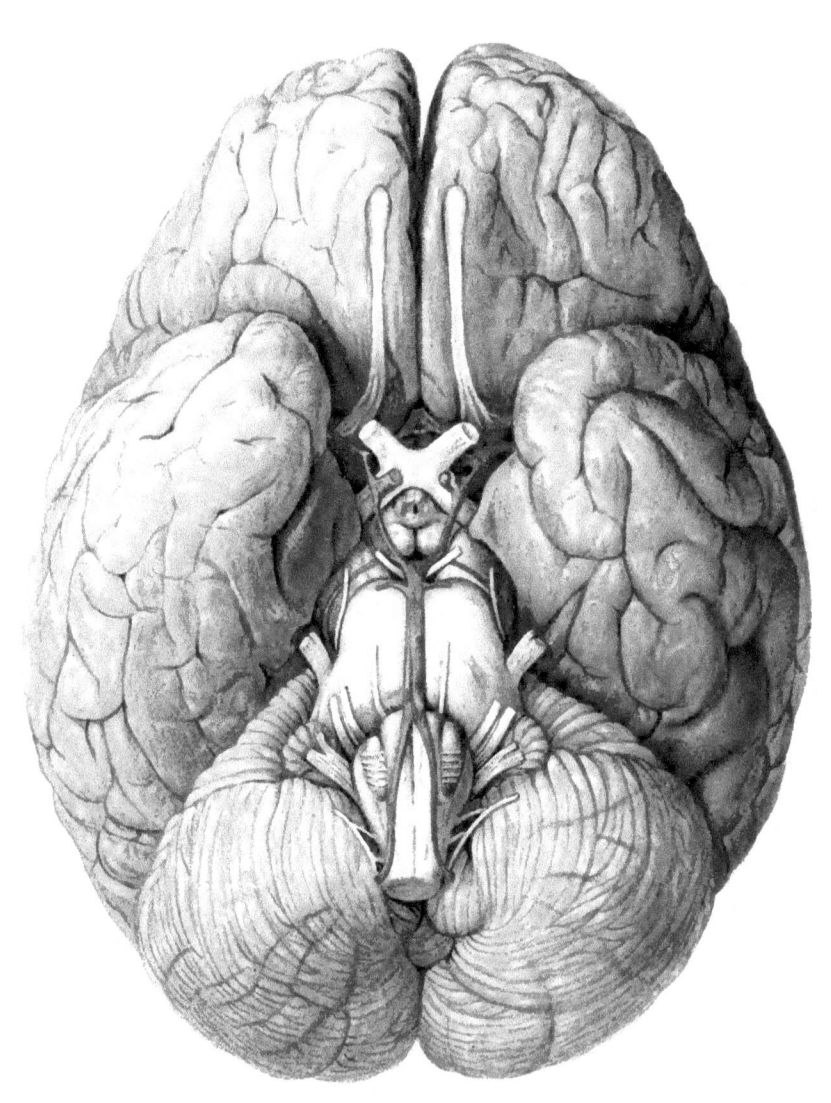

Tab. 5.

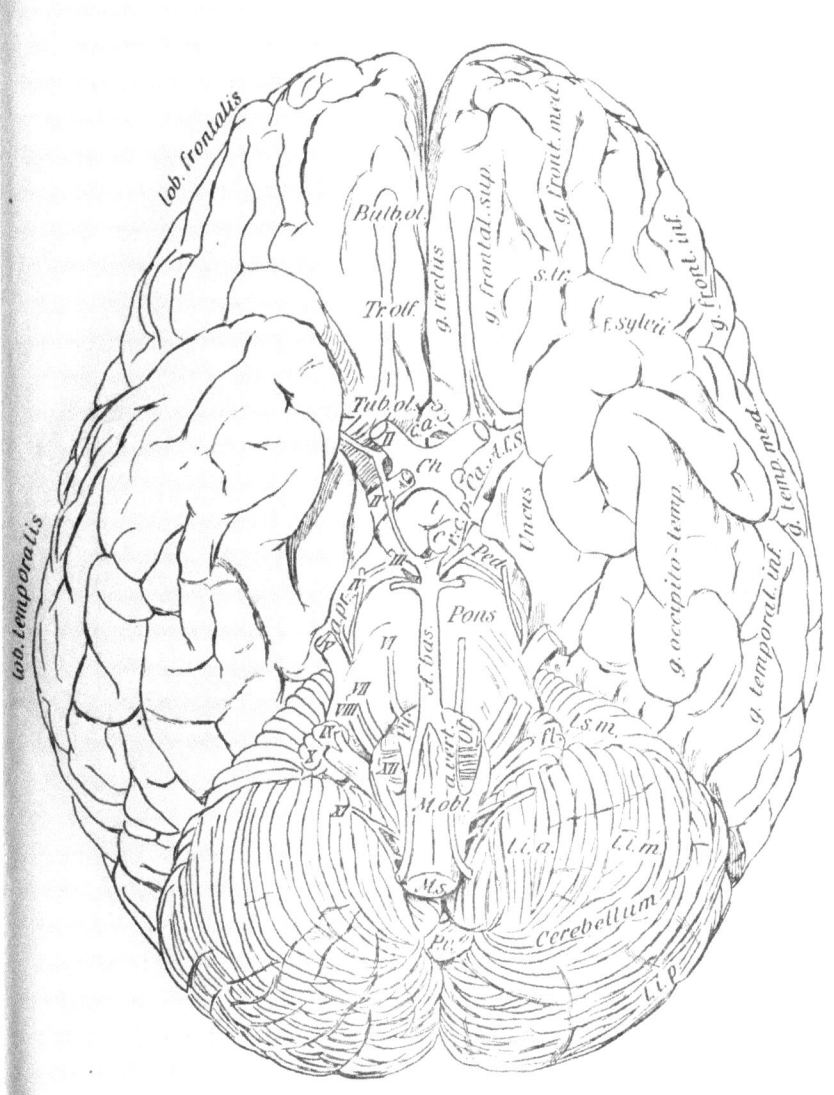

PLATE 5.

Base of the Brain.

Frontal lobe: Gyrus rectus, a part of the superior frontal convolution; middle frontal convolution (*s. tr*, triradiate fissure); inferior frontal convolution.

Temporal lobe: Uncus; occipitotemporal or falciform convolution; inferior temporal convolution.

Projecting from the interior of both hemispheres the converging crura (*Ped*), which disappear in the substance of the pons (*Pons*). Below the pons the medulla oblongata (*M. obl*) with the pyramid (*Py*) and olive (*Ol*). *Ms*, spinal cord.

The following portions of the *cerebellum* are seen: Lobus sup. med. (*lsm*); lob. inf. ant. (*lia*), medius (*lim*), posterior (*lip*); the flocculus (*fl*); and the pyramid of the inferior vermiform process (*Pv*).

Cranial nerves: Olfactory in the sulcus rectus, olfactory bulb, olfactory tract, tuber olfactorium. *II*, optic nerve; *Ch*, chiasm; *II'*, optic tract; *III*, oculomotor; *IV*, trochlear; *V*, trigeminus; *VI*, abducens; *VII*, facial; *VIII*, auditory; *IX*, glossopharyngeal; *X*, vagus; *XII*, hypoglossus; and *XI*, spinal accessory.

Arteries: Basilar, vertebral, internal carotid (*Ca*), art. profunda, art. fossæ Sylvii (*A.f.S*), *rcp*, ramus communicans post.; *c.a*, ramus communicans anterior; *c.c*, art. corporis callosi.

In the space bounded by the chiasm and converging crura the following structures are seen: Tuber cinereum (*t*), the process of which—the pituitary body—has been removed, and the corpus albicans (*c*).

PLATE 6.

Horizontal Section of the Hemispheres Immediately above the Corpus Callosum.

On the right-hand side the surface of the corpus callosum is exposed by a horizontal section. In front we see the genu (*g*); behind, the splenium (*spl*). The surface of the corpus callosum is marked by the longitudinal striæ, or nerves of Lancisi (*st. l. L*), by the rudimentary cortical convolutions, and by the chordæ transversales (*Ch. t*).

The following convolutions are included in the section: Superior (*fr. s*), middle (*fr. med*), and inferior (*fr. infer*) frontal convolutions; the central convolutions (*c. a, c. p*) with the fissure of Rolando (*s. R*) between them. The inferior parietal lobule (*par. i*) and its angular gyrus (*g. ang*); the middle and superior occipital convolutions (*oc. m, oc. s*); the cuneus (*cun*); the precuneus (*prc*); the gyrus fornicatus (*gf*); (*poc*) the parieto-occipital fissure.

The white substance of the hemisphere (centrum semiovale Vieussenii) shows the radiation of the corpus callosum (*rad. c. call*); the corona radiata (*cor. rad*); and the cingulum (*cg*).

The left side of the plate shows the body of the lateral ventricle (*cella media*). In it we see the caudate nucleus (*n. caud*); stria cornea (*str. c*); the lateral segment of the optic thalamus (*thal. o*); the lateral choroid plexus (*pl. ch. l*); and the fornix, the posterior extremity of which disappears in the descending horn, while its anterior portion joins the corpus callosum.

Tab. 6.

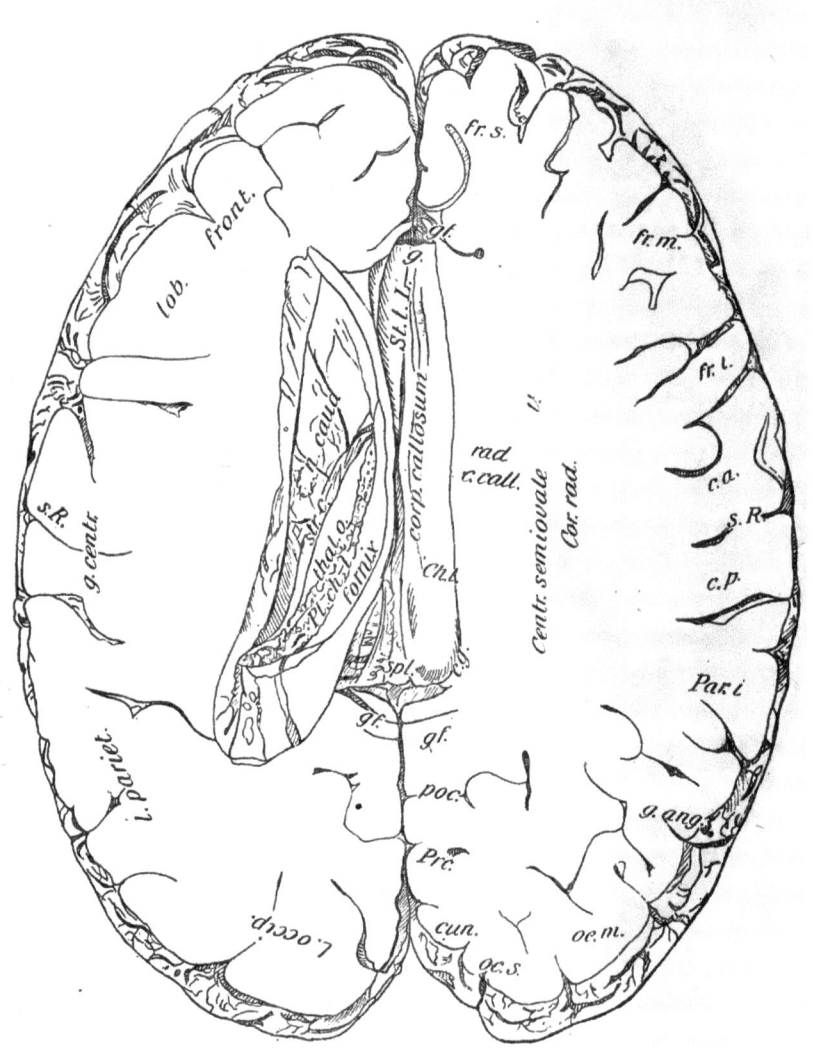

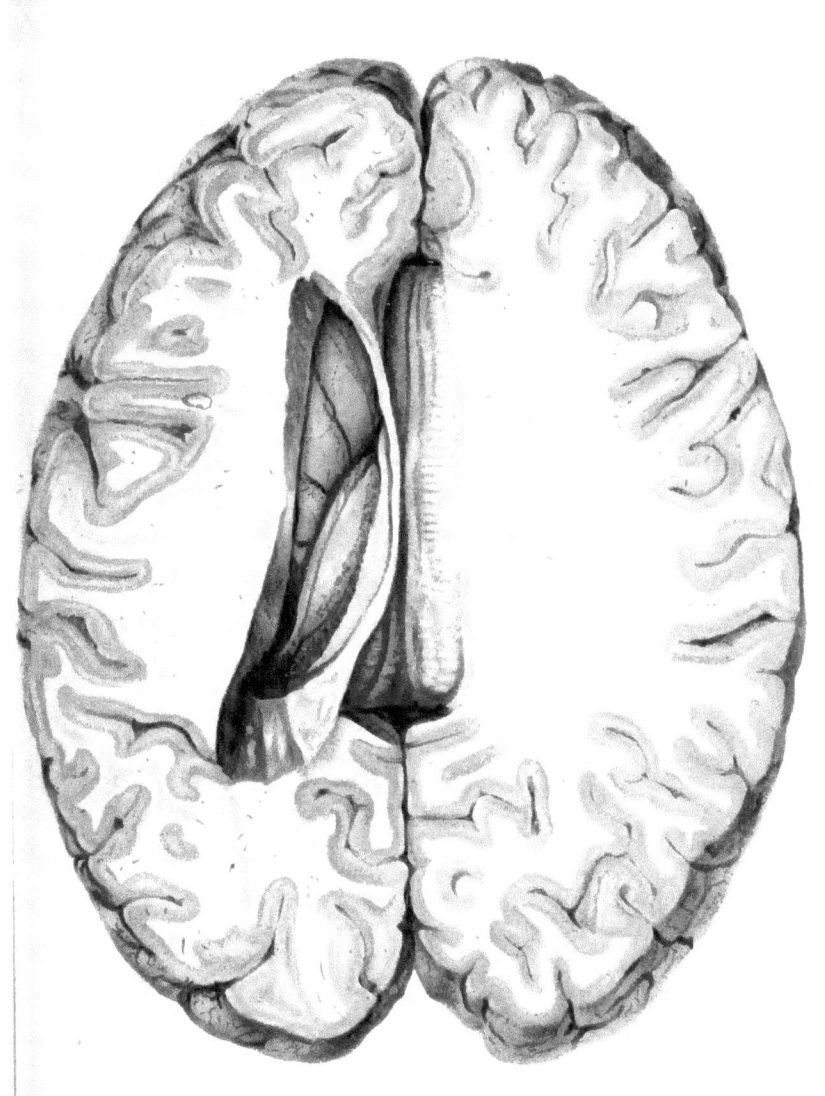

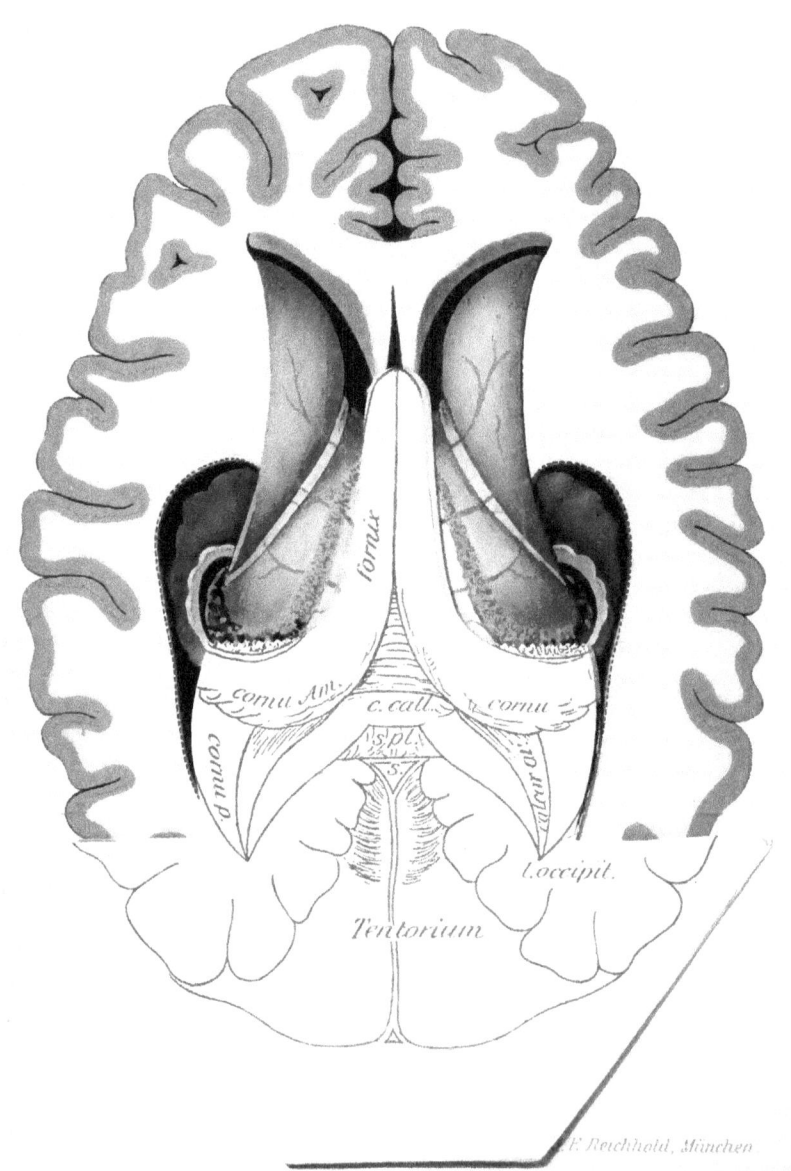

Tab. 2.

Tab. 7.

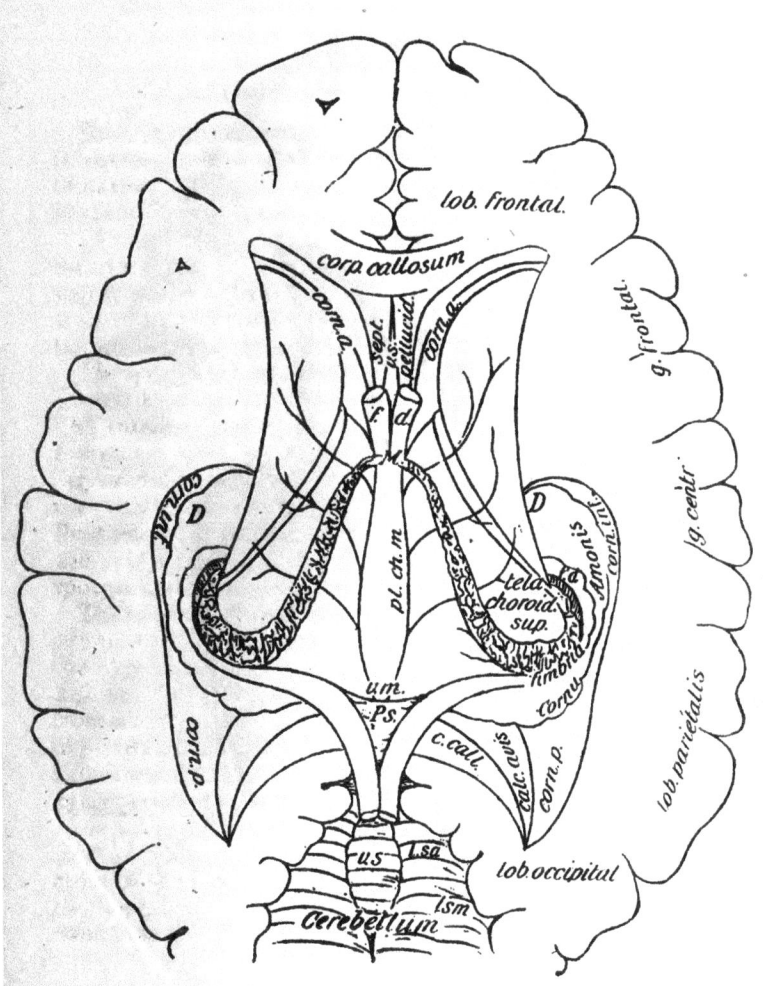

Tab. 7.

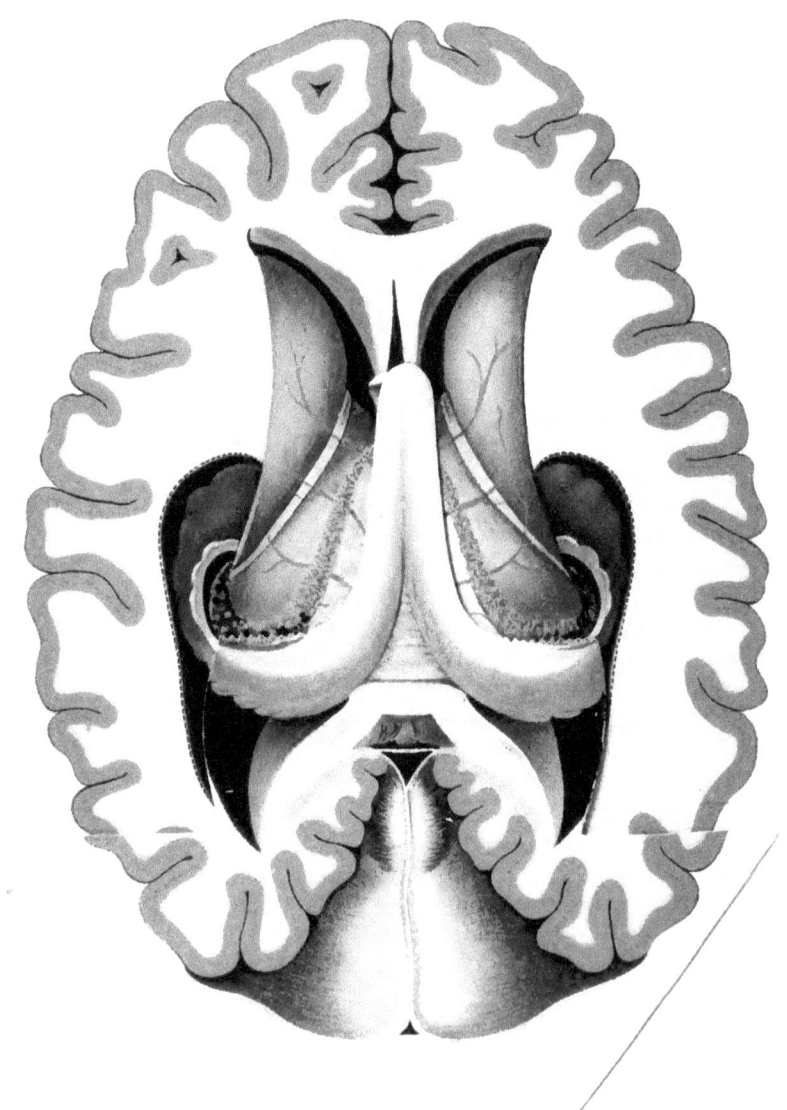

Tab. 7.

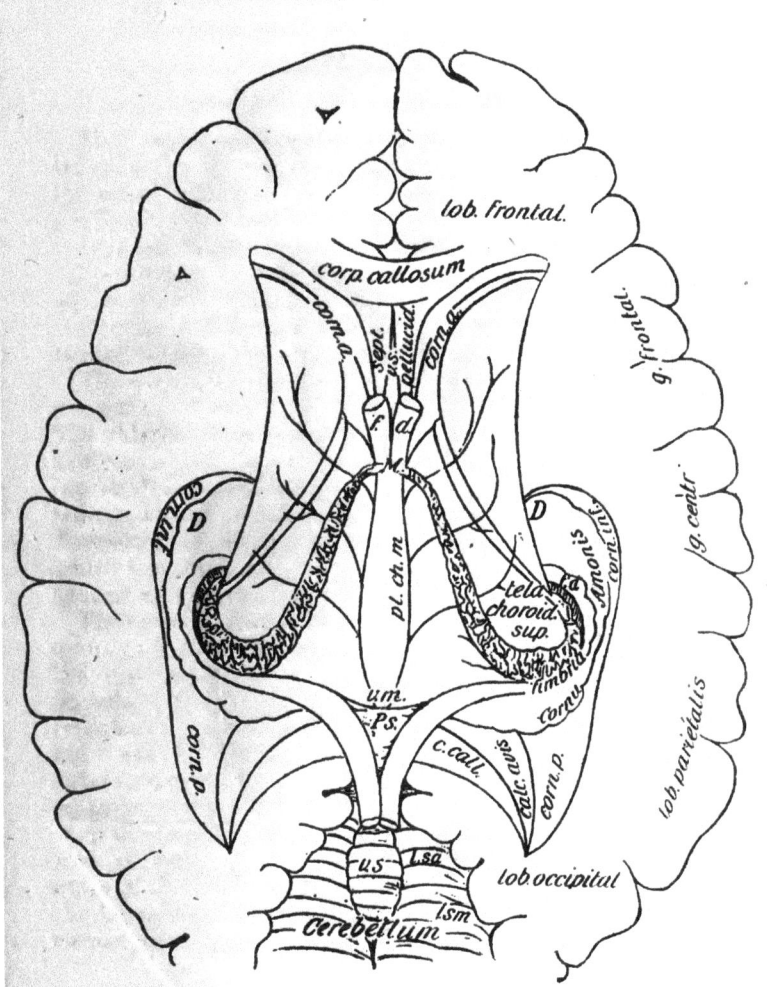

Tab. 7.

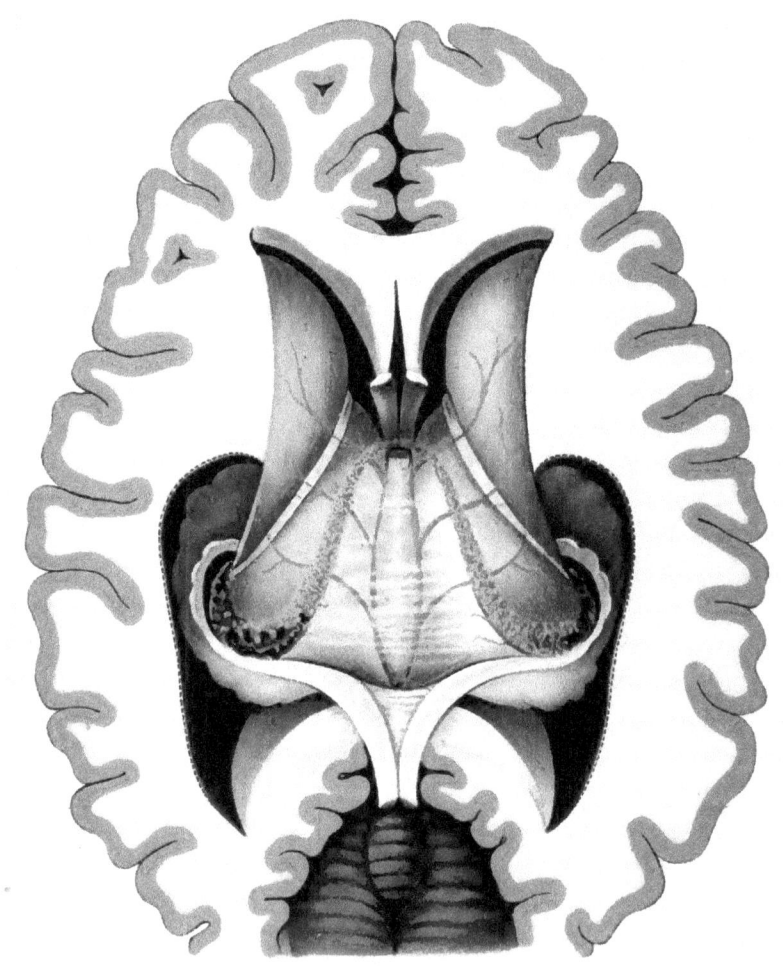

Lith. Anst. F. Reichhold, München.

Tab. 7.

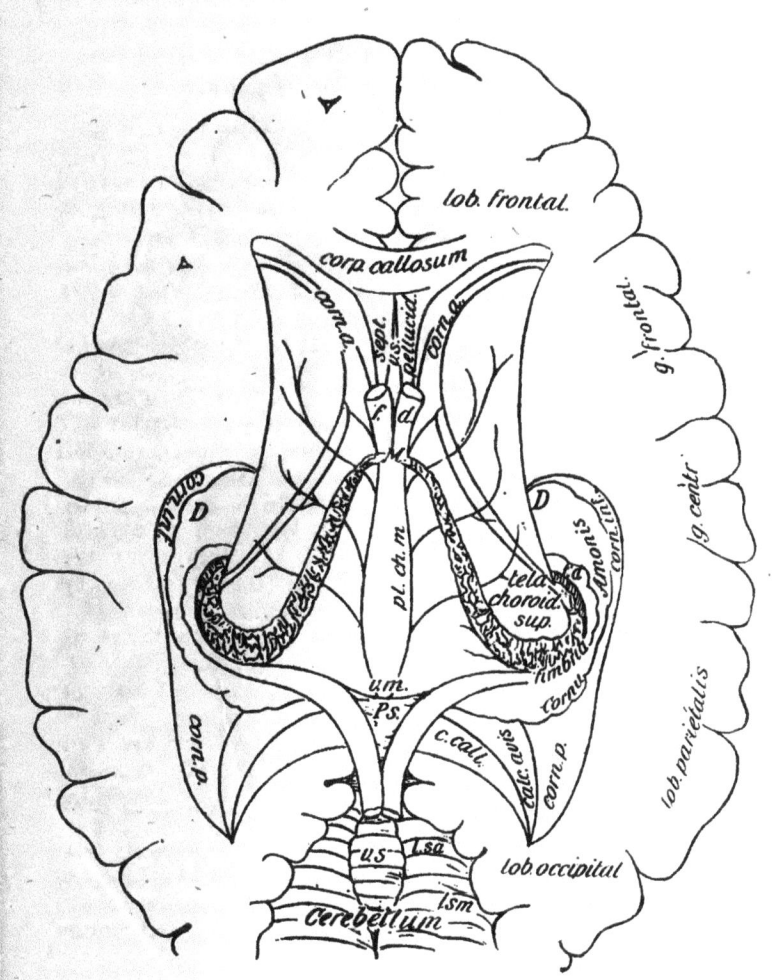

PLATE 7.

Schema of the Ventricular System.

The corpus callosum (*c. call*) has been divided through the genu, or anterior descending portion, and through the thickened posterior fold, or splenium, exposing in the median line the fornix and its two crura.

In front the interval between the genu of the corpus callosum and the most anterior segment of the fornix, which is also reflected downward to the base of the brain, is filled by two narrow bands (the septum lucidum) containing between them the fifth ventricle (*v.s*).

The section through the lateral ventricle has been made at a lower level, so that the following structures are exposed: The anterior cornu (*corn. a*) in the frontal lobe, the posterior cornu (*corn. p*) in the occipital lobe, and the descending or inferior cornu (*corn. i*) in the substance of the temporal lobe, which is here assumed to be transparent. Between the diverging occipital lobes is seen the tentorium, which is a process of the dura mater and covers the hemispheres and vermiform process of the cerebellum.

The ascending crura of the fornix arise in the descending cornu at the free border of a thickened fold in that region, the cornu ammonis (*c. Am*), where they are known as the fimbria; (*f. d*) fascia dentata; if the crura are divided in front and the entire fornix reflected backward, the descending crura of the fornix (*f.d*) are seen descending into the substance of the brain. Beneath the fornix a delicate vascular process of the pia mater, the tela choroidea superior, with the two cord-like choroid plexuses, is seen. The choroid plexuses pass immediately behind the descending crura of the fornix and enter the lateral ventricles through the foramina of Monro, and thence pass into the inferior cornua as the plexus choroidei laterales.

PLATE 8.

Horizontal Section through the Brain after the Third Ventricle Has Been Exposed.

(The section is deeper on the right than on the left.)

After the choroid plexuses of the ascending crura of the fornix (f) have been removed and the cornu ammonis divided, the cavity of the third ventricle, bounded on either side by the optic thalamus, is exposed.

On the left side is the free surface of the caudate nucleus (the caput is in the anterior horn, the tail extends outward toward the posterior horn). The caudate nucleus is separated from the optic thalamus by the narrow stria cornea ($str. c$). The anterior portion of the optic thalamus is known as the tuberculum anticum ($t. a$), its posterior projecting extremity is called the pulvinar (Pul).

In front of the descending crura of the fornix ($f. d$), at a deeper level, is the anterior commissure; behind this, in the middle of the third ventricle, the middle commissure ($c. m$); and in the posterior extremity of the ventricle, the posterior commissure (p). Immediately above the posterior commissure the tænia thalami (t), which forms the mesial border of the optic thalamus, unites with the corresponding structure of the other side. Immediately behind this is the pineal gland (E) (epiphysis), flanked by the ganglion habenulæ (h). Behind the optic thalamus are the anterior and posterior corpora quadrigemina ($qa. qp$). Behind the latter is the cerebellum (Cb), which has been divided near the surface, showing the superior vermiform process ($v. s$) in the middle and the hemispheres to either side (central white matter and peripheral cortical gray matter). lsa, lsm, lsp, lobus sup. ant., med., post.; cd, corpus dentatum.

On the right side of the plate the caput and tail of the caudate nucleus ($n. c$) are seen in transverse section. The convex middle portion has been removed. We see also the optic thalamus in cross-section, the uppermost layer having been removed (a, anterior, m, mesial, l, lateral nucleus of the optic thalamus). Laterally from the optic thalamus the lenticular nucleus ($n. l$), which with the caudate nucleus forms the corpus striatum, makes its appearance. The area of white substance to the inner side of the lenticular nucleus is known as the internal capsule ($c. i$); that on the outer side, as the external capsule ($c. e$); the internal capsule is divided into three portions: The anterior and posterior limbs (cia and cip), between them the genu (g), and the most posterior segment, the caps. int. retrolenticularis ($cirl$).

Convolutions. (See Plate 6.)

$Op fr, Op c$, frontal and central operculum; ca, anterior horn, ci, posterior horn of the ventricle; c, tail-piece of caudate nucleus; fli, inferior longitudinal bundle; spl, splenium; s, stria cornea; tap, tapetum.

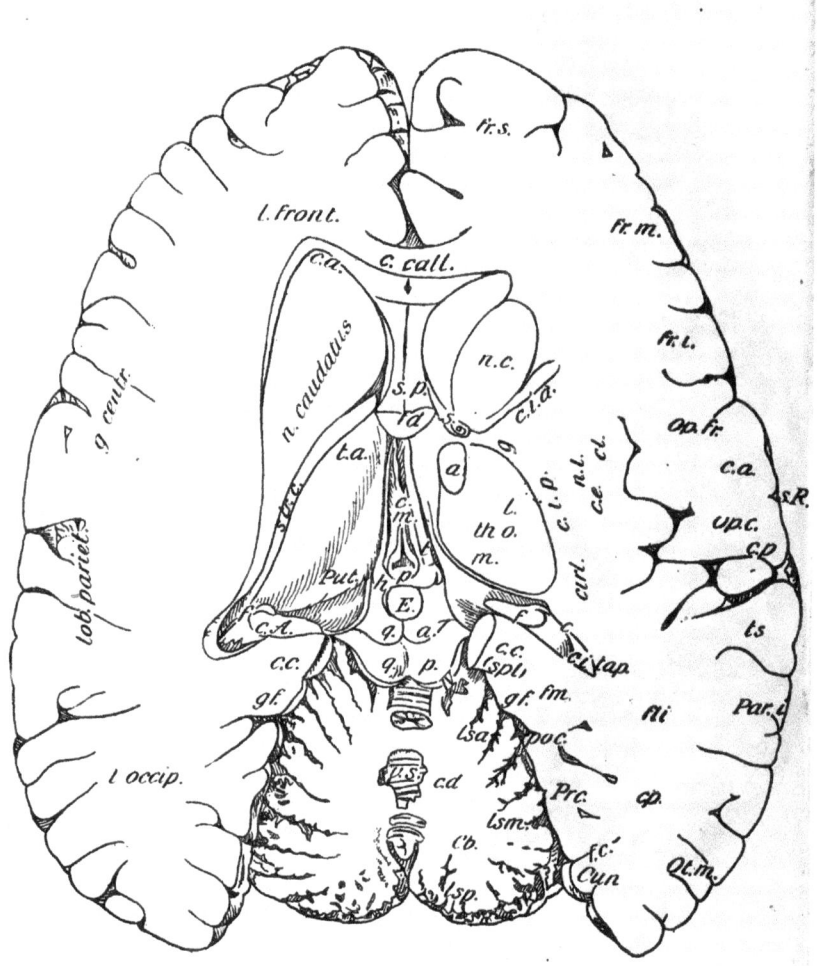

Tab. 8.

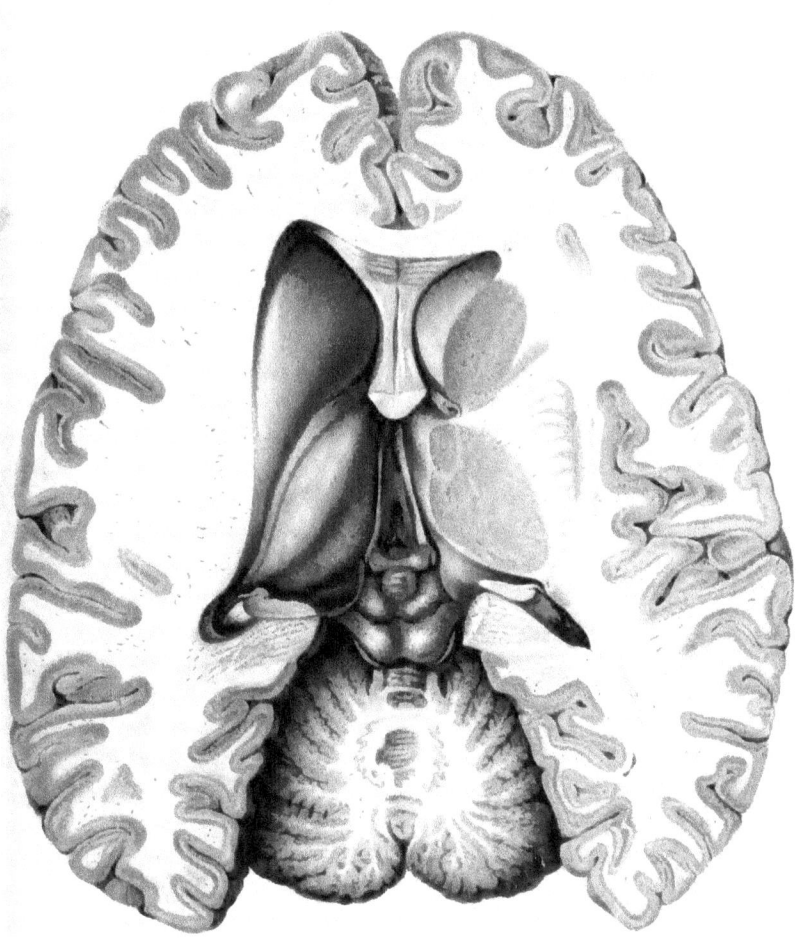

Tab. 9.

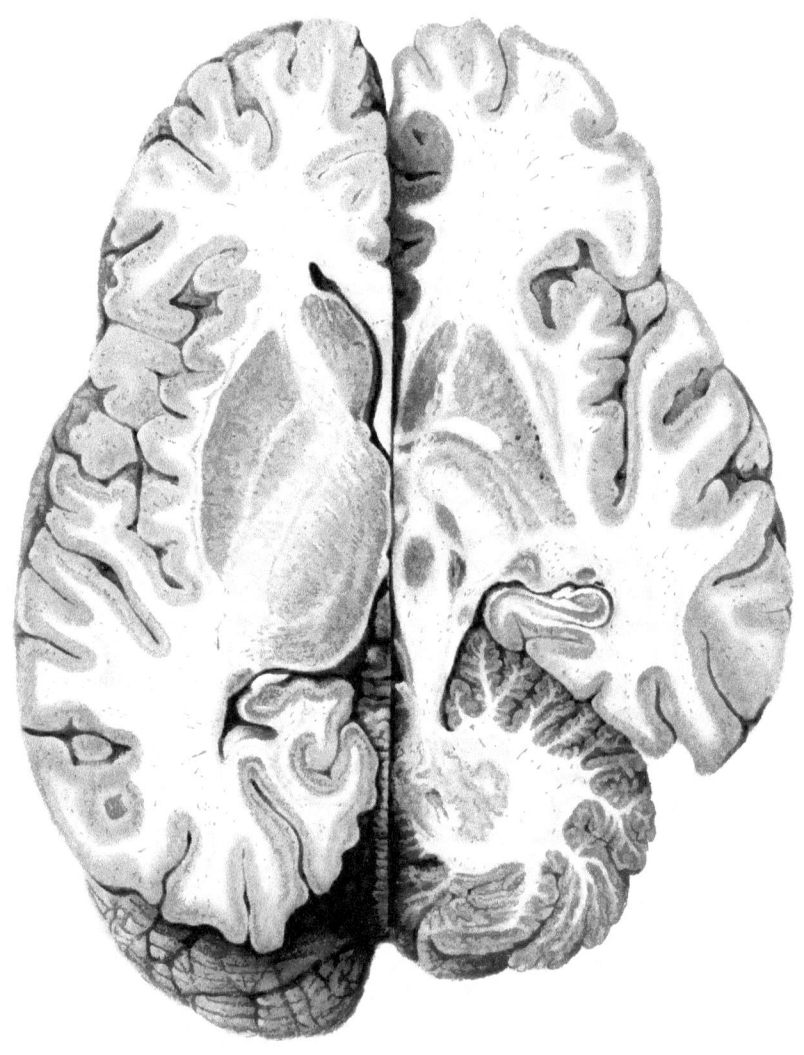

Lith. Anst. F. Reichhold, München.

Tab. 9.

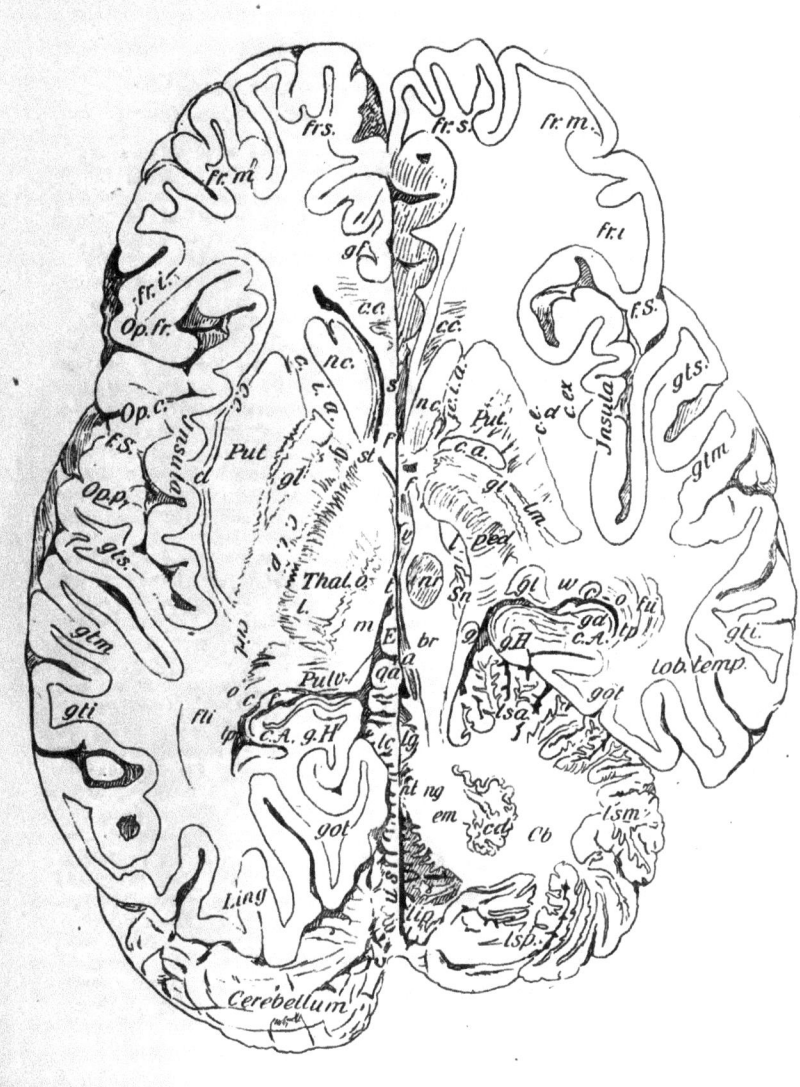

PLATE 9.
Horizontal Section through the Basal Ganglia.
(The level of the section is deeper on the right than on the left.)

On the *left* side (which represents a deeper level than the right half of plate 8), the following structures are seen in transverse section: Frontal lobe, central convolutions, temporal and occipital lobes; at the bottom of the fissure of Sylvius (*f. S*) the convolutions of the island of Reil (*ins*).

The white matter between the lenticular nucleus (*Put*) and the caudate nucleus (*nc*) is called the anterior limb (*c. i. a*), that between the lenticular nucleus (*gl*) and the optic thalamus the posterior limb of the internal capsule (*c. i. p*); the point where the two are joined is known as the knee of the capsule (*g*); its most posterior segment, as the caps. retrolenticularis (*cirl*).

Laterally from the external capsule and close to the convolutions of the insula is the claustrum (*cl*).

The lenticular nucleus is divided into an outer segment—putamen (*Put*)—and several inner segments—globus pallidus (*gl*).

The *right* side shows a broader section of the lenticular nucleus; the optic thalamus has disappeared and in its place we see the subthalamic region containing the red nucleus (*n. r*) and subthalamic body (*l*). The limbs of the capsule have separated; the posterior limb is now converted into the crusta or pes (*ped*). To the outer side are seen the lateral (*g. l*) and median (*g*) geniculate bodies.

Embedded in the white matter of the cerebellum are seen the dentate body (*c. d*) and the tegmental nucleus (*nt*). To the right of the median line (behind *a*) the fourth ventricle appears under the vermiform process; the brachium (*br*) connects the region of the corpora quadrigemina with the cerebellum.

Abbreviations.—(For the convolutions see Plate 6.) *Op. fr, Op. c, Op. p*, frontal, central, and parietal operculum; *gto, gtm, gti*, superior, middle, and inferior temporal convolutions; *got*, occipitotemporal convolution; *gH*, gyrus hippocampi; *c. A*, cornu ammonis; *gd*, gyrus dentatus; *ling*, lingula; *a*, central gray matter of the aqueduct of Sylvius; *c*, tail-piece of caudate nucleus; *cc*, corpus callosum; *ce*, external capsule; *c ex*, capsula extrema; *E*, pineal gland; *em*, embolus; *f*, fornix; *fli*, inf. long. bundle; *fu*, fasciculus uncinatus; *l*, lateral nucleus of optic thalamus; *lip*, inferior posterior lobule; *lsa, lsm, lsp*, superior anterior, middle, and posterior lobule; *m*, mesial nucleus of optic thalamus; *lm*, lamina medullaris (tænia semicircularis); *ng*, nucleus globosus; *o*, optic radiation; *ga*, corpus quadrigeminum anterius; *s*, septum lucidum; *su*, substantia nigra; *st*, stria (lamina) cornea; *t*, tænia thalami; *tp*, tapetum; *v*, bundle of Vicq d'Azyr; *vs*, superior vermiform process; *w*, Wernicke's field.

PLATE 10.

Brain-stem and Rhomboid Fossa Seen from Above.

The vermiform process of the cerebellum is divided by a sagittal section, exposing the fourth ventricle. The floor of the ventricle is formed by the rhomboid fossa, which contains the ala cinerea (a), calamus scriptorius (c), and funiculi teretes ($f.\ t$). Locus cœruleus (lc); posteriorly on either side are the restiform bodies ($c.\ rst$) and the tuberculum acusticum (ta). At the entrance of the aqueduct of Sylvius, covered by the anterior medullary velum ($v.\ a$), and frenulum (f), is the trochlear nerve (IV).

In front of the rhomboid fossa are the corpora quadrigemina anterius (qa) and posterius (qp), and the median geniculate body (gm), which receives the posterior brachium (brp). In front of the corpora quadrigemina are the optic thalami ($thal.\ opt$), the posterior segment of which has received the name pulvinar ($Pulv$), and between them the ganglion habenulæ (h) and the tænia thalami (t). The pineal gland has been removed from its pedicle. Third ventricle (III).

Behind the rhomboid fossa are the nuclei of the columns of Goll ($f.\ G$) and Burdach ($f.\ B$); the lateral column of the spinal cord ($f.\ l$); the nuclei of the columns of Goll unite above to form the clavæ (cl).

Abbreviations.—In the vermiform process of the cerebellum: lc, lobulus centralis; Cu, culmen; Dc, declive; Fc, folia cacuminis; Cb, commissura brevis; Py, pyramis; U, uvula; No, nodulus; lsp, superior posterior lobule; lip, lim, lia, inferior, posterior, middle, and anterior lobule.

Tab. 10.

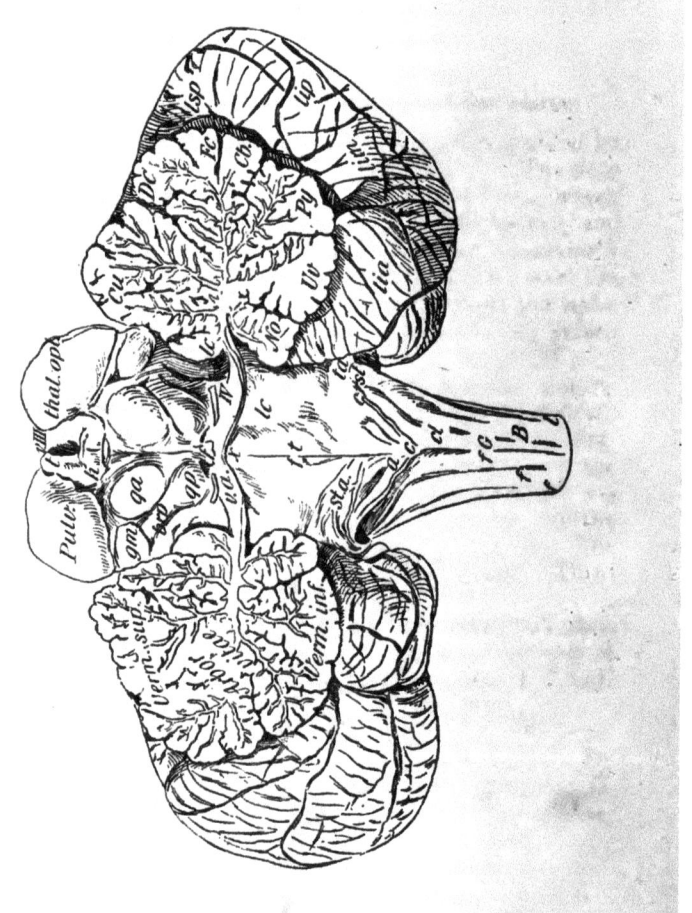

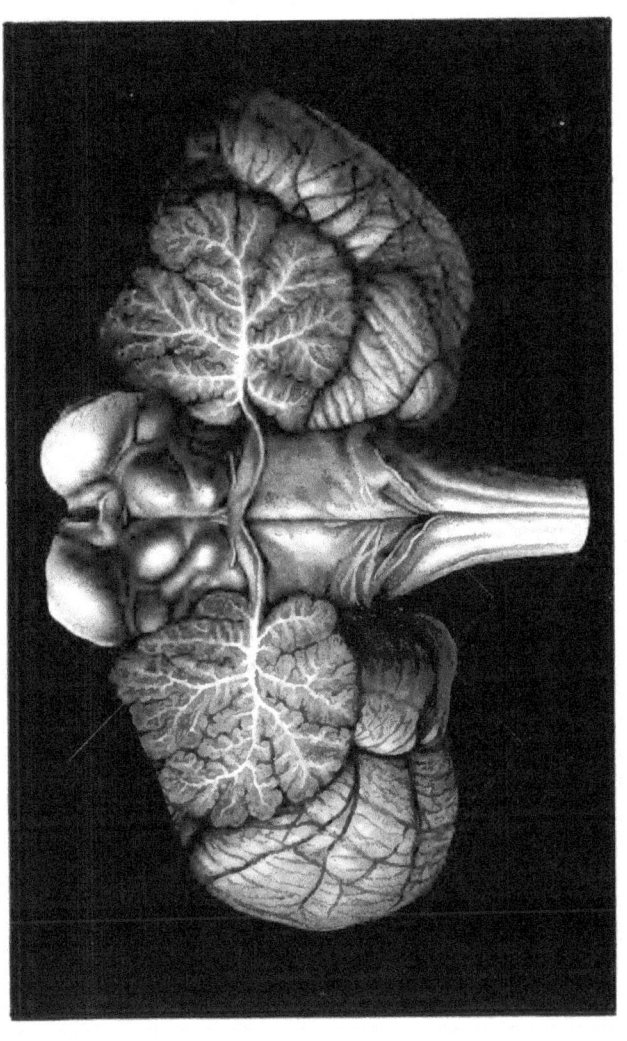

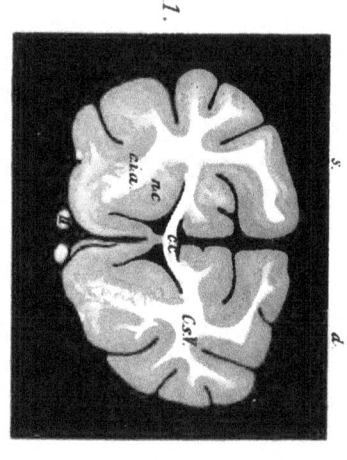

Fig. 1.

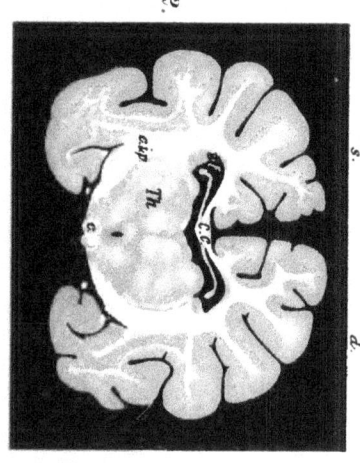

Fig. 2.

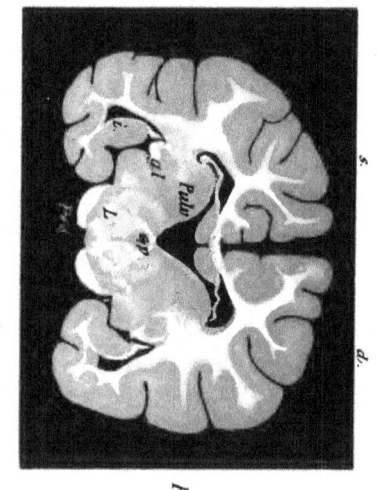

Fig. 3.

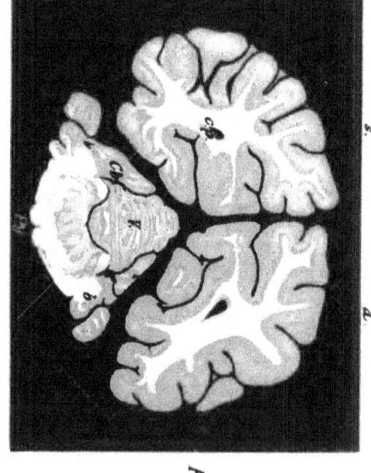

Fig. 4.

Tab. II.

PLATE 11.

Four Coronal Sections through the Brain of a Dog.

The central white matter and the cortex of the cerebral hemispheres with its convolutions are distinguished at the first glance. The white matter is relatively much smaller than in man, and the convolutions are less numerous.

FIG. 1.—*Section through the Frontal Lobes.* The head of the caudate nucleus ($n.c$), which projects into the lateral ventricle, is included in the section. The corpus callosum ($c.c$) and septum lucidum beneath it are readily recognized, as well as the cross-section of the anterior limb of the internal capsule ($c.i.a$). On the orbital surface we see the optic nerve (II) and to the outer side the olfactory bulb, which in man is rudimentary.

FIG. 2.—*Section through the Optic Thalamus ($Th.$) and the Tailpiece of the Caudate Nucleus.* Beneath the corpus callosum ($c.c$) we see the fornix (fimbria). Laterally from the optic thalamus the internal capsule,—posterior limb (cip),—which descends to the pes. (Optic tracts, corpora albicantia (c), descending horn in the temporal lobe.)

FIG. 3.—*Section through the Crura Cerebri.* The pes (Ped) projects from the surface of the hemispheres, which are separated from each other by the substantia nigra in the tegmental region (L). The termination of the optic tract in the lateral geniculate body ($g.l$) and the pulvinar ($Pulv$) are seen. The third ventricle appears beneath the posterior commissure (cp) and continues downward as the aqueduct of Sylvius.

FIG. 4.—*Section through the Occipital Lobes, Cerebellum, and Medulla Oblongata.* In the occipital lobe the posterior horn of the lateral ventricle ($c.p$), underneath the vermiform process (v) of the cerebellum (Cb), flanked on either side by portions of the hemispheres. The section of the medulla shows the brachia (b), rhomboid fossa (fourth ventricle), tegmental region, pyramids (py), and fibers of the pons.

PLATE 12.

Coronal Section through the Brain-stem of Man.

(Photographs.)

FIG. 1.—*Section through the Third Ventricle ($v.m.$).* We recognize at once the corpus callosum ($c.c$), fornix (f), lateral ventricle (vl), and caudate nucleus ($c.\,st$), and underneath the head (tuberculum anterius) of the optic thalamus (Th). Laterally from this, the posterior limb of the internal capsule (ci). Outside and below, the inner segments of the lenticular nucleus constituting the globus pallidus ($gl.p$) and a small portion of the outer segment or putamen (Put). Optic tract ($tr.o$), corpora albicantia ($c.m$), inferior convolution of the temporal lobe (uncus of the hippocampal convolution), nucleus amygdalæ ($n.a$), descending horn of the lateral ventricle, and gyrus fornicatus (qf).

FIG. 2.—*Section through the Corpora Albicantia, Posterior to Section 1.* Corpus callosum ($c.c$), fornix (f), optic thalamus (Th), caudate nucleus ($c.\,st$), internal capsule (ci), partially emerging at the base of the brain as the pes (Pd), lateral ventricles, third ventricle, hippocampal convolution ($g.H$), optic tracts ($tr.\,o$), substantia nigra (Sn), and subthalamic body ($csth$).

The corpora albicantia are connected with the optic thalami by a bundle of fibers, the bundle of Vicq d'Azyr (v); on either side the outer segments of the corpora albicantia receive the terminations of the descending crura of the fornix (f), gyrus fornicatus (qf).

FIG. 3.—*Section through the Posterior Extremity of the Third Ventricle, Shortly before its Conversion into the Aqueduct of Sylvius.* The subthalamic region, situated beneath the optic thalami (Th), unites with that of the other side; this area contains the red nucleus (nr), lateral white matter of the nucleus (Ls), and beneath it the substantia nigra (Sn). Tænia thalami (t), fasciculus retroflexus (fr).

The pes (Pd) projects freely, flanked by the lateral geniculate body (gl) with the beginning of the optic tract ($tr.o$).

Tab. 12.

Fig. 1.
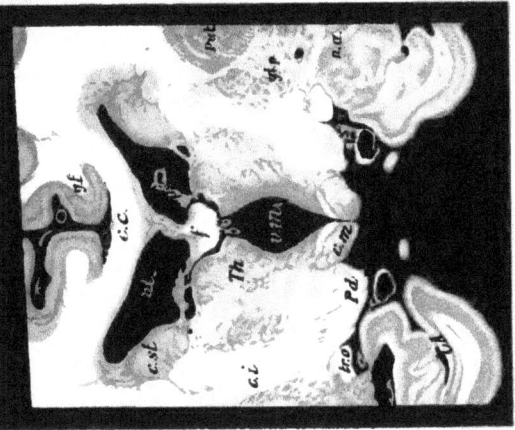

Fig. 2.
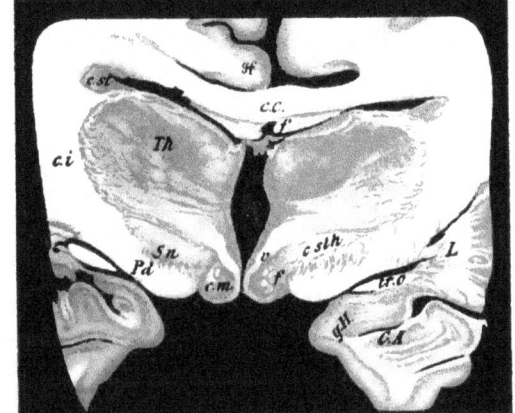

Fig. 3.
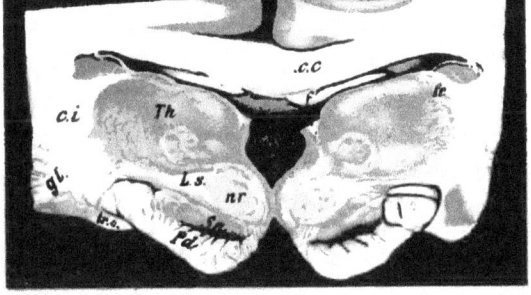

Tab. 13.

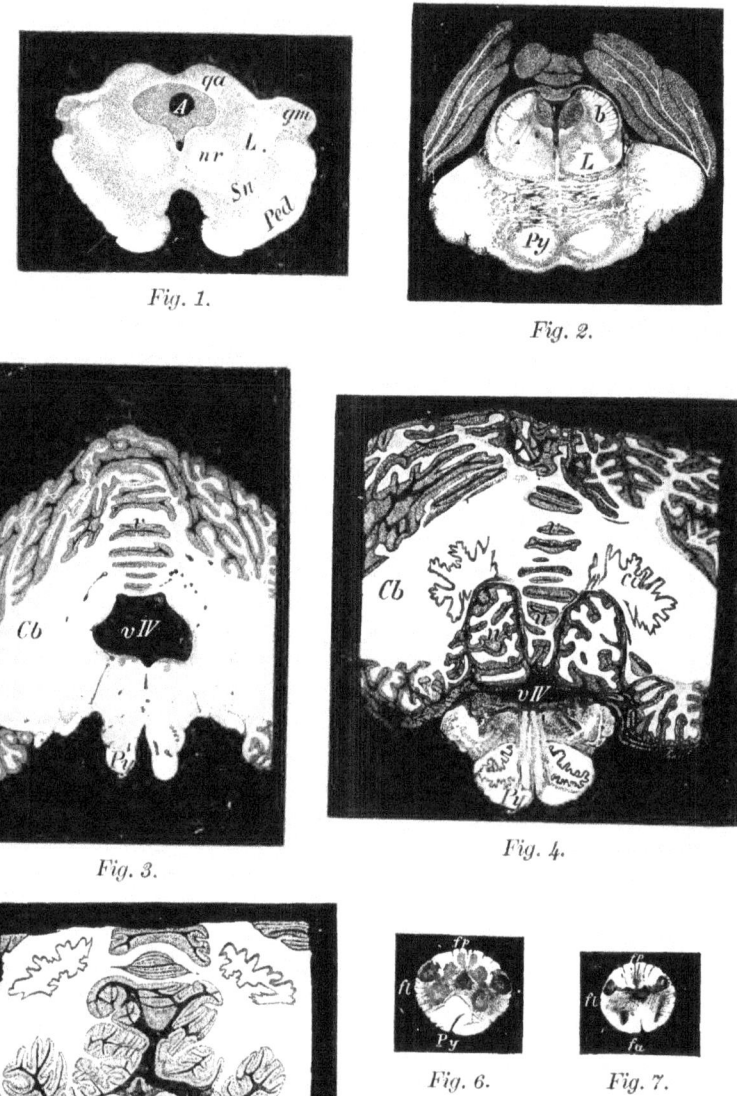

Fig. 1.

Fig. 2.

Fig. 3.

Fig. 4.

Fig. 5.

Fig. 6.   Fig. 7.

Fig. 8.   Fig. 9.   Fig. 10.

PLATE 13.

Coronal Sections through the Brain-stem. Parallel Transverse Sections through the Medulla Oblongata and Spinal Cord.

(Photographs.)

FIG. 1.—*Section through the Anterior Corpora Quadrigemina.* Beneath the corpora quadrigemina ($q.\,a$) the aqueduct of Sylvius (A), to either side the mesial geniculate body ($g.\,m$), and beneath the latter the tegmentum (red nucleus, $n.\,r$) and fillet (L); below are seen the substantia nigra and the pes. Beneath the aqueduct lies the nucleus of the oculomotor nerve.

FIG. 2.—*Section through the Middle of the Pons.* A part of the structures of the peduncle end in the pons, while another part continues as the pyramidal tract (Py) covered by the transverse fibers of the pons. The brachia (B) leave the tegmentum and after forming the lateral wall of the fourth ventricle, which is produced by the dilatation of the aqueduct of Sylvius, pass to the cerebellum. The roof of the fourth ventricle is formed by the vermiform process of the cerebellum (*lingula*), flanked on either side by the convolutions of the cerebellar hemispheres.

FIG. 3.—*Section through the Fourth Ventricle behind the Pons.* For the boundaries of the ventricle see Figure 2; the brachia have entered the white matter of the cerebellum. The section passes through the widest portion of the cerebellar hemispheres (Cb), showing both medullary and cortical substance. The pyramids (Py) stand out prominently, concealing the structures of the tegmentum (fillet, nucleus of the facial nerve, acusticus) which lie on their dorsal side.

FIG. 4.—*Section Immediately behind the Preceding.* The processus cerebelli ad medullam oblongatam (restiform bodies), which in the last section connected the cerebellum with the medulla, are now freely exposed; in the white matter of the cerebellum the corpus dentatum cerebelli ($C.\,d$) is seen; to either side of the pyramids (Py) are the olives. Uvula (U) of the vermiform process (V), nodulus (n), one of the cerebellar lobes.

FIG. 5.—*Section through the Posterior Extremity of the Rhomboid Fossa* (*Calamus Scriptorius*). The restiform bodies approach each other in the median line. The cerebellum is partially removed.

FIG. 6.—*Section through the Nuclei of the Posterior Columns* ($f.p$), *which appear in the Restiform Bodies.* Py, pyramids; fl, beginning of the lateral column of the cord.

FIG. 7.—*Section through the Decussation of the Pyramids.* The greater portion of each pyramid enters the lateral column of the opposite side.

FIGS. 8, 9, AND 10.—*Sections through the Cervical, Thoracic, and Lumbar Portions of the Cord.* The characteristic H-shape of the central gray substance is well shown (anterior horn, posterior horn). The white matter is composed of the anterior, lateral, and posterior columns ($f.a$, $f.l$, $f.p$).

PLATE 14.

Sections of the Spinal Cord in Situ.
(Photographs.)

The white matter is stained black in these preparations (medullary sheath stain). (See text, Part VI.)

Fig. 1.—*Cervical Enlargement from a Child, with Its Attachments in the Vertebral Canal (Sixth Cervical Vertebra and Surrounding Structures)* (*Magnified* × *2*). The spinal cord is surrounded by its three membranes and lodged in the bony capsule. The anterior half of the central gray matter (anterior horn) sends out the anterior motor roots ($r.a$); the posterior horn, the posterior sensory roots ($r.p$). The two roots unite and pass together through the intervertebral foramen ($f.i$), where they leave the vertebral canal to enter the soft parts as a peripheral nerve ($N.p$); before its final exit the posterior root forms the intervertebral or spinal ganglion ($g.i$) within the foramen. Body of vertebra (v), spinous process ($pr.\ sp$), vertebral arch ($a.v$), dura mater (d).

Fig. 2.—*Lumbar Enlargement Surrounded by Its Membranes (from a New-born Infant)* (*Magnified* × *10*). The outer covering is the dura mater (dm), which in the epidural space is surrounded by Breschet's venous plexus ($Pl.v$); beneath the dura mater is the subdural space; the middle envelope is formed by the arachnoid (ar); the two outer envelopes are very loosely attached to the cord, but the innermost, or pia mater (pm), which contains the blood-vessels, is closely adherent. The subarachnoid and subdural spaces are filled with cerebrospinal fluid. The anterior (ra) and posterior (rp) roots in the lumbar enlargement continue for some distance within the vertebral canal after leaving the spinal cord, which they accordingly surround on all sides; in deeper sections this bundle of nerves forms the cauda equina. In the spinal cord we see the deep anterior longitudinal fissure (Sa); the shallow posterior fissure; the anterior (fa), lateral (fl), and posterior columns (fp); the central canal ($c.c$), which is the continuation of the ventricular system; and the anterior and posterior commissures, which unite the anterior (Ca) and posterior horns (Cp) of the central gray matter.

Tab. 14.

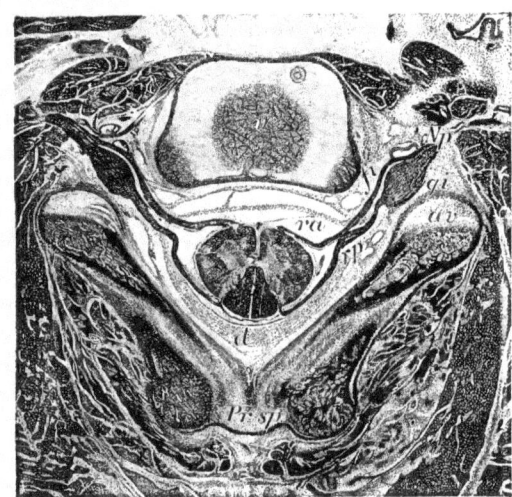

Fig. 1.

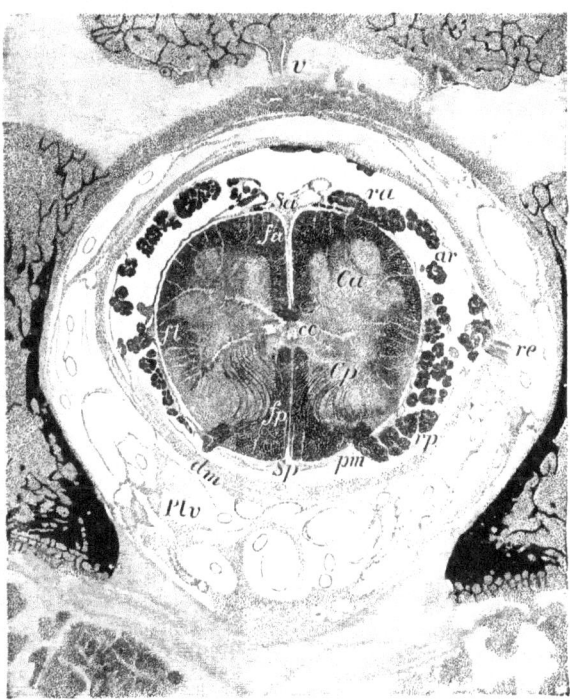

Fig. 2.

II.

DEVELOPMENT AND STRUCTURE

OF THE

NERVOUS SYSTEM.

(Part II. of Text.)

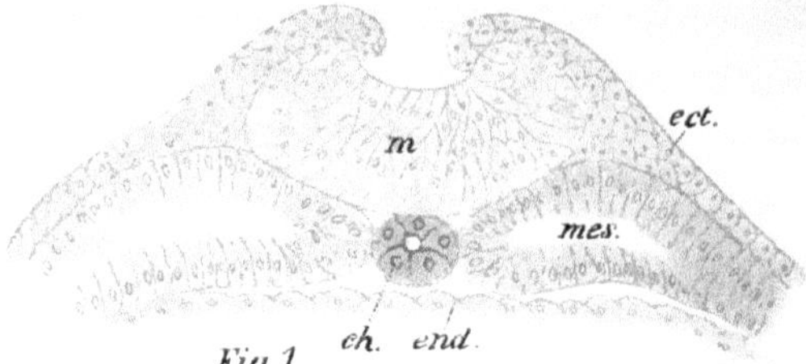

Tab. 15.

Fig. 1.

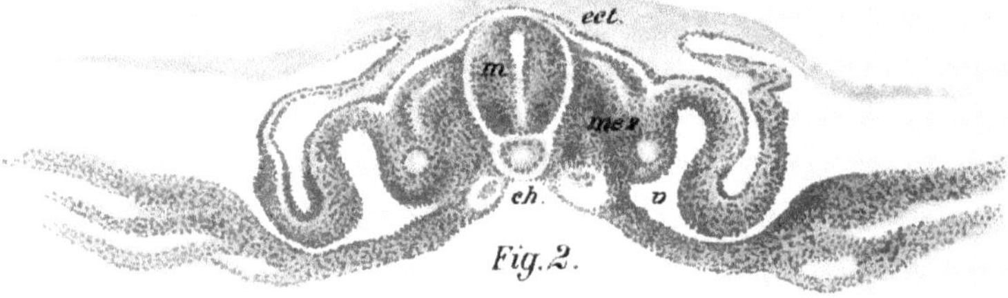

Fig. 2.

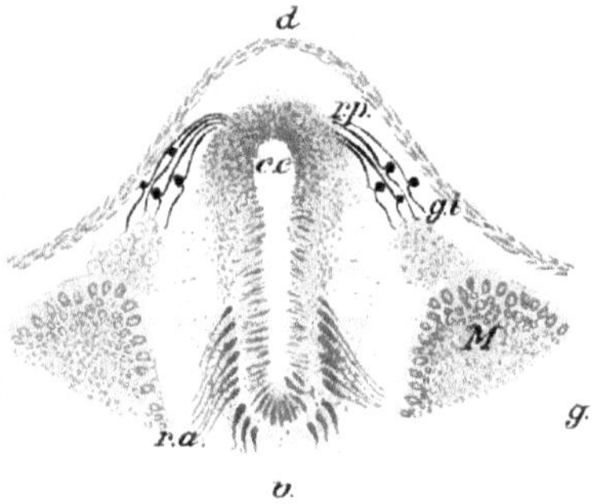

Fig. 3.

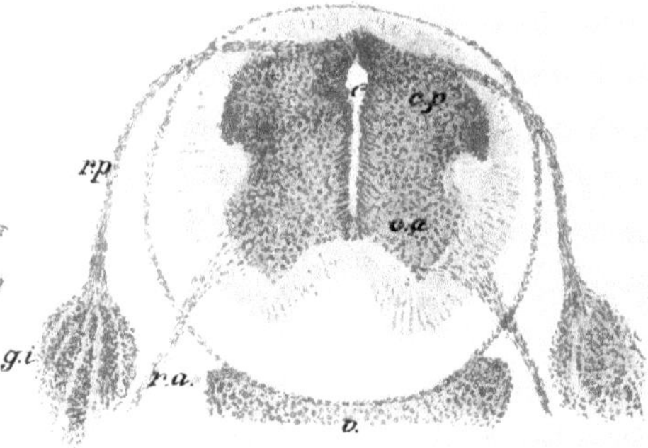

Fig. 4.

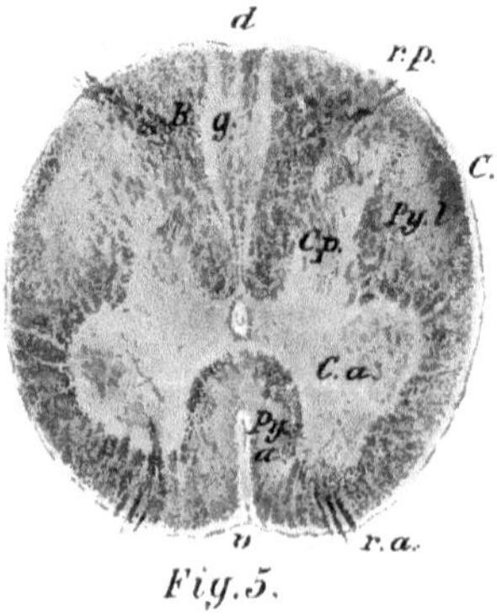

Fig. 5.

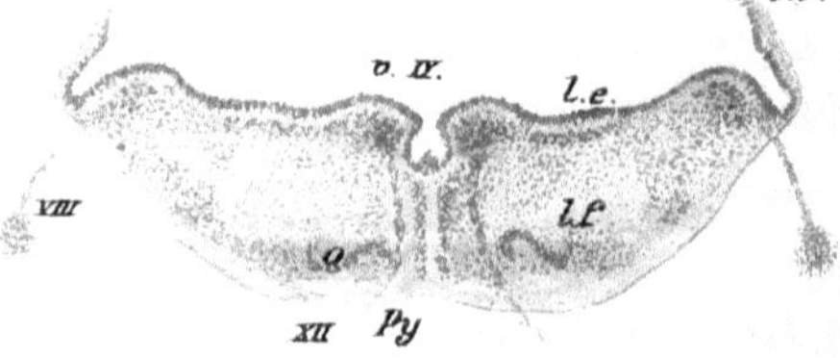

Fig. 6.

Lith. Anst. F. Reichhold, München.

PLATE 15.

Embryonal Area.

FIG. 1.—*Section through the Medullary Groove.* The medullary groove (yellow, m) is formed from the ectoderm; laterodorsally are the two primitive ganglionated cords, from the cells of which the intervertebral ganglia are developed. Mesoderm, blue; chorda dorsalis, brown; entoderm and ectoderm, red.

FIG. 2.—*Section through the Embryonal Area of a Three-day Chick Embryo.* The medullary canal (m) is closed, forming in the middle the central canal, to either side of which are the prevertebral plates. Chorda dorsalis (ch), on either side the primitive blood-vessels (v), urinary tracts, etc.

FIG. 3.—*Section through the Medullary Canal (First Month).* The stratified epithelial cells which compose the wall are differentiated into spongioblasts (supporting substance) and neuroblasts (nervous substance). On the ventral side (v) the anterior roots (ra) are beginning to grow from the neuroblasts, which form the primitive anterior horns; on the dorsal aspect the sensory posterior roots ($r.p$) pass out from the cells of the spinal ganglia ($g.i$) into the two dorsal segments of the spinal cord.

FIG. 4.—*Section through the Spinal Cord from the Second Month.* The central gray matter is better supplied with nuclei and is beginning to be differentiated from the peripheral white substance; the anterior (ca) and posterior (cp) horns are formed; roots as in figure 3; central canal (c).

FIG. 5.—*Section through the Spinal Cord from the Eighth Month.* In the white substance the various systems of nerve-fibers successively undergo the process of medullation, so that nerve tracts anatomically and functionally related reach their full development at the same time. The pyramidal tract ($Py.l$ and a) and certain portions of the posterior columns (g) are the last to become medullated. The details of the process can be studied in the figure, as the fibers already covered with the medullary sheath are stained black, while the nonmedullated portions are unstained and appear brownish in color.

FIG. 6.—*Medulla Oblongata of a Six-weeks Embryo.* Lamina fundamentalis (lf); lamina ependymica (le); lamina tegmenti (lt); *VIII*, *XII*, acusticus, hypoglossus; Py, pyramids; $v.\ IV$, fourth ventricle.

PLATE 16.
Development of the Brain.

Fig. 1.—*Brain and Cord from the Third Month.* The forebrain (*I*) is already divided into its hemispheres, and covers the interbrain and midbrain (*III*) (primitive optic thalami and corpora quadrigemina). Posteriorly the hindbrain (*IV*) (primitive cerebellum) and afterbrain (*V*) (primitive medulla). The cord shows the position of the two enlargements (*J.C* and *J.L*).

Fig. 2.—*Base of the Brain (Fourth Month).* The frontal lobe is divided from the temporal lobe (*L.f.*, *Lt*) by the fissure of Sylvius (*F.S*); the chiasm (*II*) and the pes (*Pe*) are distinguishable. Cerebellum (*C.b*), pyramids (*Py*), olives (*o*).

Fig. 3.—*Mesial Surface of the Brain (Fourth Month).* The corpus callosum (*c.c*) and fornix (*f*) are readily recognized; in front and between the two is the septum lucidum (*s.p*). The descending limb of the fornix is reflected downward and backward and ends in the corpus albicans.

Fig. 4.—*Outer Surface of the Cerebral Hemispheres (Sixth Month).* The upper surface shows a few fissures. The fissure of Rolando grows from above downward, the fissure of Sylvius (*f.S*) from below upward. At the bottom of the fissure of Sylvius the primitive island (*J*). *Cb*, cerebellum; *P*, pons; *Py*, pyramid; *o*, olive; *Mo*, medulla oblongata.

Fig. 5.—*Mesial Section through the Primitive Brain of a Two and One-half Months' Embryo.* The *roof* of the primitive ventricular cavity is formed by: Lamina tegmenti (*lt*); cerebellum (*Cb*); primitive corpora quadrigemina (*qp*, *qa*); epiphysis (*E*); tænia thalami (*t th*); pallium of the cerebral vesicle (*I*). The *floor* is formed by the bulb of the medulla (*Mo*); pons (*P*); corpus albicans (*c*); hypophysis (*H*); and in front of the latter, the lamina embryonalis. The optic thalamus (*Th*), foramen of Monro, subthalamic region, and olfactory bulb are shown.

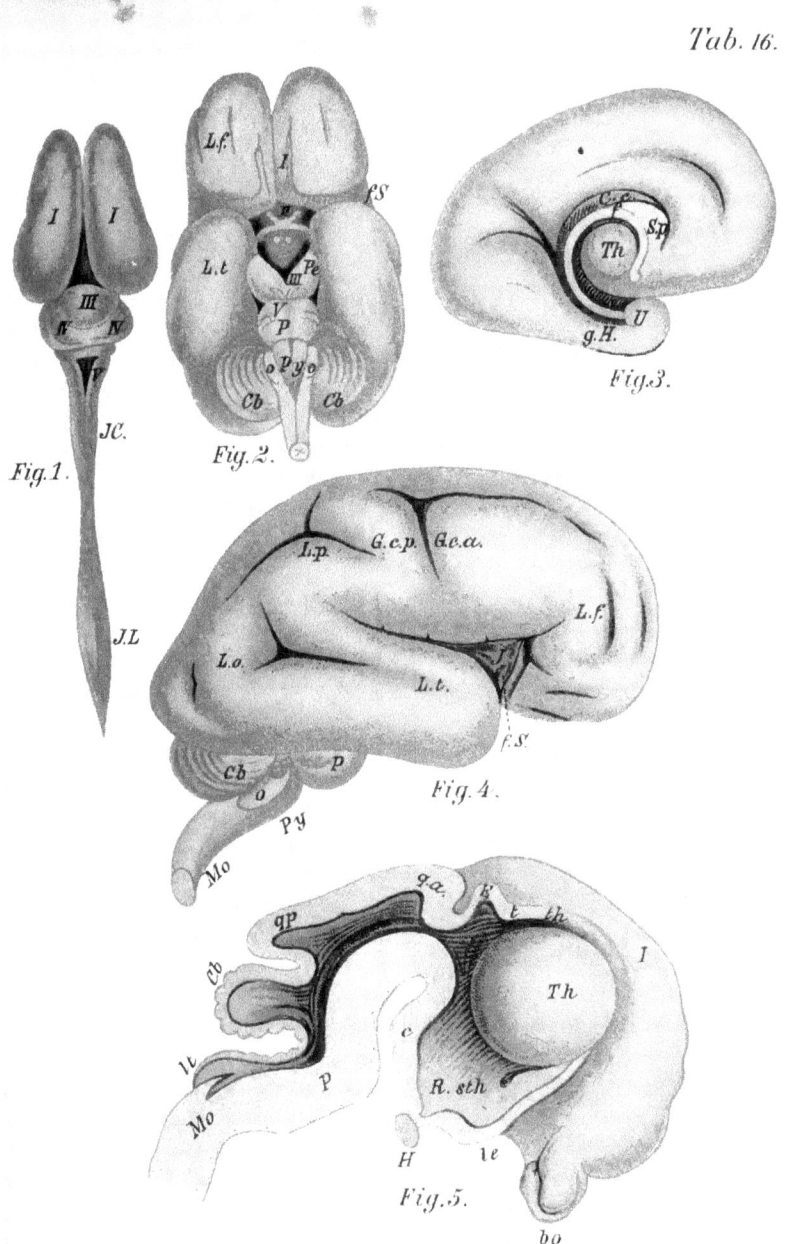

Tab. 16.

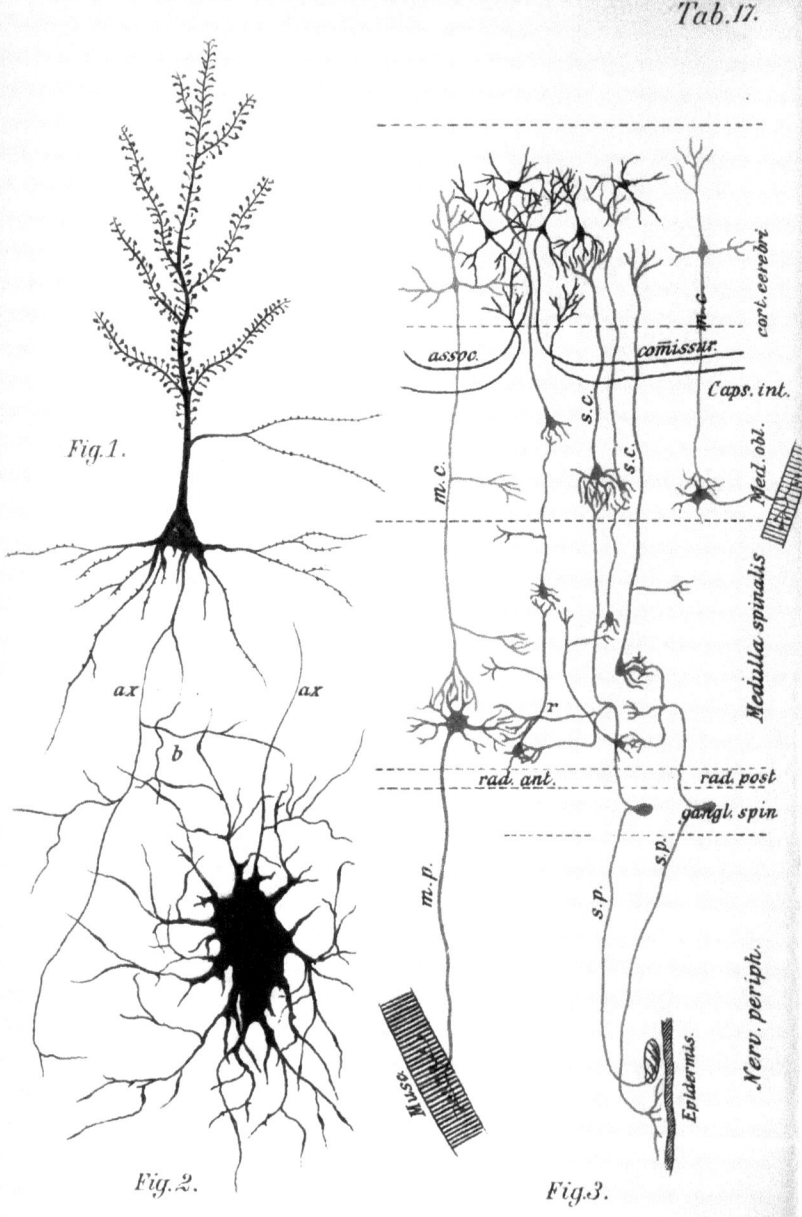

PLATE 17.

Arrangement of the Neurons.

Each neuron consists of a nerve-vessel and its process, the nerve-fiber; the cells, as well as the fiber, give off numerous protoplasmic processes. We distinguish neurons with long and with short nerve processes (Deiters' and Golgi's types).

FIG. 1.—*A Pyramidal Cell from the Cortex of the Cerebrum, with its Dendritic Ramifications (Dendrites, Protoplasmic Processes).* Each process gives off a great number of bud-like branches. The nerve-fiber of the cell, or axis-cylinder process, is designated *ax*. The terminal fibrils of the axis-cylinder process are situated at some distance from the cerebral cortex in other portions of the brain or cord, where they surround the dendrites of a ganglion cell. (Fig. 2.) This neuron begins and ends within the central organ, and is, therefore, termed a central neuron.

FIGURE 2 shows a ganglion-cell with its dendrites from the anterior horn of the spinal cord; among its ramifications are seen the terminal fibrils of the nerve-fiber belonging to the central neuron. The axis-cylinder process (*ax*) emerges from the central organ and passes to the soft parts in the periphery. The entire neuron is, therefore, called a peripheral neuron.

FIGURE 3 shows diagrammatically the manner in which these neurons unite to form the nervous pathway, especially the motor or corticomuscular. The terminal fibrils of the (red) central motor neuron (*mo*) surround the cell of the (blue) peripheral neuron (*mp*). The sensory pathway is built up in a similar manner from three or more neurons. The (brown) peripheral sensory neuron terminates with its terminal fibrils around the cell of the (green) central sensory neuron. The arrangement of the terminal fibrils in the centrifugal motor neurons is the exact opposite of that which obtains in the sensory centripetal neurons. These colored pathways are known as *projection pathways*. Within the cortex certain other neurons, colored black, indicate the numerous connections between the different parts of the cortex. They are known as the *association paths* and *commissural paths*. (For further description the reader is referred to the text, Part III.)

PLATE 18.

Glia Cells and Ganglion Cells.

FIGS. A–D.—*Glia Cells from the White Matter, a ; Gray Matter of the Cerebrum, b ; c and d, from the Cortex of the Cerebellum.* These cells are called astrocytes (silver stain).

FIGS. E AND F.—*Ganglion Cells Stained with Silver: e,* From the optic thalamus; *f,* from the cerebellar cortex (cells of Purkinje); showing numerous ramifications.

FIG. G.—*Neuroblasts with Primitive Nerve-fibers, from the Anterior Horn of a Fetus.*

FIGS. 1 AND 2.—Motor ganglion cells from the anterior horn of the spinal cord, stained with methylene-blue, showing their characteristic granulation, nucleus, and nucleolus. In some places there is marked pigmentation.

FIGS. 3 AND 4.—*Pyramidal Cell from the Cerebral Cortex Stained with Methylene-blue.*

Tab. 18.

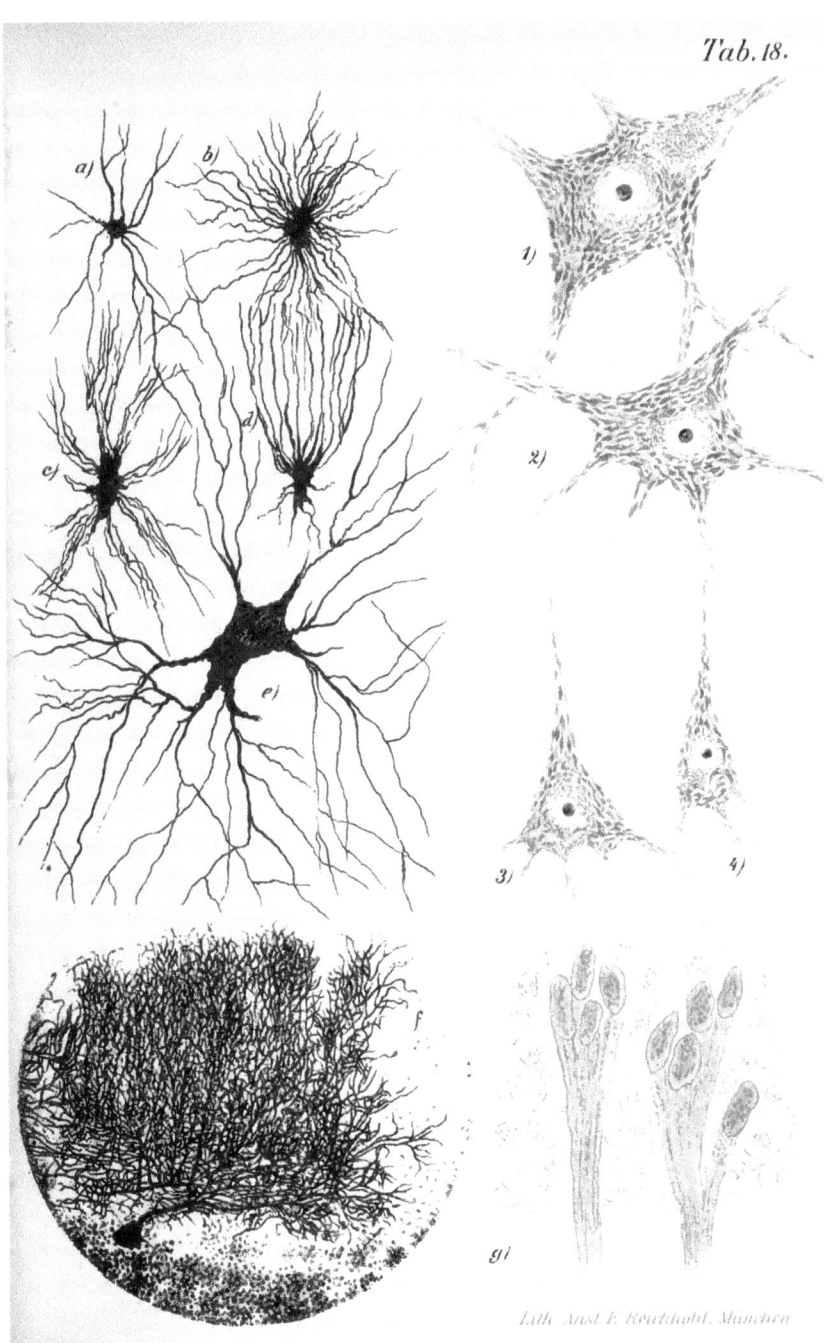

Tab. 19.

PLATE 19.

The Cerebral Cortex.

The left side of the figure shows the arrangement of the cells (the outer portions are stained with silver, the center with methylene-blue); the right side shows the arrangement of the fibers; the two portions are, of course, anatomically related.

The cells of the cortex may be divided into six layers: (1) Stratum zonale, containing small polymorphous cells of the Golgi type; (2) the first layer of small pyramidal cells; (3) the layer of medium-sized and large pyramidal cells; (4) the second layer of closely packed small pyramidal cells; (5) the second layer of medium-sized and large pyramidal cells with a few giant pyramidal cells; (6) the lowest layer of polymorphous cells lying partly within the white substance.

The nerve-fibers of the cortex for the most part pass from the cerebral medulla into the cortex; collected into bundles they enter the second layer of cells, where their terminal fibrils end; these radial bundles (radii) therefore have a vertical arrangement. They are crossed at right angles by other fibers running parallel with the surface of the cortex and forming the so-called plexus of tangential fibers—the superradial reticulum above the radii, and the interradial reticulum within the radii. The six layers are arranged as follows: (1) The stratum zonale, containing the most superficial layer of tangential fibers immediately under the pia mater; (2) the superradial reticulum, in the free upper border of which there is a robust layer of fine tangential fibers known as Bechterew-Kaes' stripe; this layer is composed entirely of very delicate transverse fibers, and contains the terminal fibrils of the radial bundles; (3) a dense collection of coarser tangential fibers (Baillarger's, Gennari's, Vicq d'Azyr's stripes, the latter being best developed in the cortex of the cuneus); (4) the interradial reticulum of tangential fibers; (5) the layer of closely packed radial bundles containing a few transverse fibers; (6) the medullary layer, containing the radiating white fibers (projection, commissural, and long association tracts) and the transverse short association bundles (Meynert's arcuate fibers).

PLATE 20.

A Cerebral and a Cerebellar Convolution.

Fig. 1.—*Cerebral Convolution from the Center of the Anterior Central Convolution* (carmin medullary sheath stain). The white matter is stained blue-black; the radial bundles (r) radiate in all directions and end in the cortex. Passing from without inward, we distinguish the following layers : The outermost subpial layer (a); the zonal layer (2); the layer of pyramidal cells, which also present a radiating arrangement and contain Baillarger's stripe; the radiation of projection fibers (r), containing the outer and inner association layer (Meynert's arcuate fibers, M); and finally the dense network of white matter (F).

Fig. 2.—*Cerebellar Convolution (Silver Stain).* From the narrow medullary substance, which is stained black, a few isolated fibers are seen passing through the granule layer (yellowish-brown) to the cortical layer proper, which is stained yellow and is also very narrow. At the base of the cortical layer we see a row of cells of Purkinje, with their elaborate arborizations. (See Plate 18.) A few moss-like fibers (r) are shown in the cortex, and some individual granule cells at g.

Tab. 20.

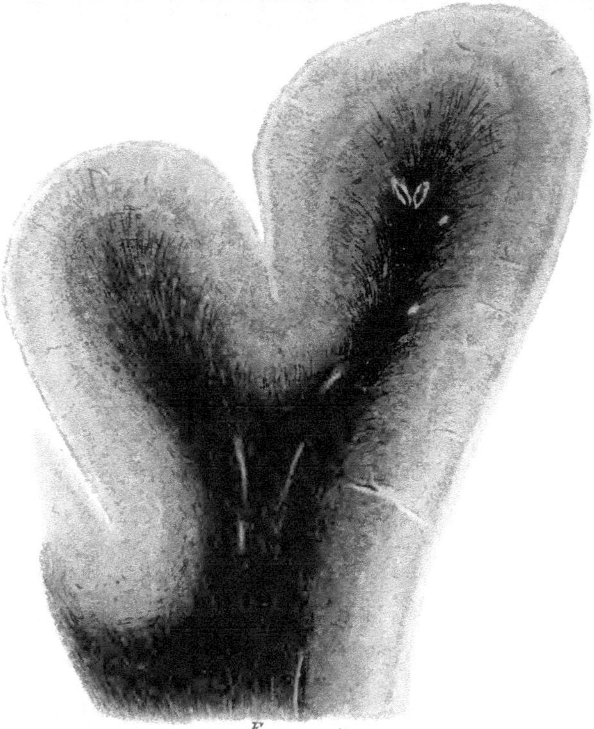

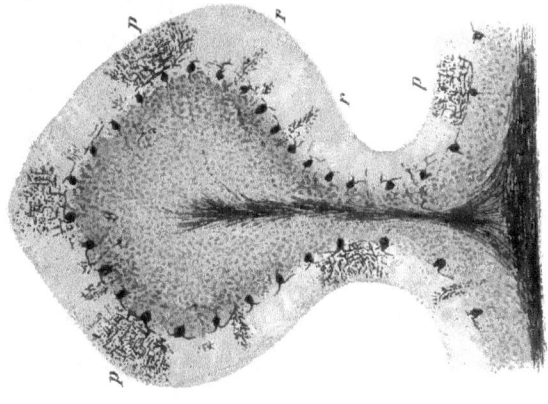

Fig. 1.

F r a

Fig. 2.

p r p r p

Lith. Anst. F. Reichhold, München

PLATE 21.

Cerebral Convolutions.

FIGURES 1 AND 2 show diagrammatically the convolutions and fissures of the cortex on the outer and mesial surfaces of the cerebral hemispheres. In the frontal lobe we recognize three convolutions ($g.$ $sup., med., inf$); behind this, separated by the sulcus centralis, the two central convolutions ($g.$ $centr.$ ant and $post$), which merge in the median line into the paracentral lobule; the parietal lobe contains an upper and a lower group of convolutions, the lower being divided into the supramarginal convolution and angular gyrus (pli courbé), while the upper is continuous on the mesial surface with the precuneus. In the occipital lobe we distinguish three convolutions (sup, med, inf); on the mesial surface the lobe is represented by the cuneus and lingula, separated by the calcarine fissure. The temporal lobe contains three convolutions ($gyr.$ sup, med, inf); on the mesial surface the occipito-temporal convolution is continuous with the lower marginal convolution (known as the hippocampal convolution), the anterior portion of which is called the uncus. The upper marginal convolution corresponds to the gyrus fornicatus.

FIG. 3.—*The Position of the Psychomotor and Psychosensory Cortical Centers in the Cavity of the Skull.* The cerebral cortex contains the motor and sensory centers for the periphery of the body. The centers which are definitely known are situated in the central convolutions, in the paracentral lobule at the base of the three frontal convolutions, in the superior temporal convolution, and in the cortex of the occipital lobe, especially on the mesial surface. The distribution and the boundaries of the various centers are clearly shown in the figure: BC, motor center for the lower, AC, for the upper, extremities; VII C, center for the muscles innervated by the facial; XII C, for those innervated by the hypoglossus nerves; M Sp C, motor, S Sp O, sensory, speech-center; S C, visual center (especially on the mesial surface, cuneus); S s, sensory sphere (trigeminus, extremities). In front of BC is the center for the movements of the trunk; in front of AC the center for movements of the head and eyes (?), at the base of the upper and middle frontal convolution. The order in BC and AC from above and in front downward and backward is as follows: hip, knee, foot (for BC); shoulder, elbow, hand (for AC). (Consult also Part IV.) The upper extremity of the central fissure is situated 5 cm. behind the coronal suture. A sagittal section through the root of the nose and the external occipital protuberance passes a little below the posterior limb of the fissure of Sylvius. The central fissure forms an angle of about 67 degrees with this line. If we divide this so-called Rolando's line into three parts, we have approximately the positions of the motor centers (leg, arm, face).

Tab. 21.

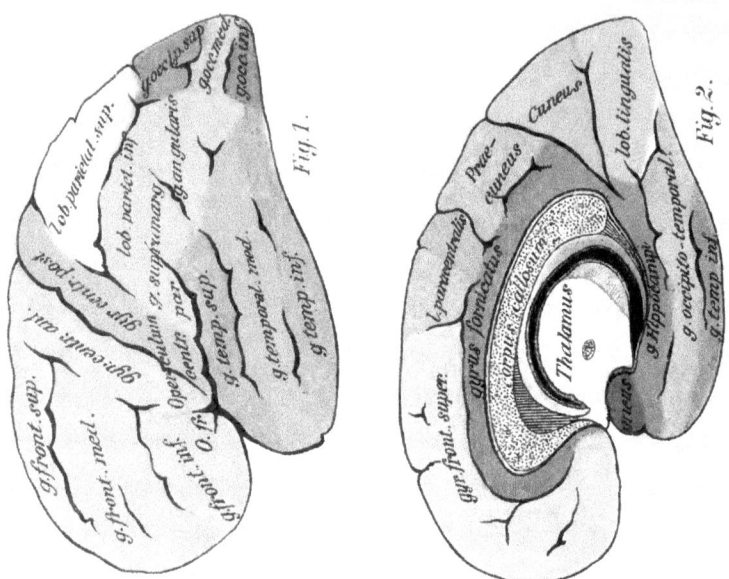

Fig. 1.

Fig. 2.

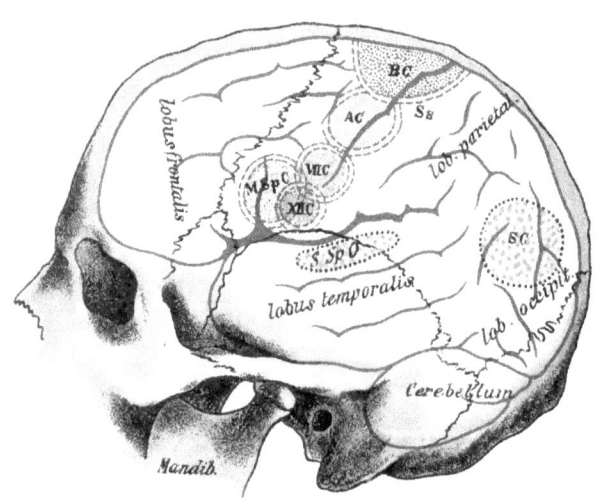

Fig. 3.

Lith. Anst. F. Reichhold, München

PLATE 22.

FIGURE 1 shows the position of the motor and sensory nuclei in which the cranial nerves originate or terminate. Their relative positions are indicated in the figure, which shows the brain-stem and medulla oblongata as seen from above.

The motor cranial nerves originate in the blue nuclei; the sensory end in the green nuclei. The cells of the green nuclei form the beginning of the sensory neuron. (See Plate 17.) The Roman numbers refer to the cranial nerves. (Vn, nasal descending motor, Vc, caudal descending sensory root of the trigeminus; Vm, motor, Vs, sensory nucleus of the trigeminus; $VIII\ c\ N$, cochlear; $VIII\ v\ N$, vestibular nerves.)

FIG. 2.—a to f show various isolated nerve-fibers, which together make up the white substance of the brain, the columns of the cord, and the peripheral nerves, and are not altogether wanting in the gray substance. Each nerve-fiber contains as its principal constituent the axis-cylinder, which is surrounded by a medullary sheath of variable thickness, the *white medullary sheath*, divided into segments by the nodes of Ranvier. The peripheral nerves are provided with an additional layer of extreme tenuity, the sheath of Schwann, situated within the medullary sheath.

(a) Medullated nerve-fibers in longitudinal section. The medullary substance is stained black and obscures the axis-cylinder, which is better seen in the transverse section (b); (c) a node of Ranvier; d and f, transverse and longitudinal sections stained with nigrosin; e, isolated fibers in the recent state, swollen from immersion in salt solution.

The axis-cylinder is composed of a large number of single so-called ultimate fibrillæ.

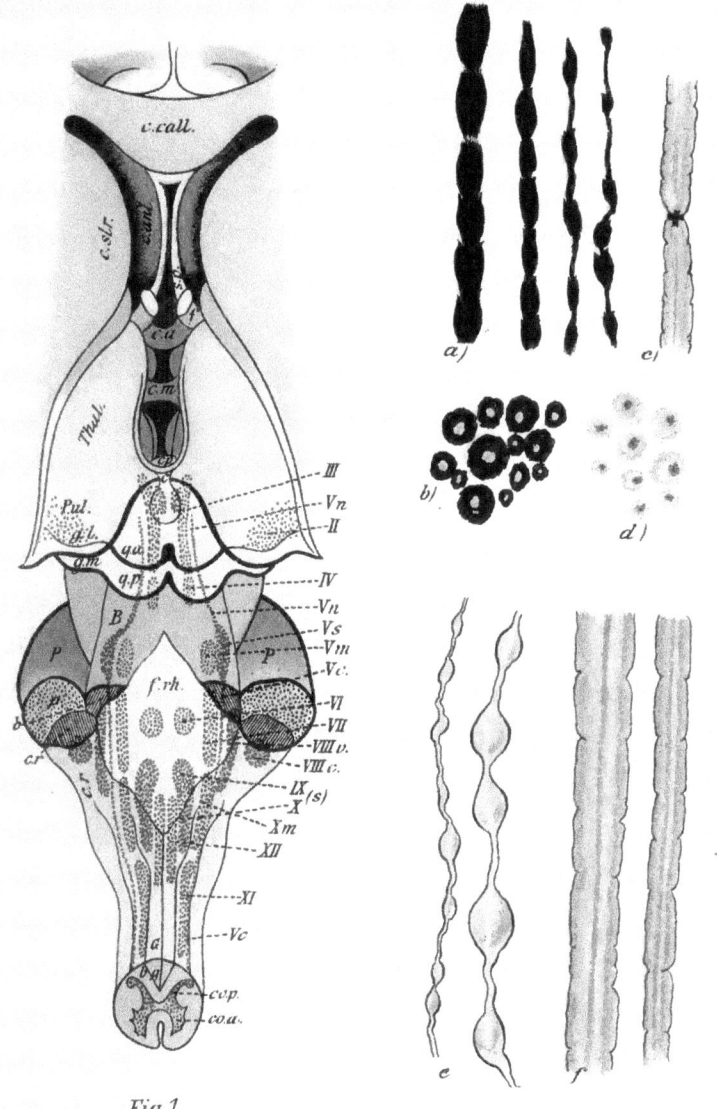

Fig. 1.

Fig. 2.

Tab. 22.

Lith. Anst. F. Reichhold, München.

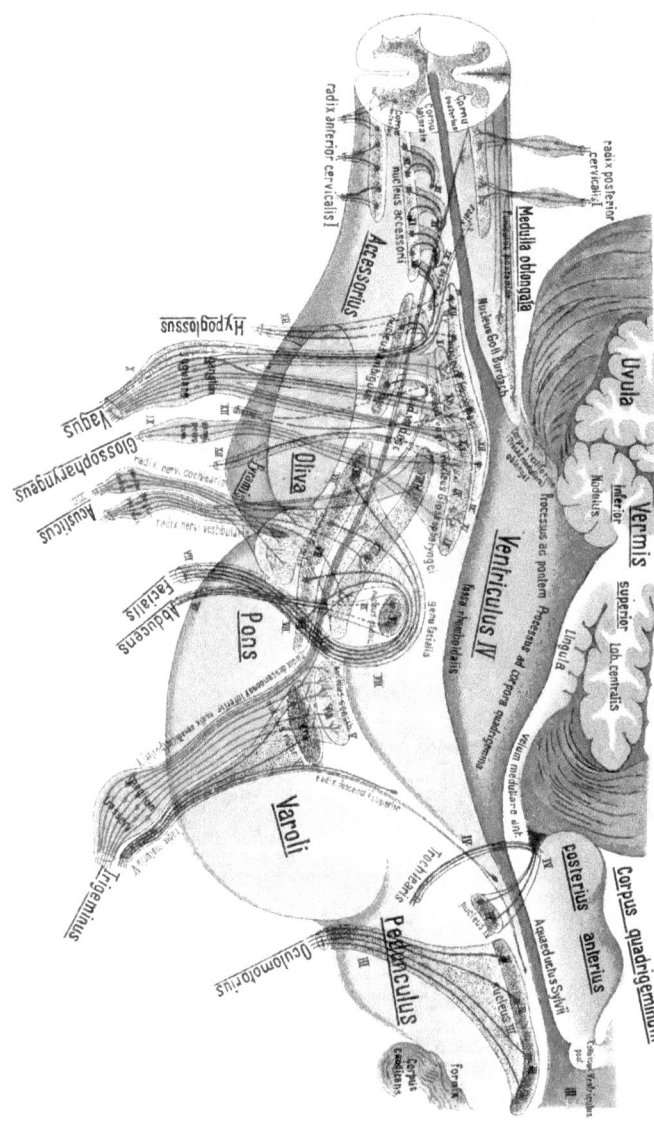

PLATE 23.

Lateral View of the Medulla Oblongata, showing, in Schematic Form, the Positions of the Nuclei and the Course of the Cranial Nerves within the white Substance.

The highest nerve is the oculomotor (III), the nucleus of which is divided into several portions and occupies an area of considerable extent in the central gray matter underneath the aqueduct of Sylvius. Posteriorly is the nucleus of the trochlear nerve (IV); it is the only cranial nerve which emerges on the dorsal surface of the brain, where it makes its appearance behind the posterior corpora quadrigemina and, after crossing that of the other side, passes to the base of the brain.

The trigeminus (V) originally consists of two distinct parts: The anterior motor portion (Vm) springs from the motor nucleus of the fifth nerve, and is probably joined by the motor nasal descending root (*radix superior*), which arises laterally from the aqueduct. The posterior sensory portion (Vs) springs from the Gasserian ganglion, and subdivides into three portions in the pons: one portion ends in the sensory nucleus of V, another passes as the caudal descending root (*radix inferior*) through the medulla oblongata to the upper portion of the cervical enlargement, and is gradually lost in this region; a third portion goes to the cerebellum. The facial nerve (VII) arises from its long nucleus, which is deeply seated. In the medulla the fibers collect and rise toward the surface to form the knee of the facial, which surrounds the nucleus of the abducens (VI) and passes first outward and finally downward to its point of exit at the base of the brain. The course of the abducens is very simple. The auditory nerve (VIII) ends as the cochlear nerve ($VIII\ c$) in the ventral, and as the vestibular nerve ($VII\ r$) in the dorsal nucleus of the auditory nerve and its immediate neighborhood. One portion continues for some distance caudad as the descending root of VIII. The sensory fibers of the glossopharyngeal and vagus arise in the jugular and petrosal ganglia, and end in the sensory nuclei of IX in the posterior extremity of the floor of the fourth ventricle (X, green); one portion continues for some distance caudad as the descending root of X (*fasciculus solitarius*). The motor fibers arise in part from the nucleus ambiguus (X, blue), in part from the nucleus of the spinal accessory.

The nucleus of the hypoglossus (XII), which is situated in the caudal dorsal segment of the medulla, sends its fibers through the substance of the medulla, on the surface of which they emerge laterally from the pyramids. The nuclei of the spinal accessory (XI) extend far down into the upper portion of the cervical enlargement. The fibers emerge on the surface of the lateral columns; $r.\ p$, highest posterior cervical roots from the spinal ganglia; $r.\ a$, highest anterior roots of the cervical enlargement.

PLATE 24.

Nuclei of the Motor Peripheral Neurons (carmin medullary sheath stain).

FIGURE 1 shows a segment of the gray anterior horn, with its motor ganglion cells, from the cervical enlargement. The cells give origin to the anterior spinal roots (*a. r*), which pass through the adjoining white substance of the anterolateral tracts (black medullated fibers seen in transverse section). The fine medullated fibers which surround the cells are in part concerned in the transmission of reflexes (reflex collaterals from the posterior roots).

FIGURE 2 represents a portion of the nucleus of the hypoglossus. The fibers of the nerve spring from the numerous large multipolar ganglion cells. The cells are surrounded by a delicate network of coarse and fine medullated nerve-fibers. Some of these fibers belong to central pathways, others effect a close connection between the two nuclei, thereby facilitating the consentaneous action of the two halves of the tongue, and subserve the transmission of reflexes. The nuclei of the facial, oculomotor, etc., are in every respect similar in structure. Thus, the peripheral motor neuron begins in these two regions, while its cells are surrounded by the terminal fibrils of the central neuron; the latter can not be seen with this stain.

Tab. 24.

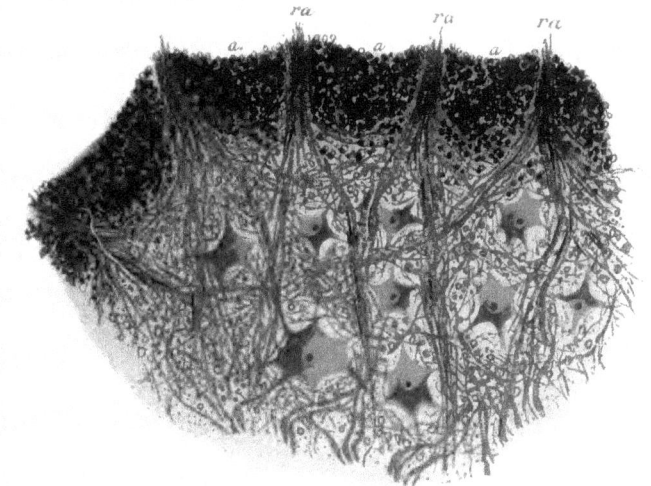

Fig. 1.

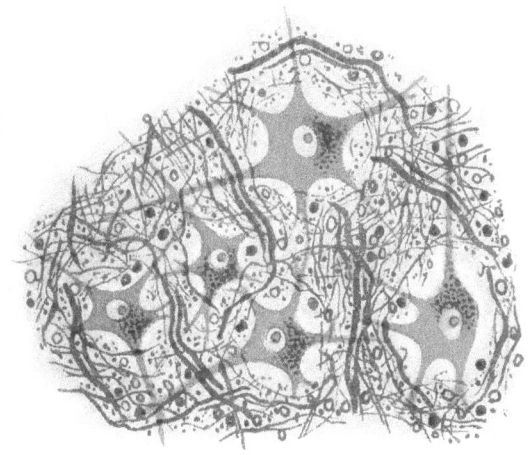

Fig. 2.

Lith. Anst. F. Reichhold, München.

Tab. 25.

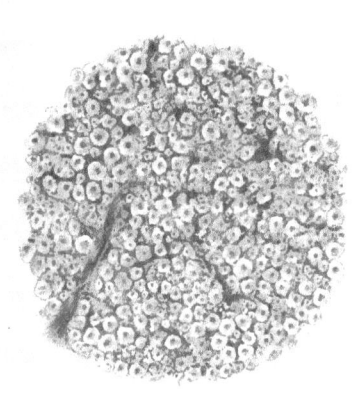

Fig. 1.

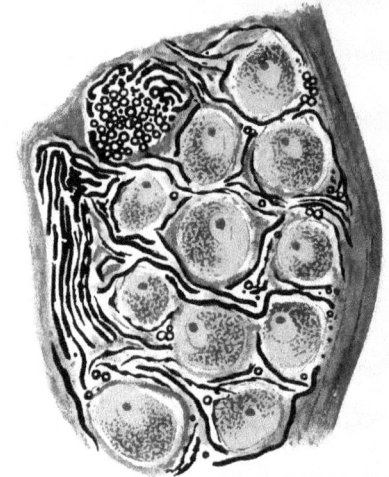

Fig. 2.

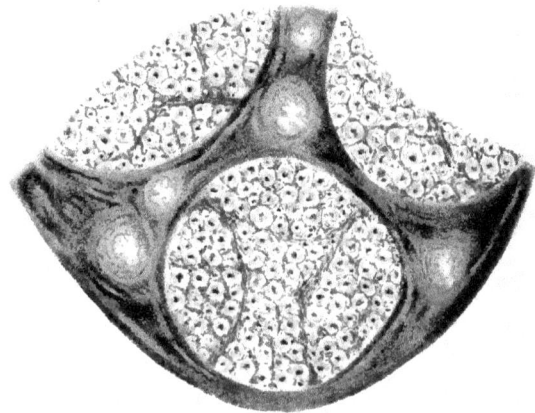

Fig. 3.

Lith. Anst. F. Reichhold, München.

PLATE 25.

Fig. 1.—*Transverse Section through the White Substance of the Spinal Cord (Lateral Column) (carmin).* The white substance is composed of closely packed medullated nerve-fibers of varying caliber, embedded in the neurogliar or sustentacular substance. As most of the nerve-fibers have a longitudinal course, they appear in this preparation in transverse section ("sun pictures"). The axis-cylinder is seen in the center of each fiber.

Fig. 2.—*Section through a Spinal Ganglion (carmin stain).* The strongly pigmented cells of the ganglia, like the Gasserian ganglion, for instance, are surrounded by the centripetal and centrifugal nerve-fibers (the centrifugal fibers correspond to the posterior roots). One fiber enters and leaves each cell (T-shaped division). These cells represent the origin of the peripheral sensory neuron.

Fig. 3.—*Cross-section of a Peripheral Nerve (nigrosin stain).* Each nerve is made up of several bundles. The entire nerve is surrounded by an envelope of connective tissue, the epineurium. The bundles are lodged in the various compartments of the perineurium, and the individual nerve bundles are again subdivided by the endoneurium, so that each compartment of the endoneurium contains a medullated nerve-fiber surrounded by the sheath of Schwann in a fibrillary sheath. The perineurium contains the blood-vessels and lymphatics. Note the variable thickness of the fibers.

PLATE 26.

Figs. 1 and 2.—*Diagrammatic Representation of the Position of the Cervical and Lumbar Enlargements.* Between the anterior longitudinal sulcus ($S.\ a$) and the anterior roots ($r.\ a$) is the anterior column, which is subdivided into the anterior (uncrossed) pyramidal tract (Pya) and the anterior ground bundle ($f.\ a$).

Between the anterior roots and the posterior roots ($r.\ p$) is the lateral column, which is subdivided into Gowers' tract (G), the direct cerebellar tract (Cb), the crossed lateral pyramidal tract (Pyl), the lateral ground bundle (fal), and the lateral boundary zone (fl).

The posterior columns are divided into the column of Goll (G) and the column of Burdach (B). The lateral posterior portion of Burdach's column corresponds to the entrance of the posterior roots (posterior (rp) and anterior (ra) root zones). The extremities of the posterior horns are capped by the zones of Lissauer (L); v, central field of the posterior columns. The gray matter is divided into anterior ($C.\ a$) and posterior horns ($C.\ p$). Between them, near the median line, are the columns of Clarke (Cl). In front of the central canal ($c.\ c$) is the anterior white ($c.\ a$), and behind it the posterior gray, commissure. The cells in the anterior horn are arranged in a mesial and a lateral group, each of which is again subdivided into an anterior and a posterior segment.

The posterior horn is bounded at its base by the substantia gelatinosa ($S.\ g$). This is continuous with the zona spongiosa, which joins the above-mentioned zone of Lissauer.

Fig. 3.—*The Central Canal and Adjoining Structures under a higher power.* The canal is lined with cylindric epithelium. We see the medullated fibers of the anterior commissure (Ca), which are distributed partly to the anterior column (fa) and partly to the anterior horn, and the more delicate fibers of the posterior commissure (Cp), which radiate into the posterior horn and into the posterior column. Sa, anterior sulcus with the blood-vessels; Sp, dorsal septum.

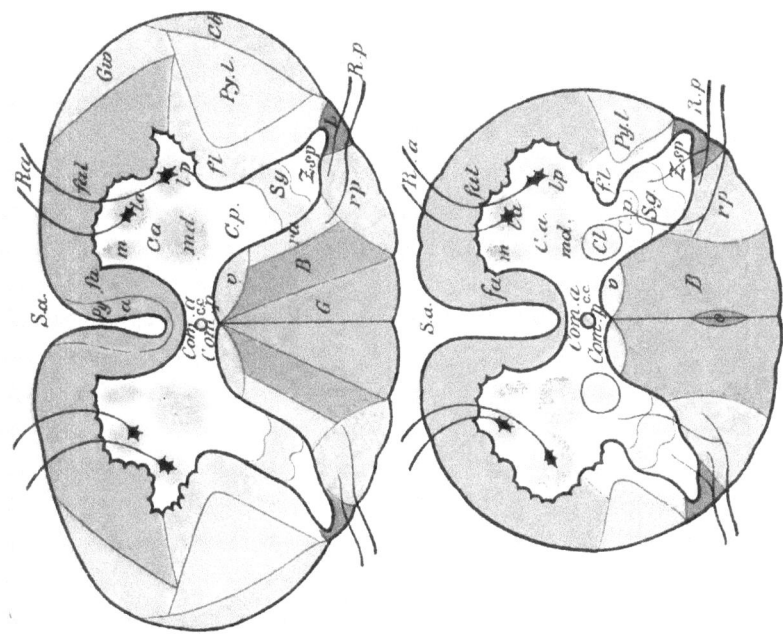

III.

TOPOGRAPHIC ANATOMY

OF THE

NERVOUS SYSTEM.

(Plates 27–53.)

PLATES 54–57, DIAGRAMMATIC REPRESENTA-
TION OF THE COURSE OF THE FIBERS.

(Part III. of Text.)

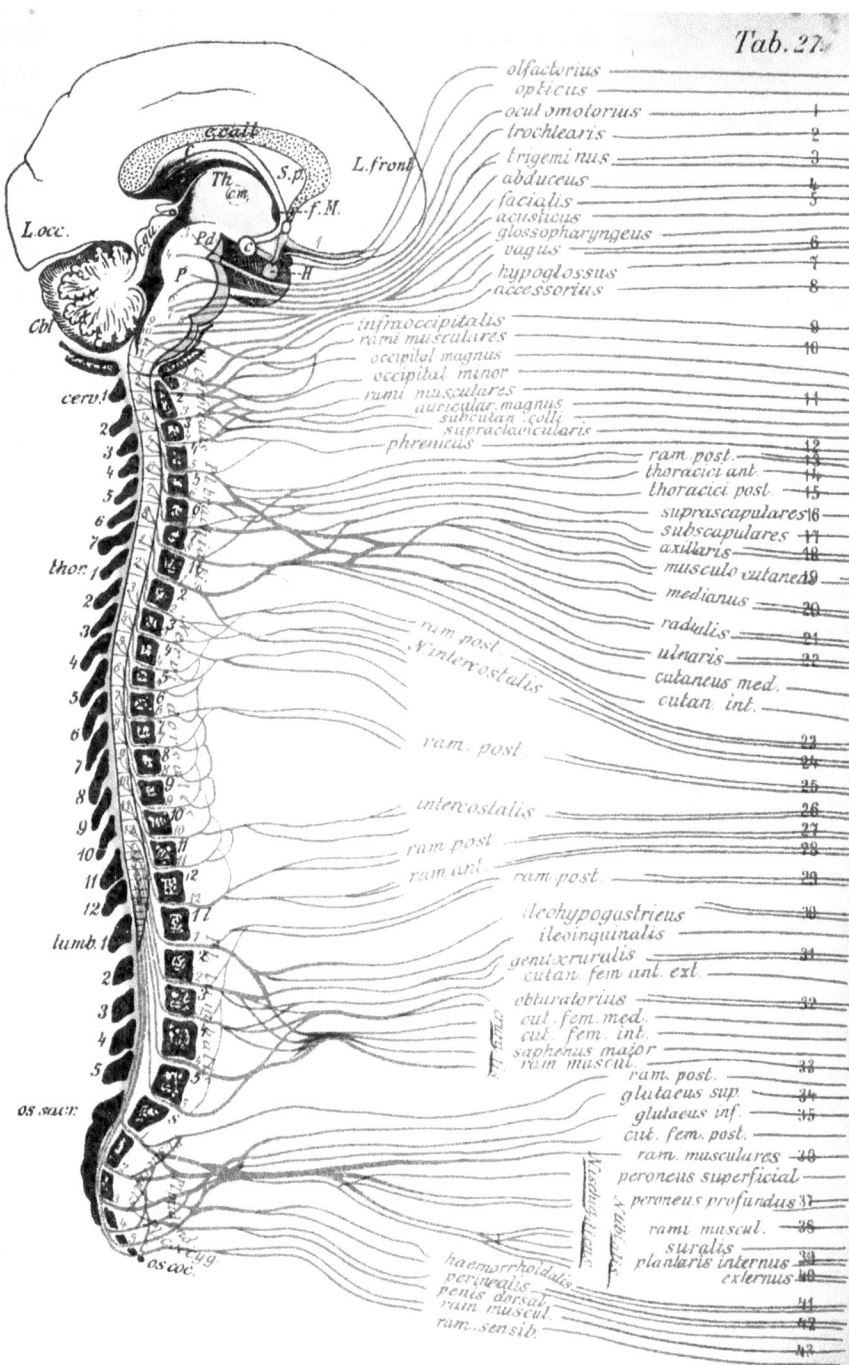

PLATE 27.

Distribution of the Cranial and Spinal Nerves.

We determine the level of the brain and cord from which the individual nerve-roots arise. A detailed description of the segments of the brain-stem and spinal cord is found in the text. (Fig. 13.) For the cutaneous areas see Figure 21 a and b. A knowledge of the relation of the individual segments of the spinal cord to the vertebral column (spinous process) and of the points of exit of the spinal nerves is of the highest importance. The nerves of the lumbar region emerge some distance below the segment from which they arise. This arrangement and the formation of the plexuses is readily seen in this plate.

The segments are marked with red numbers, the motor nerves are blue, the sensory brown, after their exit from the plexus; the explanatory text is also printed in the corresponding colors. The ultimate distribution of the cutaneous sensory nerves will be best understood by a study of figures 18, 19, and 20 in the text.

The most important motor nerves are numbered, and in the adjoining table the muscles innervated by the various nerves and the more important facts in regard to their function are given, except in those cases where the name of the muscle itself is sufficiently expressive.

1.
   - (a) Internal eye muscles (the ciliary ganglion interposed): Ciliary m. for accommodation; sphincter pupillæ for contraction of pupil.
   - (b) External eye muscles (levator palp. super.; rectus super., intern., infer.; obliquus inferior): rotation of eyeball upward, inward, and downward.
2. Superior oblique of the eye: rotation downward and outward.
3. Muscles of mastication (masseter, temporal, pterygoids, mylohyoid, digastric (ant. belly), tensor tympani, tensor et levator veli palati): lacrimal secretion (?).
4. External rectus of the eye: rotation outward.
5. Facial muscles of expression (occipitofrontalis, orbicularis oculi, orbicularis oris, zygomatic, mental, platysma, auriculares, stapedius, digastric (post. belly), etc.): salivary secretion, lacrimal secretion (?), muscles of palate (?).
6. Muscles of deglutition (constrictors, cricothyroid): gastric secretion; cardiac and respiratory movements.
7. Muscles of the tongue (sternohyoid, thyroidei).
8. Muscles of the larynx: phonation. Muscles of the palate, pharynx, esophagus (vagus): act of deglutition. Sternocleidomastoid: lateral rotation and inclination of the head. Trapezii (in part): elevation of the shoulders.
9. Posterior straight and oblique muscles of the head and nape of the neck: elevation and rotation of the head.
10. Deep posterior and anterior muscles of the back (trapezii, in part): movements of the head and neck.
11. Scaleni: elevation of the ribs; respiration. Longus colli.
12. Diaphragm: respiration.
13. Deep muscles of the neck.
14. Pectoralis major: adduction and forward movement of the arm. Pectoralis minor; subclavius.
15. Levator scapulæ, rhomboidei (nerv. dorsalis scapulæ): draw the scapulæ inward and upward. Serratus anticus major (long thoracic nerve): fixes the scapula and rotates the arm and scapula (upward and outward) beyond the horizontal.
16. Supraspinatus: elevates the arm and rotates it outward. Infraspinatus, teres minor: rotate the arm outward.
17. Subscapularis, teres major: rotate the arm inward. Latissimus dorsi: adducts the arm and draws it backward.
18. Deltoid: elevates the arm to the horizontal.
19. Biceps, flexor, and supinator of the forearm; brachialis anticus, flexor of the forearm; coracobrachialis.
20. Flexor digitorum communis (radial portion): flexes the distal phalanges. Flexor longus pollicis (distal phalanx); flexor carpi radialis; pronator teres and quadratus; palmaris longus; the thenar muscles: oppose the thumb, flex the proximal, and extend the distal phalanx. Lumbricales (1, 2, rarely 3): flex the proximal, and at the same time extend the distal phalanges.
21. Triceps: extensor of the forearm. Brachioradialis, erroneously termed supinator longus: flexor and pronator of the forearm. Extensor digitorum communis: extends the proximal phalanges. Extensor pollicis; abductor pollicis; supinator brevis; extensor carpi radialis and ulnaris.
22. Flexor digitorum profundus (ulnar portion), see 20. Flexor carpi ulnaris; hypothenar muscles; interossei: flex the proximal phalanges. Lumbricales (3 and 4), see 20. Adductor pollicis.
23. Deep muscles of the back.
24. Intercostal muscles.
25. Deep muscles of the back: extensors of the trunk.
26. Intercostal muscles.
27. Muscles of the back.
28. Intercostal muscles; abdominal muscles (rectus, external oblique): abdominal pressure.
29. Dorsolumbar muscles.
30. Transversalis and internal oblique: abdominal pressure.
31. Cremaster, transversalis, oblique.
32. Obturator externus; adductores femoris; gracilis: adductor.
33. Psoas (lumbar plexus); iliacus internus: elevate the thigh and flex the trunk. Quadriceps: extensor of the leg. Sartorius.
34. Gluteus medius and minimus: abductors of the thigh. Tensor fasciæ latæ; pyriformis; obturator internus: external rotators.
35. Gluteus maximus: extensor of the thigh.
36. Gemelli; biceps; semitendinosus; semimembranosus: flexors of the leg. Quadratis femoris: external rotator.
37. Tibialis anticus: elevates the inner border of the foot. Peronei: elevate the outer border of the foot. Extensor digitorum communis.
38. Gastrocnemius; soleus: plantar flexion of the foot. Flexor digitorum; tibialis posticus.
39. } Small muscles of the foot (flexor brevis, interossei, etc.).
40.
41. Levator ani, sphincter ani internus, sphincter vesicæ.
42. Sphincter ani, perineal muscles, bulbocavernosus, etc.
43. Sphincter ani externus.

Serial Sections through the Central Organ.

Plates 28 to 50 contain frontal sections, Plates 33 to 36 sagittal and horizontal sections, first through the entire hemisphere, then through the brain-stem, the medulla, and the spinal cord. The sections are either drawn or photographed from actual preparations stained with medullary sheath stain, and are not in any sense schematic. The order of succession of the frontal sections is shown in the accompanying diagram of the brain-stem, which is represented as though flattened out. The originally white medullary substance is, of course, stained black in all the sections. Unless it is mentioned otherwise, the sections are to be considered life-size.

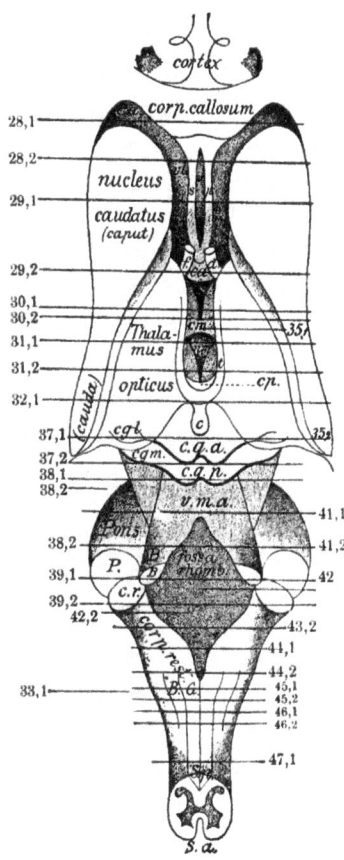

The student should carefully reconstruct the entire series by comparing each section with the sections immediately preceding and following it, and noting the position on the accompanying diagram.

[NOTE.—For the cerebral sections the brain of a sixteen-year-old boy was used. In an adult brain the white matter is more massive and more completely differentiated.]

PLATE 28.

FIG. 1.—*Frontal Section through the Genu of the Corpus Callosum and Anterior Segment of the Frontal Lobe.* The section includes the frontal lobe and its three convolutions: superior, middle, and inferior (*fr. s, fr. m, fr. i*). The tip of the anterior horn (*v. a.*) is seen in the white substance. The radiation of the corpus callosum (*Rcc*) connects all the parts of the frontal lobe with the corresponding parts of the opposite side. Laterally from the anterior cornu of the lateral ventricle (*v.a*) is the beginning of the corona radiata; *p.Cr*, its base. Centrum semiovale (*C. Vieuss*); *cg*, cingulum (association bundles); *ft*, tangential fibers; *st. s*, central gray matter of the ventricle. On the orbital surface the olfactory bulb is seen in transverse section (*I*).

FIG. 2.—*Frontal Section through the Head of the Caudate Nucleus.* Behind the genu of the corpus callosum is the beginning of the septum lucidum (*s. p*); *v*, fifth ventricle. The cut head of the caudate nucleus is seen projecting into the anterior horn (*v. a*). To the outer side the most anterior bundles of the anterior limb of the inner capsule (*c. i. a*) are closely applied to the lateral side of the caudate nucleus, in the substance of which they disappear. Note the more delicate structure of the medullary layer (centrum semiovale Vieussenii) with the interlacing bundles of fibers: (1) The radiation of the corpus callosum; (2) the corona radiata; (3) association bundles: Fasciculus occipitofrontalis (*of*); cingulum (*cg*); fasciculus arcuatus (*fa*); fasciculus uncinatus (*fu*).

ce, External capsule; *cl*, claustrum; *ft*, tangential fibers; *pes fr. i.*, base of the third frontal convolution; *sL*, nerves of Lancisi; *st. a.*, central gray matter.

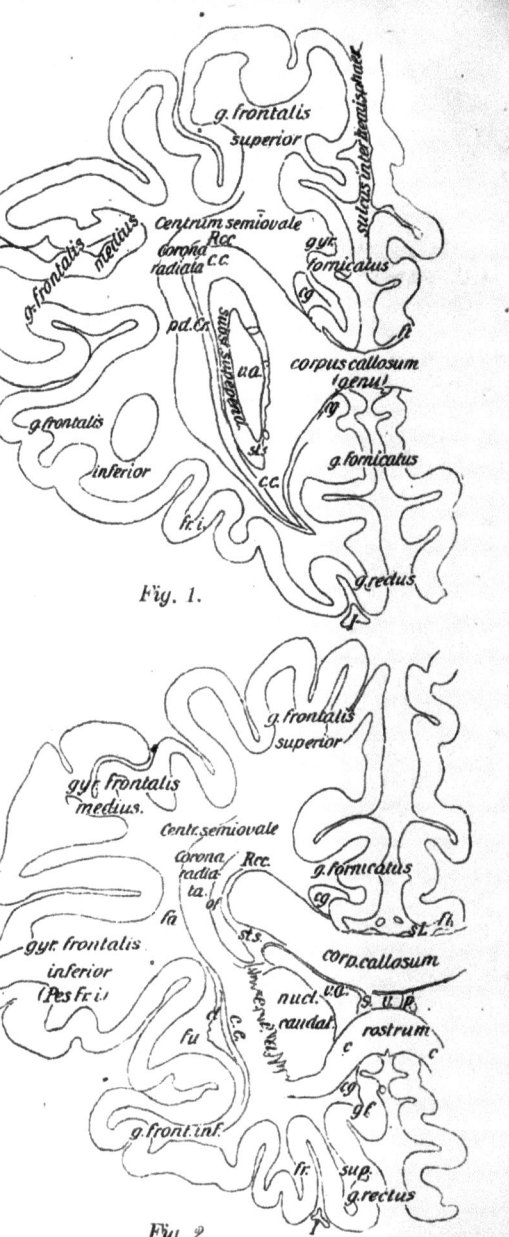

Tab. 28.

Fig. 1.

Fig. 2.
Basis

Tab. 28.

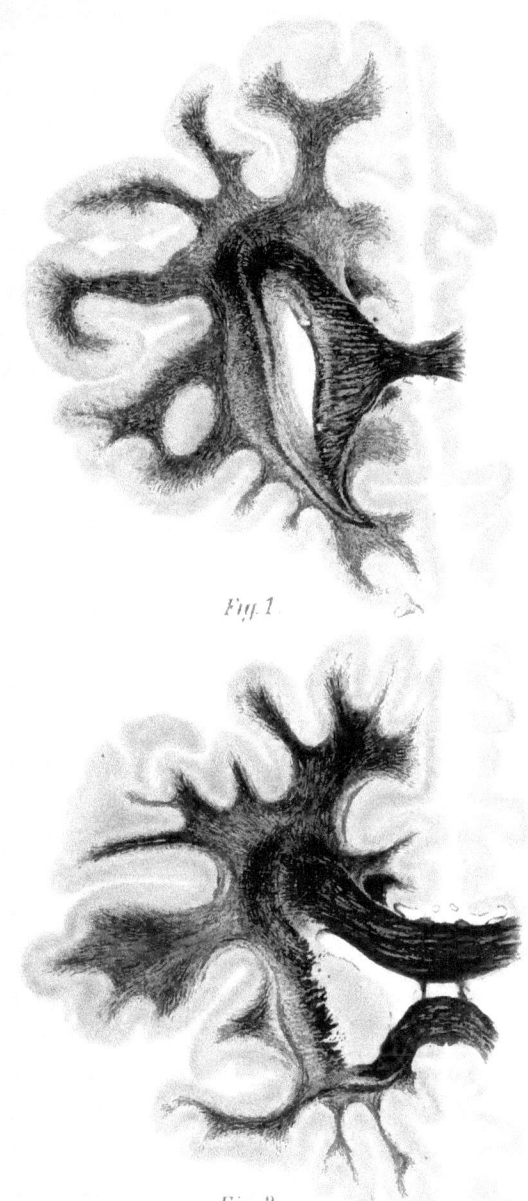

Fig. 1.

Fig. 2.

PLATE 29.

Fig. 1.—*Frontal Section through the Middle of the Septum Lucidum.* The tip of the temporal lobe is also included in the section. In the white matter the section passes through the corpus striatum, more particularly the putamen (*Put.*) or outer segment of the lenticular nucleus; the anterior limb of the capsule (*c. i. a*) breaks through the corpus striatum and thus divides it into the caudate nucleus or mesial portion, and the lenticular nucleus or lateral portion. To the outer side of the putamen is the external capsule (*c. e*); and outside of the latter, the claustrum (*cl*).

Fig. 2.—*Section through the Anterior Commissure.* The descending crura of the fornix (*f*) make their appearance. We also see the inner segments (*gl. p*, globus pallidus) of the lenticular nucleus. At the base of the brain the section has passed through the optic chiasm, to the lateral side of which the olfactory tubercle (*t. o*) is visible. The most anterior convolution of the insula (*Ins*) appears at the bottom of the fissure of Sylvius, laterally from the claustrum. In the anterior portion of the temporal lobe we see the beginning of the nucleus amygdalæ (*N. am*), which is seen better in the following section; the cortical convolutions have been cut away. The anterior commissure (*c. ant*) resembles the corpus callosum in that it connects the temporal and occipital convolutions on the basal surface. Between the crura of the fornix is seen the beginning of the third ventricle (*v. III*).

Abbreviations. —*ce*, Capsula externa, *cia*, capsula interna anterior ; *cg*, cingulum ; *cl*, claustrum ; *fa*, fasciculus arcuatus ; *fu*, fasc. uncinatus ; *inf*, infundibulum ; *of. fasc*, occipitofrontalis ; *p Cr*, foot of corona radiata; *r*, rostrum ; *Rcc*, radiation of corp. callos.; *Sbst. i*, substantia innominata ; *s L*, striæ Lancisi ; *s p*, septum pellucidum ; *stc*, stria cornea ; *sts*, substant. subependymica ; *Subst. p. ant*, Substantia perforata anterior ; *tc*, tuber cinereum ; *to*, tuber olfact.; *v*, ventriculus sept. pelluc. (fifth ventricle); *ra*, anterior horn ; *z B*, Broca's convolution ; *I*, tractus olfactorius.

Tab. 29.

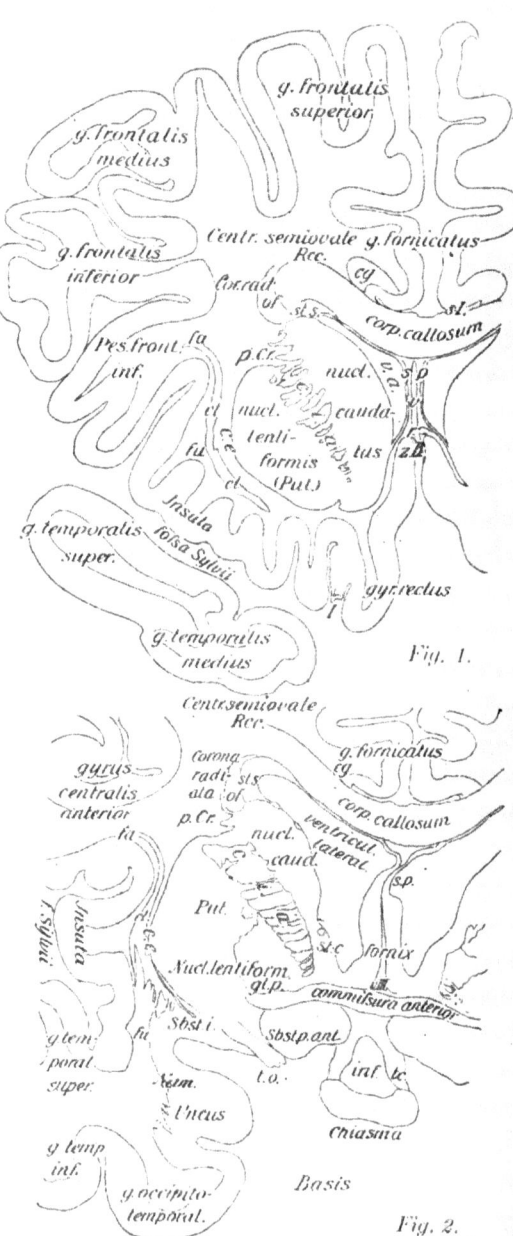

Fig. 1.

Fig. 2.

Tab. 29.

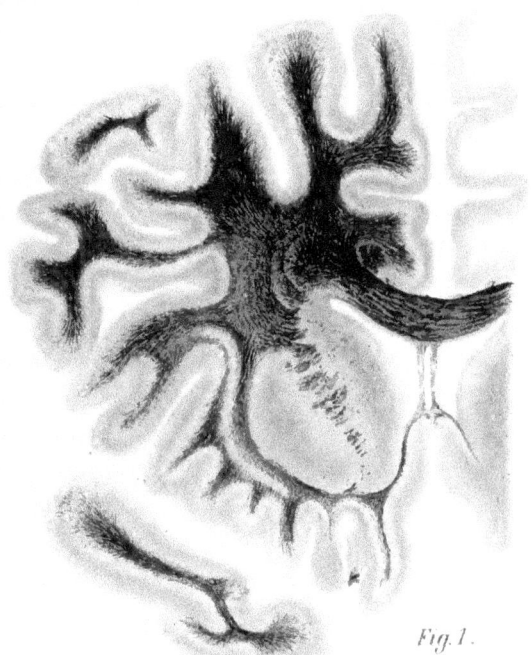

Fig. 1.

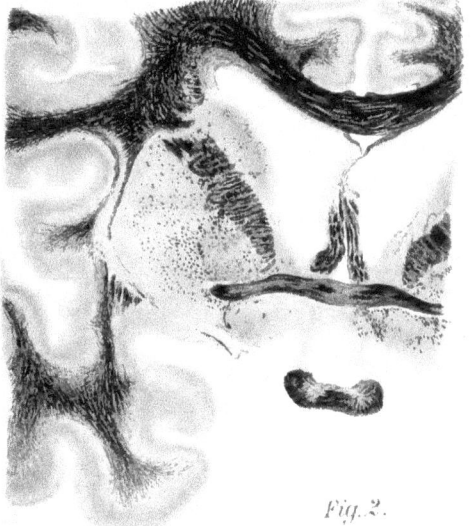

Fig. 2.

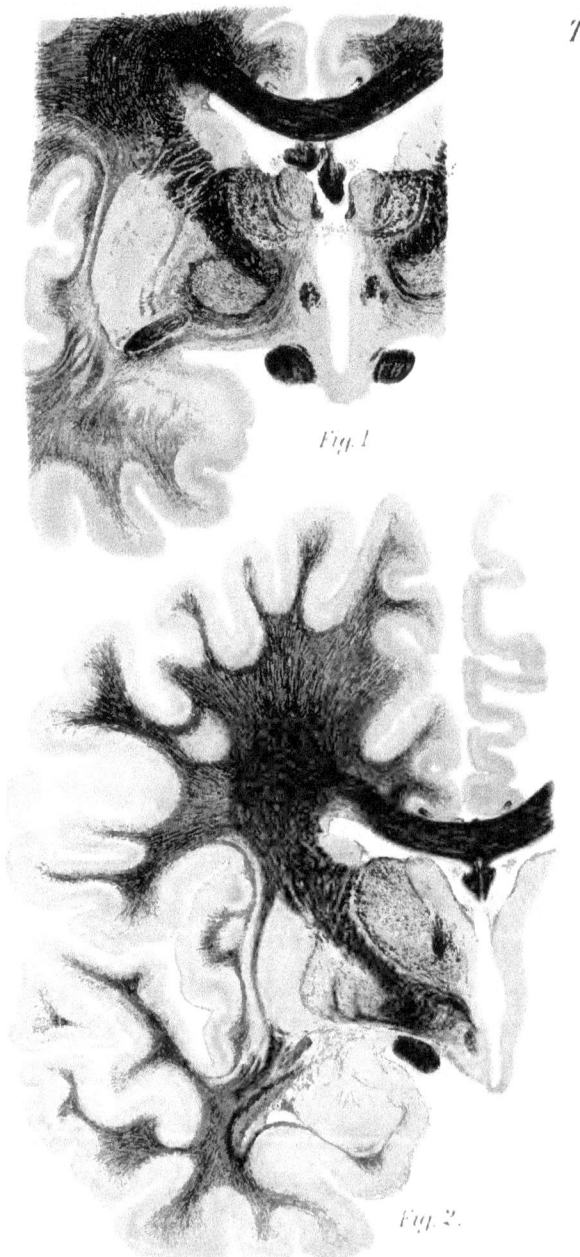

Tab. 30.

Fig. 1.

Fig. 2.

Tab. 80.

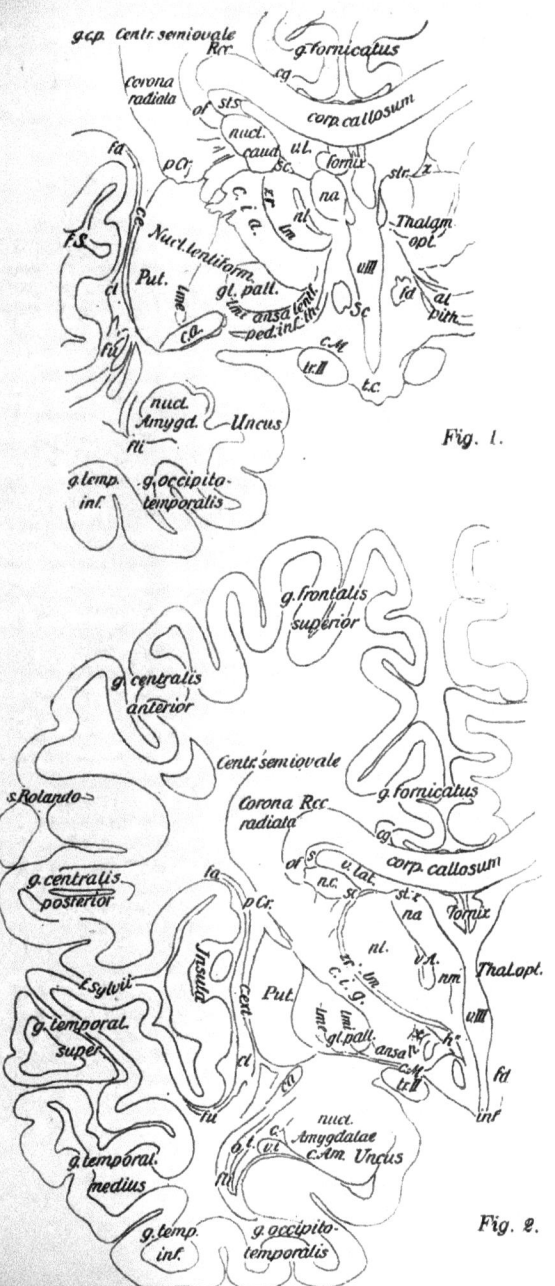

Fig. 1.

Fig. 2.

PLATE 30.

FIG. 1.—*Frontal Section behind the Anterior Commissure.* The descending crura of the fornix (*fd*) sweep backward to the corpus albicans at the base of the brain. The body of the fornix is hidden underneath the corpus callosum. (See Fig. 2.) The anterior (*na*) and lateral (*nl*) nuclei of the optic thalamus come into view, and between the optic thalami the third ventricle (*v III*) now begins to widen out.

The globus pallidus (*gl. pall*) subdivides into several segments, and with its basal fibers (ansa lentiformis) surrounds the inner capsule. The optic tracts (*tr. II*) pass backward from the chiasm to the lateral geniculate body.

As the anterior commissure (*c. a.*) also arches backward at this level, it is seen in oblique section.

FIG. 2.—*Section through the Knee of the Inner Capsule.* Beneath the most posterior portion of the upper frontal convolutions are the central convolutions, and at the bottom of the fissure of Sylvius (*f. S*) the convolutions of the insula (*ins*). In the temporal lobe (three convolutions) the nucleus amygdalæ (*N. a*) has come into view, and to its mesial side the cornu ammonis (*c. Am*), which represents the inner bulging of the Hippocampal convolution. The caudate nucleus (*n. c.*) is separated from the optic thalamus by the stria cornea. The fibers of the ansa lentiformis (*ansa lt*), which are derived from the globus pallidus (*gl. pall*), pass around and through (*x*) the lowest bundles of the knee of the inner capsule; a part of these fibers are collected into a bundle in the subthalamic region and pass to the lower field of the tegmentum (*h″*).

The optic thalamus (*Th*) is joined by the inferior peduncle of the thalamus (*ped. inf. th*, see Fig. 1), derived from the temporal lobe, and situated underneath the ansa lentiformis, with which it combines to form the ansa peduncularis. The optic thalamus has greatly increased in size, and with its upper portion (*tuberculum ant. na.*) reaches to the fornix.

It is divided into three nuclei: the anterior (*na*), lateral (*nl*), and mesial (*nm*). To its outer side lies the lamina medullaris externa (*lm*), and between this and the inner capsule the zona radicularis (*zr*).

Abbreviations.—*c*, Tailpiece of caud. nucl.; *c M*, commissura Meynert; *fd*, descending fornix; *fli*, descending long. bundle; *lma*, lamin. medullar. externa of lentic. nucleus; *lmi*, lam. medull. interna; *o*, optic radiation; *Sc*, substantia grisea centralis (central gray matter); *str. z*, stratum zonale thalami; *t*, tapetum; *vl*, lateral ventricle; *vi*, descending horn; *v III*, third ventricle. For other abbreviations see Plate 29, 8.

PLATE 31.

FIG. 1.—*Section through the Middle of the Third Ventricle.* We see the three nuclei of the optic thalamus (*Thal. o*) shown on Plate 30. From the upper (*n. a*) the bundle of Vicq d'Azyr (*v. A*) passes downward to the corpus albicans (*cp. m*). Underneath the optic thalamus the *subthalamic region* comes more plainly into view; the latter consists of the ansa lentiformis (*al*) and the tegmental portion from the ventral part of the optic thalamus. It is divided into an upper (*fh'*) and a lower (*fh''*) tegmental field, having between them the zona incerta (*zi*) or continuation of the zona radicularis thalami (*zr*), and containing besides the body of Luy (subthalamic body) (*cl*). The internal capsule (in the region of the most anterior segment of the posterior limb) (*c.i.p*) becomes gradually reinforced by constant additions from the central convolutions (motor central neurons); the mesial portion is beginning to appear at the base of the hemisphere at the crusta or pes (*P*). The lenticular nucleus has diminished in size. The descending horn (*v. i*) in the temporal lobe, on the other hand, has increased. The optic tract (*tr. o*) is seen underneath the crusta, which now projects freely. The fornix (*f*) terminates laterally in the corpus albicans (*cp. m.*).

FIG. 2.—*Section through the Central Convolutions.* The subdivision of the optic thalamus into its upper or anterior (*na*), lateral (*nl*), and mesial (*nm*) nuclei is plainly seen. Between the two latter nuclei are the fibers of the lamina medullaris interna (*mi*). On the other side the capsule is bounded by the zona radicularis, which is formed by fibers entering from the internal capsule. The subthalamic region between the crusta and the optic thalamus has widened out. It contains the corpus subthalamicum or body of Luy (*c. L*), the red nucleus (*n, r*) and its lateral white matter (*l*), and the zona incerta (*z. i*). Immediately beneath is the beginning of the substantia nigra (*Sn*). In the median line the first fibers of the oculomotor (*III*) begin to emerge.

In the descending horn (*v. i*) the tailpiece of the caudate nucleus (*c*), which is reflected toward the base of the brain, is also included in the section. The mesial wall of the lateral ventricle is formed by the cornu ammonis, gyrus dentatus (*gd*), fimbria (*f*), and inferior choroidal plexus (*pl*); the lateral wall is formed by the tapetum (*tp*).

Abbreviations.—*ce*, Capsulæ externa; *cg*. genu capsulæ int.; *cp*, capsul. int. (posterior limb); *cl*, claustrum; *fa*, fascicul. arcuatus; *fu*, fasc. uncinatus; *fli*, inferior long. bundle; *gl. p.*, globus pallidus; *nc*, caudate nucleus; *nf*, cup-shaped nucleus of Flechsig; *of*, fasc. fronto-occipital.; *o*, optic radiation; *p Cr*, foot of corona radiata; *Put*, putamen; *Rcc*, radiation of corp. callos.; *s*, subst. subependymica; *sc*, stria cornea; *sp*, septum pellucidum; *tt*, tænia thalami; *v. lat.*, lateral ventricle; *vi*, descending horn; *v. III*, third ventricle; *x*, point where the ansa lentiformis traverses the inner capsule.

Tab. 31.

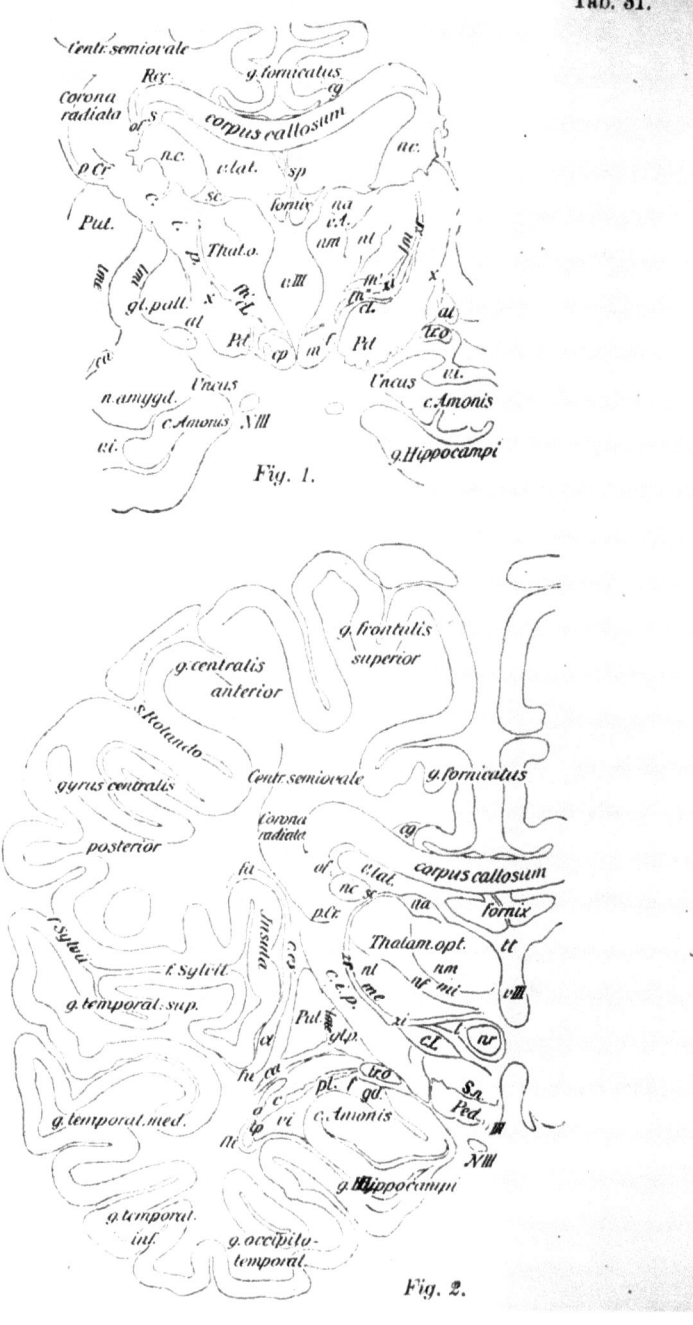

Fig. 1.

Fig. 2.

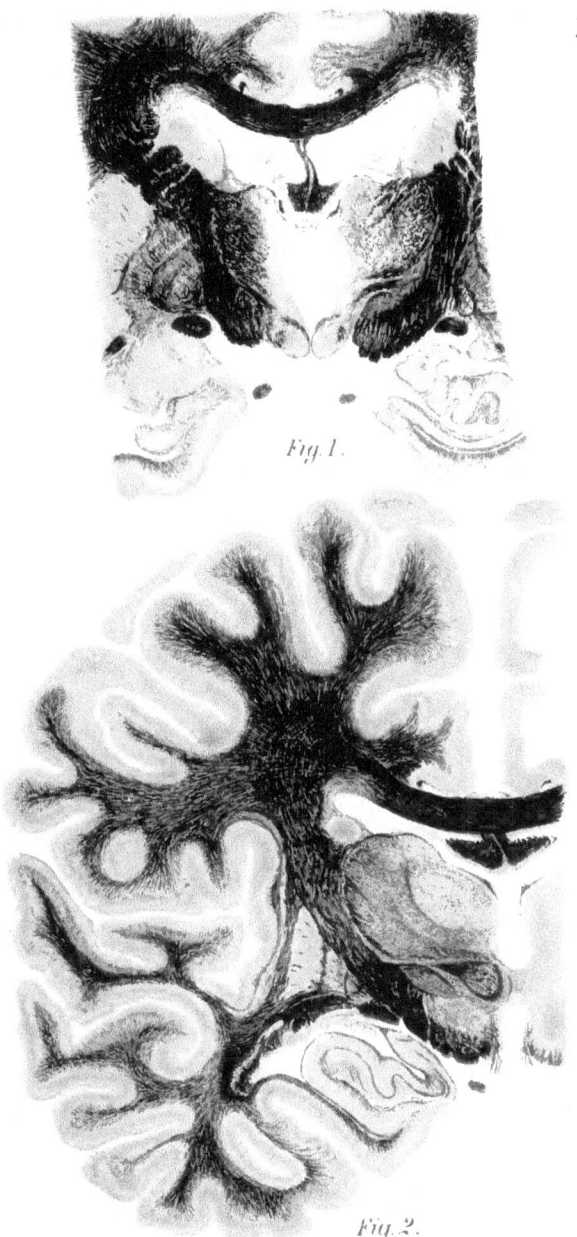

Tab. 31.

Fig. 1.

Fig. 2.

Tab. 32.

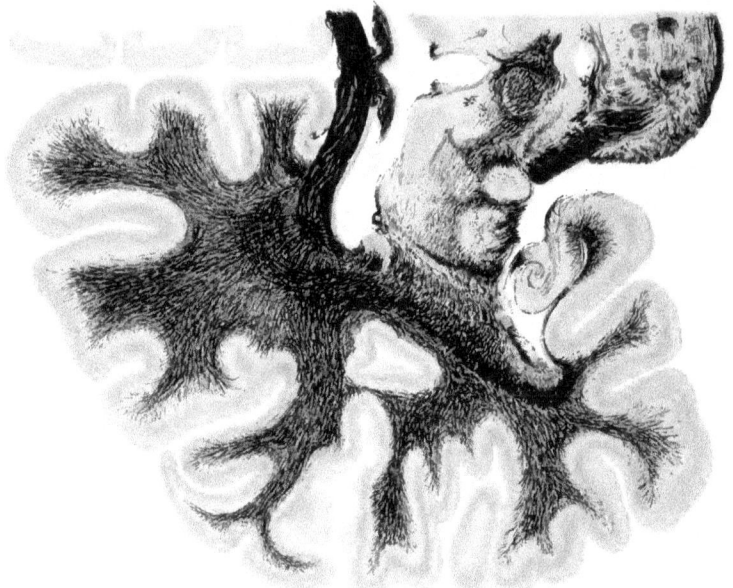

Fig. 1.

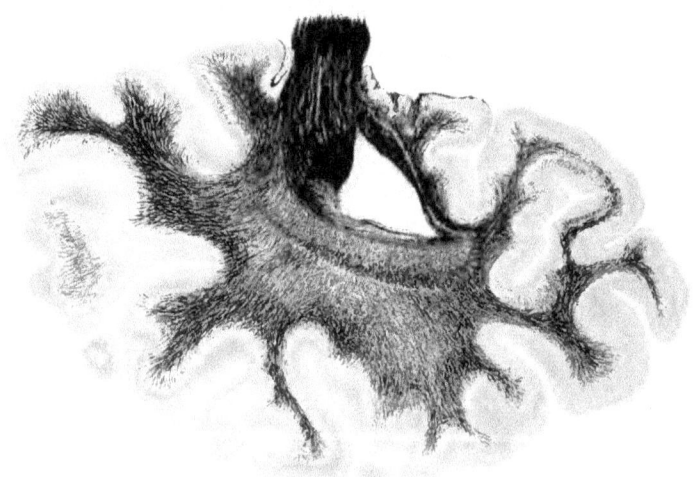

Fig. 2.

Tab. 32.

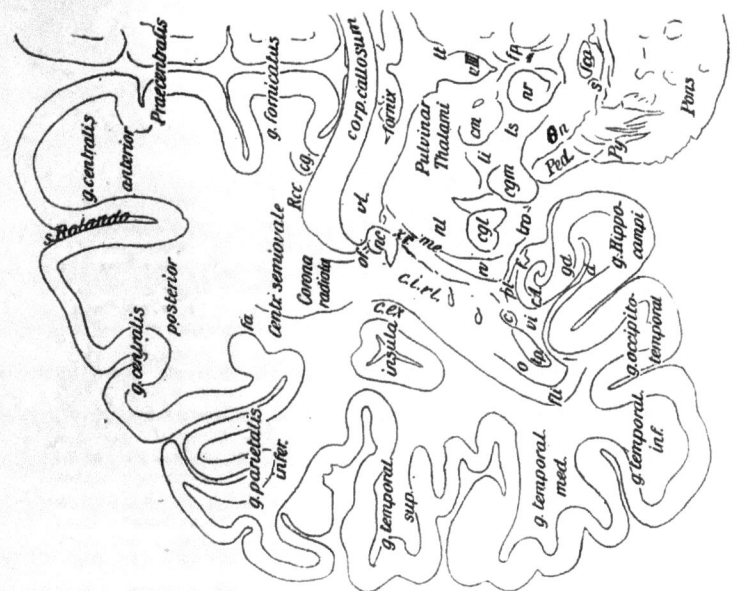

Fig. 1.

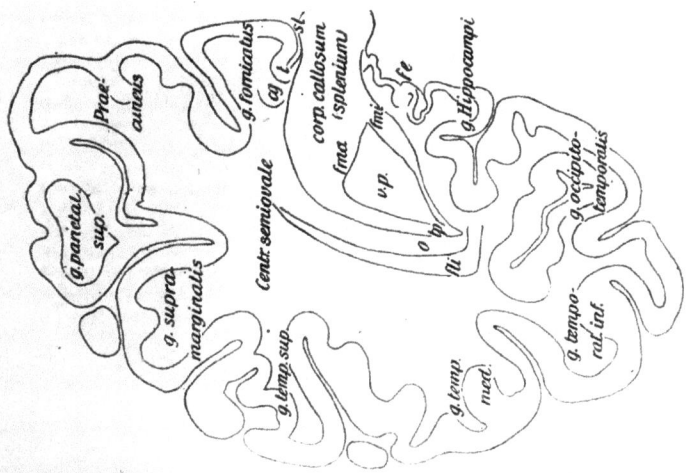

Fig. 2.

PLATE 32.

FIG. 1.—*Section through the Pulvinar Thalami.* The brain-stem emerges more and more from the hemisphere. The cerebral peduncle (*Ped*) is entirely free, while the pulvinar is still attached by its upper and posterior peduncles. Wedged in between the cerebral peduncle and the internal capsule (posterior segment, *cirl*) we find the lateral geniculate body (*c. g. l*), in which the optic tract (*tr. o*) terminates, and the mesial geniculate body (*c. g. m*).

The descending horn (*r. i*) is apparently opened up so that its formation by the invagination of the cortex of the hippocampal convolution is readily seen. From the free border of the latter the fimbria (*f*) begins its course upward. To the outer side of the lateral geniculate body the optic radiation (*o*) begins in the triangular field of Wernicke (*w*) and passes to the cortex of the occipital lobe. The subthalamic region has been replaced by the important tegmental region; the subthalamic body has disappeared, the fillet (upper, *ls*, and lower, *li*) has increased in width, and the red nucleus (*n. r*) has become larger. The third ventricle is about to become the aqueduct of Sylvius. The peduncular fibers nearest the median line are surrounded by the first transverse fibers of the pons; the lenticular nucleus has disappeared.

FIG. 2.—*Section through the Parietal Lobe.* The brain-stem together with the pulvinar is completely separated from the hemisphere. The picture resembles the first section through the frontal lobe.

The section includes the splenium of the corpus callosum; the tapetum (*tp*), to the lateral side of the posterior horn of the lateral ventricle (*v. p*); the optic radiation (*o*), which passes from the primary optic centers (lateral geniculate body, inferior corpora quadrigemina, pulvinar) to the occipital lobe. To its outer side is the inferior longitudinal bundle (*fli*).

Abbreviations.—*c*, Cauda; *c. ex*, capsula externa; *cg*, cingulum; *cirl*, capsula intern. retrolenticularis; *cm*, cella media; *d*, diverticulum subiculi; *fc*, fasciola cinerea; *fca*, foramen cæcum anterius; *fli*, inferior long. bundle; *fma*, forceps major; *fmi*, forceps minor; *fp*, posterior long. bundle; *gd*, gyrus dentatus; *me*, lamina medullaris externa; *nc*, caudate nucleus; *nl*, nucleus lateralis; *of*, fasc. fronto-occipital.; *pl*, plexus choroideus inferior; *Py*, fibers of pyramids; *Rcc*, radiation of corp. callos.; *s*, accessory fillet; *Sn*, substantia nigra; *t*, tænia tecta; *tp*, tapetum; *tt*, tænia thalami; *vl*, lateral ventricle; *v III*, third ventricle; *zr*, zona radicularis.

PLATE 33.

FIG. 1.—*Section through the Occipital Lobe.* The cortical visual center lies chiefly in the neighborhood of the calcarine fissure in the cuneus and lingula. Here the fibers of Gratiolet's optic radiation (*o*) gradually make their entrance. The association fibers are represented by the inferior longitudinal bundle (*ls*), the fasciculus transversus cunei (*t*), and the stratum calcarinum (*str*).

Abbreviations.—*c,* Remains of the forceps of the corpus callosum; *vp,* remains of the posterior horn of the ventricle.

FIG. 2.—*Sagittal Section through the Brain-stem* (two millimeters to one side of the median line). The section shows: The optic thalamus (inner wall of the third ventricle, *v. III*), the posterior commissure (*cp*), the anterior and posterior corpora quadrigemina (*cqa* and *cq p*) with the central gray matter of the aqueduct (*e*), from which the oculomotor (*III*) arises. Underneath is the tegmental region containing the red nucleus (*nr*), the decussation of the brachia (*dbr*), and the anterior brachium which passes from that point to the cerebellum; *l. m,* fillet. In the pons is the pyramidal tract (*Pyr*) which emerges as the pyramids (*Py*). Above the pyramidal tract the trapezoid body (*ctz*) in transverse section, and above the pyramid the olive (*ol. inf*). Beneath the floor of the fourth ventricle (*ventr. IV*) are the following structures: The locus cœruleus (*lc*), the knee of the facial nerve (*g. VII*) with the nucleus of the abducens immediately beneath it, the fibers of this nerve (*VI*) passing down to the base of the brain, the dorsal longitudinal bundle (*fd*), and the striæ acusticæ (*st. a*). In the medulla oblongata the nucleus of the hypoglossus (*n, XII*), the funiculus gracilis (nucleus of Goll, *n. G*), the internal arcuate fibers (*fai*), the posterior (*fp*) and anterior (*fa*) columns of the spinal cord, and the decussation of the pyramids (*D. pyr*). We see also *IV,* trochlear nerve; *Ch,* chiasm; *cpm,* corpus albicans; *fr,* fasciculus retroflexus; *tc,* tuber cinereum; *tt,* tænia thalami; *v,* bundle of Vicq d'Azyr.

FIG. 3.—*Sagittal Section through the Brain-stem and Corpus Callosum* (six millimeters to one side of the median line).

Abbreviations.—*al,* Ansa lentiformis; *c. dent.,* corpus dentatum; *c L,* corpus Luys; *c. rst,* corpus restiforme; *fs,* fasciola cinerea; *fl,* flocculus; *fh',* Forel's tegmental bundle; *l. sup. a,* lobus superior anterior; *ll, lm,* laqueus lateralis and laqueus medialis; *m,* motor nucleus of fifth nerve; *nr,* nucleus ruber; *Py,* pyramidal tract; *qa, qp,* anterior and posterior corp. quadrigemina; *s,* sensory nucleus of fifth nerve; *Sn,* substantia nigra; *V,* trigeminus.

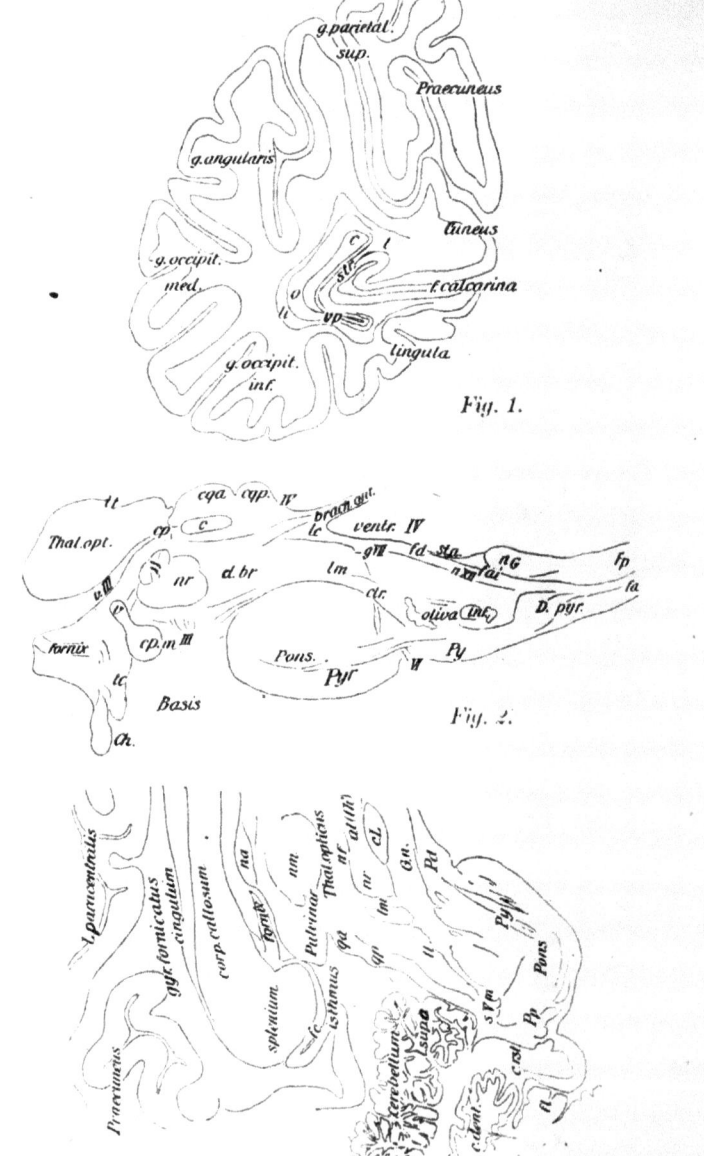

Tab. 33.

Fig. 1.

Fig. 2.

Fig. 3.

Tab. 33.

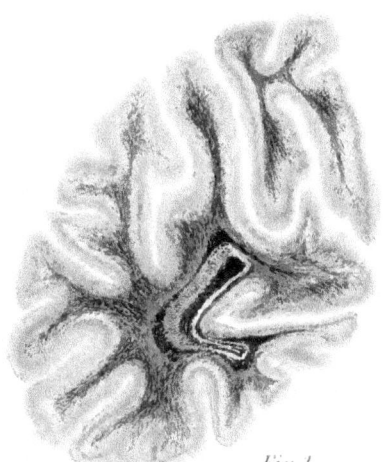

Fig. 1.

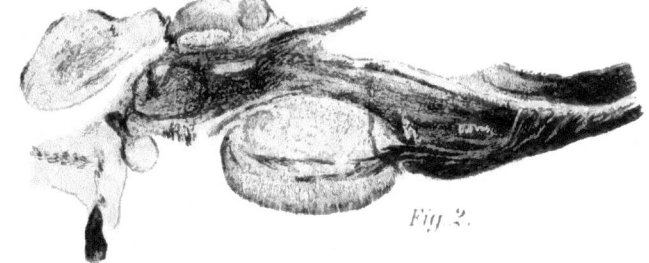

Fig. 2.

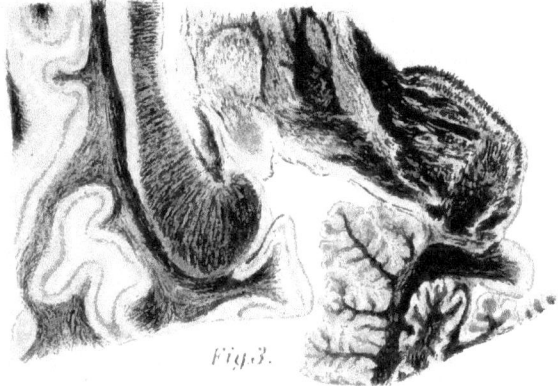

Fig. 3.

Tab. 34.

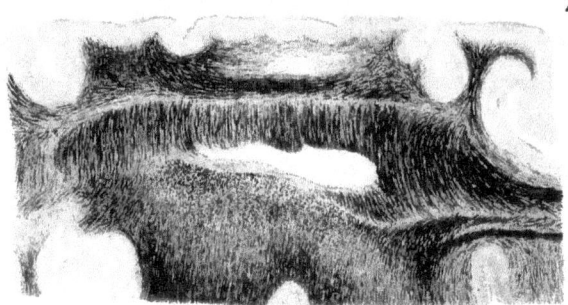

Fig. 1.

Fig. 2.

Fig. 3.

Tab. 34.

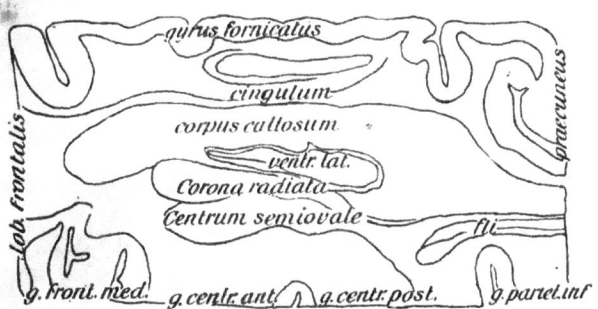

Fig. 1.

Fig. 2.

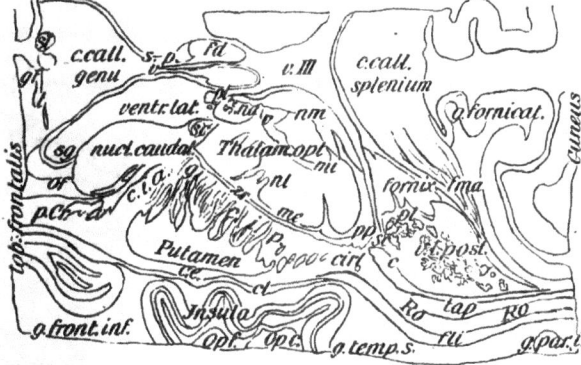

Fig. 3.

PLATE 34.

Fig. 1.—*Horizontal Section Immediately above the Corpus Callosum.* The lateral ventricle (*ventr. lat.*) is laid open from above; the section passes through the foot of the corona radiata.

Fig. 2.—*Horizontal Section through the Center of the Corpus Callosum.* The caudate nucleus and optic thalamus are cut near the surface. To either side we see the inner capsule (anterior limb, *cia*), knee (*g*), posterior limb (*cip*), and the outer segment of the lenticular nucleus of which the putamen is seen between the fibers of the capsule. To the outer side of the latter is the foot of the corona radiata (*pes Cor. rad*).

Fig. 3.—*Horizontal Section Immediately below Figure 2.* The putamen has increased in size; the most posterior segment of the inner capsule, the pars retrolenticularis (*cirl*), has come into view and is joined by Gratiolet's optic radiation (*Ro*); to the outer side is the inferior longitudinal bundle (*fli*); to the mesial side, the tapetum (*tap*), which forms the lateral wall of the posterior horn.

Abbreviations.—*c*, Tailpiece of the caudate nucleus; *c. call*, corpus callosum; *cex*, external capsule; *cia*, internal capsule (anterior limb); *cirl*, internal capsule, pars retrolenticularis; *cip*, internal capsule (posterior limb); *cl*, claustrum; *fd*, descending limb of the fornix; *fli*, inferior longitudinal bundle; *fma*, forceps major; *g*, knee of the inner capsule; *g.f*, gyrus fornicatus; *me*, lamina medullaris externa; *mi*, lam. med. interna; *na*, nucleus anterior; *nl*, nucleus lateralis; *nm*, nucleus medialis; *of*, fascicul. occipitofrontalis; *p Cr*, foot of corona radiata; *pl*, plexus choroid. lat.; *pp*, pedunculus post. thalami; *Ro*, optic radiation; *sg*, substant. grisea subependymica; *sc*, stria cornea; *sl*, striæ Lancisi; *sp*, septum pellucidum; *sz*, stratum zonale; *t*, tænia tecta; *tap*, tapetum; *v*, fifth ventricle; *v. ant*, anterior horn; *vl post*, posterior horn; *zr*, zona radicularis.

PLATE 35.

Fig. 1.—*Horizontal Section through the Middle of the Optic Thalamus.*

Figs. 2 and 3.—*Sections through the Base of the Optic Thalamus.* For lettering not included in the next paragraph see Plate 34.

Abbreviations.—*r. A*, Cornu ammonis; *ca*, anterior horn; *cm*, cella media; *cp*, commissura posterior; *E*, pineal gland; *f*, fornix; *fh'*, Forel's tegmental bundle; *fmi*, forceps minor; *g*, central gray matter; *gd*, gyrus dentatus; *gl. pall*, globus pallidus; *gscc*, gyrus subcallosus; *lme, lmi*, lamina medullaris ext. and interna of lenticular nucleus; *nf*, cup-shaped nucleus of Flechsig; *pm*, plexus choroid. med.; *Pulv*, pulvinar thalami; *r*, fascicul. retroflexus; *spl cc*, splenium; *tt*, tænia thalami; *v*, bundle of Vicq d'Azyr; *v III*, third ventricle; *w*, Wernicke's lateral field of pulvinar.

Tab. 35.

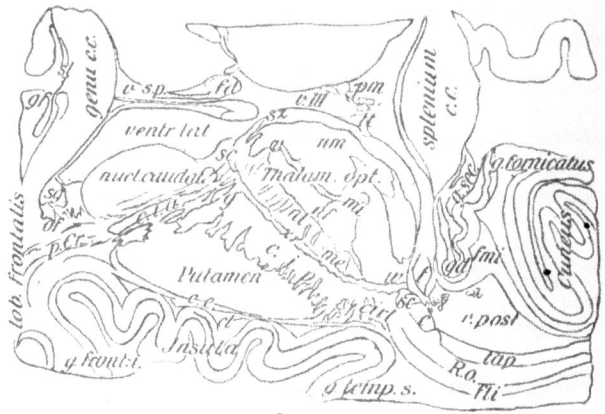

Fig. 1.

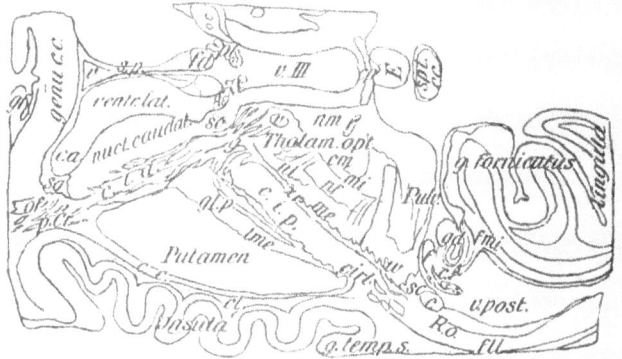

Fig. 2.

Fig. 3.

Tab. 35.

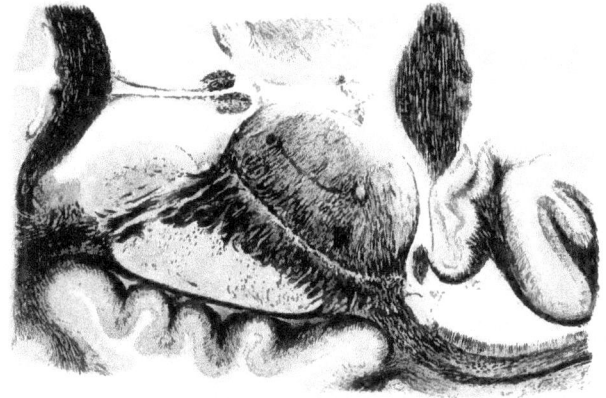

Fig. 1.

Fig. 2.

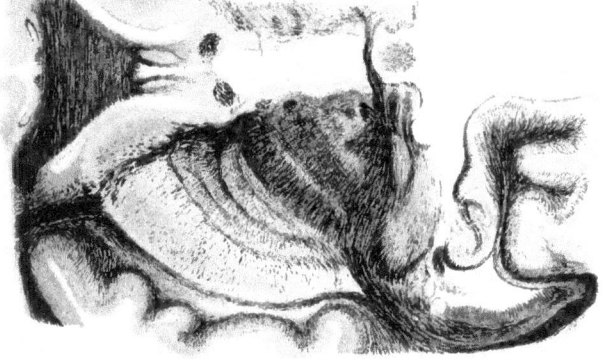

Fig. 3. Lith. Anst. F. Reichhold, München

PLATE 36.

FIGS. 1 TO 3.—*Horizontal Sections through the Subthalamic Region and Corpora Quadrigemina.* In these sections the pes separates from the hemisphere as the continuation of the posterior limb of the capsule; the posterior commissure makes its appearance.

For the lettering not included in the following paragraph see Plates 34 and 35.

Abbreviations.—A, Aquæductus Sylvii; al, ansa lentiformis; ba, brachium anticum; bp, brachium posticum; $c.ant$, commissura anterior; sg, central gray matter; $cing$, cingulum; cm, corpus mammillare; fh'', field h″ of tegmentum (ansa lenticularis); fu, fasciculus uncinatus; g, central gray matter of third ventricle; $gfr.i$, gyrus frontalis inferior; gl, corpus geniculatum lateral; $gl.p$, globus pallidus; gti, gyrus temporalis inferior; gts, gyrus temporalis superior; gm, corpus geniculatum mediale; ll, laqueus lateralis; lm, laqueus medialis; lt, lamina terminalis; $N\,III$, fibers of oculomotor; $N\,IV$, decussation of trochlear nerve; nr, nucleus ruber; p, fascicul. longitud. posterior; rcc, rostrum corpor. callosi; s, accessory fillet; $Sb.\,in$, substantia innominata; Spa, Spp, substantia perforata anterior and posterior; tc, tuber cinereum; tro, tractus opticus; cx, point where ansa lentiformis traverses the knee of the internal capsule; $z\,B$, Broca's convolution; zi, zona incerta.

Tab. 86.

Fig. 1.

Fig. 2.

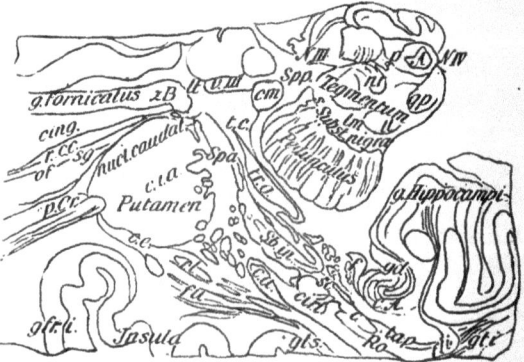

Fig. 3.

Tab. 36.

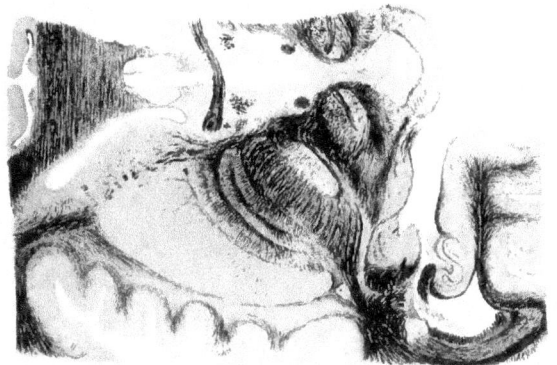

Fig. 1.

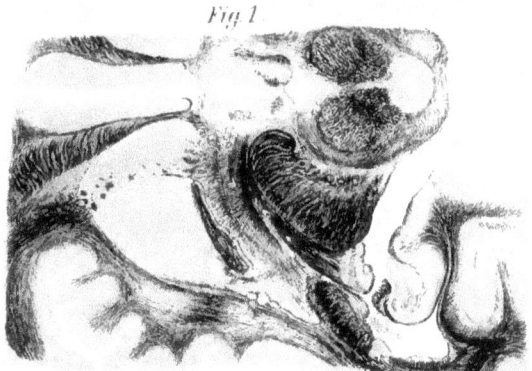

Fig. 2.

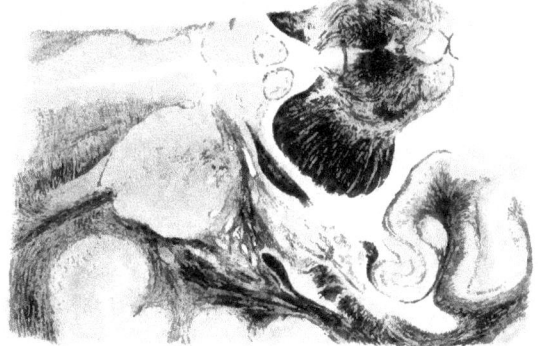

Fig. 3.

Tab. 37.

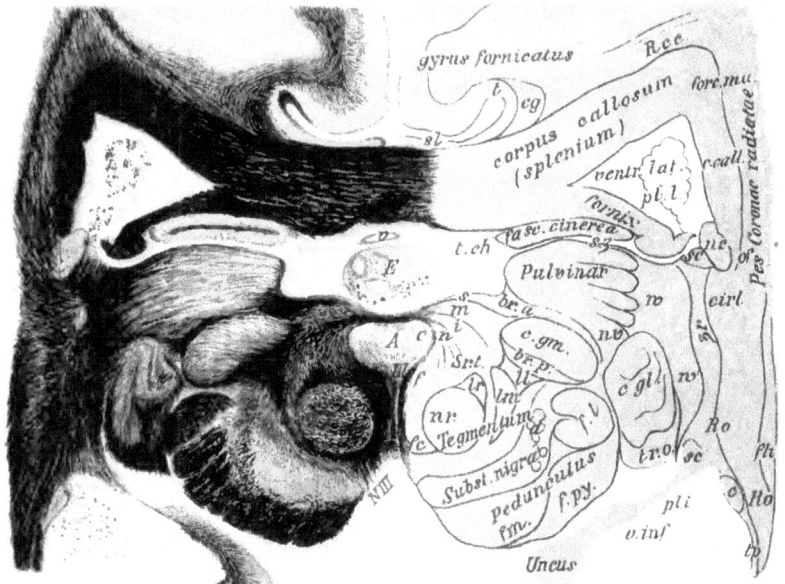

Fig. 1.

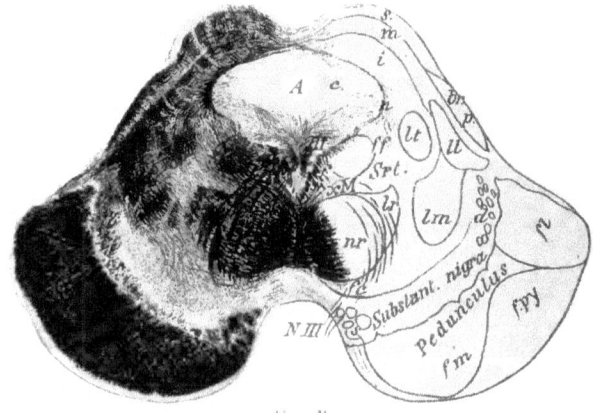

Fig. 2.

Lith. Anst. F. Reichhold, München.

PLATE 37.

FIG. 1.—*Vertical Section through the Anterior Corpora Quadrigemina and Pulvinar.* The optic thalami (pulvinar) are widely separated by the anterior quadrigemina. Above the corpora quadrigemina is the pineal gland (E), above that the large vein of Galen (v) and the tela choroidea ($t.\ ch$), and above this, finally, the splenium of the corpus callosum and fornix.

In the central gray matter (c) the aqueduct of Sylvius (A), with the nucleus of the oculomotor (III) beneath it and the nasal root of the fifth nerve (n) on its lateral side.

In the corpora quadrigemina we distinguish a superficial (s), a middle (m), and a deep (i) layer of white matter. Under these layers are the tegmentum and the red nucleus ($n.\ r$), which approach each other from either side; to their outer side is the upper sensory fillet ($l.\ m$), which is joined by the lower fillet ($l.\ l$) from the corpora quadrigemina and the posterior brachium (bp). To the lateral side of these structures we find the mesial ($c.\ g.\ m$) and lateral ($c.\ g.\ l$) geniculate bodies. Separated from the tegmentum by the substantia nigra, which is recognized by its darkly pigmented cells, is the crusta (pedunculus), which contains in its central portion the motor pyramidal tract (fpy). The optic tract ($tr.\ o$) passes to the lateral geniculate body, the anterior corpus quadrigeminum, and finally to the pulvinar, where it ends. From this point the fibers of the optic radiation (Ro) pass through the lateral white matter (w) toward the center and finally to the occipital lobe. For further details see the photograph on Plate 40, 2.

FIG. 2.—*Section between the Anterior and Posterior Corpora Quadrigemina.* The tegmental region is completely separated from the pulvinar and lateral white matter. The fillet (lm, upper, and ll, lower lateral) passes toward the base of the brain beneath the red nuclei (nr). From the depths of the white matter (i) the fountain-like tegmental radiation ($f.f$) rises to the median line, where the fibers decussate in Meynert's tegmental decussation (xM) in the raphe. Immediately beneath the nucleus of the oculomotor ($n.\ III$) in the central gray matter (c) is the posterior longitudinal bundle (f), which can be plainly recognized in this section. On its outer side fibers from the optic thalamus are seen passing to the substantia reticularis (Srt). The divisions of the oculomotor nucleus (ventral and dorsal nuclei) can be seen. The posterior brachium ($br.\ p$) contains fibers running from the posterior corpus quadrigeminum to the mesial geniculate body. Fibers coming from the striate body end in the substantia nigra. The fillet which unites the corpora quadrigemina with the optic thalamus (lt) contains fibers which pass from the anterior nucleus in the corpora quadrigemina to the optic thalamus. The crusta contains the following structures: The lateral (oval or Türck's) bundle (fl), the pyramidal tract (fpy), and the mesial pontine bundle (fm). The latter is surrounded by the accessory tract of the fillet, Spitzka's bundle from the pyramidal tract, which is regarded as the central pathway of the motor cranial nerves; the central pathway of the sensory cranial nerves is supposed to correspond to the scattered bundle of the fillet (d) which descends from the fillet to the highest segment of the pes.

Abbreviations.—*c. call*, Corpus callosum; *cirl*, capsule int. retrolenticularis; *cg*, cingulum; *E*, pineal gland; *fc*, Forel's tegmental decussation; *fli*, fascicul. longitud. inf.; *forc. ma*, forceps major; *lr*, lateral white matter of red nucleus; *n*, nasal or upper root of fifth nerve; *nc*, nucl. caudatus; *nv*, nucleus ventralis thalami; *N. III*, oculomotor; *of*, fascicul. occipitofrontalis; *pl l*, *pl. i*, plexus choroideus lateralis, inferior; *tp*, tapetum; *t*, tænia tecta; *sc*, stria cornea; *sl*, striæ Lancisi; *sz*, stratum zonale; *v, vena magna*; *v. inf*, descending horn; *zr*, zona radicalis.

PLATE 38.

FIG. 1.—*Section through the Posterior Corpora Quadrigemina.* On the basal aspect the section includes the anterior portions of the pons which surround the crusta. The posterior corpora quadrigemina ($q. p$) are joined by a part of the inferior lateral fillet (ll). By the side of the nasal, descending root of the trigeminus (n) we see the trunk of the trochlear nerve (IV), which begins at this point. The tegmentum contains the decussation (dbr) of those fibers of the brachia (br) which arise in the red nuclei and enter the cerebellum (processus cerebelli ad corpora quadrigemina).

The posterior longitudinal bundle (f) comes in relation on its outer side with the substantia reticularis tegmenti (Srt). Underneath the decussation of the brachia is the superior horizontal fillet (lm) connecting the cortex and optic thalami (central sensory pathway), and to the outer side of the latter the inferior fillet (ll) from the corpora quadrigemina (central auditory pathway).

Most of the peduncular fibers end in the pontine ganglia, mesial and lateral pontine tracts (fm, fl). The pyramidal tract (fpy) only passes through.

FIG. 2.—*Section through the Middle of the Pons.* The aqueduct has widened out and become the fourth ventricle ($v. IV$). Its roof at this point is formed by the anterior medullary velum ($v. m. a$) and the lingula (l) (from the vermiform process of the cerebellum), and to either side by the massive brachia (br), which have just emerged from their decussation.

In the tegmental region we see the posterior longitudinal bundle (f); the substantia reticularis (Srt), to the lateral side of the raphe (R), in which numerous central pathways undergo decussation; the central tegmental pathway ($c.t$); superior (mesial) and inferior (lateral) fillets ($l. m$ and $l. l$). Embedded among these fibers are numerous nuclei (upper olive ($o. s$), nuclei of the substantia reticularis, etc.); to the lateral side of the tegmentum the motor (m) and sensory (s) nuclei of the fifth nerve and its roots, which are joined above by the nasal (motor?) root of the fifth nerve (n) (near the latter the pigmented cells of the locus cœruleus, li). It is further reinforced by a bundle of fibers from the neighboring white matter of the cerebellum corresponding to the direct sensory cerebellar tract (sc), and by a crossed bundle (c) from the nucleus of the opposite side. The sensory caudal root of the fifth nerve ($V. c$) passes downward.

The pyramids (Py) pass from the crusta through the pons covered by the superficial and deep pontine fibers. The processus cerebelli ad pontem (Prp) begin in the cerebellar cortex ($Cb. cort$) and terminate in the pontine ganglia of the opposite side after decussating in the raphe (R). They communicate with the mesial and lateral pedunculopontine pathway.

Abbreviations.—A, aqueduct of Sylvius; c, central gray matter; $ctrp$, corpus trapezoides; d, scattered bundles of fillet; R, raphe (decussation); s, accessory fillet.

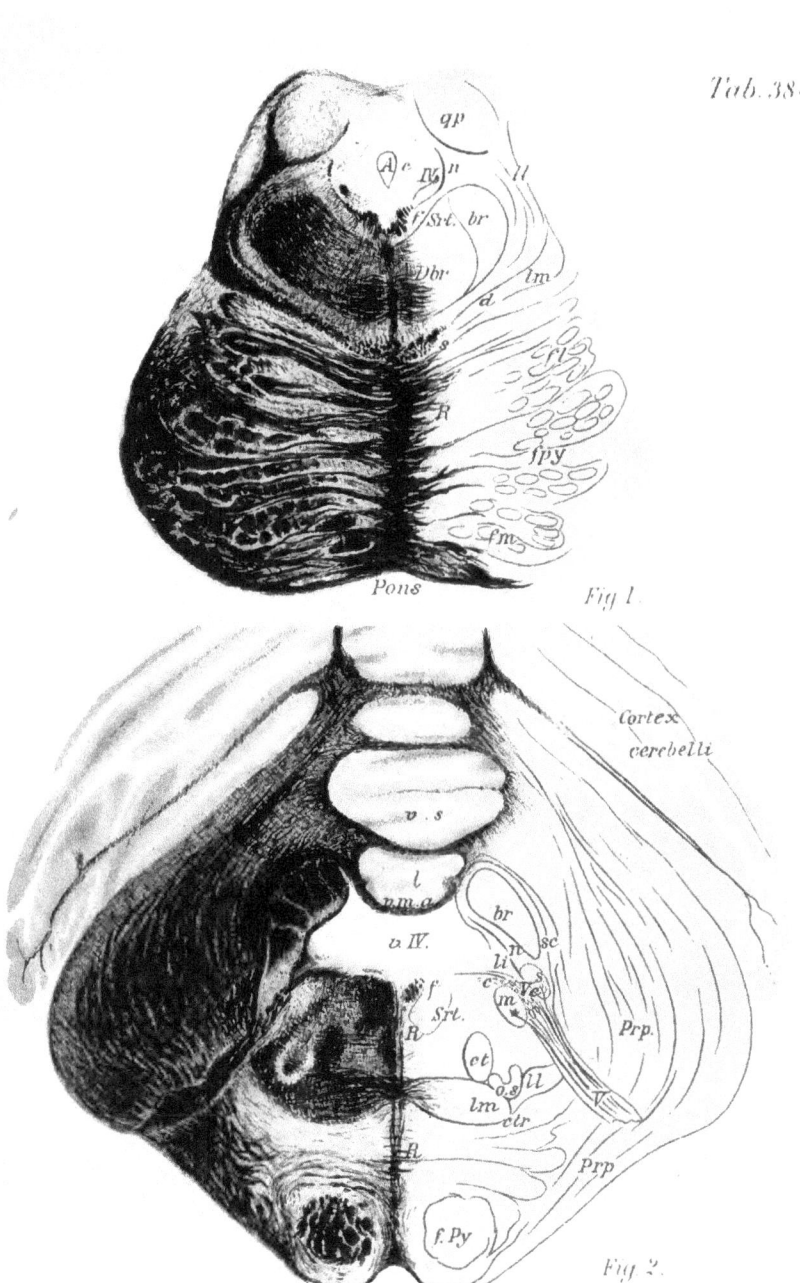

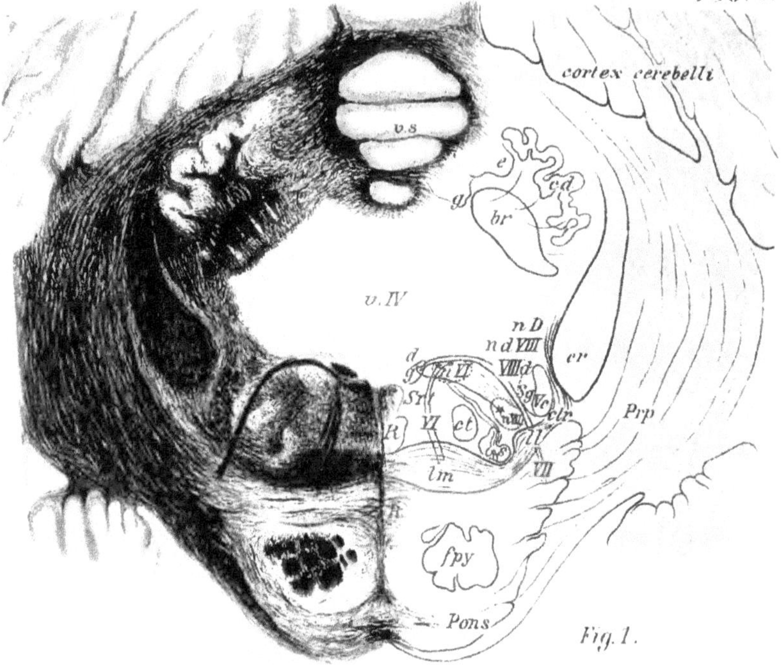
cortex cerebelli
v.s
e
cd
g
br
v. IV
n D
n d VIII
VIII d
cr
Srt
Vc
ctr
Prp
R
VI
ct
lm
VII
fpy
Pons

Fig. 1.

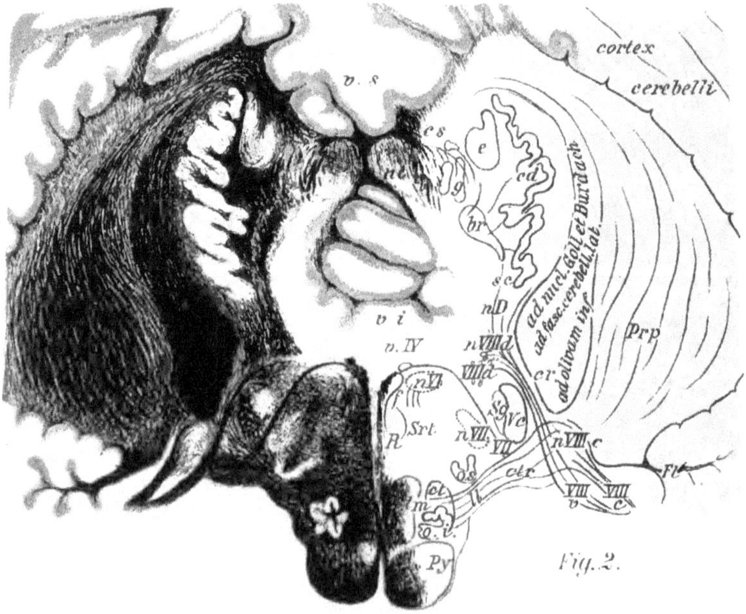
cortex
cerebelli
v. s
c s
e
cd
g
br
ad nucl. Goll et Burdach
ad fasc. cerebell. lat.
ad olivam inf.
s c
n D
v i
v. IV
n VIII d
VIII d
cr
Prp
n VI
Srt
R
n VII
VII
Vc
n VIII c
Fl
ctr
VIII v
VIII c
ct
lm
o. i.
Py

Fig. 2.

PLATE 39.

Fig. 1.—*Section through the Posterior Extremity of the Pons.* In the tegmentum the nuclei of the facial (*n. VII*) and abducens (*n. VI*) have made their appearance. The fibers of the facial (*VII*), after surrounding the nucleus of the abducens, as shown on the right-hand side, collect into a compact bundle at the knee (*g*) and pass first horizontally, and then downward to emerge at the medulla (*VII*); the course of the abducens is more simple. Its nucleus is connected with the superior olive (*o. s*).

Srt, substantia reticularis; *Lm*, superior fillet; *ll*, inferior fillet, etc., as heretofore. The caudal descending root of the trigeminus (*V. c*) joins with the sensory root and passes downward by the side of the trunk of the facial nerve. To the outer side the broad processus cerebelli ad pontem (*pr. p*) appear with the restiform bodies (*cr*) lying between them and the brachia, as will appear more plainly in the next section.

Fig. 2.—*Section through the Nuclei of the Auditory Nerve.* In the white matter of the cerebellum (*Cb*) the section has passed through the corpus dentatum (*c. d*), and in the white matter of the vermiform process through the tegmental (*n. t*) and other nuclei. The auditory nerve (*VIII*), makes its entrance to the mesial side of the flocculus (*Fl*). The cochlear branch (*VIII c*) terminates in the ventricular auditory nucleus (*n. VIII c*) to the lateral side of the restiform body (*c. r*) (shown schematically on the right-hand side); the vestibular branch (*n. VIII v*) ends in the dorsal nucleus of the auditory nerve (*n. VIII d*) and in Deiters' nucleus (*n. D*) or continuation of the locus cœruleus. From the ventral nucleus of the auditory nerve the trapezoid body (*c. tr*) passes transversely through the mesial (*L. s*) fillet to the lateral fillet (*ll*) of the other side, also to the superior olive (*o.s*); another portion of the central auditory pathway reaches the same region by way of the striæ acusticæ. (See Plate 42.) The pyramids (*Py*) have emerged from the pons. Beginning of the inferior olive (*o. i.*).

Abbreviations.—*br*, Brachium; *cd*, corpus dentatum cerebelli; *ct*, central tegmental tract; *ctr*, corpus trapezoides; *e*, embolus; *f*, fasciculus longitudinalis posterior; *g*, nucleus globosus; *n. D*, nucleus Deiters et Bechterew; *Prp*, processus cerebelli ad pontem; *R*, raphe; *s. C*, direct sensory cerebellar tract (Edinger); *sg*, substantia gelatinosa; *Srt*, substantia reticularis tegmenti; *vi*, *vs*, vermis inferior and superior; *v. IV*, fourth ventricle.

PLATE 40.

FIG. 1.—*Section through the Right Optic Thalamus at the Level of the Middle Commissure* (behind the section shown on Plate 31, Fig. 1). The three nuclei of the optic thalamus are easily recognized (nucl. anterior, a; medial., m; lateral., l). A robust bundle of fibers (v), known as the bundle of Vicq d'Azyr, passes from the anterior nucleus (which is shown in transverse section in Plates 35 and 36) downward to end in the corpus albicans of the same side (its termination is clearly shown in the unstained section 2, Plate 12). Underneath the optic thalamus is the subthalamic region with the ansa lenticularis—Forel's field, h'' of the tegmentum ($An. l$); subthalamic body ($c. L$), the fibers of which after traversing the internal capsule (ci) terminate in the globus pallidus ($gl.p$) of the lenticular nucleus; underneath is the substantia nigra ($S. n$). P, pes.

The lateral zone of the lateral nucleus (zona reticularis) is joined by the corona radiata coming from the internal capsule ($c. i$). The middle commissure ($c. m$) contains only a few nerve-fibers.

FIG. 2.—*Section through the Anterior Corpora Quadrigemina on the Left Side* (in front of the section shown on Plate 37, Fig. 1). The lateral geniculate body ($c. g. l$) and anterior corpus quadrigeminum ($c. q. a$) contain numerous terminal fibrils from the fibers of the optic nerve (tro). The pathway for the pupillary reflex must be sought in this region, between this point and the oculomotor nucleus ($N III$). The emerging oculomotor fibers (III) mark the beginning of the crusta or pes (Ped). Its mesial segment contains Spitzka's accessory bundle (s), which probably contains the central pathway for the motor cranial nerves, and passes from the pes upward to the tegmentum to undergo decussation later in the raphe.

Abbreviations.—AS, Aqueduct of Sylvius; $c. Am.$, gyrus hippocampi; cc, corpus callosum; cst, nucl. caudatus; f, post. long. bundle; fim, fimbria; li, ls, lateral and mesial fillets; nam, nucl. amgydalæ; nl, lenticular nucleus; nr, red nucleus; *Putamen teg, thal,* fibers to the optic thalamus; tro, tractus opticus; u, uncus; $vl, v. III$, lateral and middle ventricles.

Tab. 40.

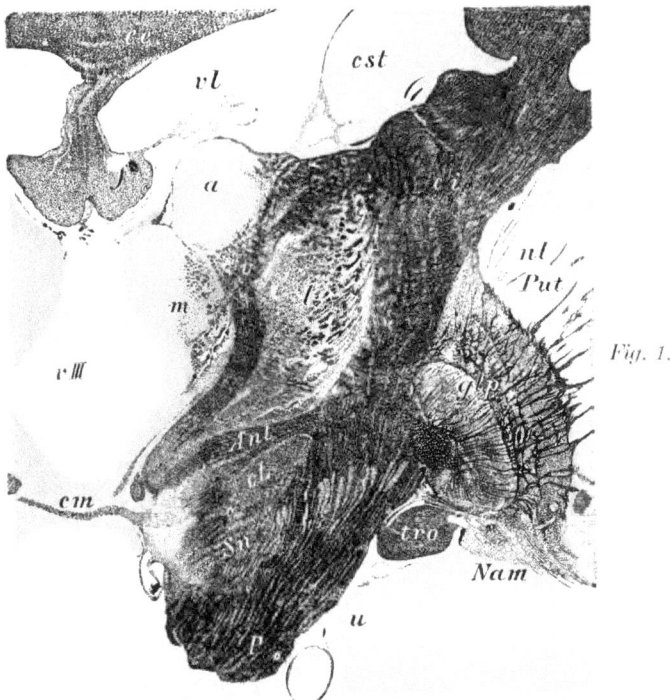

Fig. 1.

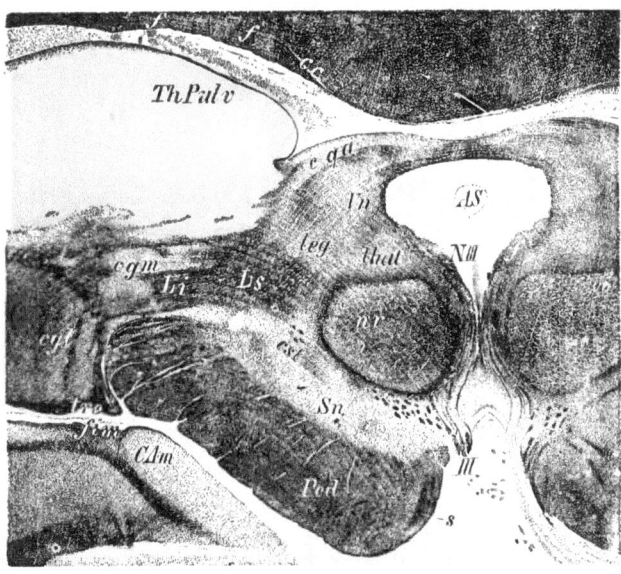

Fig. 2.

Tab. 41.

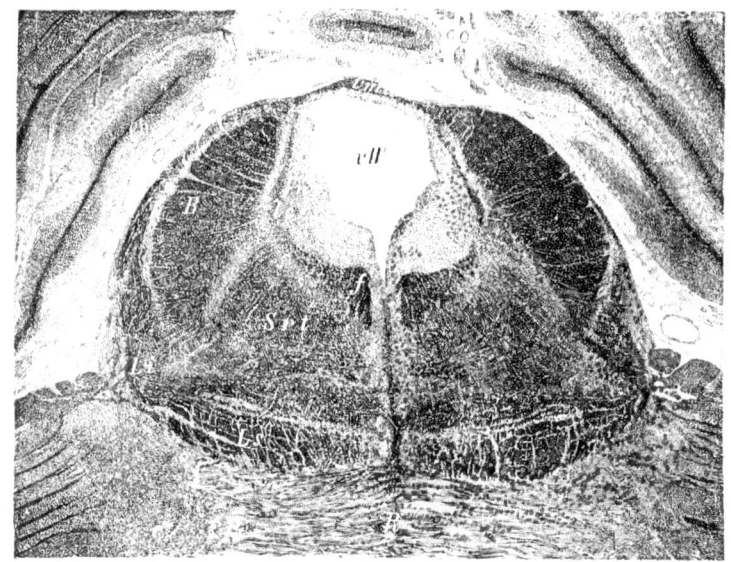

Fig. 1.

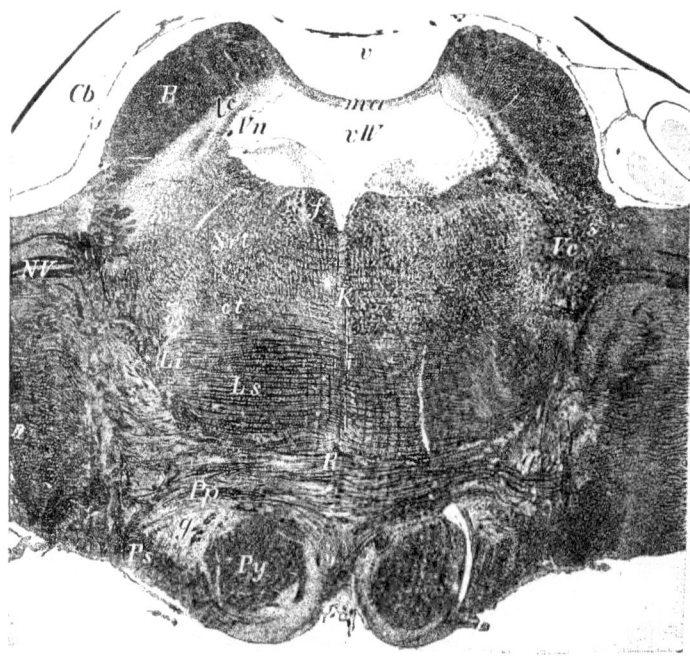

Fig. 2.

PLATE 41.

Fig. 1.—*Section through the Tegmentum behind the Posterior Corpora Quadrigemina* (behind the section on Plate 38, 1). The aqueduct is just beginning to widen out into the fourth ventricle (*r IV*).

Note the structure of the substantia reticularis (*Srt*), which contains descending fibers from the optic thalami and ascending fibers from the anterolateral columns of the spinal cord. The mesial superior fillet (*L. s*, main fillet) subdivides into numerous bundles. To its outer side is the inferior fillet (*L. i*), part of which ascends to the posterior corpora quadrigemina. Further out is the nucleus lateralis (of the optic thalamus).

Brachia (*B*), nasal root of the trigeminus (*Vn*), posterior longitudinal bundle (*f*); the heavy decussation of fibers in the raphe (*R*) of the tegmentum is plainly seen (the region contains central sensory and motor decussating pathways); *l. c*, locus cœruleus, containing deeply pigmented cells.

Abbreviations.—*P*, Pons; *Cb*, cerebellum; *v*, superior vermiform process.

Fig. 2.—*Section through the Nuclei of the Trigeminus* (in front of the section shown on Plate 48, 2). Note the details of the tegmentum and of the nuclei of the trigeminus. The caudal descending root with its various bundles (*V c*) is very plainly seen in this section lying between the motor (*m*) and sensory (*s*) nuclei. Central tegmental pathway (*ct*), substantia reticularis tegmenti (*Sr. t*), pontine ganglia (*g*) between the superficial (*Ps*) and deep (*Pp*) pontine fibers. The raphe of the tegmentum (*K*) and of the pontine fibers (*R*) contains numerous decussating fiber tracts. Underneath the superior olive (*o. s*) at *L. i*, the transverse fibers of the trapezoid body and inferior fillet (central auditory pathway) are seen.

Abbreviations.—*B*, Brachium; *Cb*, cerebellum; *lc*, locus cœruleus; *N V*, trigeminus fibers; *Py*, pyramidal tract; *ma*, anterior medullary velum; *v*, vermis sup.; *Nv*, nasal root of trigeminus.

PLATE 42.

FIG. 1.—*Section through the Right Tegmental Region at the Level of the Nucleus of the Facial Nerve.* Compare this figure with Plate 39, 1. The fibers of the nerve ascend singly from the deeply seated nucleus (*n. VII*).

We can also see a bundle of fibers running from the superior olive (*ol. s*) to the nucleus of the abducens (*N. VI*), although the latter is better seen in more anterior sections. Passing down from the cerebellum we see the restiform body (*Cr*) and the processus cerebelli ad pontem (*Cb*).

The fibers of the facial (*g. VII*) unite at the knee to form the nerve-trunk, which occupies a deeper position underneath the ependyma of the floor of the fourth ventricle (*v. IV*). The adjacent ventral nucleus of the auditory nerve is joined to the fillet by the trapezoid body (through *Li*).

On the outer side of the trunk of the facial lies the descending root of the trigeminus (*V. c*); immediately in front of it is the substantia gelatinosa (*S. g*), which represents the beginning of the posterior horn of the spinal cord. On the dorsal side we find the dorsal nucleus of the auditory nerve (*n. VIII*), and Deiters' nucleus (*N. D*), with the vestibular nerve (*VIII v*), which enters at this point; superior and inferior fillets (*L. s, L. i*). Substantia reticularis (*Sr. t*); central tegmental pathway (*c. t*); raphe (*K*); pontine ganglia (*g*); pontine fibers (*P*).

FIG. 2.—*Section through the Ventral Nucleus of the Auditory Nerve on the Left Side.* (Following Plate 39, 2.) The restiform body (*cr*) has emerged from the white matter of the cerebellum and forms the lateral wall of the fourth ventricle (*v. IV*). To its lateral side is the semicircular ventral nucleus of the eighth nerve (*n. v. VIII*), in which the cochlear nerve disappears. The nucleus extends some distance upward and presents a large transverse section as high up as the level shown in Plate 39, 2. Of the fibers forming the central pathway, we can recognize the striæ acusticæ (*str. a*), which cover the floor of the fourth ventricle, running from the median line. They decussate in the raphe (*K*) and continue their course in the lateral fillet. Dorsal nucleus of the eighth nerve (*n. VIII d*); descending root of the eighth (*a. d*); on the mesial side the nucleus of the glossopharyngeal (*n. IX*); the nucleus of the facial (*n. VII*); the substantia reticularis (*Sr. t*); the central tract of the tegmentum (*c. t*); mesial fillet (*L*); pyramid, posterior longitudinal bundle (*f*); and flocculus (*fl*) of the cerebellum.

Vc, descending root of the trigeminus. At *fol* the cerebello-olivary fibers from the restiform body pass down through the nucleus of the lateral column situated in this region. Laterally under *K*, nucleus reticularis tegmenti; *f*, fasciculus longitudinalis posterior.

Tab. 42.

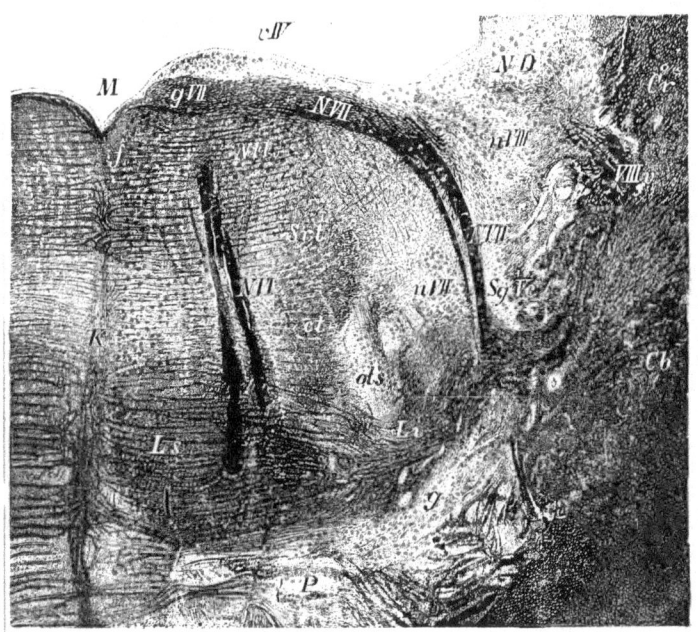

Fig. 1.

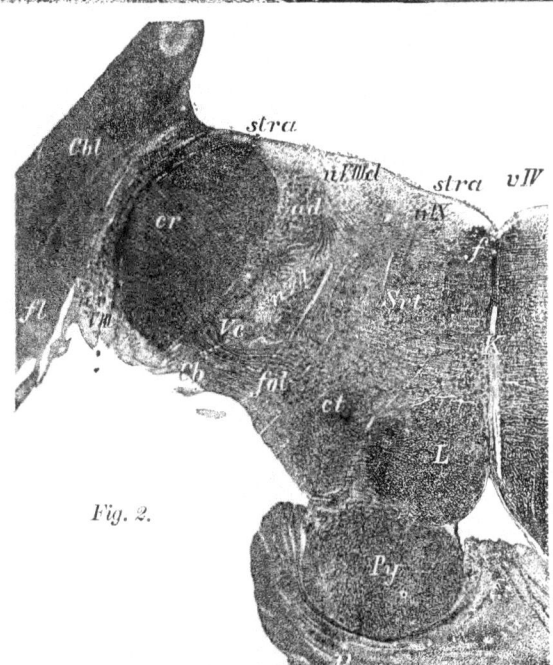

Fig. 2.

Tab. 43.

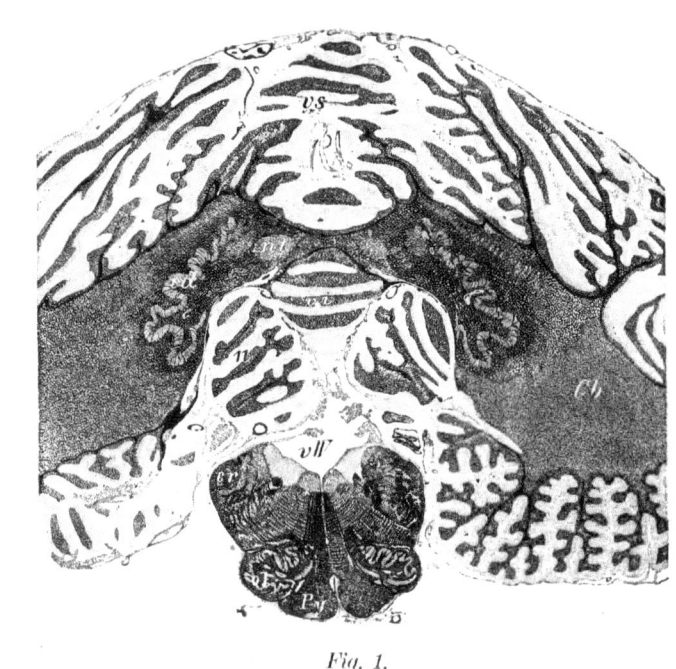

Fig. 1.

Fig. 2.

PLATE 43.

Fig. 1.—*Section through the Cerebellum and Medulla Oblongata* (posterior portion of the rhomboid fossa). The lateral walls of the fourth ventricle ($v. IV$) at this point are formed by the pia-arachnoid, as the restiform bodies (cr) have become completely separated from the cerebellar hemispheres. The roof of the ventricle is formed by the vermiform process (V); superior ($v.s$) and inferior vermiform processes ($v. i$).

In the cerebellum we see the corpus dentatum ($c. d$) and the tegmental nucleus ($n. t$). The cortex of the hemispheres has been cut away. Nodulus (n).

In the medulla we see the pyramids (Py), olives (ol), restiform bodies (cr), and the internal arcuate fibers which leave the latter structures at this point.

Fig. 2.—*Section through the Medulla Oblongata at the Level of the Glossopharyngeovagus Nucleus.* By the side of the pyramids (Py) the inferior olives (ol) have made their appearance. The cerebellar fibers (fol) pass out from the restiform bodies (cr) to the olive of the opposite side. Between the olives in the "interolivary layer" the superior fillet (L) is seen close to the raphe (K). Dorsally it comes into relation with the posterior longitudinal bundle (f). The space between the latter and the restiform body is occupied by the substantia reticularis ($S. r. t$) of the tegmentum, while on the dorsal side the sensory nuclei of the ninth and tenth nerves are seen; on the outer side of these the dorsal nucleus of the eighth ($n. VIII d$). In front of the restiform body is the descending root of the ninth and tenth, the solitary bundle (s), and under this the descending root of the trigeminus ($V. c$) to the lateral side of the substantia gelatinosa ($S.g$). The fibers of the ninth and tenth emerge on the surface of the medulla by the side of the solitary bundle. To their mesial side in the tegmentum is a group of cells known as the nucleus ambiguus ($n. a$), or motor nucleus of the vagus, which can also be seen in the following sections. $ol. m$, Mesial olive; $ol.p$, posterior accessory olive; Cb, fibers of the restiform body belonging to the direct cerebellar tract; nf, nucleus arciformis, surrounded by the external arcuate fibers, which emerge at the raphe and, sweeping over the pyramids, join the restiform body.

PLATE 44.

Fig. 1.—*Section through the Medulla at the Level of the Nuclei of the Tenth and Twelfth Nerves.* To the mesial side of the nucleus of the tenth nerve that of the hypoglossus (*XII*) makes its appearance in the floor of the fourth ventricle. The fibers of this nerve pass upward from the posterior longitudinal bundle (*f*) and fillet (*L*). To the outer side of the olives the external arcuate fibers (*fac*) pass from the restiform body to the fillet of the same side, while the internal arcuate fibers (*fai*) pass through the substantia reticularis and connect the fillet with the mesial segment of the restiform body of the other side, after traversing the descending root of the trigeminus (*Vc*); hence they cross in the raphe. Above the inferior olives (*ol*) is the posterior olive, and to its mesial side the internal or accessory olive (*ol. m*). The direct cerebellar tract (*Cb*) is contained in the restiform body and continues downward toward the pyramids. *fiol*, cerebello-olivary and interolivary fibers.

Fig. 2.—*Section through the Calamus Scriptorius in the Medulla.* The restiform bodies (*c. r*) are gradually reduced in size as more and more fibers are given off, and, approaching each other in the median line, close the rhomboid fossa (*v. IV; dorsally*, the tænia of the fourth ventricle). The nuclei of the posterior columns, the mesial nucleus, or nucleus of Goll, and lateral nucleus, or nucleus of Burdach (*n. f. p*), appear in the restiform bodies. From these nuclei the internal arcuate fibers (*fai*) descend in massive bundles to the fillet (*L*) of the other side. The nucleus of the hypoglossus (*n. XII*) and the central canal (*cc*) occupy a deeper position. Termination of the nucleus of the tenth.

Pr, Pyramids; *L*, fillet; *Srt*, substantia reticularis; *S. g*, substantia gelatinosa; *V. c*, descending root of the trigeminus; *Cb*, direct cerebellar tract; *s*, solitary bundle; *ol*, olives; *f*, posterior longitudinal bundle, etc., as in former plates. *K*, raphe of the tegmentum; *fac*, external arcuate fibers.

Tab. 44.

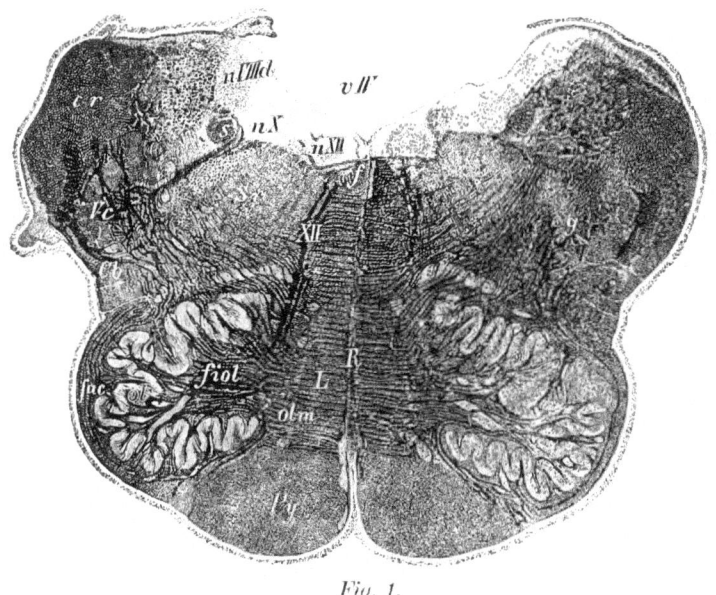

Fig. 1.

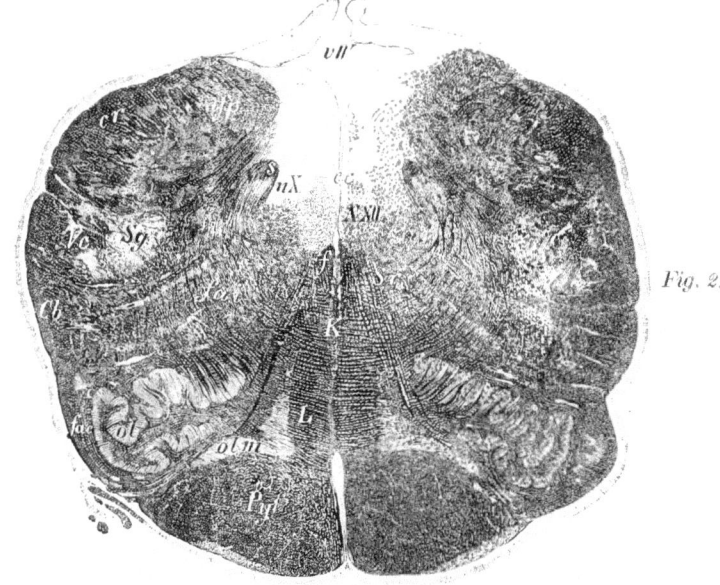

Fig. 2.

Tab. 45.

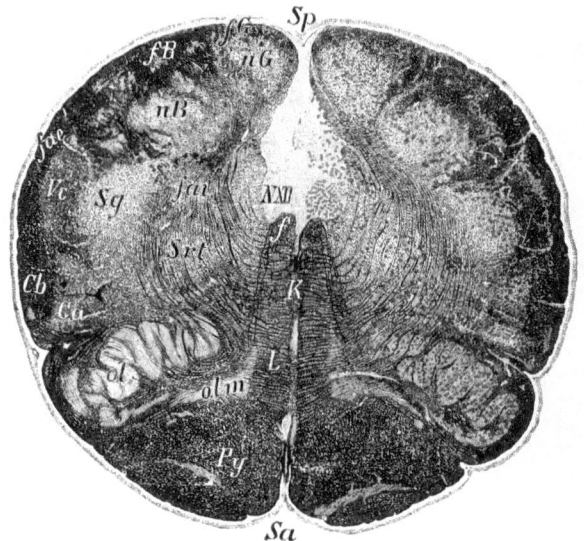

Fig. 1.

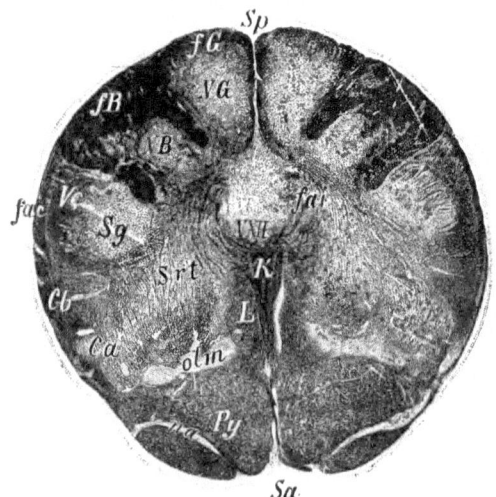

Fig. 2.

PLATE 45.

FIG. 1.—*Section through the Nuclei in the Posterior Columns.* Above the nuclei of Goll (*n. G*) and Burdach (*n. B*) the corresponding funiculi (gracilis and cuneatus) are plainly seen sharply separated from each other. The central canal, and with it the nucleus of the hypoglossus (*XII*), have descended further into the substance of the medulla. The internal (*fai*) and external (*fae*) arcuate fibers are plainly visible. Everything else as in the preceding sections, except that the olives (*ol*) are considerably diminished in size. *Ca*, beginning of the anterior horn of the spinal cord; *Sg*, beginning of the posterior horn.

FIG. 2.—*Section through the Medulla below the Olives.* After the olives have disappeared, the medulla becomes considerably smaller. The nuclei of Goll (*n. G*) and Burdach (*n. B*) are smaller, while the corresponding funiculi (gracilis and cuneatus) are larger. The nucleus of the hypoglossus has disappeared, and that of the spinal accessory makes its appearance in the anterior horn (*Ca*).

The area occupied by the direct cerebellar tract is clearly outlined, and is joined on its dorsal side by the substantia gelatinosa (*S. g*), on the outer side of which we see the descending root of the trigeminus (*V. c*). *fai* and *fae*, internal and external arcuate fibers; *S. rt*, substantia reticularis; *L*, fillet (considerably reduced in size); *K*, decussation of the fillet; *Py*, pyramids; *olm*, internal secondary olive as on Plate 44. Between the columns of Goll the posterior longitudinal sulcus (*S. p*), and between the pyramids the anterior longitudinal sulcus (*S. a*). In the pyramids the arciform nucleus (*n. a*).

PLATE 46.

Fig. 1.—*Section Immediately above the Decussation of the Pyramids*. The pyramids (*Py*) occupy a deeper position and tend to approach each other, thus separating the narrow layer of the fillet (*fa*) into two portions. The posterior longitudinal bundle (*f*) is still visible at the summit of the pyramids. The internal arcuate fibers (*fai*) are plainly seen emerging from the nucleus of Goll (*n. G*) to pass to the fillet of the opposite side (decussation of the fillet).

The nuclei of the posterior columns (*n. G.* and *B.*) have diminished, while the substantia gelatinosa (*S. g*) has become more massive (beginning of the posterior horn, *corn. p*). In the substantia reticularis tegmenti (*Srt*) the region between the remains of the fillet and longitudinal bundle corresponds to the beginning of the anterior horn (*corn. a*). The fibers of the substantia reticularis on the outer side of the anterior horn, the anterolateral ground bundle (*fl*), and Gowers' tract (*G*), the direct cerebellar tract (*Cl*) being situated more posteriorly. In the middle we see the nucleus of the twelfth nerve, which disappears at this point. The accessory olives have disappeared. The spinal portion of the eleventh nerve arises in cells situated in the lateral portion of the anterior horn. For the remaining letters see Plate 45.

Fig. 2.—*Section through the Decussation of the Pyramids*. The nuclei of the posterior columns have disappeared, and the posterior segment is entirely occupied by the posterior columns (column of Goll and column of Burdach, *f. G. B*).

The pyramids, after undergoing decussation, traverse the substance of the anterior horn (*D. Py*) and enter the lateral column of the other side; the decussation of the fillet has disappeared. The posterior horn (*S. g*) is plainly seen. The other structures are the same as in the preceding cut.

C.a, Anterior horn; *c.c*, central canal; *S.a*, posterior sulcus; *fal*, lateral column; *N XI*, spinal accessory nerve emerging at the lateral surface of the cord. Its nucleus is situated in the anterior horn (*Ca*); *ra*, highest anterior root of the first cervical nerve.

Tab. 46.

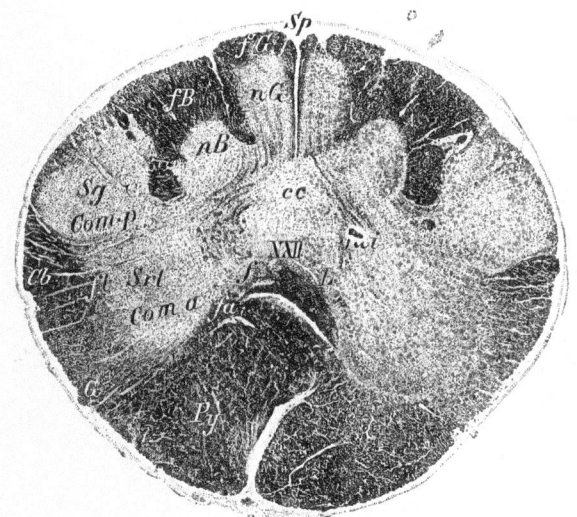

Fig. 1.

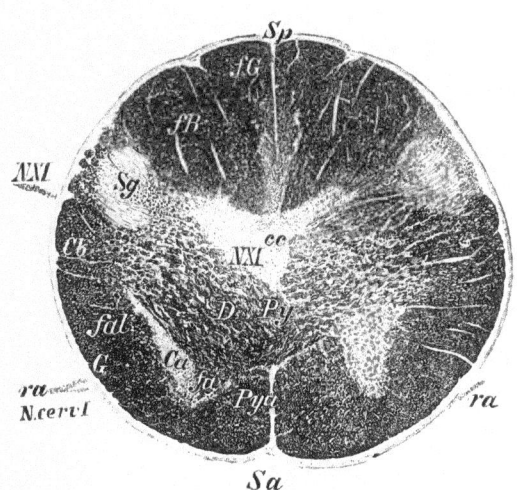

Fig. 2.

Tab. 47.

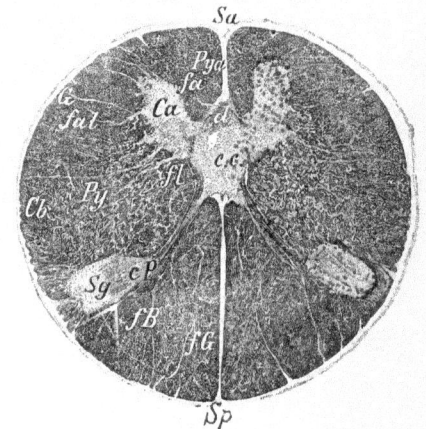

Fig. 1.

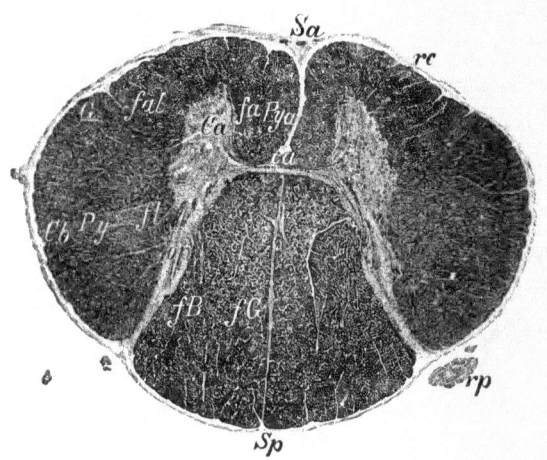

Fig. 2.

PLATE 47.

Beginning with this plate the sections are shown inverted, according to the usual custom. The dorsal segment ($S. p$) is below; the ventral ($S. a$), above.

FIG. 1.—*Section through the Spinal Cord immediately below the Decussation of the Pyramids.* The pyramids (Py) have for the most part disappeared from the anterior column, and are now contained in the lateral column of the other side. The anterior column now contains the uncrossed pyramidal tract ($Py. a$) and the anterior ground bundle (fa), consisting partly of the posterior longitudinal bundle. The lateral column contains the crossed or lateral pyramidal tract (Py); the anterolateral ground bundle (fal) and Gowers' tract (G) being the continuation of the fibers of the substantia reticularis tegmenti; the direct cerebellar tract ($C. b$), consisting of the restiform bodies (ventral portion). The posterior columns contain the column of Goll ($f. G$) and the column of Burdach ($f. B$).

At the bottom of the anterior longitudinal sulcus ($S. a$) we see the anterior commissure (d), the spinal continuation of the decussation of the pyramids, and dorsally the central canal ($c. c$) and the posterior commissure.

The anterior horn ($C. a$) and the posterior horn ($c. p$) are now fully formed. In the posterior horn the substantia gelatinosa ($S. g$), which is visible in higher sections, is still very well represented. The roots of the highest cervical nerves here emerge from the anterior horn (anterior roots), and the posterior fibers enter the lateral portion of the column of Burdach (the posterior roots enter the posterior root-zone).

FIG. 2.—*Section through the Spinal Cord at the Level of the Fourth Cervical Nerve.* Lettering as in Figure 1. The substantia gelatinosa ($c. p$) in the posterior horn is now much reduced in size and appears smaller and smaller in succeeding sections. Origin of the phrenic nerve in the cells of the anterior horn (Ca). rp, Posterior roots.

PLATE 48.

FIG. 1.—*Section through the Cervical Enlargement at the Level of the Seventh Cervical Nerve (Plexus Brachialis).* Owing to the vigorous development of the gray matter, the anterior horn (*C. a*) has materially increased in width. The arrangement of the structures is the same as in Plate 47, Figure 1. The anterior horn contains the cells for the motor peripheral neurons for the muscles of the arm at this level, especially of the muscles of the forearm. The ganglion cells are divided into a small mesial (*m*), and a lateral (*l*) group. The lateral and mesial groups are again subdivided into anterior (*l. a*) and posterior (*l. p*) segments. It is probable that the true motor ganglion cells are situated in the lateral groups. Behind the motor-cell groups are the so-called "middle cells" (*c*), which are surrounded by the terminal fibrils of numerous collaterals from the posterior roots and from the lateral columns. The posterior roots (*r. p*) and their course can be studied better on Plate 52, Figure 1.

FIG. 2.—*Section through the Thoracic Portion of the Spinal Cord at the Level of the Third Thoracic Nerve.*

FIG. 3.—*Section through the Thoracic Portion of the Cord at the Level of the Sixth Thoracic Nerve.* The peripheral neurons for the intercostal muscles emerge from the anterior horn, which is narrower at this point than in the cervical enlargements. At the base of the posterior horn the first indications of the columns of Clarke (*Cl*) are seen. *cc*, Central canal.

The columns of Goll gradually disappear as we go further down the cord. The relations of other structures are the same. *r. a*, Anterior roots; *r. p*, posterior roots.

Abbreviations.—*Ca*, Anterior horn; *ca*, anterior commissure; *Cb*, direct cerebellar tract; *cc*, central canal; *cl*, columns of Clarke; *cp*, posterior horn; *fa*, anterior column (ground bundle); *fal*, lateral column (ground bundle); *fB, fG*, columns of Burdach and Goll; *G*, Gowers' tract; *L*, boundary zone of Lissauer; *ra, rp*, anterior and posterior roots; *Sa, Sp*, anterior and posterior longitudinal sulcus; *Py*, lateral pyramidal tract; *Pya*, anterior pyramidal tract.

Tab. 48.

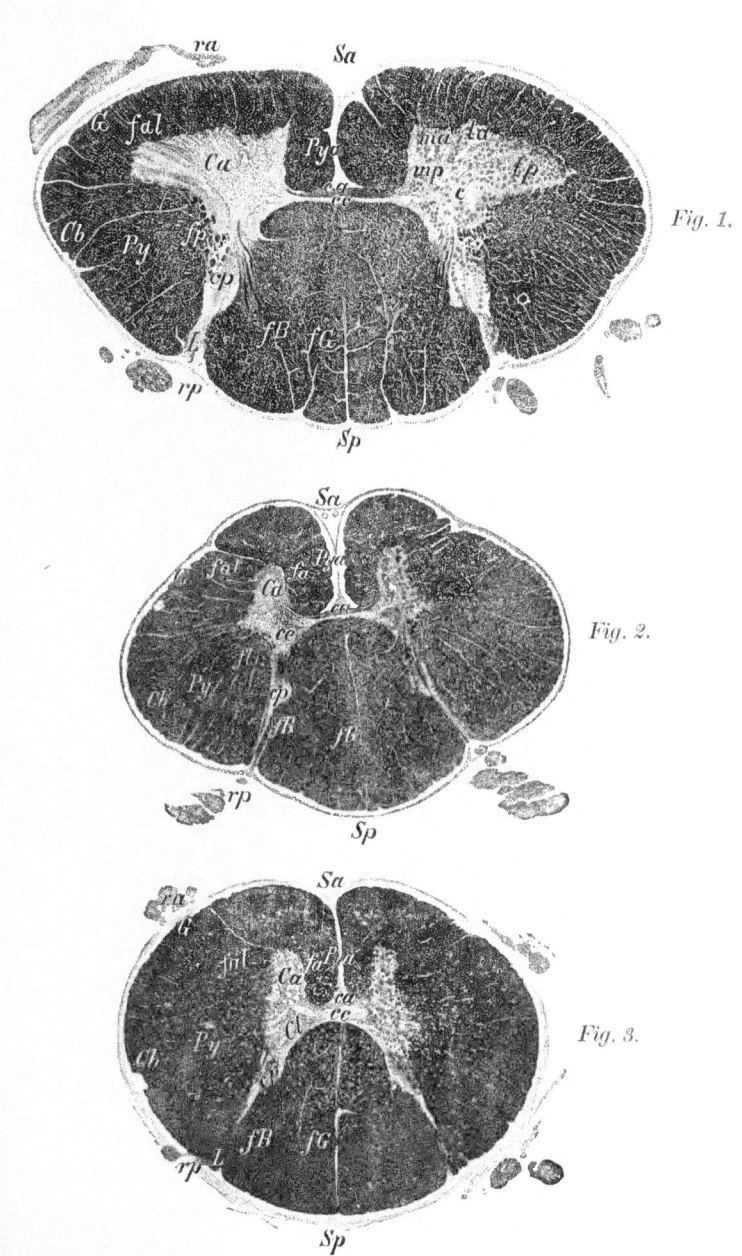

Fig. 1.

Fig. 2.

Fig. 3.

Tab. 49.

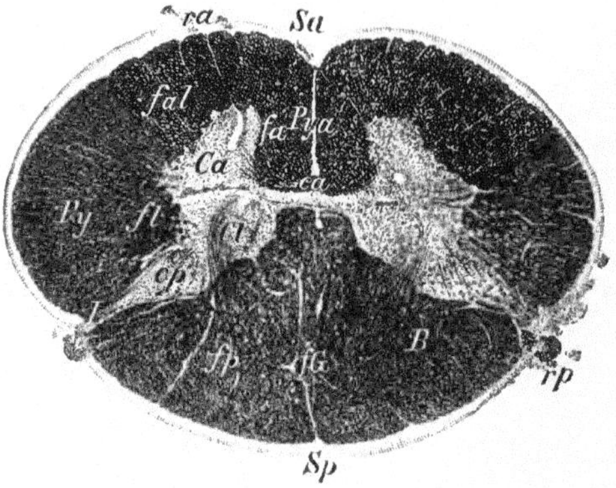

Fig. 1.

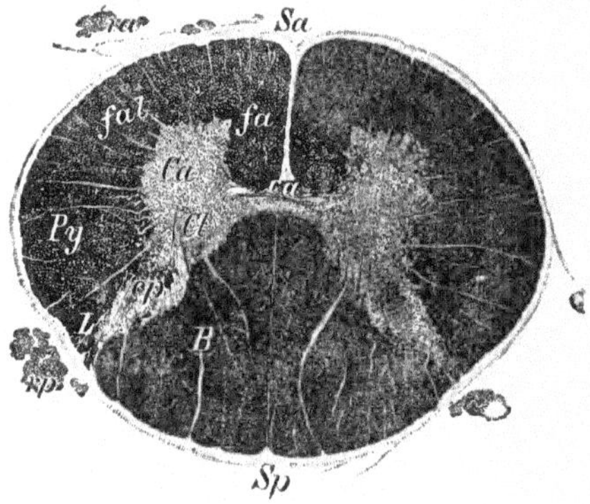

Fig. 2.

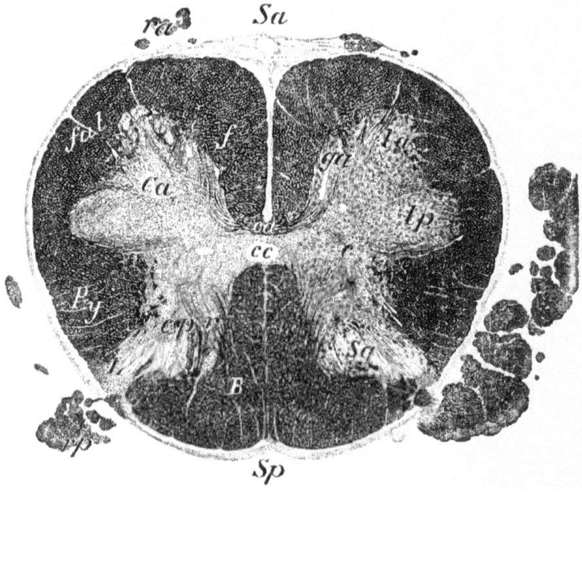

Fig. 3.

PLATE 49.

FIG. 1.—*Section through the Thoracic Portion of the Cord at the Level of the Eleventh Cervical Nerve.* The anterior horn ($C.a$) again increases in size and its contour is altered. The cells of the columns of Clarke ($C.l$) have become larger and are quite conspicuous. Fibers from these cells enter the direct cerebellar tract (Cb, Plate 48) of the same side, and pass by way of the restiform bodies to the tegmental nucleus of the opposite side in the cerebellum. Below the origin of the direct cerebellar tract the lateral pyramidal tract (Py) appears at the periphery of the cord. The anterior pyramidal tract becomes smaller and smaller and is gradually lost in the upper portion of the lumbar cord; the remaining columns of the cord are similarly decreased in size, having given off a portion of their fibers at higher levels.

FIG. 2.—*Section through the Upper Portion of the Lumbar Cord at the Level of the Second Lumbar Nerve.*

FIG. 3.—*Section through the Lower Portion of the Lumbar Cord at the Level of the Fourth Lumbar Nerve.* The anterior and posterior horns appear very massive; the gray matter is almost in excess of the white matter. The cell-groups in the anterior horn, like their homologues in the cervical enlargement, are divided into a mesial group (anterior and posterior, ga) and very much larger anterior (la) and posterior (lp) lateral groups. c, Intermediate zone. The peripheral neurons for the muscles of the leg are given off from the lateral group. The posterior roots ($r.p$) are collected into massive bundles and enter the posterior root-zones; their collaterals and shorter branches (radii) arch backward into the posterior horn. Sg, substantia gelatinosa in the posterior horn; B, column of Burdach. For remaining letters see Plate 48.

PLATE 50.

Fig. 1.—*Section through the Middle Sacral Portion of the Cord at the Level of the Third Sacral Nerve.* The termination of the lateral pyramidal tract (Py) is seen in the white substance of the lateral column. The gray matter is relatively greatest at this level. The broad anterior horn (Ca) contains the motor ganglion cells of the peripheral neuron for the small muscles of the feet, and, at a somewhat deeper level, those for the anal and vesical muscles and for the fibers which subserve the reflex and automatic activity of these organs. B, Column of Burdach; Sg, substantia gelatinosa of the posterior horn.

Fig. 2.—*Section through the Cauda Equina and the Conus Medullaris.* Lying within the dural sac are the motor and sensory roots for the nerves of the lower extremity, which emerge from the cord at a higher level and continue for some distance within the vertebral canal; the constituents of the crural nerve ($Pl. l$) in the lateral, those of the sciatic ($Pl. s$) in the mesial, portion. The former, after their exit from the cord, form the lumbar, the latter the sacral, plexus. In the center of the figure we see the conus medullaris ($C. m$), which forms the tip of the spinal cord.

Fig. 3.—*Section through the Posterior Root and Spinal Ganglion from the Lumbar Portion of the Cord.* The mixed nerve ($N.p$) coming from the periphery divides at the distal boundary of the ganglion, its sensory portion ($r.a$) entering the ganglion and terminating in its cells. Although the magnification is low, a portion of the darkly pigmented cells of the ganglion can be made out. The fibers from these cells collect into a bundle and form the posterior root ($r.p$), which enters the spinal cord, especially the posterior root-zone in the posterior column. fa, Afferent, fe, efferent, fibers; c, cells of the ganglion.

Tab. 50.

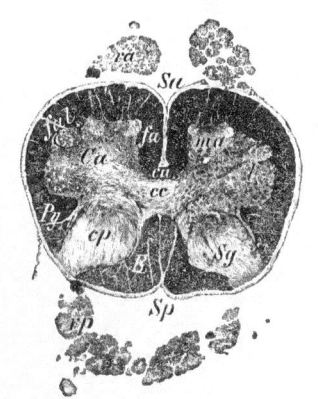

Fig. 1.

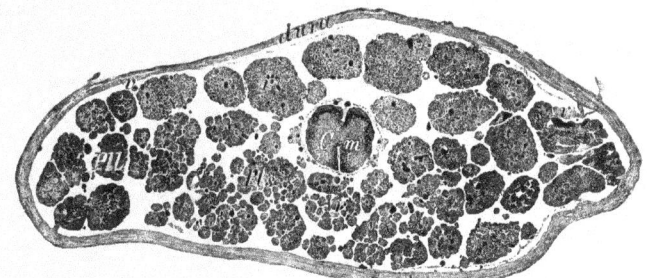

Fig. 2.

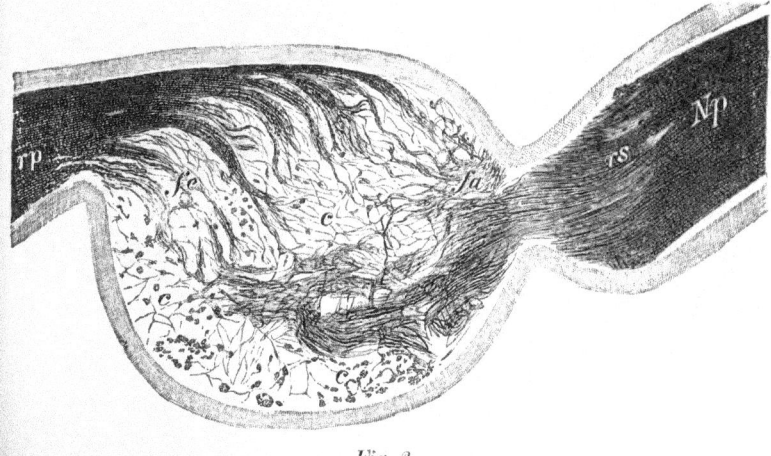

Fig. 3.

Tab. 51.

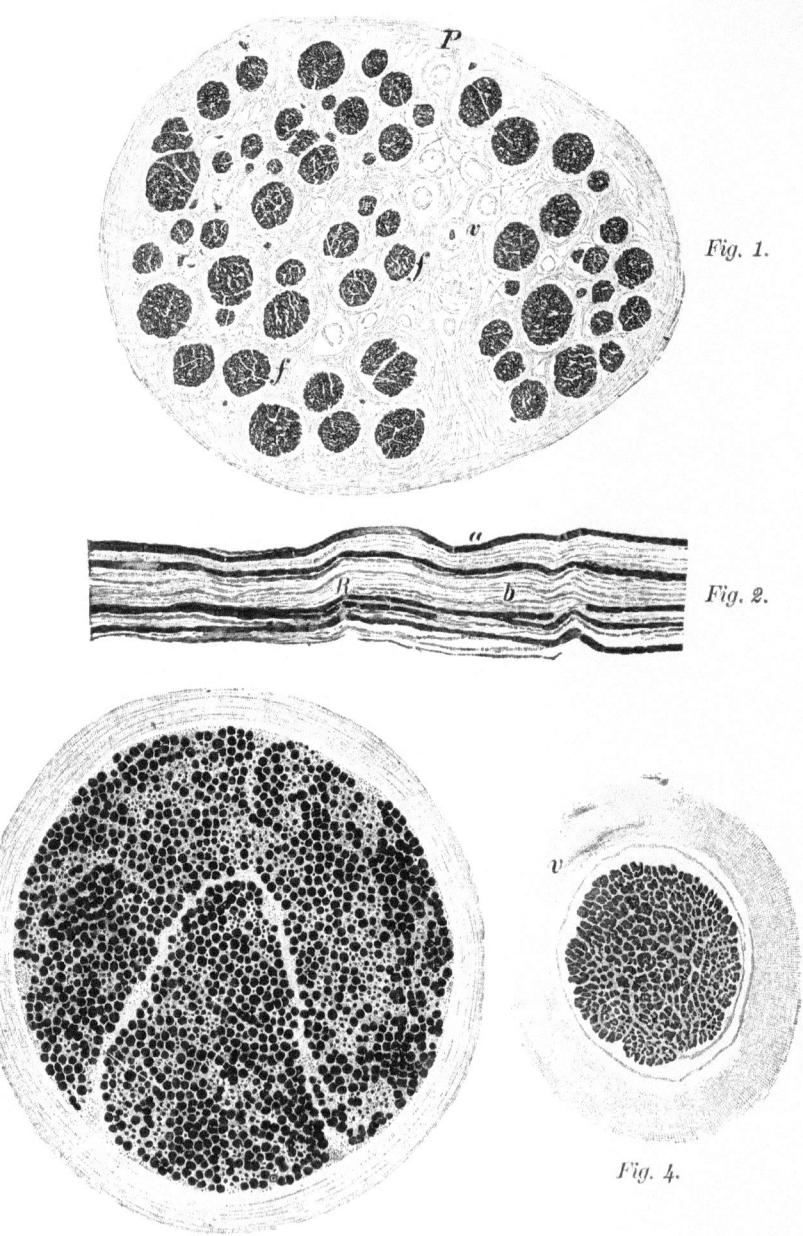

Fig. 1.

Fig. 2.

Fig. 3.

Fig. 4.

PLATE 51.

Fig. 1.—*Transverse Section through the Entire Sciatic Nerve at its Point of Exit (Great Sciatic Foramen).* With a lower power the numerous bundles (*f*) of different sizes which make up the nerve are plainly seen, surrounded by the epineurium (*P*). The blood-vessels are seen among the cells in the perineural connective tissue.

Fig. 2.—*Longitudinal Section of a Nerve Bundle from the Sciatic Nerve.* For further description see Figure 3.

Fig. 3.—*Transverse Section of a Nerve Bundle from the Sciatic Nerve.* With a higher power it appears that the bundle is composed of medullated fibers (black) of varying sizes. In the various nerve bundles numerous very delicate nerve-fibers with barely perceptible medullary sheaths are seen scattered without any apparent order among the fibers of the largest caliber. The nerve bundle is subdivided into separate compartments by the endoneural connective tissue.

Fig. 4.—*Transverse Section of a Normal Optic Nerve and Sheath* (low power). This nerve also consists of numerous bundles which contain the minute nerve-fibers. The optic nerve contains more than 400,000 individual fibers.

PLATE 52.

The Gray Matter of the Spinal Cord.

The two photographs present the right half of a section through the cervical portion, and the left half of a section through the lumbar portion of the cord under high power. For the lettering see Plate 48, Figure 1, and Plate 39, Figure 3.

Note especially the vast number of fibers which enter into and emerge from the horns. The anterior horn receives:

1. Fibers from the anterior commissure (decussating fibers from the anterior pyramidal tract and decussating central sensory fibers).

2. Fibers from the anterolateral column (terminal motor fibers, collaterals from the lateral pyramidal tract, and sensory central collaterals from the anterolateral tract).

3. Fibers from the posterior horn (reflex collaterals and other posterior root-fibers) which pass to the middle zone and to the anterior horn.

From the anterior horn emerge the anterior motor roots (ra), which arise from the groups of motor ganglion cells and emerge in bundles at the surface of the anterolateral column. They are derived principally from the lateral cell groups.

The posterior horn receives from the posterior column massive arching bundles (r) containing the collaterals and all the short tracts of the posterior roots (rp). The substantia gelatinosa ($S. g$), situated at the posterior extremity of the posterior horns, is capped by the boundary zone of Lissauer (L), consisting of delicate posterior root-fibers, and immediately in front of Lissauer's zones we see the zona spongiosa of the posterior horns. (See Plate 26.)

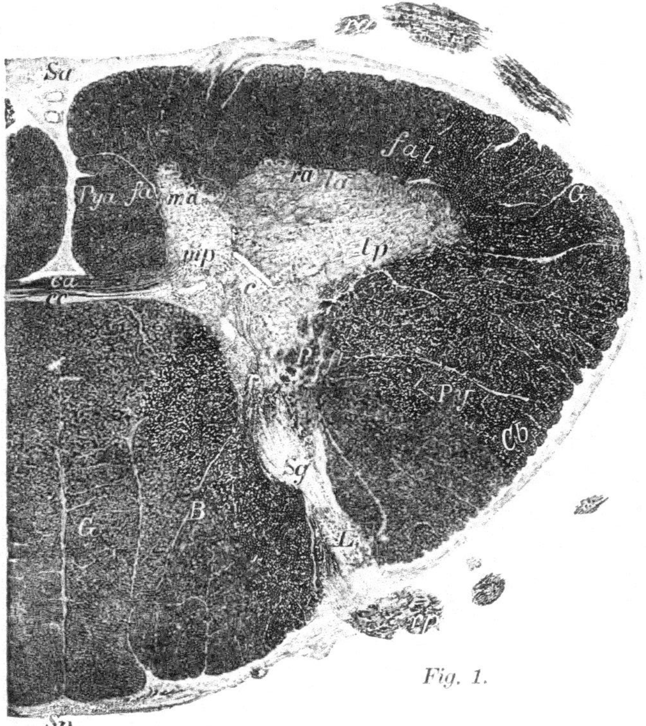
Sa
Pya
fa
ma
ra
la
fal
G
mp
lp
ca
cc
c
p
Py
Cb
Sg
B
G
L
rp
Sp

Fig. 1.

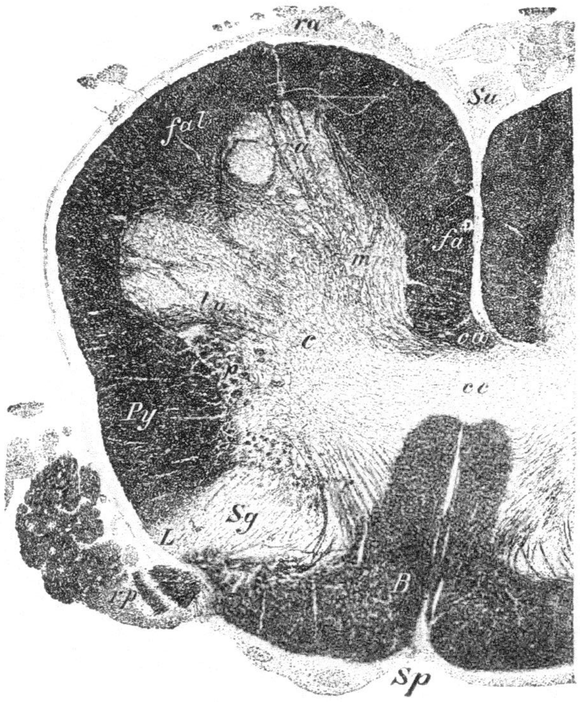
ra
Su
fal
a
fa
m
la
c
ca
p
cc
Py
Sg
L
rp
B
Sp

Fig. 2.

Tab. 53.

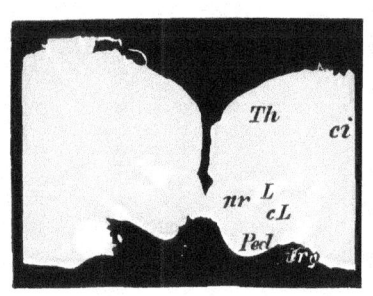
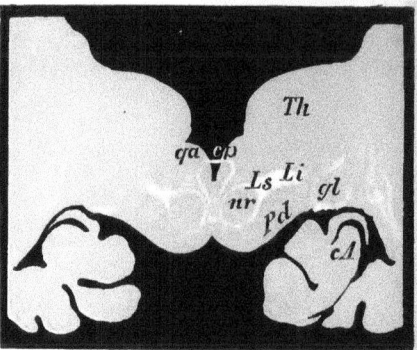

Fig. 1. Fig. 2.

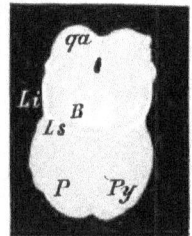
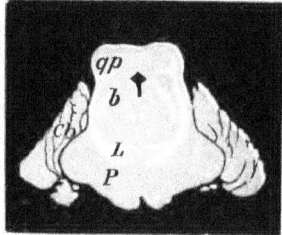
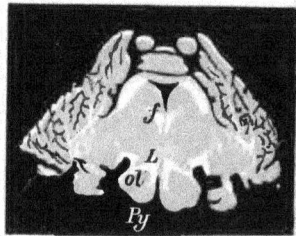

Fig. 3. Fig. 4. Fig. 5.

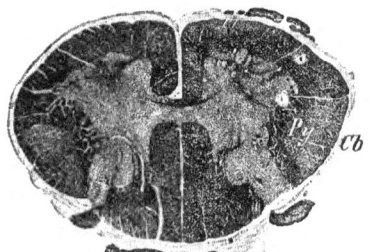
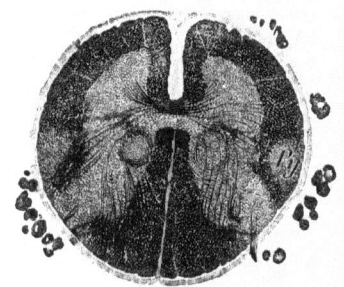

Fig. 6. Fig. 7.

PLATE 53.

Process of Medullation in the Fetal Brain. (Photographs.)

This plate belongs immediately after Plate 15. It has, however, been introduced at this point for the sake of greater clearness.

Figures 1 to 5 represent sections through the unstained brain-stem of an eight months' fetus. Nearly all the fibers which in the fully formed brain are medullated—that is to say, white when unstained—appear nonmedullated in these sections. On the other hand, certain important tracts, which are evidently quite old in a genetic sense, can be readily picked out even with the naked eye by the presence of the nerve sheath, their glistening white color contrasting with the gray of the remaining brain-stem. The most important of these pathways are: The radiation to the red nucleus ($n.\ r$) (Fig. 1, L), the ansa lenticularis (cL), and the fillet ($Ls.\ i$). In addition to these, the posterior longitudinal bundle (f), the brachia (b), the nasal trigeminus root, the peripheral cranial nerves, the optic tract (tro), the posterior commissure (cp), are medullated. The pyramidal tract has not yet become medullated.

FIGS. 1 AND 2.—*Section through the Middle and Posterior Segments of the Optic Thalamus.* Note the crusta (motor pyramidal tract, etc.), which has not yet become medullated.

FIG. 3.—*Section through the Anterior Corpora Quadrigemina.*

FIG. 4.—*Section through the Middle of the Pons.*

FIG. 5.—*Section through the Medulla Oblongata.* Bundles of fibers which early become medullated ascend from the region of the fillet above the levels shown in section 1, and after joining the ansa lenticularis and traversing the globus pallidus (probably without interruption), enter the so-called tegmental radiation (the earliest medullated fiber tract of the cerebral medulla, sensory pathway; see text, Part IV), to end in the cortex of the posterior central convolution and of the parietal lobe.

FIGS. 6 AND 7.—*Sections through the Cervical and Thoracic Portions of the Spinal Cord from a New-born Infant.* The pyramidal tract (Py), which is not medullated, is readily distinguished from the fully developed direct cerebellar tract (Cb). (For the corresponding segment of the spinal cord see Plate 14, Fig. 2—medullary sheath stain.)

PLATE 54.

Schema of the Most Important Nerve Tracts from a Clinical Point of View.

The following pathways and their relative position in both halves of the cord are indicated in the transverse sections of the cerebral hemispheres, crura, pons, cerebellum, medulla oblongata, cervical and lumbar enlargement.

1. *Motor Pathway.*—Central neuron complex (pyramidal tract), red; peripheral, blue. Note the decussations of the central pathways (*d VII, d XII, dp,* decussations of the facial and hypoglossus fibers and of the pyramids).

Abbreviations.—*Py,* Pyramidal tract; *Pya, Pyl,* anterior and lateral pyramidal tracts.

2. *Sensory Pathway.*—Peripheral neuron, brown; central (tract of the fillet), green; centrocortical, yellow.

Abbreviations.—*Cb,* Direct cerebellar tract; *Cr,* restiform body; *c trap,* trapezoid body; *Ll, lm,* lateral and mesial fillet; *L,* superior fillet; *c.l,* subthalamic body.

3. The pathway uniting the red nucleus (nucl. ruber) with the cerebellum (brachium, *b,* and corpus dentatum, *cd*) is colored brown.

4. The cerebello-olivary tracts are yellow. The rest explains itself.

Tab. 54.

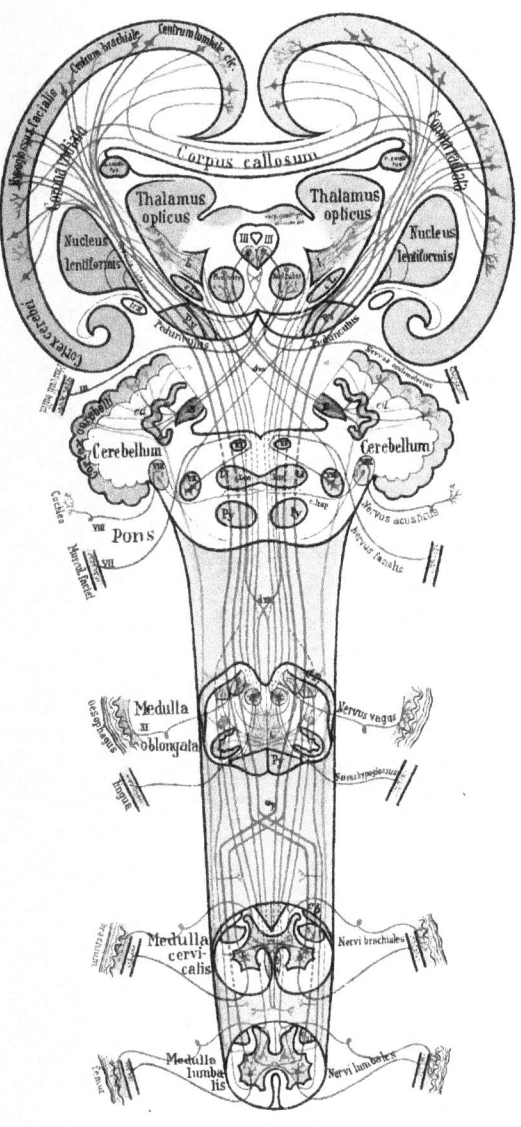

Lith. Anst. F. Reichhold, München.

Tab. 55.

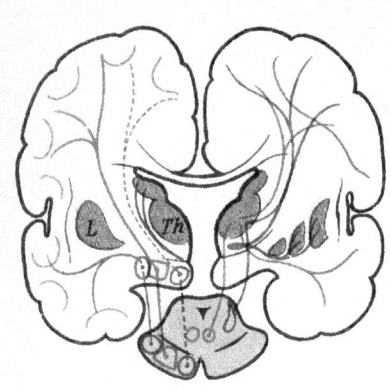

Fig. 1.

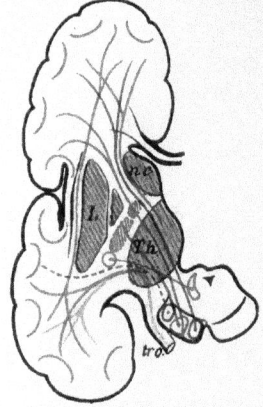

Fig. 2.

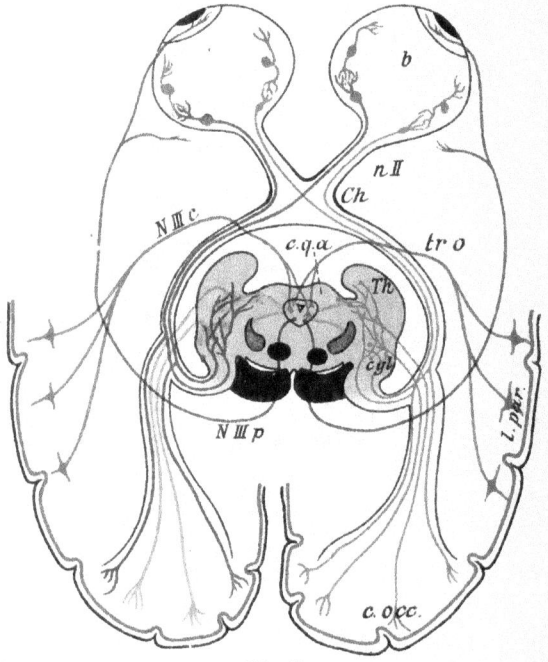

Fig. 3.

Lith. Anst. F. Reichhold, München.

PLATE 55.

Figures 1 and 2 show the manner in which the tegmentum and crusta are formed from the tracts of the cerebral hemispheres.

Figure 1 shows the hemisphere in frontal section; Figure 2, in a horizontal section.

The left side of Figure 1 shows the formation of the crusta, the right side that of the tegmentum.

Crusta: Frontal pontine tract (dotted blue line); pyramidal tract (red); temporo-occipital pontine tract (blue).

Tegmentum: Tract of the fillet (blue); optic thalamus—red nucleus—(brown); ansa lenticularis (green).

The sections of the hemispheres show diagrammatically: The short and long association tracts (brown); the fibers of the corona radiata running to the optic thalamus—upper and lower peduncles—(brown).

Figure 2 shows in addition the optic radiation—occipital cortex, optic centers, optic tracts (yellow).

FIG. 3.—*Schema of the Optic Nerve and the Oculomotor Tract with their Connections (the Fibers of the Left Optic Tract are colored).* Optic nerve: peripheral neuron (brown), in the retina (*b*, bulbus); central neuron (green), in the optic nerve (*n. II*) as far as the chiasm (*Ch*) (decussation of the nasal bundles), thence to the optic tract (*tr. o*), to the lateral geniculate body (*cgl*), pulvinar (*Th*), and to the anterior corpus quadrigeminum (*cqa*), where the tract breaks up into terminal fibrils. From this point the pathway follows the optic radiation (yellow, green) to the cuneus in the occipital lobe (it is doubtful whether fibers pass directly from the tracts to the cortex) (collaterals?).

Oculomotor: Central neuron (red), from the cortical center (*g.*, angularis?), containing both crossed and uncrossed fibers to the nucleus of the oculomotor nerve in the floor of the aqueduct.

Peripheral neuron (blue): From this point as peripheral neuron to the muscles of the eyeball (fibers also originate on the opposite side for the internal rectus).

Pupillary reflex arc: Fibers of the optic nerve—corpora quadrigemina, hypothetical reflex collaterals (dotted yellow line), nucleus of oculomotor, peripheral nerve (blue), sphincter pupillæ (the ciliary ganglion is interposed).

PLATE 56.

FIG. 1.—*General View of the Projection Paths.* The projection paths which connect deeper portions of the brain with the cortex, after leaving the cerebral cortex unite to form the corona radiata and enter the internal capsule. Thence some of the fibers forming the corona radiata enter the optic thalamus (brown) (anterior, posterior, superior, inferior peduncles). The frontal and temporal pontine pathway, which reaches the cerebellum through the middle cerebellar peduncle of the other side, is colored blue. The pyramidal tract is red, the sensory tract of the fillet green, the cerebello-olivary tract violet, the optic radiation yellow, the brachia brown.

FIG. 2.—*Schema of the Position of the Sensory Nerve Tracts.* The peripheral sensory neuron is brown, the centrocortical green. The arrangement of the cells, the course of the fibers, their manner of termination, the collaterals, reflex arcs, etc., are readily seen in the figure.

I, Olfactory pathway; *II*, visual pathway; *VIII*, auditory pathway; *V*, *IX*, gustatory pathway or pathway of cutaneous sensation.

Tab. 56.

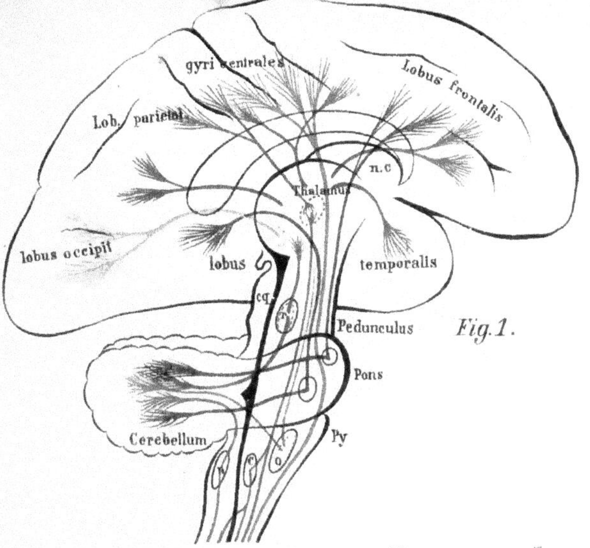

Fig. 1.

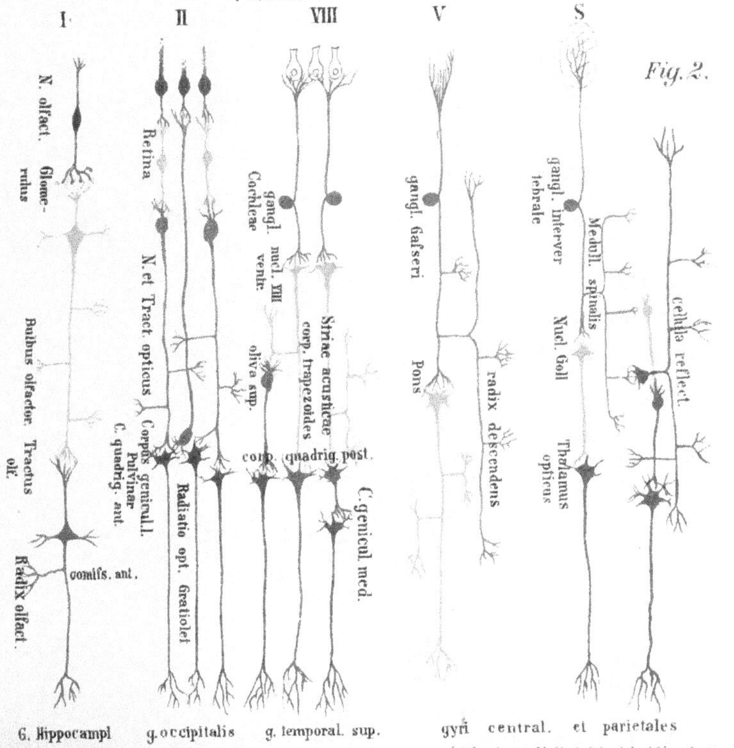

Labels in Fig. 1: gyri centrales, Lobus frontalis, Lob. parietal, n.c, Thalamus, lobus occipit, lobus, temporalis, cq, Pedunculus, Pons, Cerebellum, Py

Fig. 2.

I.   II.   VIII   V   S

Column I: N. olfact., Glomerulus, Bulbus olfactor., Tractus olf., Radix olfact., comiss. ant., G. Hippocampi

Column II: Retina, N. et Tract. opticus, Corpus geniculi l., Pulvinar, C. quadrig. ant., Radiatio opt. Gratioleti, g. occipitalis

Column VIII: gangl. nucl. VIII Cochleae ventr., oliva sup., Striae acusticae corp. trapezoides, corp. quadrig. post., C. genicul. med., g. temporal. sup.

Column V: gangl. Gasseri, Pons, radix descendens

Column S: gangl. Intervertebrale, Nucl. Goll, Medull. spinalis, Thalamus opticus, cellula reflect., gyri central. et parietales

Lith. Anst F. Reichhold, München.

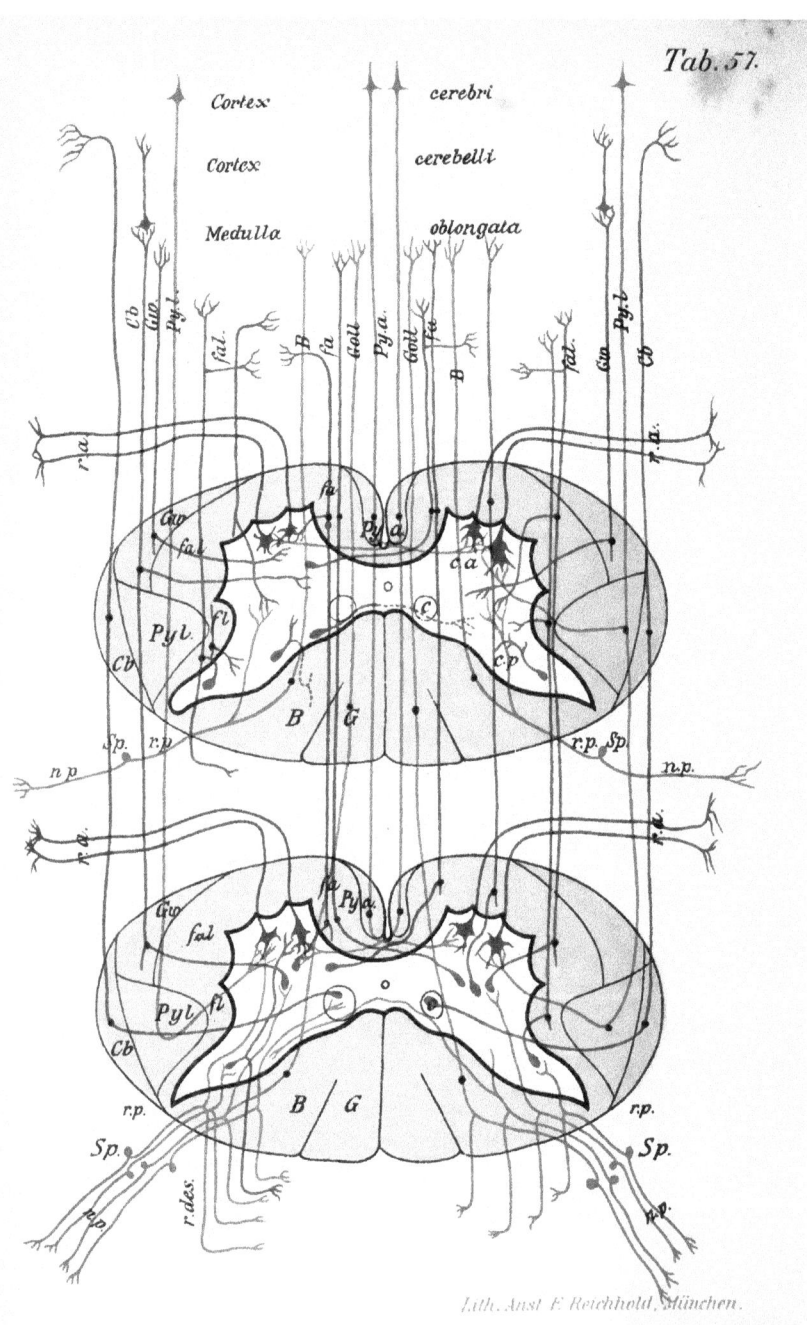

PLATE 57.

Schema Showing the Course of the Fibers in the Spinal Cord.

I. MOTOR PATHWAY.

(*a*) *Central neuron* (red): Lateral pyramidal tract (*Py.l*) and anterior pyramidal tract (*Py.a*); terminal fibrils in the anterior horn (*ca*).

(*b*) *Peripheral neuron* (blue): Cell in anterior horn, anterior root (*r.a*), motor nerve muscle.

II. SENSORY PATHWAY.

(*a*) *Peripheral neuron* (brown): sensory nerve (*N.p*), spinal ganglion (*Sp*), posterior root (*r.p*) of the spinal cord. In the posterior root-zone of the posterior cord each fiber divides into an ascending and a descending branch (short and long fibers). The short tracts are reflected into the posterior horn (*cp*) and consist of: (1) Reflex collaterals going to the anterior horn, short reflex arc, long reflex arc. (A green neuron is interposed.) (2) Fibers running to the cells in the middle zone of the gray matter. (3) Fibers running to the cells of the columns of Clarke (*c*). (4) Fibers running to the central, and especially to the mesial cells in the anterior horn (commissural cells). (5) Fibers running to cells in the posterior horn.

The long tracts (6) first enter the columns of Burdach (*B*), and higher up the columns of Goll (*G*), and pass to the funiculus gracilis and funiculus cuneatus in the medulla oblongata (at this point the fillet begins).

(*b*) *Central neuron* (green): Its beginning corresponds to the cells named under 2 to 6, where the peripheral neuron ends.

1. From the cells mentioned under *a* ("Strangzellen") arise the fibers of the anterolateral ground bundle (*fal*) and (*fa.*) of the same side (ground bundle of the anterolateral columns), and those of Gowers' tract (*G*).

2. From the cells under 3: The direct cerebellar tract (*Cb*) of the same side.

3. From the cells under 4: Fibers which, after decussating in the anterior commissure, ascend in the anterolateral column (*fa*) of the other side.

4. From the cells under 5: Fibers running to the lateral ground bundle (*fl*) and to the ventral field of the posterior columns. (See Plate 26, 1.)

The figures also show the manner in which the collaterals are given off and the termination of the central short tracts of the anterolateral column (which soon reenter the gray matter) in the internal cells ("Binnenzellen"), colored green (Golgi), in the posterior horn. The decussation which takes place in the posterior commissure is not perfectly understood as yet. It appears that the posterior roots also contain a few scattered centrifugal fibers which have their neuron cells in the anterior horn, but their existence in man has not as yet been definitely established.

IV.

GENERAL PATHOLOGIC ANATOMY

OF THE

NERVOUS SYSTEM.

ILLUSTRATED BY INDIVIDUAL EXAMPLES.

(Part IV. of Text.)

SPECIAL PATHOLOGY OF THE BRAIN.

(Part V. of Text.)

Secondary Diseases of the Nervous System.

PLATE 58.

Fig. 1.—*Section through the Cerebral Cortex and Meninges in Epidemic Cerebrospinal Meningitis.* The preparation is taken from a soldier aged twenty-three, who was suddenly taken ill with general febrile symptoms, vomiting and headache, and pain and rigidity in the back of the neck. Continuous fever ranging about 104° F.; herpes labialis; the diagnosis was confirmed by a leukocytosis of 36,000. The mental condition gradually became worse, motor irritative phenomena (twitching of the muscles of the face and of the arms, especially on the right side) and delirium made their appearance. The patient died after six days in deep coma, with marked persistent rigidity of the nuchal and dorsal muscles.

Autopsy.—Purulent infiltrations in and upon the soft membranes of the brain and spinal cord, especially over the convexity of the hemispheres, and most marked about the middle of the left central convolutions. The pus contained the diplococcus lanceolatus. The purulent infiltration (colored red) dips down into the fissures and accompanies the pial vessels into the cortical substance. The effect of the inflammatory products on the cortical cells is to throw them at first into a morbid state of irritation and later to abolish their activity.

Fig. 2.—*Cerebral Cortex in Tubercular Meningitis.* In a woman thirty years old in an advanced stage of pulmonary tuberculosis the following symptoms appeared twenty days before death: Rise in the fever-curve, headaches, delirium, increasing coma, ptosis of the eyelids, dilatation of the pupil, convulsions.

Diagnosis.—Miliary tuberculosis.

Autopsy.—Small grayish-white nodules are scattered over the soft membranes. The base is covered with a gelatinous exudate containing tubercles, in which the oculomotor nerve is embedded. The preparation shows one of these miliary tubercles taken from the bottom of a sulcus; the growth of the tubercle has gradually encroached on the cell-layer of the cortex. These solitary tubercles are apt to increase in size, especially in children, until they form large tumors. (See Plate 62.) In this case we have a disseminated form of tuberculosis.

Tab. 58.

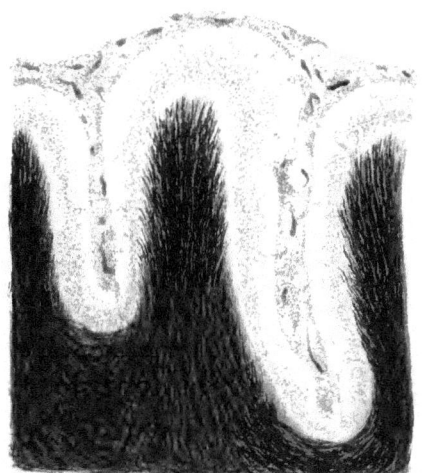

Fig. 1.

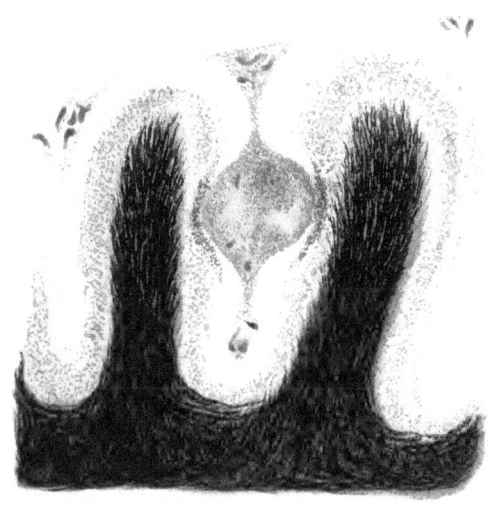

Fig. 2.

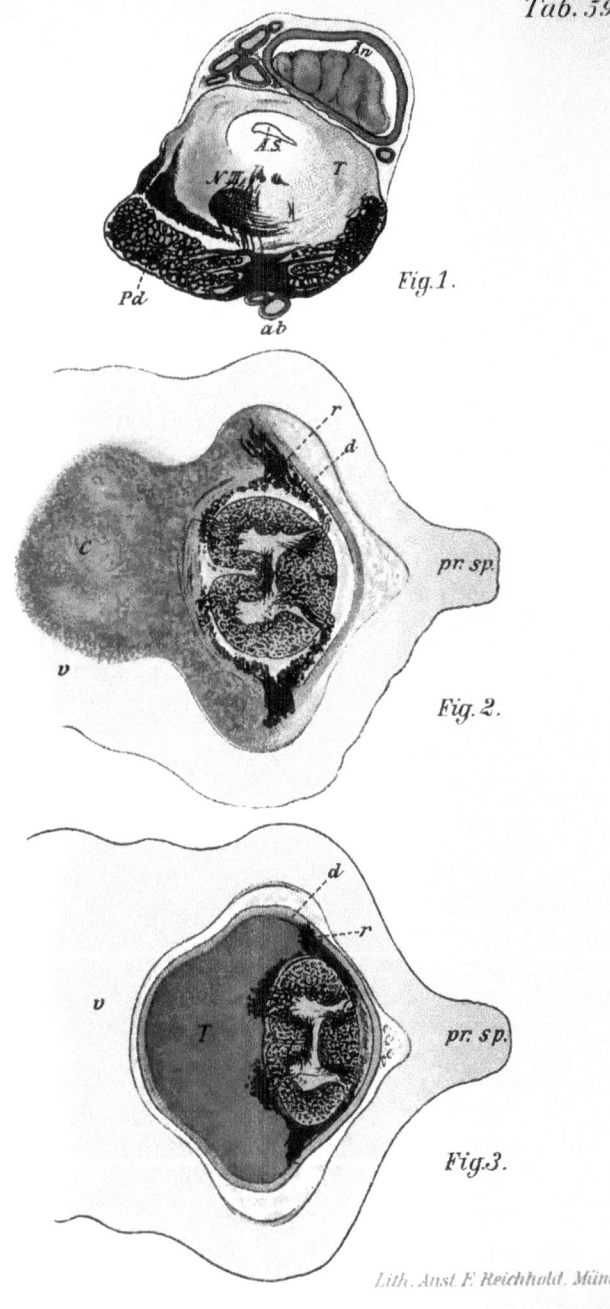

Tab. 59.

Fig. 1.

Fig. 2.

Fig. 3.

Lith. Anst. F. Reichhold, München.

PLATE 59.

Fig. 1.—An *aneurysm* (*An*) situated immediately above the corpora quadrigemina has led to softening, especially of the right half of the tegmentum (*T*) and of the region about the corpora quadrigemina. The patient, a man of fifty-three, presented the following symptoms: Headache, attacks of vertigo, paresis of the left arm and leg, marked hemianesthesia of the same side, paralysis of the muscles of the right eye (ptosis, paralysis of the sphincter pupillæ, superior rectus, etc.).

Abbreviations.—*AS*, Aqueduct of Sylvius; *N III*, oculomotor nerve; *ab*, basal artery.

Fig. 2.—*Caries of a Vertebra.* The specimen was taken from a woman forty-five years of age who was taken ill with pains in the back and ribs, accompanied with increasing weakness in the legs. At the end of three months she was barely able to stand, and slight disturbances of the vesical function and of sensibility made their appearance. Tendon reflexes increased; irregular fever; nothing abnormal in the vertebral column. Eventually paralysis of the legs resulted, and contractures appeared. The appearance of a cold abscess in the thorax gave the *diagnosis:* Compression of the spinal cord by caries of the vertebral column.

Autopsy.—Carious focus in the eighth thoracic vertebra (*C*); exuberant granulations and masses of caseous material completely filled the vertebral canal and compressed the spinal cord and emerging roots (*r*). *v*, Body of vertebra; *pr. sp*, spinous process; *d*, dura mater.

Fig. 3.—A *tumor* (*T*) which developed on the inner surface of the dura (*d*) in the vertebral canal in a woman thirty-eight years of age, and gave rise to severe pains, referred especially to both legs, in the course of three months led to complete spastic paralysis of the legs, complete anesthesia in those members (the only trace of sensation was that contact with cold water gave the sensation of heat), incontinence of urine, etc. Death from cystitis and pyelitis.

Diagnosis.—Compression of the spinal cord (carcinoma?). The tumor proved to be a sarcoma which filled the vertebral canal at a level corresponding to the interval between the second and sixth thoracic vertebræ.

Abbreviations.—*v*, Body of vertebra; *r*, posterior roots; *d*, dura mater; *prsp*, spinous process.

PLATE 60.

Fig. 1.—*Brain Abscess.* A woman of fifty-six who for years had complained of persistent, dull headache and attacks of vomiting, developed gradually increasing fever and fell into a typhoid state, with marked rigidity of the neck, trismus, opisthotonos, vomiting, and violent headache. The patient's conversation was confused; she could not find the right name for ordinary objects with the use of which she was perfectly well acquainted, such as fork, candle, etc. (optic aphasia).

At the autopsy an abscess was found in the left occipital lobe, the white matter of which had been largely destroyed.

The specimen shows a horizontal section through the occipital lobe. *Prc*, Precuneus; *c*, cuneus; *o s*, superior occipital convolution; *Pc*, inferior parietal convolution (pli courbé).

Fig. 2.—*Tubercle in the Pons.* Male, aged fifty. Complained of headache and vertigo for the past year. During the last six weeks there occurred attacks of vertigo, staggering gait (cerebellar ataxia), vomiting, pain, rigidity in the neck. Right side, paresis of the muscles of the face, arm, and leg; left side, paralysis of the trigeminus and facial (facial anesthesia) (hemiplegia alternans). Inability to rotate the eyes first to the left, and later also to the right; diplopia. Later, paralysis of the muscles of the pharynx and of the vocal cords; cachexia; death after eight weeks. No other signs of tuberculosis.

Diagnosis.—Tumor of the base of the brain in the region of the pons.

Specimen.—Large tuberculous tumor (T) in the left half of the pons; above it, in the tegmental region (tg), a purulent focus; the fourth ventricle has been pushed upward; the median raphe (R) has been displaced to the right. Destruction of the middle peduncle of the cerebellum (Prp), of the pyramidal tract (Py), of the trigeminus, and of the region of its nucleus and of the nucleus of the facial nerve. (Consult Plates 38 and 39 for letters.)

Tab. 60.

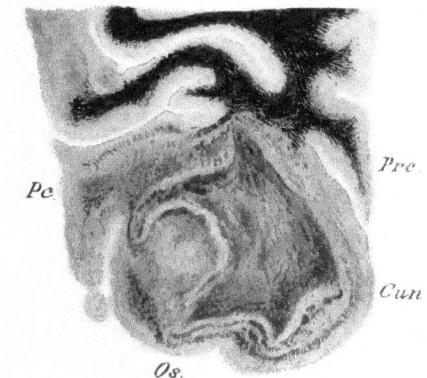

Fig. 1.

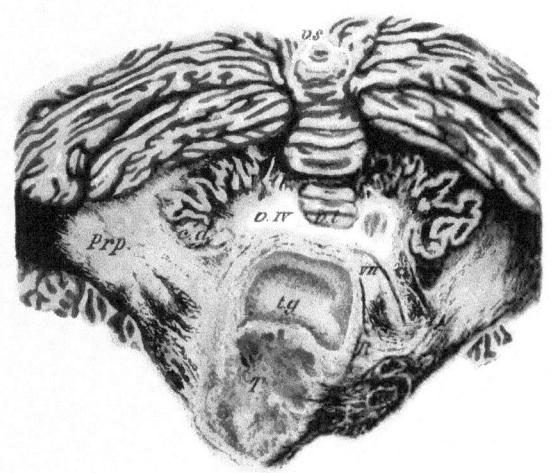

Fig. 2.

Lith. Anst. F. Reichhold, München.

Tab. 61.

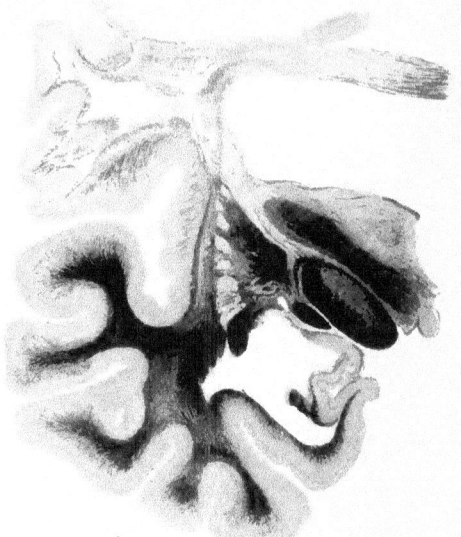

Fig. 1.

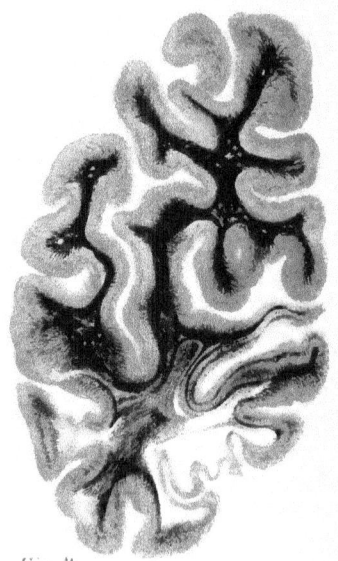

Fig. 2.

PLATE 61.

FIG. 1.—*Chronic Hydrocephalus.* Section through the middle of the brain of an idiot eighteen years old, the subject of congenital hydrocephalus. The lateral ventricle (*ventr. lat*), the descending horn (*v.inf*), and the third ventricle (*v.m*) are very much dilated. Flattening of the cortical convolutions; marked reduction in the thickness of the corpus callosum (*cc*), of the radiation of the corpus callosum, and of the association fibers, the projection fibers being comparatively best preserved. (Consult Plate 38, Fig. 2, for letters.)

FIG. 2.—*Acute Hemorrhagic Encephalitis.* Section through the left occipital lobe of a woman sixty-six years of age. The patient was seized with fever and vomiting and presented meningitic symptoms. The most marked symptom was a constant right-sided hemianopsia; the patient was unable to see any object on her right side until it was carried beyond the middle of the visual field to the left side. Death occurred at the end of thirteen days after increasing coma, rigidity of the neck, and delirium.

Autopsy.—Softening of the basal portion of the temporal lobe, of the mesial and basal cortical convolutions of the left occipital lobe, with numerous pinhead-sized hemorrhages.

The specimen shows hemorrhagic encephalitis with softening of the cuneus (*cun*), of the lingula (*ling*) and its white matter, and of the optic radiation. *g.ang*, Gyrus angularis; *Præc*, precuneus; *fc*, calcarine fossa.

PLATE 62.

FIG. 1.—*Subcortical Cerebral Focus after Hemorrhage. Secondary Degeneration.* A woman forty-two years of age had an apoplectic attack which left the following residua: Total motor aphasia, total right-sided hemiplegia of the face, arm, and leg, slight hemianesthesia.

Autopsy.—Extensive destruction of the white matter under the central convolutions by an old hemorrhage.

Specimen.—The focus (f) includes the white matter of the posterior central convolution (cp), the lateral portion of the centrum semiovale, and the upper portion of the internal capsule (ci). From the focus the secondary degeneration has spread to the corpus callosum (cc), to the internal capsule (x), and to the lateral nucleus of the optic thalamus (Tho). At the surface of the pes (ped) the seat of the degenerated pyramidal tract is represented by two bright spots separated by the transverse fibers of the ansa lenticularis. (See Plate 31 for further explanations.)

FIG. 2. — *Embolic Softening. Secondary Degeneration.* Section through the occipitoparietal lobe of a man forty-five years of age. The patient suffered from mitral stenosis and had had several apoplectic attacks due to embolism. One of these attacks left him with a pronounced right-sided homonymous hemianopsia.

Autopsy.—Numerous cysts due to emboli and scars were found all over the brain.

Specimen.—Softening of the cuneus (cun) and of the lingula ($ling$) and its white matter. Secondary degeneration of the inferior longitudinal bundle and Gratiolet's optic radiation (o). (Compare Plate 33, Fig. 1.)

Tab. 62.

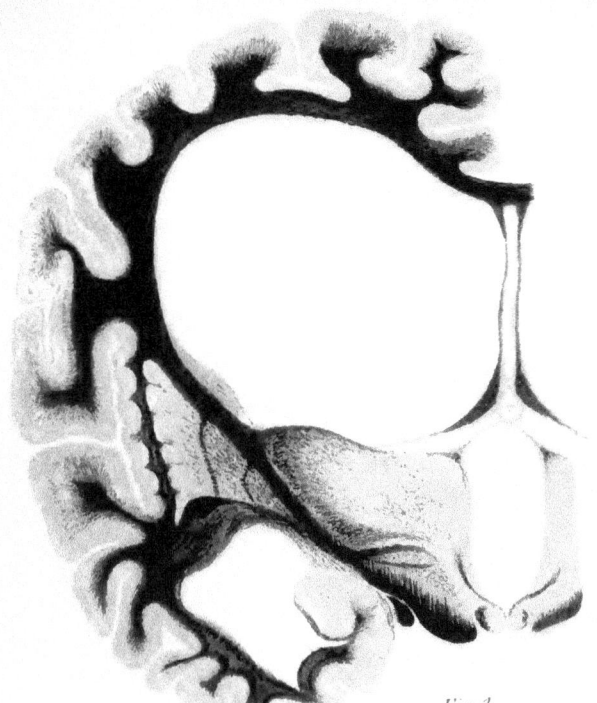

Fig. 1.

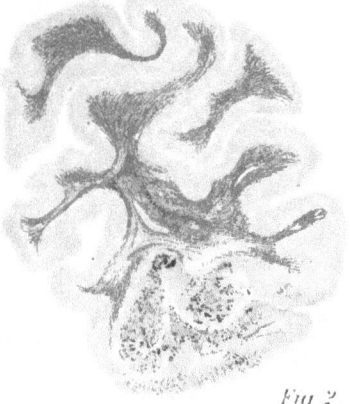

Fig. 2.

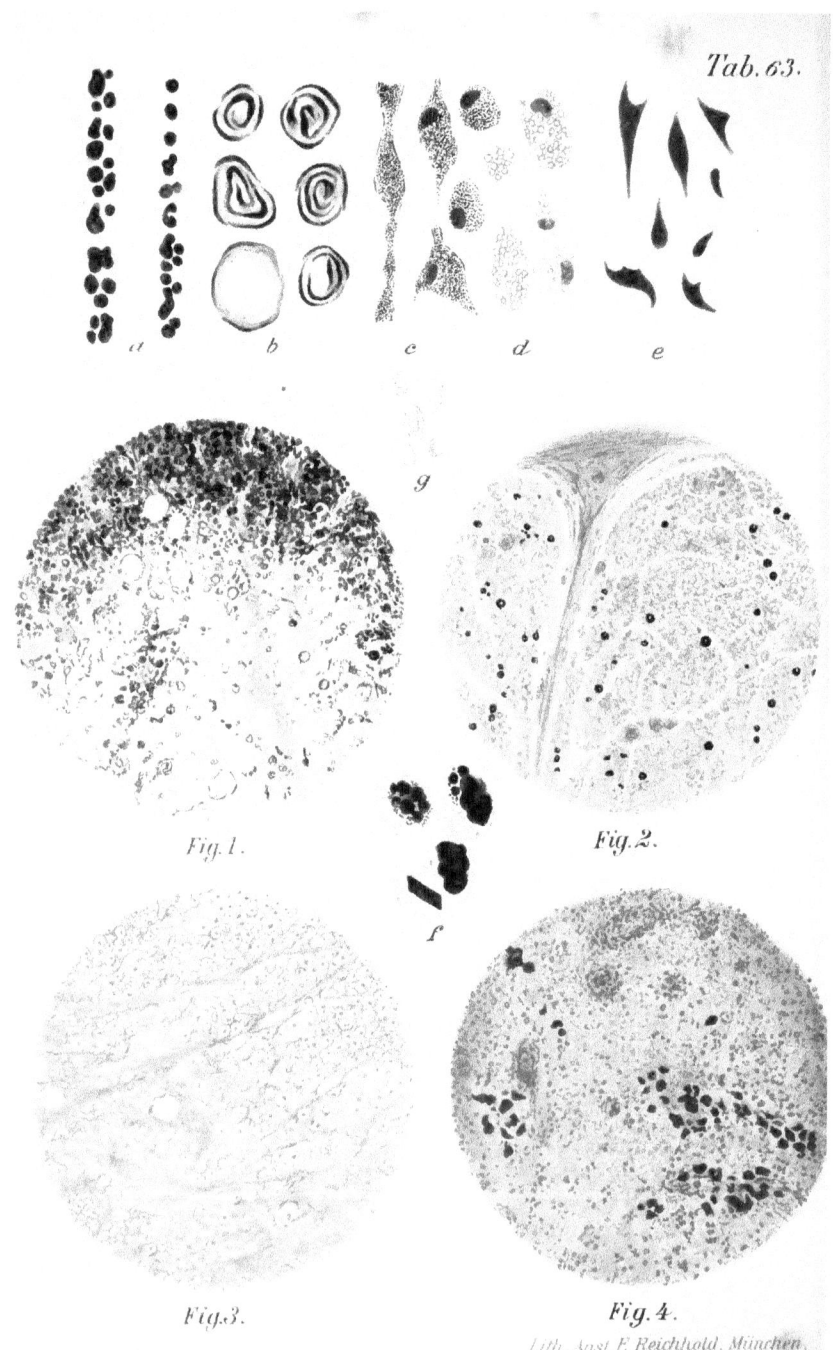

PLATE 63.

Figs. A to F.—*Products of Degeneration of Nerve-cells and Fibers.* (*a*) Degenerating nerve-fibers (longitudinal section from a case of alcoholic neuritis); (*b*) swollen and degenerating fibers, transverse section from a case of acute myelitis; (*c*) fibers and cells from the cerebral cortex, filled with fat droplets, treated with osmic acid (from a case of thrombotic softening); (*d*) fatty granule cells, unstained; (*e*) atrophic ganglion cells from the nucleus of the hypoglossus (from a case of bulbar palsy); (*f*) cells containing blood pigment, fragments of hemoglobin (from a case of cerebral hemorrhage); (*g*) corpora amylacea from the posterior column (from a case of tabes dorsalis).

Fig. 1.—*Specimen of Acute Myelitis.* (One hundred and fifty diameters). Taken from the case shown in Plate 75, Figure 1. The microscope shows in the lateral cord myelitic foci separated by areas of normal tissue. Instead of the closely packed nerve-fibers stained blue-black we see vacuoles; the fibers present all the stages of degeneration.

Fig. 2.—*Specimen of Acute Neuritis.* Portion of a nerve bundle from the sciatic nerve from a case of alcoholic neuritis. Great destruction of nerve-fibers; only a few bluish-black fibers remained. The sites of the medullary sheath can be recognized in the connective-tissue stroma and in the thickened sheath of Schwann.

Fig. 3.—*Specimen of Chronic Sclerosis.* Section through the lateral column from a case of amyotrophic lateral sclerosis. In consequence of the gradual disappearance of the pyramidal tracts the neurogliar tissue is greatly increased; here and there a few isolated nerve-fibers are seen in transverse section.

Fig. 4.—*Specimen of Chronic Myelitis.* Section through the lateral column from an old case of myelitis. Complete loss of the nerve-fibers, dense network of neurogliar tissue, indurated sheaths of blood-vessels surrounded by the remains of old hemorrhages (fragments of blood pigment), characterize this myelitic "scar."

PLATE 64.

Diseases of the Muscle-fibers.

Fig. 1.—Transverse section of a normal muscle composed of bundles of equal size, presenting a polygonal shape in transverse section and containing a few cells.

Figs. 2 and 3.—*Transverse and Longitudinal Sections of Muscle in Spinal Muscular Atrophy (Biceps).* There is a marked variation in the thickness of the individual fibers; some of them have disappeared entirely, others are much reduced in size (p). The muscle nuclei are much increased and form the so-called "lines *or verses* of nuclei" ("Kernzeilen"). The transverse striation of the protoplasm is lost in the degenerated fibrils; the protoplasm itself has undergone degeneration. n, Normal fibrils; h, hypertrophic fibrils.

Fig. 4.—*Juvenile Muscular Atrophy (Dystrophia Muscularis Progressiva) (Quadriceps Extensor).* Whole bundles of muscle-fibers are destroyed, the nuclei are increased in number, and many fibers are hypertrophic. Transverse striation is preserved for some time in spite of the atrophy of the fibers. The intervals between the remaining muscular fibers are frequently filled with fat (pseudohypertrophy). At h so-called "hypertrophic" muscle-fibers; n, normal fibers.

Fig. 5.—*Neurotic Muscular Atrophy (opponens pollicis).* The section shows marked diminution in the size of the fibrils and increase in the number of nuclei. The transverse striation persists for some time.

Fig. 6.—*Unstained Muscle-fibers.* (a) Degenerative muscular atrophy (quadriceps extensor from a case of lumbar myelitis). The muscle is granular and cloudy, the fibrils are broken up, the transverse striation has disappeared, and the fibers are reduced in thickness, but not uniformly. Eventually the disintegrated protoplasm is absorbed and nothing but the empty tube of sarcolemma remains. (b) Neurotic muscular atrophy, slight diminution in the thickness of the fibers with "lines of nuclei" and well-marked transverse striation (see above).

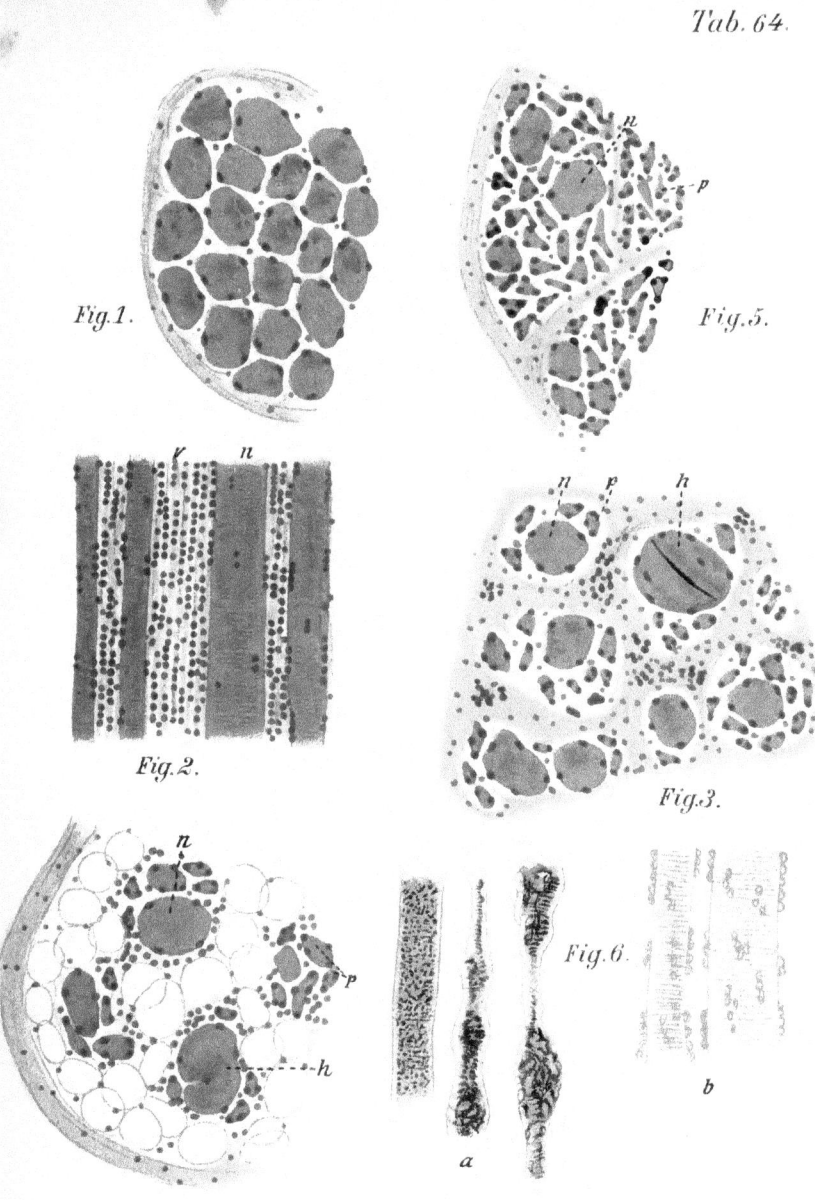

Tab. 64.

Tab. 65.

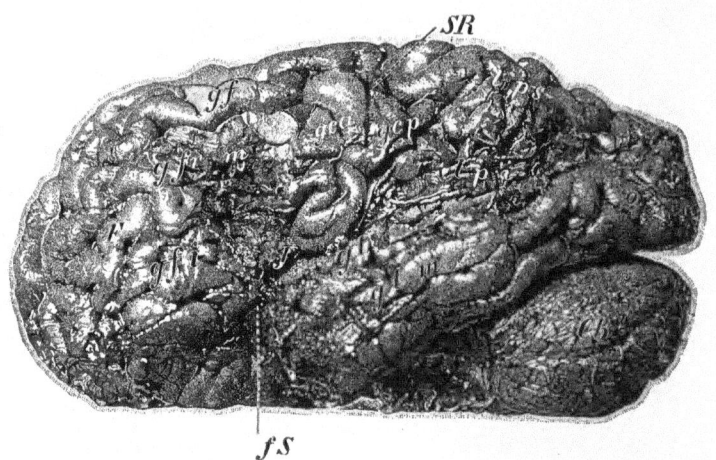

Fig. 1.

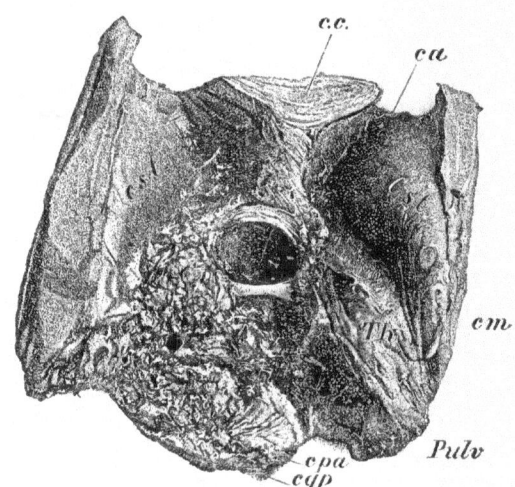

Fig. 2.

PLATE 65.

Fig. 1.—Left hemisphere from a man fifty-six years of age, who, after several attacks of apoplexy, was left with a permanent complete spastic paralysis of the right facial and hypoglossus and of the right arm, and with weakness of the right leg (right-sided hemiplegia). He had also lost the power of voluntary speech (motor aphasia); inability to understand spoken and written language (word-deafness, loss of visual memory pictures). The dementia gradually increased and death occurred after three years.

The photograph shows the outer surface of the left hemisphere. A large portion of the cortical convolutions is destroyed (porencephalus). The following portions of the cortex have been converted into connective tissue: The posterior portion of the middle and inferior frontal convolution (*g. fr. m* and *i*), the superior and middle temporal convolutions (*g. t. s* and *m*), the inferior parietal lobule (*l. p. i*), the greater portion of the anterior and posterior central convolutions, especially the lower half (*g. c. a* and *p*), and the central portion of the occipital lobe (*o*). The destructive process extends underneath the cortex and involves large portions of the insula (*I*) and of the white matter of the hemispheres. *f. S*, Fissure of Sylvius; *S. R.* fissure of Rolando; *Cb*, cerebellum.

Fig. 2.—*View of the Interior of the Third Ventricle after Removal of the Corpus Callosum and Fornix.* The left optic thalamus and surrounding structures (corpora quadrigemina, internal capsule) are completely destroyed.

A man fifty years of age had a stroke of apoplexy; when he recovered, after three days of coma, he was paralyzed on the right side (face, arm, and leg); at the same time there was oculomotor paralysis of the left eye (hemiplegia alternans). There was no disturbance of speech, but there was a right-sided hemianesthesia.

The focus was found to be very extensive and due to hemorrhage. Under the optic thalamus of the left side the subthalamic region, and further out the posterior limb of the internal capsule, were destroyed. Also the left anterior corpus quadrigeminum (*c. q. a*) and the tegmental region, including the left oculomotor nucleus. *Th*, Optic thalamus; *Pul*, pulvinar; *c. m*, middle commissure, central portion; *c. a*, anterior horn of the lateral ventricle; *C. st*, corpus striatum; *c. c*, corpus callosum; *cq p*, left posterior corpus quadrigeminum.

PLATE 66.

FIG. 1.—*Section through the Anterior Corpora Quadrigemina.* The left tegmental region (*f*) is completely destroyed; the left corpus quadrigeminum (*cqa*) is atrophied. The region about the nucleus of the left oculomotor (*N. III*), underneath the aqueduct of Sylvius (*A. S*), is likewise destroyed. Complete absence of the constituents of the tegmentum, red nucleus (*n. r*), superior and inferior fillet (*L*), substantia reticularis, etc.; the entire left half of the crusta (*ped x*) is atrophied. Clinical symptoms as in Plate 65, Figure 2: Hemiplegia alternans.

FIG. 2.—*Section through the Medulla Oblongata of a Young Girl, the Subject of Hereditary Tuberculosis.* The patient was taken ill quite suddenly with headache, vomiting, and increasing weakness of the right leg, and later of the right arm. This was soon followed by paralysis of the left facial and hypoglossus (hemiplegia alternans), and paralysis of the muscles of the pharynx. Sudden death. At the autopsy a tumor was found in the pons which had spread far into the medulla (*Tub*) and destroyed the pyramids (*Py*) and the facial and hypoglossus (*XII*) nerves at their points of exit. The tumor proved to be a solitary tubercle containing large numbers of giant cells.

FIG. 3.—So far we have considered *focal diseases* of the brain. The specimen before us shows a system disease —namely, *chronic progressive ophthalmoplegia.* The cells of the oculomotor nucleus (*N. III*) are the seat of a primary degeneration, and the fibers of the oculomotor nerve (*N. III*), which normally form a massive bundle at their point of exit on the surface of the brain, have also disappeared. (Compare the corresponding normal section, Plate 40, Fig. 2.)

The disease occurred in a woman suffering from tabes dorsalis. Paralysis of all the ocular muscles had gradually developed. *c. p,* Posterior commissure; *S. n,* substantia nigra; *n. r,* red nucleus; *Ped,* crusta; *L,* fillet.

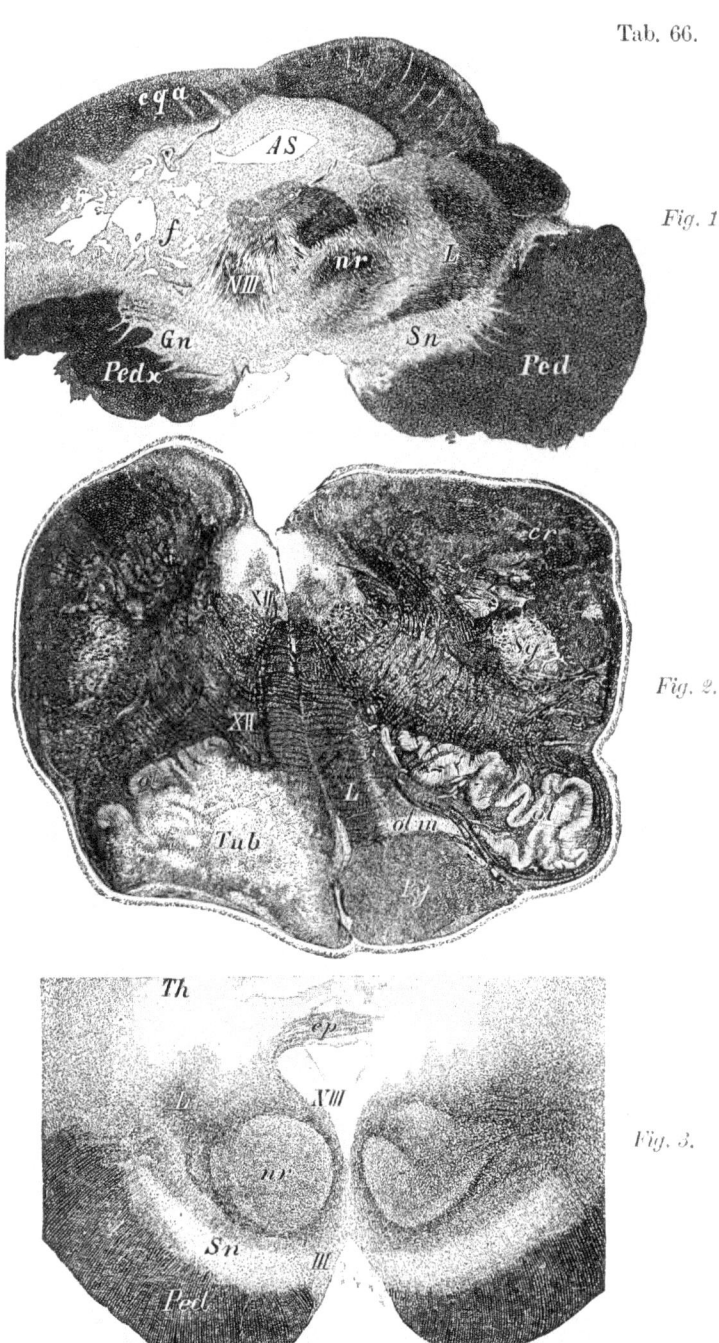

Tab. 66.

Fig. 1.

Fig. 2.

Fig. 3.

Tab. 67.

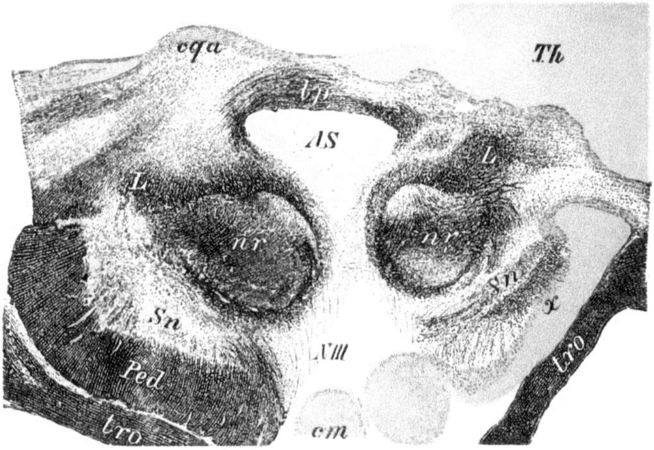

Fig. 1.

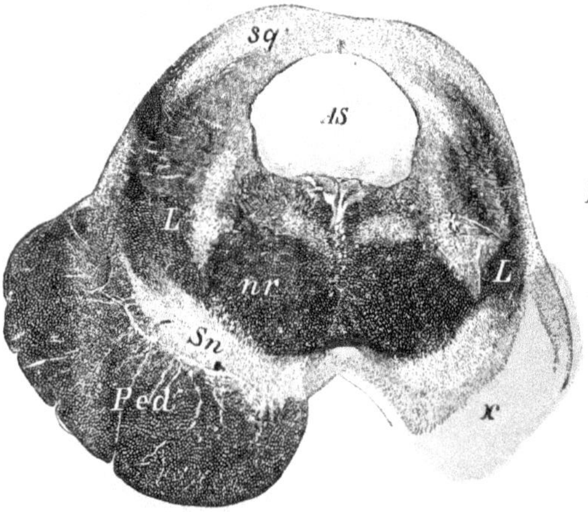

Fig. 2.

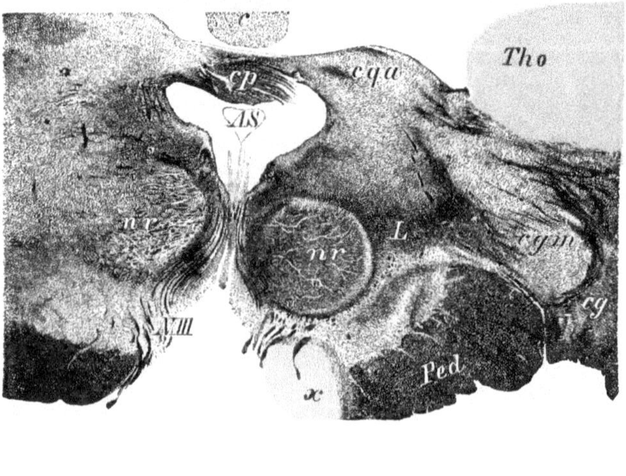

Fig. 3.

PLATE 67.

Secondary Degenerations of the Crusta.

Figures 1 and 2 present transverse sections through the anterior corpora quadrigemina and the parts immediately below these structures. There is complete atrophy of the fibers in the right half of the crusta (x). The specimens were taken from a case with extensive primary destruction of the cerebral cortex. As the fibers in the crusta have their neuron cells in the cortex, they necessarily undergo a secondary descending degeneration if these cells are destroyed.

The tract of the fillet (L) on the right side is narrower than on the left, but the degeneration is not complete (simple nondegenerative atrophy). The neuron cells of the fibers in the fillet are not situated in the cortex, but, in part at least, in the funiculus gracilis and cuneatus, while others are probably to be sought in the subthalamic region and in the optic thalamus. (The clinical symptom in this case was a total left-sided hemiplegia.) The red nucleus (nr) is also atrophic. The anterior and posterior brachia have disappeared.

Abbreviations.—*tr. o*, Optic tract; *S. n*, substantia nigra; *L*, fillet; *c. q. a*, anterior corpus quadrigeminum; *Ped*, crusta.

FIG. 3.—*Section through the Anterior Corpora Quadrigemina in Total Secondary Atrophy of the Mesial Fibers of the Crusta (Frontal Pontine Tract)* (x). This partial degeneration of the crusta (*Ped*) was secondary to an embolic softening focus which had destroyed the anterior limb of the capsule and the lenticular nucleus. There were no clinical symptoms.

Abbreviations.—*A. S*, Aqueduct of Sylvius; *c.g.m*, mesial geniculate body; *c. g*, lateral geniculate body; *c*, pineal gland; *L*, fillet; *c. q. a.* anterior corpora quadrigemina; *nr*, red nucleus; *N. III*, oculomotor.

These and the following examples of secondary degenerations in the brain and spinal cord are particularly important from a neurological point of view, because they enable us to follow the course of the various pathways almost as accurately as could be done in actual experimental work. They represent in man the experimental work done on animals. It is for this reason that we have described them here at some length. They are well adapted to illustrate once more the text in Part III.

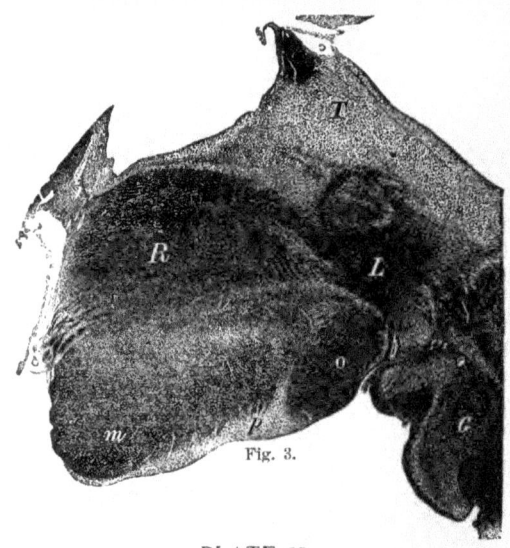

Fig. 3.

PLATE 68.

Secondary Degenerations of the Crusta.

FIG. 1.—*Section through the Third Ventricle (Middle Commissure).* Beneath the optic thalamus (*Th*), which has been cut away, are the constituents of the subthalamic region, the subthalamic body (*c. L*), white matter of the nucleus (*L*) and, underneath, the internal capsule (*ci*, posterior limb), above the point where it becomes the pes. On the right side the middle portion (*x*) of the internal capsule is degenerated in consequence of a lesion (hemorrhage) which has destroyed the central convolutions.

The degenerated areas correspond to a portion of the pyramidal tract. *tro*, Optic tract; *cm*, middle commissure; *f*, fornix; *v III*, third ventricle.

FIG. 2.—*Section through the Anterior Corpora Quadrigemina, from the same Case.* The figure shows the position of the degenerated pyramidal tract (*Py*) in the middle of the crusta (*Ped*). A large portion of the tract, however, which in this case is not totally degenerated, occupies a larger area situated laterally from the diseased portion. (See Fig. 3.)

Clinically there was a left-sided hemiparesis of the face, arm, and leg. *A.S*, Aqueduct; *L*, fillet; *cgm*, lateral geniculate body; *cqa*, anterior corpus quadrigeminum; *III*, oculomotor; *nr*, red nucleus; *Sn*, substantia nigra.

FIG. 3.—In this case, which belongs to Plate 62, Figure 1, there is a *pure degeneration of the pyramidal tract* (*p*). To its lateral side we see the oval bundle of Türck (*o*) in the crusta; *m*, the mesial pontine tract; *T*, optic thalamus; *R*, red nucleus; *L*, superior fillet; *g*, lateral geniculate body.

Owing to the secondary shrinking which always takes place, these cases of degeneration do not represent accurately the entire extent of the degenerated bundle.

Tab. 68.

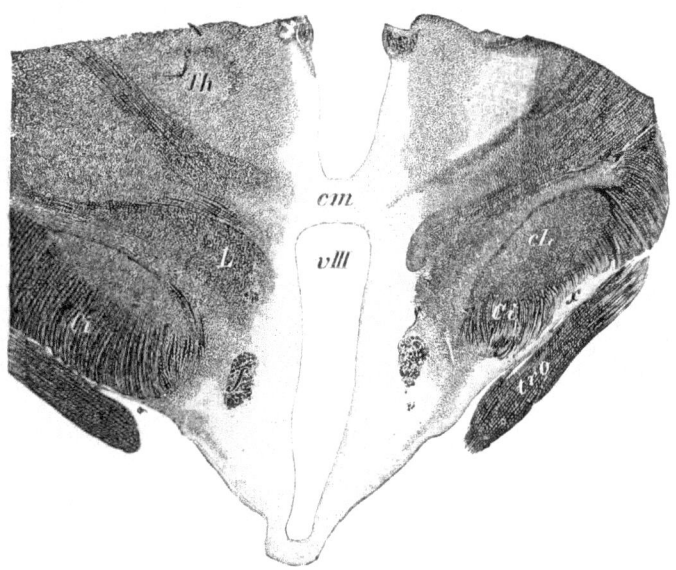

Fig. 1.

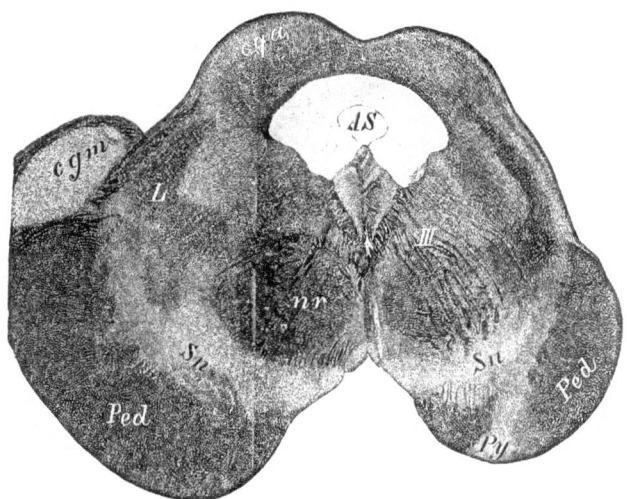

Fig. 2.

Tab. 69.

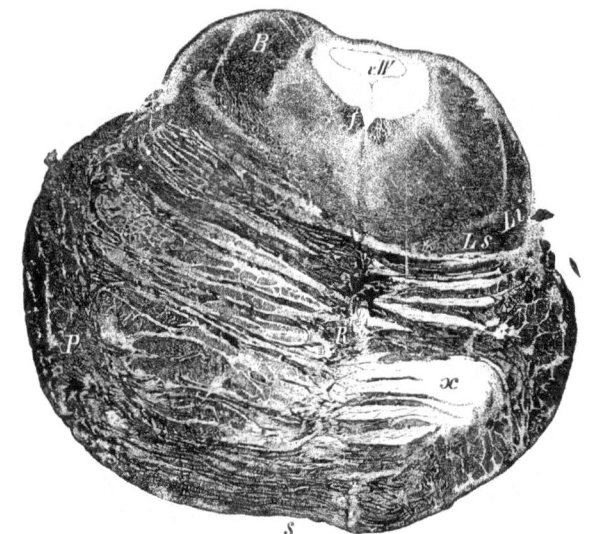

Fig. 1.

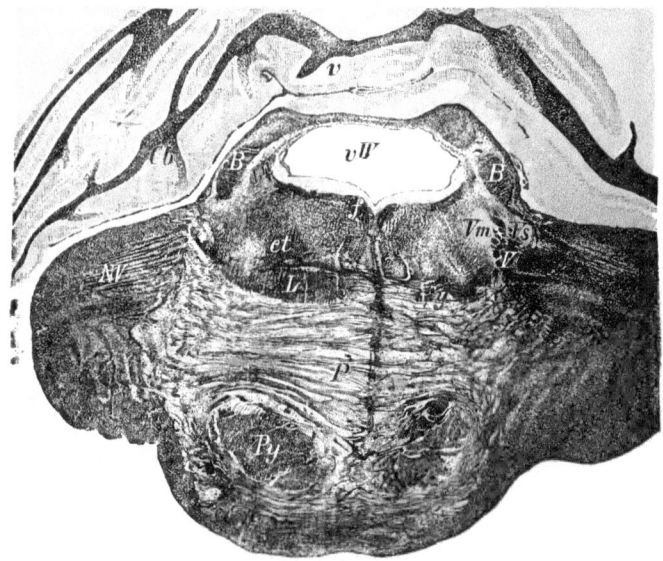

Fig. 2.

PLATE 69.

Secondary Degenerations of the Pons.

FIG. 1.—*Section through the Anterior Half of the Pons.* The section belongs to the case shown on Plate 67, Figures 1 and 2. On the left side the peduncular fibers collected in numerous bundles are seen traversing the transverse pontine fibers (P). On the right-hand side (x) these fibers, as well as the pontine ganglia, are completely wanting; hence the enormous diminution in the width of the right side of the pons. We learn from this section that the secondary degeneration does not confine itself to the fibers connecting two ganglion systems directly continuous with one another by their neurons, but extends also to their cells. The fillet (Ls, i) is atrophic.

Abbreviations.—B, Brachium; $v. IV$, aqueduct of Sylvius; f, posterior longitudinal bundle.

FIG. 2.—*Section through the Middle of the Pons, with Extensive Secondary Degenerations in the Tegmental Region.* The specimen belongs to the case shown on Plate 65, Figure 2. (The photograph is inverted so that the left, diseased half is shown on the right side.) The degeneration includes the two brachia (B) (in part on the right side at z); the neuron cells are in the red nucleus, which has been destroyed. The central tract of the fillet ($c. t$) in the right half of the tegmentum, the entire superior fillet (y) (neuron cells in the destroyed subthalamic region and in the optic thalamus?), the right pyramidal tract (Py) and other tracts, the substantia reticularis, and other structures. Vm, Motor, Vs, sensory, nucleus of the trigeminus; between the two the descending root (Vc); f, posterior longitudinal bundle; v, superior vermiform process; P, pontine ganglia; Vn, nasal root of the trigeminus.

PLATE 70.

Secondary Degenerations in the Medulla Oblongata.

Fig. 1.—*Section through the Medulla Oblongata below the Pons.* The entire left pyramidal tract (x) has undergone secondary degeneration, owing to primary destruction of the posterior limb of the internal capsule by hemorrhage (right-sided hemiplegia); the fillet (L) is reduced in size.

Note in this section the course of the striæ acusticæ (*stra*) on the left side, from the central nucleus of the auditory nerve over the floor of the fourth ventricle to the raphe, where they undergo decussation and pass to the fillet. *Cb*, restiform body; *NVII*, nucleus of facial nerve; *Nx*, nucleus of vagus; *Py*, pyramidal tract.

Fig. 2.—*Medulla Oblongata in Infantile Cerebral Paralysis.* The specimen was taken from a man thirty years of age, who from his earliest infancy (congenital? acquired?) presented the marks of arrested development in the entire right half of the body. The right arm was paretic, and there was a moderate contracture of the flexor muscles. There was also weakness of the right leg. Epileptiform attacks. Athetosis.

		Arm.	Forearm.
Length of arm	Right, 29 cm. Left, 31 "		
Circumference		Right, 21 cm. Left, 24 "	Right, 19 cm. Left, 24 "
Circumference of thigh	Right, 35 cm. Left, 39 "		
Calf	Right, 29 cm. Left, 32 "		

Autopsy.—The left central convolutions were rudimentary (agenesis?). The entire left pyramid (x) was atrophied, as was the left fillet (y), although there was no true degeneration, evidently because the disease made its appearance at a time when medullarization had not yet begun. The raphe (k) is displaced to the left; the right pyramid is almost hypertrophic (topical compensation). *cr*, Restiform body; *ol*, inferior olive; *XII*, nucleus of hypoglossus.

Fig. 3.—*Medulla Oblongata in Atrophy of the Fillet.*—The right fillet ($L.\ x$) and the internal arcuate fibers (*fai*, y) of the substantia reticularis (*s. r*) of the *left side* (!) show a descending degeneration. These arcuate fibers correspond to the direct communication with the fillet of the opposite side, which, with the funiculus gracilis and funiculus cuneatus (*n. G*), appear in the restiform body (*Cr*). The pyramid (*Py. x*) and the olives (*ol*) of the same side are also degenerated.

The chief clinical symptom was hemianesthesia of the left half of the body. (See Plate 65, Fig. 2, to which this specimen belongs.)

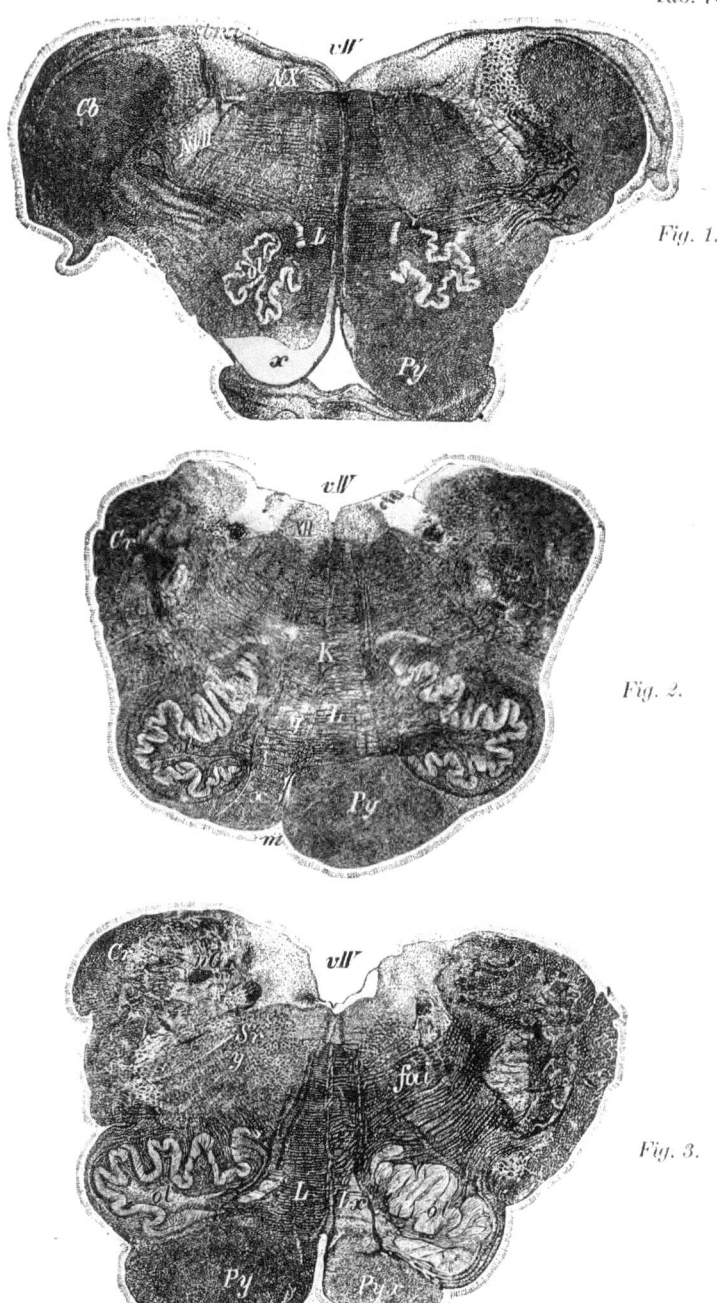

Tab. 70.

Fig. 1.

Fig. 2.

Fig. 3.

Tab. 71.

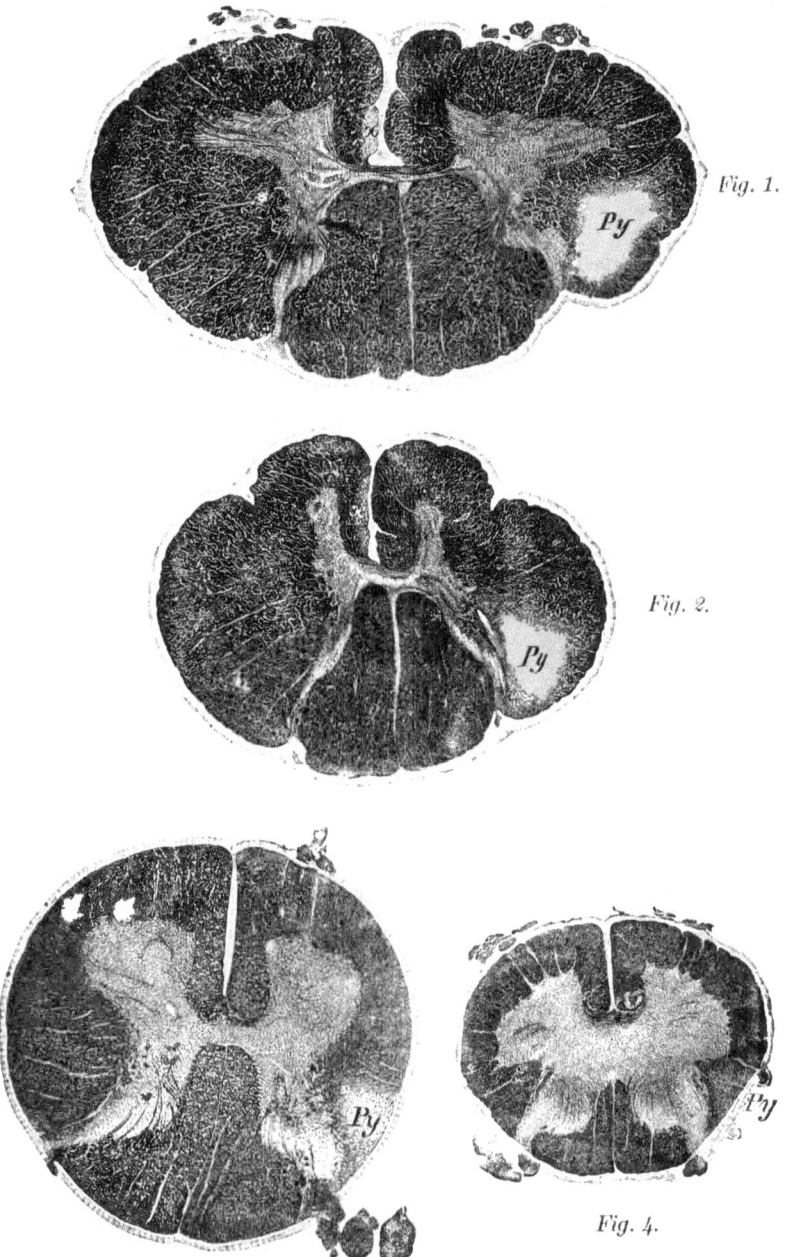

Fig. 1.

Fig. 2.

Fig. 3.

Fig. 4.

PLATE 71.

Descending Degeneration of the Pyramidal Tract in the Spinal Cord after a Focal Lesion of the Cerebrum.

The specimens belong to the case illustrated on Plate 70, Figure 1, where the left pyramid shows secondary degeneration throughout. This degeneration can be traced in the spinal cord through the entire course of this tract—that is to say, below the decussation of the pyramids in the lateral column of the opposite (right) side (crossed fibers), and in the anterior column of the same side (uncrossed fibers).

In the cervical and thoracic portions of the cord the lateral pyramidal tract (Py) is bounded on the outer side by the direct cerebellar tract, which is still preserved. In the lumbar portion of the cord the cross-section is wedge-shaped and extends to the periphery. The degeneration of the anterior pyramidal tract (x) can be traced into the lower thoracic portion of the cord. In the right anterior horn the destruction can be seen with the microscope. The degeneration, therefore, involves the central motor neuron complex, the entire pyramidal tract, so that the entire right side of the spinal cord is considerably diminished in size.

FIG. 1.—*Cervical Portion (Sixth Cervical Nerve)*.
FIG. 2.—*Thoracic Portion (Third Dorsal Nerve)*.
FIG. 3.—*Lumbar Portion (Second Lumbar Nerve)*.
FIG. 4.—*Sacral Portion*.

PLATE 72.

Descending Degeneration in the Spinal Cord in Diseases of the Spinal Cord.

FIG. 1.—*Lower Cervical Portion of the Cord.*

FIG. 2.—*Lower Thoracic Portion.* (The figure is inverted so that the right half appears on the left side.)

FIG. 3.—*Upper Lumbar Portion.* The specimens were taken from a man forty years of age who fell and sustained a fracture of a cervical vertebra, followed by contusion of the lower cervical portion of the cord. The following symptoms were present: Complete spastic paraplegia of the legs, muscular atrophy and paralysis of the small muscles of the hand, anesthesia, incontinence of urine.

Autopsy.—Below the point of compression in the cervical portion of the cord there was found a descending degeneration of both lateral pyramidal tracts (Py) and anterior pyramidal tracts (Pya), and of a comma-shaped area (r, Schultz' area, containing descending fibers arising from the gray matter) in the columns of Burdach and a central area ("clearing") in the columns of Goll. Note that the anterior pyramidal tract on the right side is considerably smaller than on the left (individual variation). In the thoracic and lumbar portions of the cord the pyramidal tracts on both sides are degenerated. The degeneration of the posterior columns has disappeared (short pathways).

FIG. 4.—*Lumbar Portion of the Cord in Compression of the Thoracic Portion.* The specimen was taken from the case shown on Plate 59, Figure 3. *Sarcoma of the dura mater.* Below the seat of compression there was descending degeneration of the pyramidal tracts (Py) on both sides, and some degeneration in the marginal zone of the antero-lateral column (fal) (descending branches of the central sensory neurons arising in the gray matter) (middle zone).

Note the great number of fibers entering the anterior horns from the posterior horn and posterior roots.

Tab. 72.

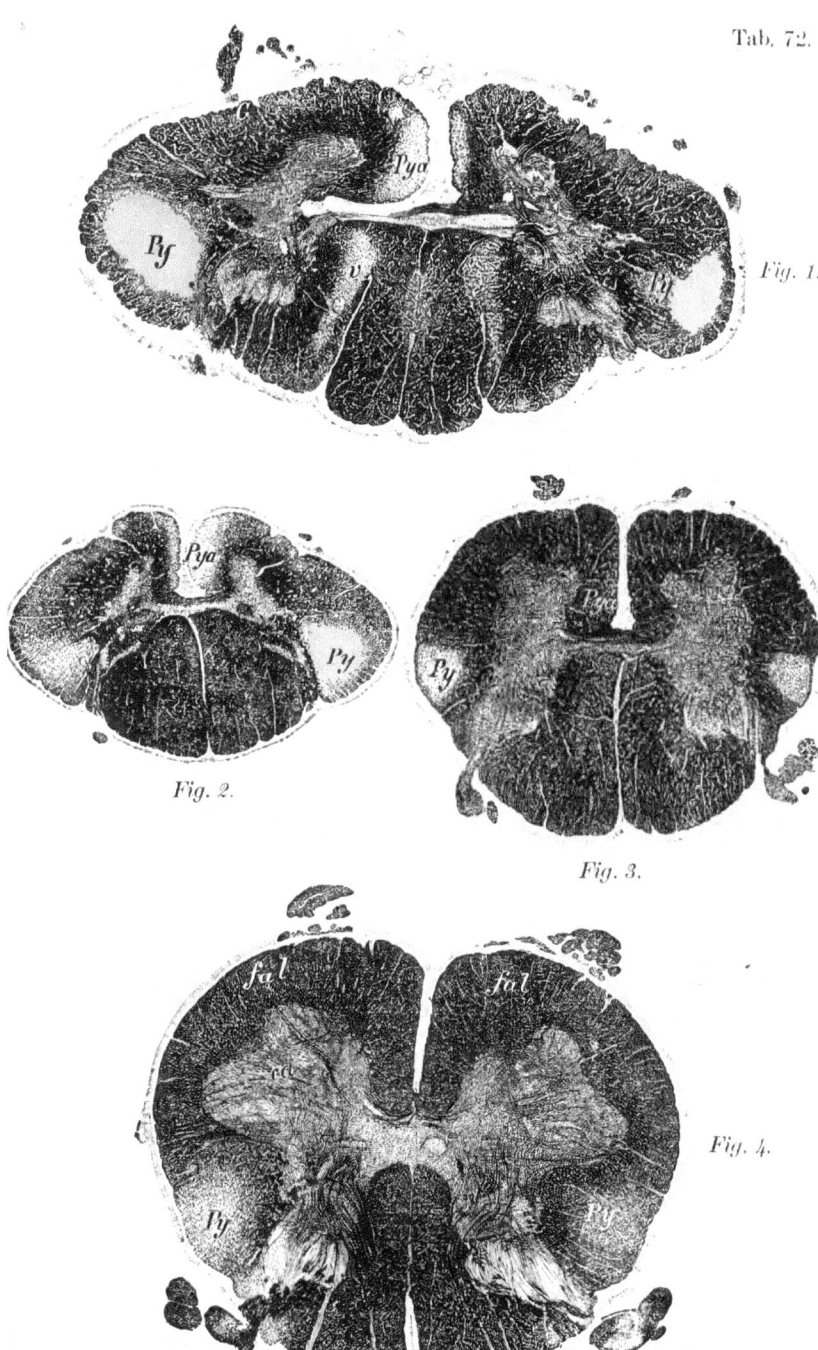

Fig. 1.

Fig. 2.

Fig. 3.

Fig. 4.

Tab. 73.

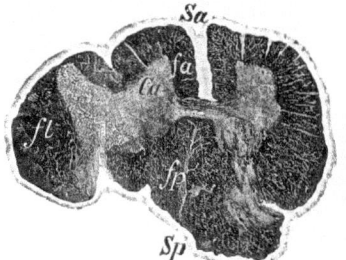

Fig. 1.

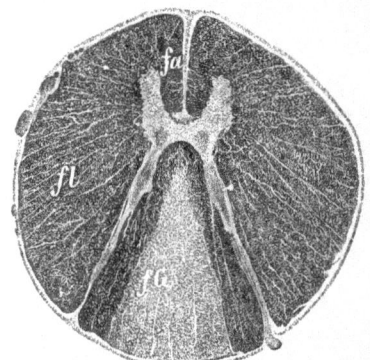

Fig. 2.

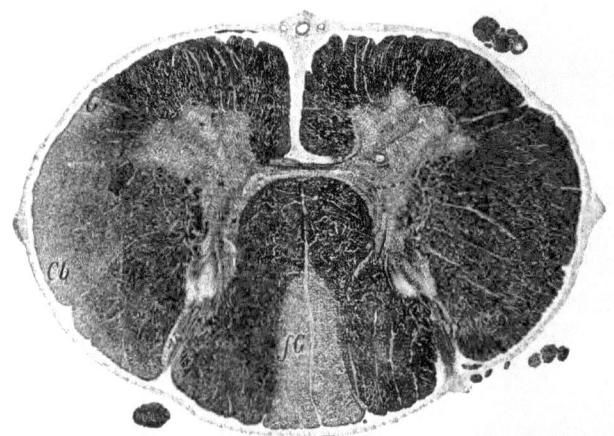

Fig. 3.

PLATE 73.

Ascending Degeneration of the Spinal Cord.

A soldier twenty-two years of age fell and crushed the lower thoracic portion of the vertebral column and suffered a contusion of the lumbar cord. Complete flaccid paralysis of the legs ensued, and was followed by a rapidly developing degenerative muscular atrophy. Disturbance of sensation, bladder, and rectum, and loss of patellar reflex. The patient died two months later of cystitis.

Fig. 1.—*Upper Contused Portion of the Lumbar Cord.*

Fig. 2.—*Middle Thoracic Portion.* There is a secondary ascending degeneration of the columns of Goll (fG) (neuron cells in the spinal ganglia).

Fig. 3.—*Lower Cervical Cord.* The degenerated columns of Goll (fG) present a distinct, wedge-shaped outline. They occupy a much smaller area than in deeper sections.

In addition we note an ascending degeneration of the left direct cerebellar tract (Cb) and of Gowers' tract (G) on the left side. It is readily seen in Figure 1 that the gray matter and the columns of Clarke, where the neuron cells of these tracts are situated, have suffered a much greater destruction on the left than on the right side.

The columns of Goll, therefore, contain the long sensory pathways from the lower extremities, and are joined higher up by the long sensory pathways from the trunk and upper extremities (column of Burdach).

Abbreviations.—Ca, Anterior horn; fa, anterior column; fl, lateral column; fp, posterior column; Sa, anterior sulcus.

PLATE 74.

Ascending Degeneration in the Cervical Portion of the Cord and Medulla Oblongata.

FIG. 1.—*Ascending Secondary Degeneration in the Upper Cervical Portion in Primary Acute Myelitis situated about the Middle of the Thoracic Cord.* As a result of the interruption of the fibers which takes place in the thoracic cord the following regions, containing long pathways, are degenerated: Column of Goll (*f. G*), direct cerebellar tract (*Cb*), Gowers' tract (*G*), and the marginal zone of the anterior column.

FIG. 2.—*Section through the Decussation of the Pyramids.* Ascending degeneration in chronic (syphilitic?) myelitis situated in the thoracic cord. The columns of Goll (*f. G*), the direct cerebellar tract (*Cb*), and Gowers' tract (*G*) are degenerated.

FIG. 3.—*Section through the Medulla Oblongata at the Level of the Inferior Pole of the Olive.* The preparation belongs to the case illustrated on Plate 73, and represents a section immediately below that shown in Figure 3.

We note ascending degeneration of the columns of Goll (*f. G*) in which the funiculi graciles (nuclei of Goll, *n G*) have made their appearance. The degeneration has not extended to the contiguous fibers of the fillet (internal arcuate fibers, *fai*), which therefore represent a new, independent neuron. In the direct cerebellar tract (*Cb*) the degeneration is evidently also confined to the left side. Owing to the obliquity of the plane of section the right olive only is included.

Abbreviations.—*L*, Fillet; *f. a. i*, internal arcuate fibers; *ol. m*, mesial accessory olive; *ol*, inferior olive; *Sg*, substantia gelatinosa; *fB*, *fG*, columns of Burdach and Goll; *n B*, *n G*, funiculi gracilis and cuneatus.

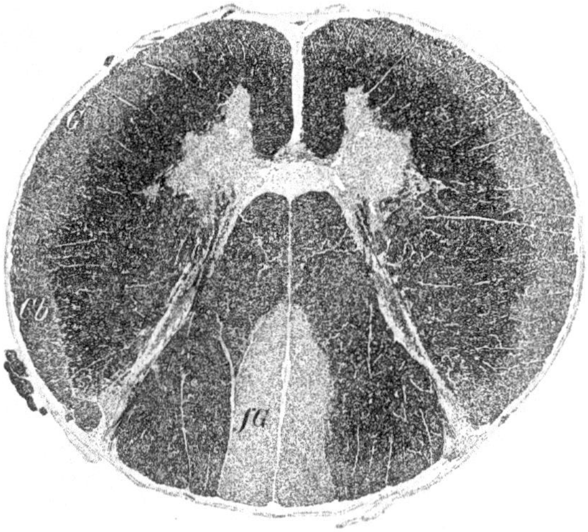

Tab. 74.

Fig. 1.

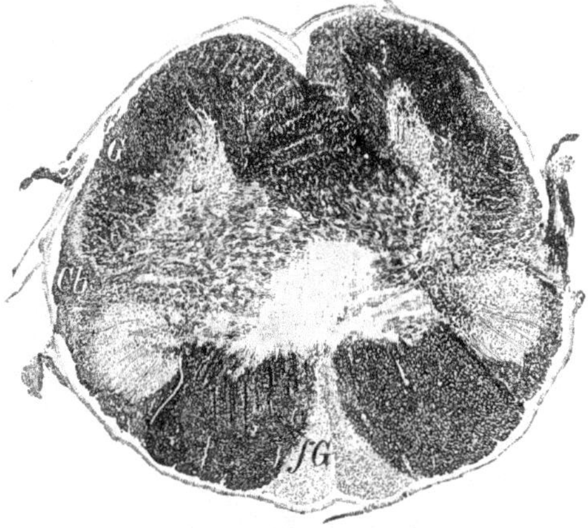

Fig. 2.

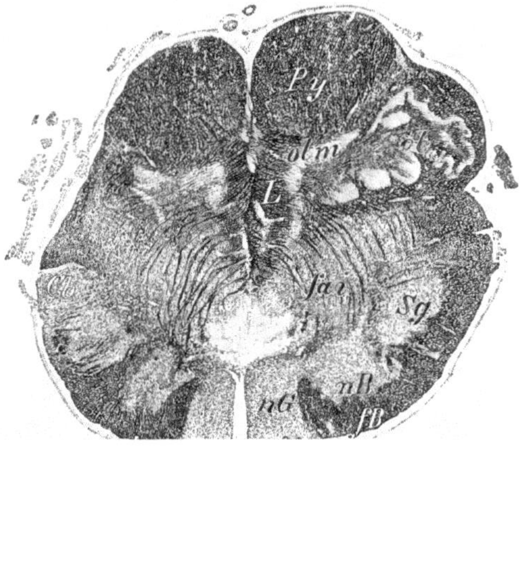

Fig. 3.

V.

SPECIAL PATHOLOGY

OF THE

Spinal Cord and of the Peripheral Nerves.

(Part V. of Text.)

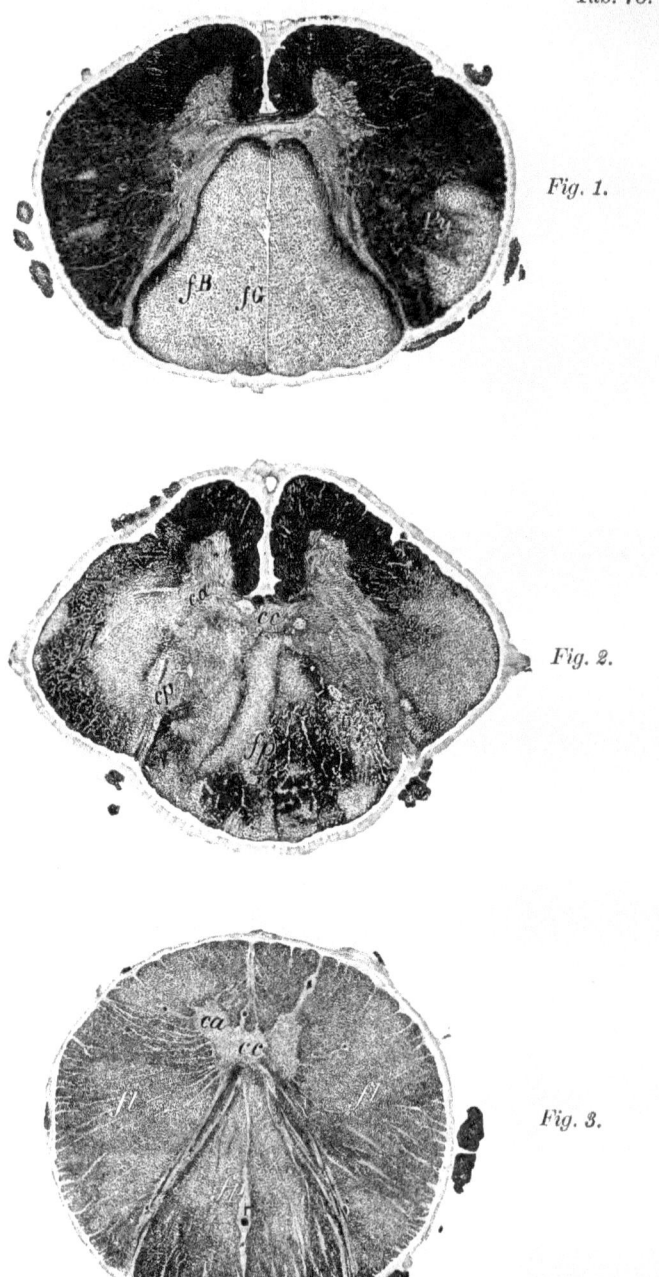

Tab. 75.

Fig. 1.

Fig. 2.

Fig. 3.

PLATE 75.

Various Forms of Myelitis.

Fig. 1.—*Columnar Acute (toxic) Myelitis.* (Cervical portion of the cord.) A man forty-two years of age, after a severe attack of erysipelas, developed a rapidly increasing paresis of the arms and legs, accompanied by painful sensations. The paralysis was never complete. There was slight disturbance of sensation and of the vesical function; pain-sense remained normal. Toward the end there was paralysis of the diaphragm. The disease lasted only four months.

Diagnosis.—Multiple neuritis (?).

Autopsy.—Extensive myelitic degeneration of the posterior columns (*f. G, f. B*), extending from the cervical to the thoracic portion of the cord. Myelitic foci in the lateral columns (*Py*), especially in the cervical region. Slight neuritic changes. This case proves, among other things, that the posterior columns are not essential to cutaneous sensation.

Fig. 2.—*Chronic (syphilitic?) Myelitis.* (Cervical region.) A man forty-eight years of age, suspected of lues, developed a slowly progressive weakness of the legs, without pain, which after a year and a half culminated in total paraplegia and loss of all sensation. Knee-jerks exaggerated. Incontinence.

The specimen shows a diffuse myelitic degeneration involving the entire transverse section of the cord. It was most extensive in the region including the seventh, eighth, and ninth thoracic segments. Below the lesion there was descending degeneration of the pyramidal tract. (For the changes above the lesion consult Fig. 2 on Plate 74, which belongs to this case.)

Fig. 3.—"*Compression Myelitis.*" Carcinoma in the third thoracic vertebra led to compression of the cervical cord, followed by marked degeneration in every part of the cross-section.

The specimen was taken from a woman forty-two years of age, who was suddenly seized with violent neuralgic pains in the back. She rapidly developed a progressive paresis of the legs and became completely bedridden. There were disturbances of the bladder and of sensation. After three months the paraplegia had become complete. Contractures formed, and the patient suffered continuously from violent pain which could hardly be controlled by opium. The disease lasted six months.

Abbreviations.—*ca, cp,* Anterior horn, posterior horn; *cc,* central canal; *fl, fp,* lateral column, posterior column.

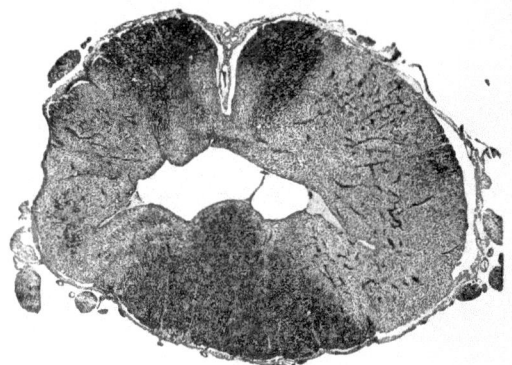

Fig. 4.

PLATE 76.
Syringomyelia.

FIG. 1.—*Hydromyelia, Upper Thoracic Region.* (Specimen of Professor v. Strümpell.) A man thirty-five years of age, the subject of hereditary disease, developed a slowly increasing weakness and stiffness of the legs, and later of the arms. The tendon reflexes were exaggerated; muscular spasms appeared and gradually grew worse. No atrophy. Sensation normal.

Diagnosis.—Spastic spinal paralysis.

Autopsy.—Hydromyelia with degeneration of the pyramidal tract. The central canal throughout the spinal cord was converted into a wide cavity filled with fluid (hydromyelus). Congenital (?).

FIGS. 2 AND 3.—*Sections through the Upper and Middle Thoracic Portions of the Cord from another case of Syringomyelia.* The cavity extends partly into the anterior and into the posterior horns, involving the entire extent of the latter. The clinical course was as follows: A man forty years of age developed slowly progressive weakness and emaciation of the right, and later of the left, hand and right arm. The muscles of the ball of the thumb, the hypothenar muscles, and the interossei were the first to undergo degenerative atrophy. Pain-sense and temperature-sense were completely lost in the arms. The tactile sense was normal. Trophic disturbances made their appearance in the hands. Inflammatory necrotic processes in the phalanges, nails, and joints.

Figure 2 shows a partial descending degeneration of the column of Goll (x), due to destruction of the posterior column (x) by extension of the cavity seen in Figure 3.

FIG. 4.—*Syringomyelia and Multiple Sclerosis.* In addition to the cavity formation there are extensive sclerotic areas in the anterolateral and posterior columns, where the medullary sheaths of the fibers have been destroyed. The diseased portion, therefore, appears white.

Abbreviations.—*ca*, Anterior horn; *cb*, direct cerebellar tract; *cc*, central canal (or, more accurately, cavity); *fa, fl, fp*, anterior, lateral, and posterior columns; *fB, fG*, columns of Burdach and Goll.

Tab. 76.

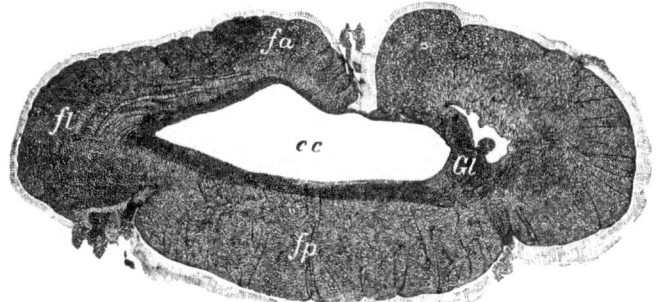

Fig. 1.

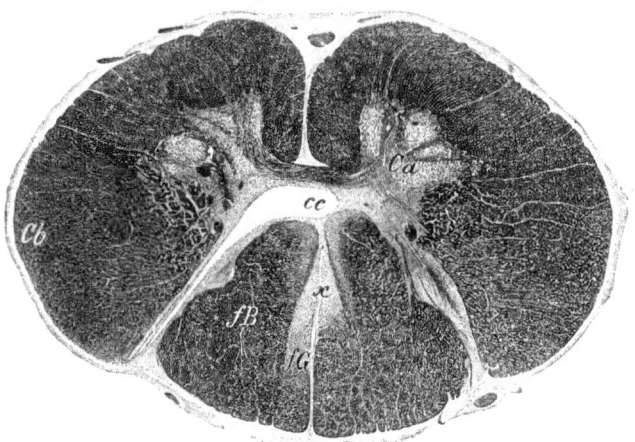

Fig. 2.

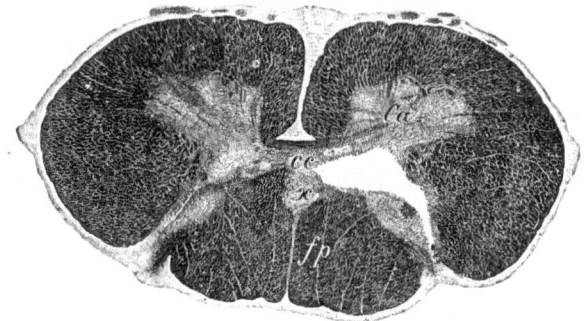

Fig. 3.

Tab. 77.

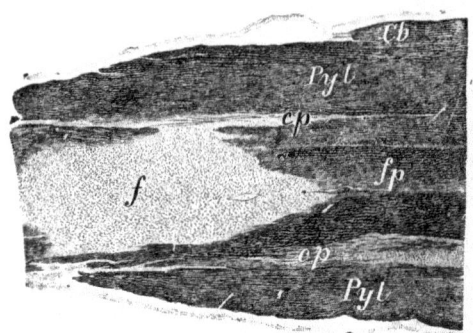

Fig. 1.

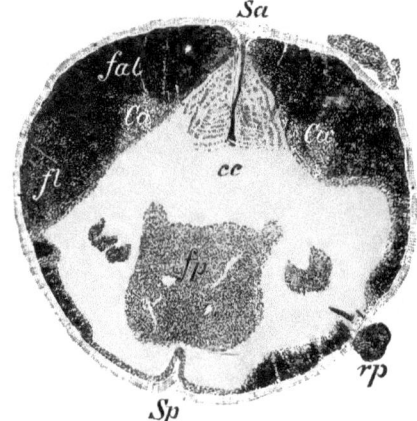

Fig. 2.

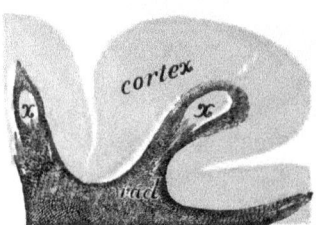

Fig. 3.

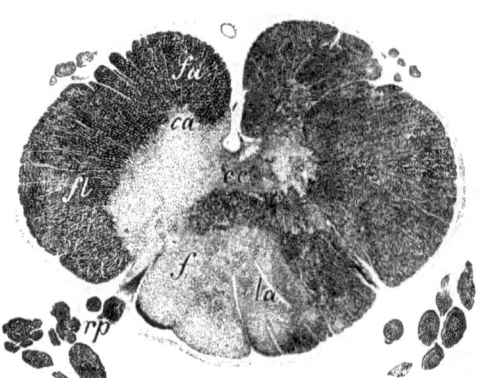

Fig. 4.

PLATE 77.

Multiple Cerebrospinal Sclerosis.

A woman twenty-five years of age had for several months noticed increasing weakness of the hands, with tremors and inability to grasp objects (intention tremor). Later there were added stiff, uncertain gait, nystagmus, scanning speech, optic-nerve atrophy (white, pale fundus), and exaggeration of the reflexes. Sensation was normal; slight vesical disturbance. In the course of three years the woman became completely bedridden and finally died of pneumonia.

Autopsy.—Irregularly scattered sclerotic foci in the brain and spinal cord, where the medullary sheaths of the nerve-fibers were partially destroyed. The axis-cylinders in some parts were preserved.

Fig. 1.—*Longitudinal Section through the Thoracic Region, showing a Sclerotic Focus (f) in the Posterior Columns, which are included in the Section.*

Figs. 2 and 4.—*Cross-sections through the Thoracic Region.* In Figure 2 almost the entire cross-section is involved, a portion of the anterolateral columns alone being preserved; all of the gray matter of the anterior and posterior horns is involved.

Figure 4 shows a smaller focus (f) in the posterior columns and in the posterior and anterior horns, especially of the left side.

Fig. 3.—*Section through the Cortex of the Cerebral Hemispheres.* The radiating fibers of the white matter (*rad*) contain two small sclerotic foci (*x*).

Similar foci were also found in the brain-stem, the pons, the medulla oblongata, etc.

Abbreviations.—*ca*, Anterior horn; *cb*, direct cerebellar tract; *cc*, central canal; *cp*, posterior horn; *fal*, anterolateral column; *fl*, lateral column; *fp*, posterior column; *Pyl*, lateral pyramidal tract.

PLATE 78.

FIG. 1.—*Section through the Medulla Oblongata from a case of Chronic Bulbar Paralysis with Amyotrophic Lateral Sclerosis.* A man thirty-six years of age developed a slowly progressing atrophy and paralysis of the small muscles of both hands; soon a marked disturbance in the speech (bulbar speech) made its appearance. The movements of the tongue and lips became slower, the corresponding muscles atrophied, and marked fibrillary contractions appeared in the tongue. The patient's gait also became stiff and labored. At the end of two years there were complete atrophy and paralysis of the tongue and lips and of the muscles of deglutition. Speech had become impossible. The arms were completely atrophied, and the legs spastic and paralyzed. Death from inspiration pneumonia.

The preparation shows marked destruction of the cells and fibers in the nucleus of the hypoglossus (XII); light spots in the pyramids (Py). Many of the cells in the nucleus of the facial nerve were also destroyed. L, Fillet; ol, olive; Cr, restiform body.

FIG. 2.—*Section through the Lower Cervical Cord in Amyotrophic Lateral Sclerosis.* The clinical course was quite similar to that which has just been described, except for the absence of bulbar symptoms in the uncomplicated form. Thus we have slowly increasing degeneration, muscular atrophy of the upper extremities, beginning in the thenar and interossei muscles, and spastic paralysis of the legs. Sensation and vesical function are not affected. The reflexes are increased. The specimen shows wide-spread destruction of cells and fibers in the anterior horn (Ca), which is much reduced in size. The pyramidal tracts on both sides are degenerated.

FIG. 3.—*Section through the Anterior Horn of the Cervical Cord in Spinal Muscular Atrophy.* (Professor v. Strümpell's case.) A man thirty-five years of age, the subject of an hereditary disease, developed atrophy and paralysis of the thenar and interossei muscles. In the course of a year the atrophy extended to all the muscles of the arms, of the shoulder-girdle, and to the costal and nuchal muscles. The muscles showed fibrillar contractions and the reaction of degeneration. Sensation normal. No bulbar phenomena. No disturbance of the gait.

In the preparation we see that the anterior horn (cornu a) is much shrunken; extensive destruction of cells. The anterior roots are also very atrophic. (Compare with Plate 52, Fig. 1.) In the anterior horn we see a dense network of cicatricial neurogliar tissue. The lateral column is normal. B, Column of Burdach; ca, anterior commissure; fa, fal, anterior and lateral columns; G, column of Goll; Py, lateral pyramidal tract.

Tab. 78.

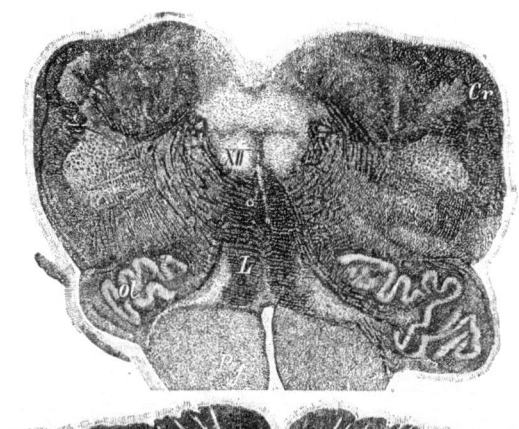

Fig. 1.

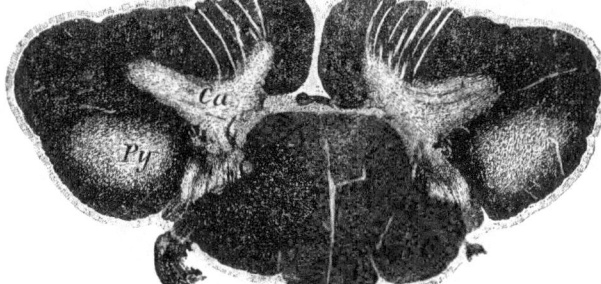

Fig. 2.

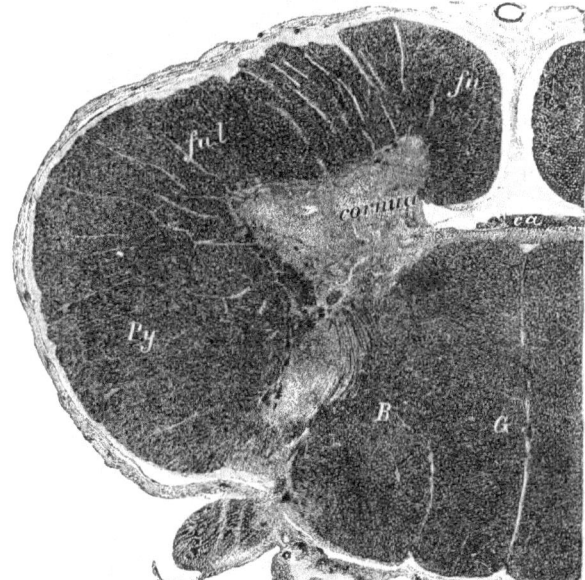

Fig. 3.

Tab. 79.

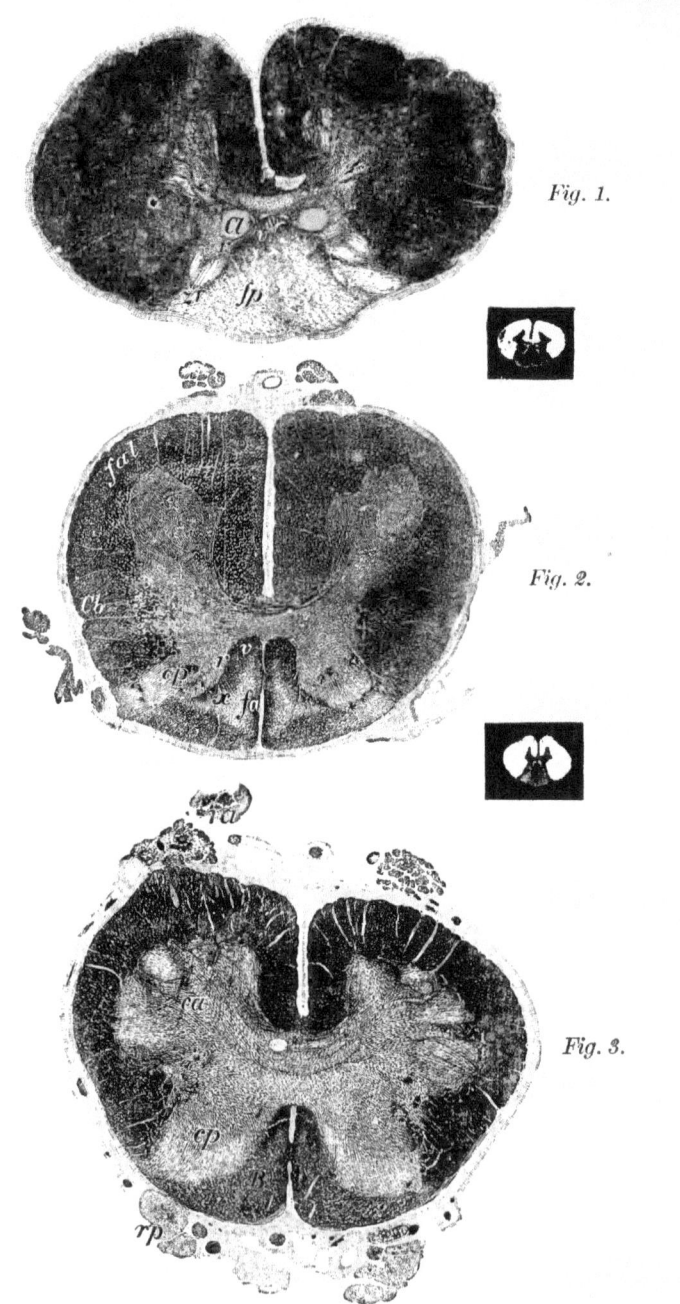

Fig. 1.

Fig. 2.

Fig. 3.

PLATE 79.
Tabes Dorsalis (Thoracic and Lumbar Portions).

In tabes the nerve-fibers of a part of the peripheral sensory neuron degenerate. Usually those of the lower extremity are affected; more rarely those of the arm and of the face (fifth nerve). The primary seat of the disease is not yet definitely known (neuron cells in the spinal ganglia?). It is probable that certain reflex paths (collaterals from the posterior roots) are the first to become diseased, then the posterior roots (see Plate 83, Fig. 5, for their course), both the short fibers which enter the columns of Clarke in the posterior horn and the long fibers which enter through the lumbar roots and ascend in the columns of Goll; the peripheral portions of the neuron, the sensory cutaneous nerves, are always involved in the degenerative process.

FIG. 1.—*Section through the Lower Thoracic Region.* The posterior columns (fp) are very much paler than normal; the greater part of the ascending and descending fibers from the posterior roots contained in the posterior columns is degenerated. The ventral portion (v) of the posterior columns is not derived from the posterior roots, and it regularly escapes in tabes. The short tracts which enter the posterior horn from the posterior columns at r are also entirely destroyed (compare the normal section, Plate 49, Fig. 1). Owing to the destruction of the fibers, the columns of Clarke (Cl) appear as broad, round, sharply circumscribed areas.

FIG. 2.—*Section through the Upper Lumbar Region from another case.* The degeneration is confined to symmetrical areas (d) in both posterior columns, separated by a small area (oval outline, fa) of intact tissue. There is also a so-called "marginal degeneration," or degeneration of the short tracts which ascend and descend in the marginal portions of the anterior (fol) and lateral columns, being derived from cells in the gray matter (central neuron). Cb, Cerebellar tract; ep, posterior horn; r, absent radii.

FIG. 3.—*Section through the Lower Lumbar Region from a third case.* In addition to the uniform degenerated area in the posterior cords (B), the ventral aspect being normal, we recognize degeneration of the posterior roots ($r.p$), the anterior roots ($r.a$) presenting the normal black color. Ca, cp, Anterior and posterior horns.

PLATE 80.
Tabes Dorsalis (Cervical Region).

FIG. 1.—*Section through the Cervical Spinal Cord.* (From case on Plate 79, Fig. 1.) The column of Goll (fG), which represents the continuation of the long ascending posterior root-fibers of the lumbar cord, is completely degenerated. The columns of Burdach (fB) also present a central light area (long fibers from the thoracic and cervical roots). The zone of Lissauer (L), at the tip of the posterior horn, which contains the outermost root-fibers of small caliber, is also degenerated. Rp, Posterior roots; r, radii.

The specimens were taken from a man, aged fifty, who for six years had been suffering from a distressing sense of pressure in the epigastric region, which later developed into a typical girdle-pain extending around the entire body. During the last four years his gait became gradually more uncertain, and neuralgic pains frequently appeared in the legs (lancinating pains). Paresthesia was present. The pupillary and patellar reflexes were abolished. There were marked ataxia and distinct disturbance of sensation in the legs (delayed pain-sense). Disturbance of vesical function. Later a chronic effusion developed in the left knee-joint (arthropathia tabetica). The knee was flexed, and the ataxia became so great that the patient had to keep his bed altogether.

FIG. 2.—*Section through the Cervical Region in so-called "High Tabes."* The peripheral sensory neurons of the upper, as well as of the lower, extremities are diseased, so that almost the entire posterior column in the cervical region is degenerated (column of Goll, FG, and of Burdach, FB). In addition there is a slight symmetrical affection of the pyramidal lateral tract (Py) (the color is faint). We therefore have a combined form of tabes.

FIG. 3.—*Section through the Highest Portion of the Cervical Cord (Tabes Combiné).* This is another case of "high tabes" in which only a small portion of the posterior columns (B, G), corresponding to the posterior external segment, is preserved. There is also a plainly marked degeneration of the direct cerebellar tract (Cb) on both sides (tabes combiné). The most pronounced clinical symptom in this case was muscular paresis, and the pupillary reflex was preserved (!). Hence a provisional diagnosis of "pseudotabes" was made.

Tab. 80.

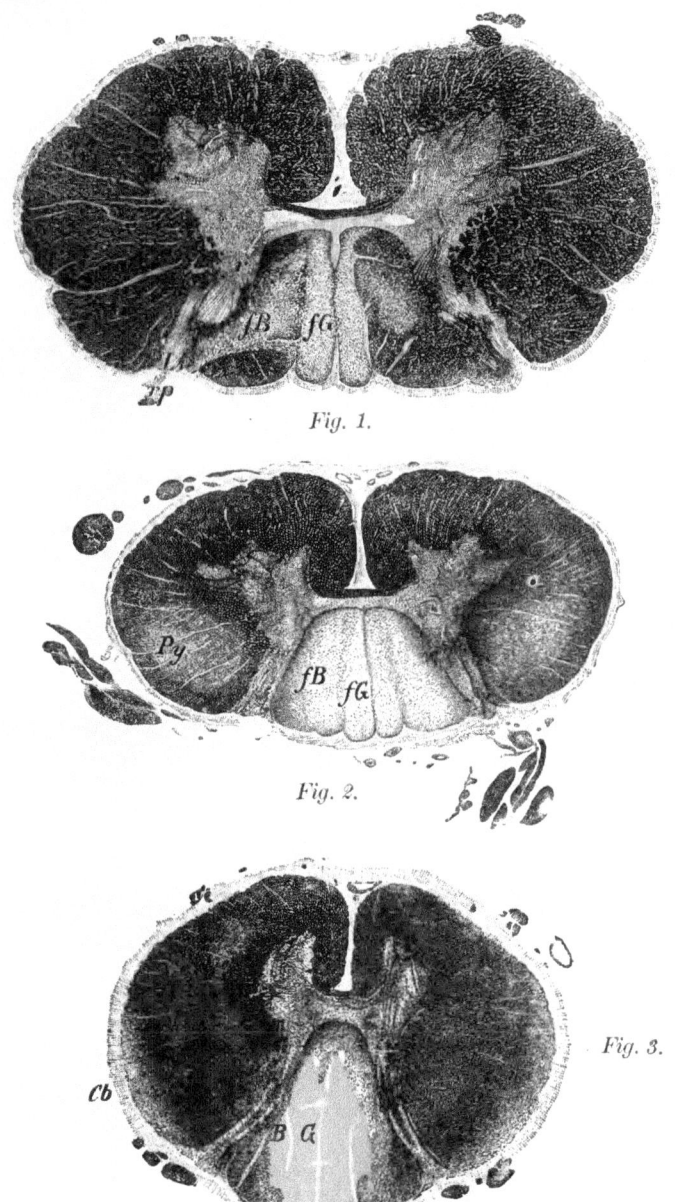

Fig. 1.

Fig. 2.

Fig. 3.

Tab. 81.

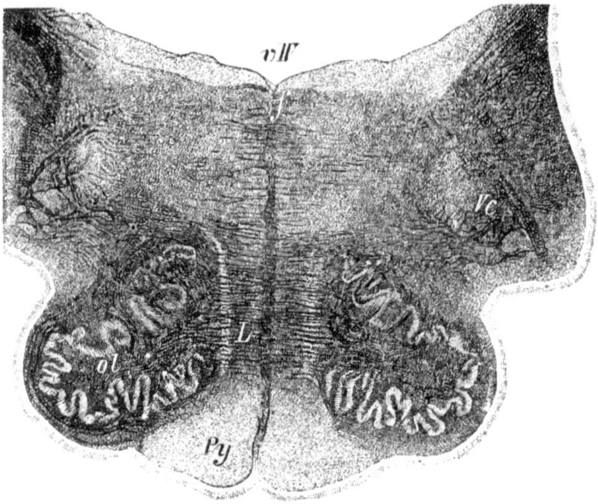

Fig. 1.

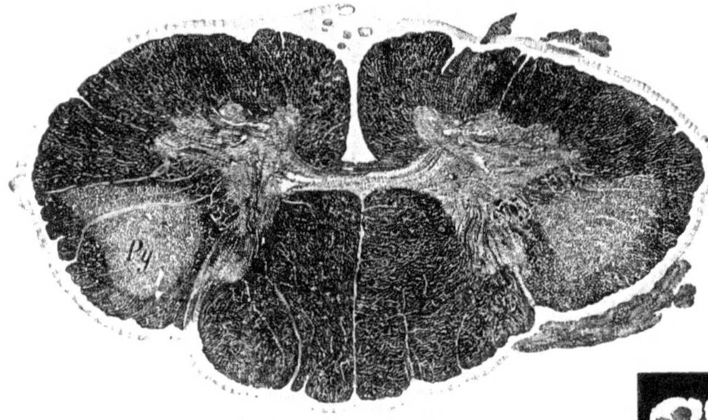

Fig. 2.

Fig. 3. 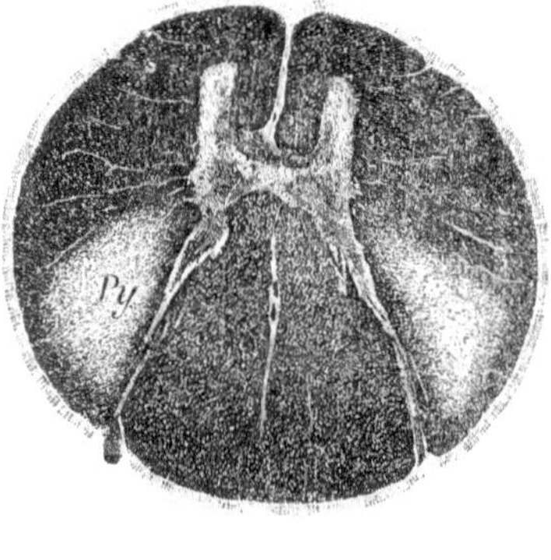 Fig. 4.

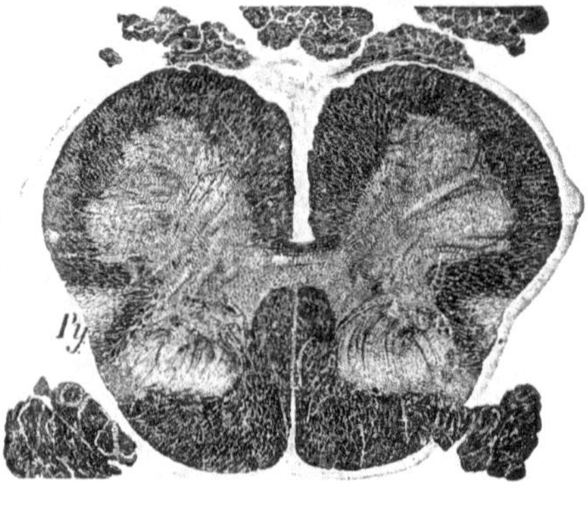

PLATE 81.
Spastic Spinal Paralysis.

A woman sixty-three years of age had noticed for the last two years increasing weakness of the arms and legs. The paresis gradually went on to complete paralysis of the arms and legs; the muscles became rigid and offered a slight spastic resistance to passive movements. The knee-jerks were increased. There was no muscular atrophy and no disturbance of sensation or vesical function. Finally, after three years, there developed complete paralysis of all the voluntary muscles of the skeleton—the muscles of the eye, face, pharynx, tongue, back of the neck, arm, trunk, and leg; everything else was normal. Anatomically, a symmetrical degeneration of the entire pyramidal tract, from the cortex through the internal capsule, brain-stem, medulla oblongata, and spinal cord (central motor neuron complex), was found.

Fig. 1.—*Section through the Medulla Oblongata.* Both pyramids (Py) are degenerated and pale in color. A large portion of the nerve-fibers is destroyed. *f*, Posterior longitudinal bundle; *L*, fillet; *ol*, olive; Vc, descending root of the trigeminus.

Fig. 2.—*Section through the Cervical Cord.* Bilateral degeneration of the lateral pyramidal tract (Py) with slight atrophy of the walls in the anterior horn. This slightly resembles amyotrophic lateral sclerosis.

Fig. 3.—*Sections through the Middle of the Thoracic Cord.* Degeneration of the lateral pyramidal tract (Py).

Fig. 4.—*Sections through the Lumbar Cord.* The diseased pyramidal tract (Py) has gained the periphery.

PLATE 82.

Combined System Disease.

There are other cases besides combined tabes in which, instead of one neuron complex, forming an anatomic and physiologic unit, becoming diseased, several different neuron complexes are attacked at the same time by a primary degeneration. It is not as yet definitely known where the degenerative process begins in these cases: whether the neuron cell or the neuron-fiber becomes primarily diseased. The clinical course consists in a slowly progressive spastic paresis and ataxia of the legs and arms, with more or less pronounced disturbances of sensation and vesical function. No muscular atrophy. A similar disease forms the foundation of hereditary ataxia. (See text.) The following sections were taken from the spinal cord in a case of this kind:

FIG. 1.—*Section through the Cervical Cord.* A symmetrical disease of the lateral (Py) and anterior (Pya) pyramidal tracts, of the direct cerebellar tract (Cb), columns of Goll (fG), and the central portion of the columns of Burdach (fB).

FIG. 2.—*Section through the Lower Thoracic Cord.* The same as Figure 1. In the posterior column the degeneration is less marked and is confined to the central portion. Pya, Cb, Py, as above.

FIG. 3.—*Section through the Lumbar Cord.* The lateral pyramidal tracts (P) still exhibit marked degeneration; in the posterior column (fp) there is only a narrow area of degeneration.

Tab. 82.

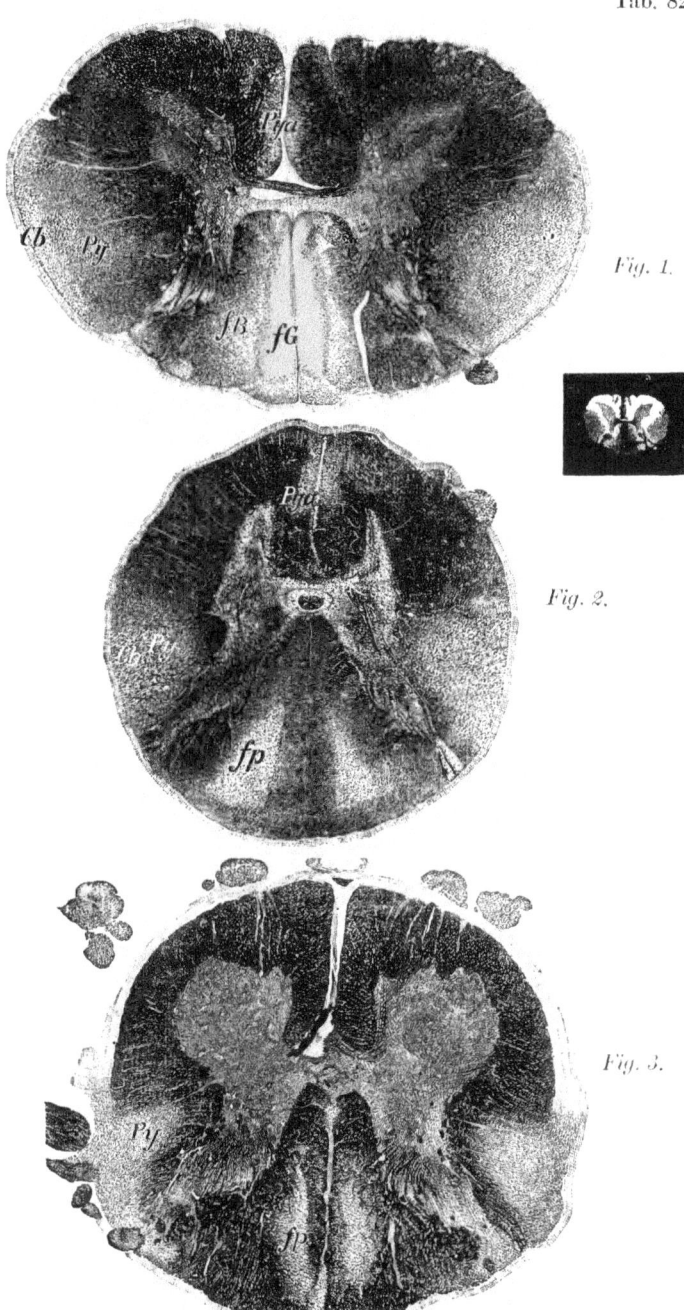

Fig. 1.

Fig. 2.

Fig. 3.

Tab. 83.

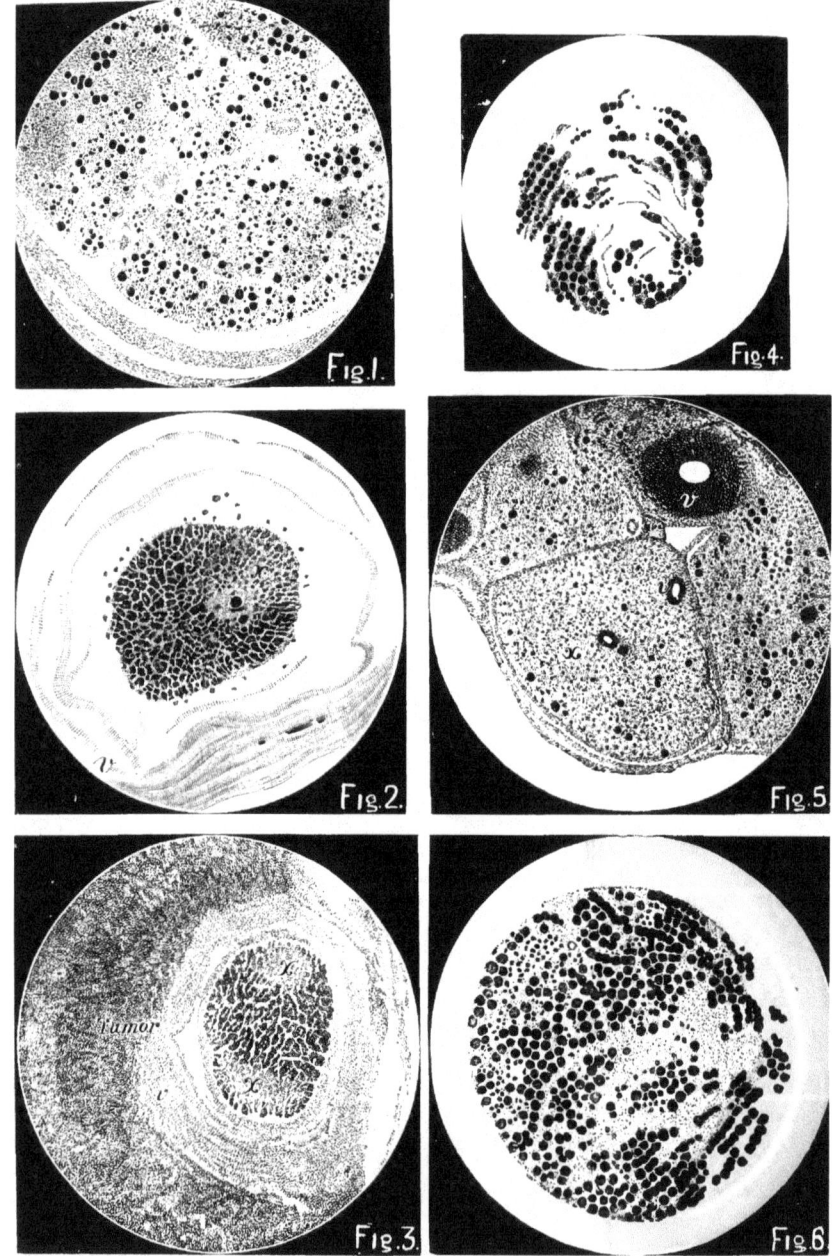

PLATE 83.

Degenerations of the Peripheral Nerves.

FIG. 1.—*Ascending Secondary Degeneration of the Sciatic Nerve after Amputation of the Leg.* A high amputation of the leg had been performed on a man fourteen years before. The figure shows the margin of a nerve bundle in which the greater part of the nerve-fibers is destroyed. The coarser fibers especially show a marked secondary ascending degeneration, due to the primary disease in the neuron cells situated in the lumbar cord, caused by the loss of function. The smaller fibers are better preserved. (Compare the normal cross-section, Plate 51, Fig. 3.)

FIG. 2.—*Descending Degeneration of the Right Optic Nerve after Destruction of the Left Lateral Geniculate Body and the Left Anterior Corpus Quadrigeminum.* The optic nerves contain fibers whose neuron cells are situated for the most part in the retina, and, in addition, fibers which have their cells in the above-named subcortical optical centers. The latter, therefore, undergo descending, the former ascending, degeneration. We see in this section a degenerated area (x) in the form of a sector. (Compare the normal optic nerve, Plate 51.) v, Sheath of the optic nerve.

FIG. 3.—*Compression Neuritis of the Optic Nerve.* In a patient suffering from acromegaly a malignant tumor of the pituitary gland, which surrounded the optic nerve, led to partial degeneration (x, x). v, Sheath of the optic nerve (dural sheath).

FIG. 4.—*Motor Nerve Branch in Spinal Muscular Atrophy.* Note the marked, wide-spread destruction of fibers. (Belonging to case shown on Plate 78, Fig. 3.)

FIG. 5.—*Posterior Root From the Lumbar Cord in Tabes Dorsalis.* (From the case shown on Plate 79, Fig. 3.) The anterior bundle (x) of posterior roots contains scarcely more than ten normal fibers. To the right of it there is another in a somewhat better state of preservation. V, Blood-vessels.

FIG. 6.—*Bundle From the Peroneal (External Popliteal) Nerve in Neurotic Muscular Atrophy.* Note the irregular distribution of the areas of fiber degeneration, especially in the central portions of the bundle. The spinal cord is probably also involved (motor cells in the anterior horn).

PLATE 84.

Multiple Neuritis.

FIGS. 1 AND 2.—*From a case of grave Alcoholic Polyneuritis.* (Fig. 1 from the crural nerve; Fig. 2 from the sciatic nerve.)

A heavy drinker, forty years of age, rather suddenly developed an increasing weakness of the legs which rapidly went on to complete paralysis. There was marked tenderness, the patellar reflexes were abolished, sensory disturbances were present, and muscular atrophy developed. His condition became worse after injections of strychnin. The arms also became involved; the irregular disturbances persisted. Death after two and a half months.

Marked destruction of fibers is seen in all the peripheral nerves. Some bundles contain scarcely more than six to ten normal fibers. (Compare Plate 51, Fig. 2.) The degeneration extends as far as the roots in the spinal cord.

FIG. 5.—*Transverse Section of the Cervical Cord from the same case.* The atrophy of the anterior roots ($r. a$), which traverse the anterolateral column, is plainly seen. There is also a well-marked degenerated area in the mesial portion (m) of the anterior horn, due to the degeneration of the anterior roots which enter at this point. There is a slight anterior degeneration in the column of Goll (long fibers of the posterior roots, $r. p$).

FIG. 3.—*Postdiphtheric Neuritis.* Transverse section through a bundle from the crural nerve, showing advanced degree of degeneration of the fibers, from a boy fifteen years old who, after recovering from pharyngeal diphtheria, was suddenly seized with paralysis of the pharyngeal muscles and progressive paralysis of the legs. The knee-jerks disappeared within ten days. There was little pain and only slight disturbance of sensibility. Death from paralysis of the vagus.

FIG. 4.—*Longitudinal Section through a Nerve Bundle from the Sciatic Nerve, from a case of Infectious Multiple Neuritis (Landry's Paralysis).* The products of disintegration (myelin granules) of a part of the degenerated nerve-fibers are still visible. The nerve-fibers are seen in all stages of degeneration.

The specimen is taken from a case in which the etiology remained doubtful. A woman thirty years of age who had probably had a severe acute disease (fever?) presented complete paralysis, first of the legs and then of the arms (ascending paralysis). The patient was in a very low condition and almost unconscious when she came under medical treatment, two days before her death. The spinal cord was not examined.

Tab. 84.

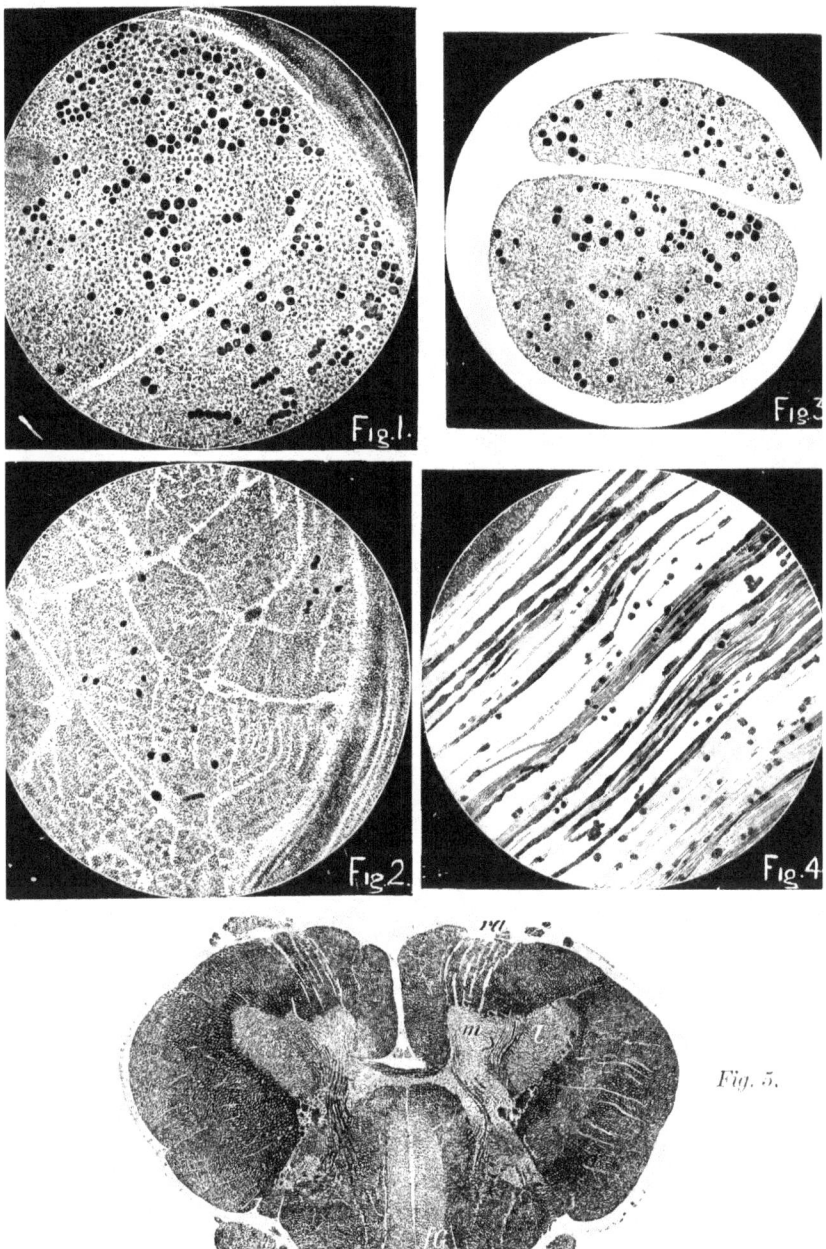

PART I.

MORPHOLOGY OF THE NERVOUS SYSTEM.

(Plates 1 to 14.)

THE nervous system of man consists of—
1. The **central organ,** comprising brain and spinal cord, and the **peripheral nerves** which spring from them.
2. The **sympathetic nervous system,** consisting of the main trunk of the sympathetic nerve and its plexuses.

These two parts communicate with each other by numerous nerve paths.

The brain and the spinal cord are contained in the cranium and vertebral column, respectively, and from these bony receptacles the nerves issue into the soft tissues. The ganglionated cords of the sympathetic lie on each side of, and anterior to, the vertebral column.

The brain and spinal cord are invested by three membranes, termed the meninges. The outer of these is the **dura mater,** a tough, fibrous membrane in close relation with the bone and performing the function of a periosteum to the interior of the skull. It surrounds the brain and cord like a sac, and furnishes tubular sheaths to the nerves at their points of exit, where the membrane terminates and is attached to the edges of the foramina at the base of the skull. The dura contains the large sinuses which collect the venous blood from the brain and empty into the jugular vein. These *venous sinuses* are: The superior and the inferior falciform (longitudinal), the cavernous, petrosal, transverse, etc.

The dura mater sends processes into the interior of the cerebrum. The *falx cerebri* (processus falciformis major) occupies the median sagittal line, being attached in front to the crista galli, and divides the upper half of the cranium into two equal parts. The *tentorium* occupies a horizontal plane and forms the roof of the posterior fossa of the skull.

The dura loosely invests the brain and cord, leaving an interval filled with lymph which is known as the subdural space.

The second envelope is formed by a delicate membrane known as the **arachnoid**. It is more intimately adherent to the brain than to the cord; in the brain it bridges over the convolutions without dipping down into the sulci. On each side of the falx cerebri are seen the Pacchionian bodies, which consist of exuberant masses of connective tissue derived from the arachnoid. Beneath the arachnoid is the subarachnoid space, which is subdivided into numerous compartments communicating with one another and containing the cerebrospinal fluid.

The innermost envelope is formed by the **pia mater**, the term "soft membranes" being applied to this membrane and to the arachnoid. The pia closely invests the nerve substance and dips down into all the fissures and cavities in the brain, as the tela choroidea inferior. It conveys the numerous blood-vessels which supply the brain and cord.

The **brain** consists of the two large **cerebral hemispheres**, the brain-stem, and the cerebellum; the direct continuation of the brain-stem is the **spinal cord**. The axis of the latter is nearly perpendicular to the plane of the cerebellum, as the brain-stem is bent at an angle of almost 90 degrees.

The weight of the brain in the adult is 1300 to 1400 grams. In man it averages 1360, in woman 1220; a variation as low as 900 grams is not considered abnormal.

THE CEREBRAL HEMISPHERES.

The two cerebral hemispheres communicate only on their median surfaces; they consist of a reddish-gray layer of cortical substance, the *cortex cerebri*, which is disposed on the surface, and a central *white matter*, or medullary substance, situated under the cortex.

The surface of the cortex is thrown into numerous vermiform convolutions or gyri, marked off by fissures or **sulci,** an arrangement that greatly increases the surface area of the brain. The fundamental type of the convolutions is constant, but there are numerous individual variations.

Each cerebral hemisphere is divided into several lobes, each lobe comprising several convolutions and a portion of the white matter.

In the anterior fossa lodges the **frontal lobe**, which forms the anterior pole of the cerebrum and is marked by two principal fissures (sulc. front. sup. and inf.), which divide it into three convolutions or gyri (gyr. front. sup., med., and inf.). The posterior boundary of the frontal lobe is formed by the *central sulcus* or *fissure of Rolando*, which commences a little behind the middle of each hemisphere and runs downward and forward. This fissure divides the two "*central convolutions*" (gyr. centr. ant. and post.) (ascending frontal and ascending parietal convolutions).

Posterior to the central convolutions is the parietal lobe, which is divided by the intraparietal sulcus into the superior and inferior parietal lobules (lob. pariet. sup. and inf.).

The posterior pole of the brain is formed by the occipital lobe, which is contiguous to the parietal.[1] Like the frontal lobe, it is divided into three convolutions (gyr. occip. med., sup., and inf.); the under surface of the occipital lobe rests on the tentorium.

[1] Occasionally the division between the parietal and occipital lobes is abnormally deep, owing to the unusual development of the so-called "Simian fissure."

The middle fossa of the skull accommodates the temporal lobe, which is subdivided into three convolutions (gyr. temp. med., sup., and inf.) by three fissures (sulc. temp. sup., med., and inf.). In front and above it is divided from the frontal lobe and the central convolutions by a broad and deep sulcus, the **fissure of Sylvius,** while it is directly continuous behind with the inferior convolutions of the parietal lobe. Hence the inferior parietal lobule comprises two convolutions, arching from before backward, known as the supramarginal and angular gyri (*pli courbé*).[1]

At the bottom of the fissure of Sylvius is another lobe, the **island of Reil,** with its small convolutions, covered over by the adjoining lobes, especially the temporal and central. [NOTE.—More correctly, the part of the inferior frontal convolution in front of the ascending limb of the fissure of Sylvius.] The convolutions which overlap the island are collectively known as the *operculum,* which is again subdivided into the operculum frontale, centrale (or Rolando), and parietale.

The convolutions hitherto described can be seen on the external convex surface of the hemisphere. On the mesial surface of the hemispheres the continuation of the superior frontal convolution can be seen. The *central convolutions* run together in the *paracentral lobule,* and the *parietal lobe* is continued as the **precuneus.** The latter is separated from the mesial surface of the occipital lobe by the *parieto-occipital fissure.* The mesial surface of the occipital lobe is divided into the **cuneus,** and beneath this and separated from it by the deep calcarine fissure, the *lobulus lingualis.*

On the under surface of the temporal lobe the *inferior temporal* joins the *occipitotemporal* convolution, and to the mesial side of the latter and separated from it by the occipitotemporal fissure is the *inferior marginal convolution,*

---

[1] Many anatomists count three convolutions, gyrus **marginalis, angularis,** and **præoccipitalis.** The convolutions in this portion of the brain are subject to frequent variations.

the *gyrus hippocampi*, which terminates anteriorly in the *uncus*. The orbital surface of the frontal lobe is marked by the following fissures: The **sulcus rectus (olfactory sulcus)** and, external to it, the *triradiate fissure*, which forms part of the middle frontal convolution.

In the central portion of the median surface of the hemispheres, which is surrounded by the above-mentioned convolutions, the arrangements are somewhat different. Above, the cortex ends in the **gyrus fornicatus**, and below in the **gyrus hippocampi** (upper and lower marginal convolutions). Underneath the upper marginal convolution the white matter of the brain projects from the interior of the two hemispheres and forms the **corpus callosum**.

Above the lower marginal convolution the white matter also projects from the hemispheres, and converging from either side, forms the **crusta** (or **pes**), the ventral portion of the cerebral peduncle, which begins at this point.

Between the corpus callosum and the cerebral peduncle is a series of deeply placed structures and spaces which will be described more in detail later on. Thus the entire intermediate portion, which is surrounded by the marginal convolutions, is not covered with cortical substance.

The corpus callosum, which connects the two hemispheres, forms a robust layer of white fibers; the larger central portion is nearly horizontal; the anterior extremity, or *genu*, is reflected downward and then backward to the base of the brain; posteriorly it ends in a thick rounded fold, the *splenium*. The mass of white matter in the interior of each hemisphere forms the nucleus of the lobes we have described. The upper half, down to the level of the corpus callosum, is formed chiefly by the radiating fibers of the corpus callosum, and a section at this level is known as the **centrum semiovale Vieussenii** (centrum ovale majus). The basal portion contains in its substance a grayish-red mass the size of a goose's egg,—the *corpus striatum*,—which is divided into the *lenticular nucleus*, or lateral portion, and the *caudate nucleus*, or mesial portion.

These two parts are divided by the layer of white fibers which we have already described as emerging from the base of each hemisphere—namely, the ventral portion of the cerebral peduncle, or crusta pedunculi.

In the interior of each hemisphere is a system of cavities filled with lymph—the **ventricles.** The roof of the lateral ventricle is formed by the centrum ovale, which is, therefore, also called the tegmentum ventriculorum.

The free upper surface of the corpus striatum projects from the white matter and bulges from without and below into the lateral ventricle.

This portion of the lateral ventricle, which lies between the lateral portion of the corpus callosum and the surface of the corpus striatum, is known as the *cella media* (body of the lateral ventricle). The ventricle is continued into the frontal lobe as the *anterior horn*, and into the occipital lobe as the *posterior horn*, while the descending horn dips down into the temporal lobe. The anterior and posterior horns are surrounded on every side by white matter, and thus lie buried in the white matter of the hemispheres. The descending horn, on the contrary, is open toward the median line, the opening being effected by a reflection on itself of the lower marginal convolution, the gyrus hippocampi, which therefore projects into the descending horn and forms a thick rounded fold, the **cornu ammonis.** The free edge of the cortical layer of the gyrus hippocampi is really formed by the narrow gyrus dentatus (**fascia dentata** or **fascia Tarini**). This arrangement is clearly seen in Figure 1.

At the free border of the cornu ammonis is the beginning of the **fimbria,** or terminal portion of the white matter belonging to the gyrus hippocampi, or, more specifically, of the gyrus dentatus. The fimbria passes backward and upward from the anterior extremity of the descending horn, along with the superficial corrugated portion of the cornu ammonis (digitationes cornu ammonis). At the junction of the descending horn with the cella media the fimbria leaves the cornu ammonis and, joining with that of the opposite side, forms the ascending limb of the fornix (crus ascendens fornicis) and unites with the lower posterior segment of the corpus callosum in the central triangular interval, known as the lyra. The fornix (or " cortical medulla "

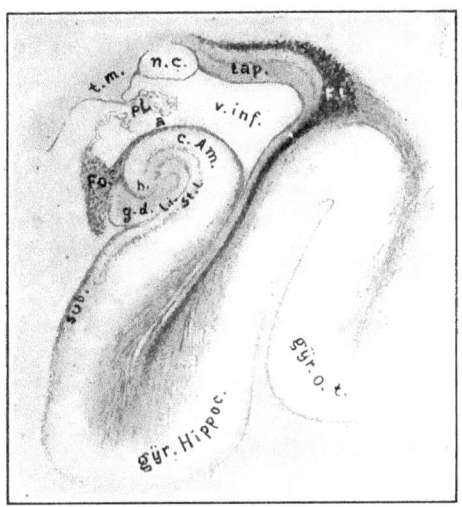

Fig. 1.—Section through the lower marginal convolution (medullary sheath stain): *a*, Alveus; *c. Am*, cornu ammonis; *F. l*, fascicul. longitud. inf.; *Fo*, fornix; *g. d*, gyrus dentatus; *gyr. Hippoc.*, Hippocampal gyrus; *gyr. o. t*, occipitotemporalis; *h*, hilus of gyr. dentat.; *l. i*, lamina med. involuta (tangential fibers); *n. c*, caudate nucleus (tailpiece); *pl*, plexus choroid. inf.; *st. l*, stratum lacunosum; *sub*, subiculum; *tap*, tapetum; *t. m*, tænia medullar.; *v. inf.*, inferior ventricle (descending cornu).

of the hemisphere) passes along the under surface of the corpus callosum, with which it is united, to a point just behind the genu, where it leaves the corpus callosum and again takes a downward course, after dividing into the two descending limbs or *anterior pillars* of the fornix (crura descend. fornicis). At the base of the brain the anterior pillars of the fornix are reflected backward and end in the corpora albicantia.

It follows that between the genu of the corpus callosum and the anterior pillars of the fornix there remains an open space which is occupied by two slender folds, the septum lucidum, bounding a small cavity, the ventricle of the septum lucidum (*fifth ventricle*). To either side of each

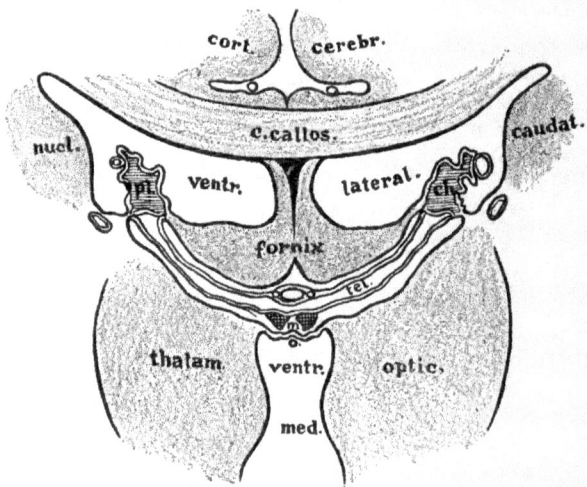

Fig. 2.—Schema of the ventricles of the brain (coronal section): Pl. ch, Plexus choroideus lateralis ; tel., tela choroidea ; m, plexus choroidea med.; o, membrana obturatoria ventr. III. (anterior commissure).

septum and underneath the corpus callosum is the lateral ventricle.

In the floor of the lateral ventricles, therefore, the surface of the corpus striatum is seen projecting from the white matter of the hemispheres. The broadest anterior portion, which lies toward the anterior horn, is known as the caput, or *head* of the corpus striatum, or in transverse section as the caudate nucleus. From the caput it runs backward and downward and forms the narrow *tail*, which, at the junction of the descending horn with the body, sweeps downward and finally forward to form part of the roof of the descending horn.

To the mesial side of the corpus striatum and parallel with it is a narrow band of white fibers, the lamina cornea, which contains a large vein. It separates the corpus striatum from a large structure, the optic thalamus, which lies to its mesial and posterior side and presents, in transverse section, a grayish-red mass similar to that of the corpus striatum. At the base of the brain the optic thalami gradually approach each other and the median line; the cavity between them is known as the **third** (or middle) **ventricle.** The bodies of the lateral ventricles directly communicate with the third ventricle by means of the foramina of Monro, two slit-like apertures situated immediately behind the anterior pillars of the fornix.

The roof of the third ventricle would be formed by the fornix and superimposed corpus callosum were it not for the fact that a process of the pia mater passes under the splenium of the corpus callosum (great transverse fissure) and penetrates into the third ventricle, which is open at this point. This vascular prolongation of the pia spreads out under the fornix in a thin layer (velum interpositum) which forms the roof of the third ventricle, and is known as the **tela choroidea superior.** It contains at its center two cord-like granular structures, the **choroid plexuses** (plex. choroidei med.), which pass from the third to the lateral ventricles in the foramen Monro as **plexus choroideus lateralis** (the choroid plexuses of the third ventricle). Here they are closely applied to the lateral border of the optic thalamus, and, passing backward, finally enter the descending horn, where they become continuous with the pia mater, which enters through the foramen of Monro.

As has been stated, the white matter is encroached upon in the central portion of each hemisphere by the gray masses of the corpus striatum and optic thalamus, which increase more and more in size as the base of the brain is approached. The white fibers as they descend from the centrum semiovale pierce the corpus striatum and form the *anterior limbs* of the *internal capsule* (capsula Reilii), dividing the lateral portion or lenticular nucleus from the caudate nucleus. Another bundle of white fibers passes downward as the *posterior limb* of the internal capsule, and separates the lenticular nucleus from the optic thalamus. The anterior and posterior limbs unite to form the *genu* of the internal capsules. Part of the fibers of the internal capsule enter the corpus striatum and optic thalamus and disappear in these structures; others are continued downward toward the base of the brain, where they emerge in the form of the above-mentioned *crusta* or *pes*.

The lenticular nucleus, which is wedged in between the internal capsule and the island of Reil, is divided into several portions: a larger lateral portion, the **putamen**, and several median segments not related morphologically to the putamen, together forming the **globus pallidus**. The putamen and the caudate nucleus together really form the corpus striatum.

Outside of the putamen the white matter of the hemispheres is continued downward in a thin layer as the *external capsule;* between this and the white matter of the insula (capsula extrema) there is a narrow strip of gray matter running parallel with the insula and known as the **claustrum.**

Below the lenticular nucleus the white matter, which at this point is reduced, by the encroachment of the gray matter, to two narrow strips, the internal and external capsules, begins to expand, reaching its greatest development posteriorly in the white matter of the temporal lobe. Under the anterior portion of the lenticular nucleus, embedded in the mass of white matter between the frontal and temporal lobes, is a small roundish mass of gray matter, the **amygdaloid nucleus.**

The upper and mesial surface of the optic thalamus may be exposed by removing the corpus callosum with the fornix and velum interpositum. It presents in front a small prominence, the **anterior tubercle**, and projects backward and outward to form a prominent mass, the **pulvinar.**

The median surfaces of the optic thalami form the lateral walls of the third ventricle. Along the upper inner margin of the optic thalami is seen the *tænia medullaris*, which ascends from the interior of the brain and, passing backward in the form of the *pedunculus conarii* (or *stria pinealis*), decussates with the corresponding structure of the other side. To each side of the point of intersection lies the small *ganglion habenulæ (trigonum habenulæ)*. Resting upon the decussation, but not in any way connected with it, is found the **pineal gland** (epiphysis, conarium, glandula pinealis, etc.).

The cavity of the third ventricle is traversed by three short bundles of fibers connecting the two halves of the brain. Immediately in front of the anterior pillars of the fornix, near the floor of the ventricle, is the robust white **anterior commissure.** In the middle of the third ventricle is the **gray** or **middle commissure,** which is easily torn, while immediately below and in front of the decussation of the peduncles of the pineal body is the **posterior commissure.**

Beneath the optic thalami is a region into which a part of the white fibers from the lenticular nucleus, the optic thalamus, and the inner capsule project, and which is known as the regio subthalamica. It contains the oval **corpus subthalamicum** (subthalamic body) and the beginning of the **red nucleus** (nucleus ruber), which extends further backward into the mesencephalon.

The third ventricle ends in front, between the two anterior pillars of the fornix; its cavity is more or less funnel-shaped, and diminishes in size toward the base of the brain, where it is continued into the **infundibulum.**

The latter is closed by the **pituitary body**, which is lodged in the sella turcica of the sphenoid bone. Owing to the gradual encroachment of the median surfaces of the optic thalami, the posterior portion of the ventricle is more shallow than the anterior. It is traversed by the posterior commissure, and continued backward in the form of a narrow canal, the **aqueduct of Sylvius**.

The lower halves of the optic thalami form a continuous mass, but their upper posterior portions (pulvinar) are forced apart by the **corpora quadrigemina**, which rise to the surface behind the posterior commissure. There are two anterior and two posterior quadrigemina. On each side they send out the *anterior (superior)* and *posterior (inferior) brachia*, which terminate in the *corpus geniculatum laterale (externum)* and *medialei (internum)*, between the corpora quadrigemina and the pulvinar. From the substance of the corpus geniculatum laterale a bundle of white fibers, the **optic tract**, takes its course toward the base of the brain. Beneath the corpora quadrigemina the ventricular system is continued as the aqueduct, the immediate surrounding of which is formed by the gray matter, which also covers the surface of the optic thalami and forms the lining of the third ventricle.

Beneath the corpora quadrigemina is the **tegmentum**, formed by the union of the fibers from the subthalamic region. Under the tegmentum the converging crura cerebri emerge from the hemispheres and form the continuation of the white matter of the internal capsule; underneath the tegmentum they unite to form the crusta. Between the tegmentum and the crusta is a brownish, crescentic mass, the **substantia nigra**. Behind the corpora quadrigemina and covered by the tentorium is the **cerebellum**, occupying the interval between the cerebral hemispheres and overlapped by the occipital lobes. It lies in the posterior fossa of the cranium, and consists of a central portion, the *vermiform process* (vermis), flanked on each side by the hemispheres of the cerebellum.

THE CEREBRAL HEMISPHERES.

The cerebellum is connected with the corpora quadrigemina by the superior cerebellar peduncles, which pass through the tegmental region. They are directly connected with the vermiform process of the cerebellum by means of the thin anterior medullary velum and the lingula. Underneath the superior medullary velum forms the roof of the aqueduct, which is bounded on each side by the diverging superior peduncles, and at this point widens out into the *fourth ventricle*. The communications of the ventricular system are shown in Figure 3.

The floor of the fourth ventricle is formed by the **rhomboid fossa,** and beneath it are found the structures of the medulla oblongata, which correspond to continuations of the crura cerebri (tegmentum and crusta).

The roof of the fourth ventricle is formed by the inferior vermiform process. The tela choroidea inferior, a process of the pia mater, projects into the ventricle from behind.

The hemispheres of the cerebellum, like those of the cerebrum, consist of a superficial cortex of gray matter and a central mass of white fibers. They are subdivided into a great number of small convolutions,

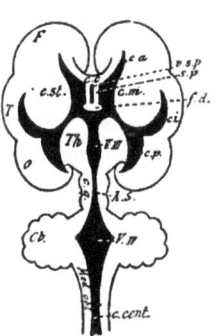

Fig. 3.—Schema of the ventricles (longitudinal section): *c. a*, Anterior horn; *c. m*, cella media; *c. i*, descending horn; *c. p*, posterior horn of lateral ventricle; *V. III*, third ventricle; *A. S*, aqueduct of Sylvius; *V. IV*, fourth ventricle; *c. cent.*, central canal. For remaining letters see p. 12.

running for the most part parallel with one another and grouped into lobules. Each lobule communicates by means of a section of the vermiform process with the corresponding lobule of the other hemisphere.

The upper surface is divided into two lobes, the lob. sup. ant. and post. (semilunaris), connected by the superior vermiform process (lob. central., monticulus, folia cacuminis).

On the under surface, from before backward, are the following lobules: flocculus, tonsilla, lob. cuneiformis, and lob. inf. post. Communication is established between these lobules by means of the inferior vermiform process, the corresponding portions being the nodulus, uvula, pyramis, and commissura brevis. In the interior of the white matter of the cerebellum is the **corpus dentatum cerebelli**, and in the white matter of the vermiform process the **nucleus tegmenti**, while between these are other smaller masses of gray matter (embolus, nucleus globosus).

Passing forward from the white matter of the cerebellum are the converging superior peduncles that have already been mentioned, while below, two bundles of white fibers, the **middle cerebellar peduncles**, pass backward around the crura cerebri, uniting at the base of the brain to aid in the formation of the **pons Varolii**. Finally, the **inferior cerebellar peduncles** pass backward to the medulla oblongata and form the **restiform bodies**. The superior peduncles form the lateral boundaries of the anterior half of the rhomboid fossa, while the restiform bodies bound the posterior half, the convergence of these two bundles of white fibers giving it its characteristic rhomboid shape.

The floor of the fourth ventricle is covered with a thin layer of gray matter (central gray matter); the center is traversed by white medullated fibers, the **striæ acusticæ**, which meet in the median line at an obtuse angle. Underneath the layer of gray matter are the continuations of the tegmental structures, while the succeeding layer is formed by the structures of the crusta inclosed and surrounded by the pontine fibers derived from the cerebellum. In the intervals between these interlacing bundles of fibers are numerous smaller masses of gray matter (nuclei), and this entire collection of structures, together with the nerves which emerge in this region, is included in the term **medulla oblongata**.

At the base of the brain the **pyramidal bodies**, consisting of white matter, emerge at the inferior border of the pons as the continuations of the crusta. They are flanked laterally by the **olivary bodies,** which in transverse section appear as crumpled leaves of gray matter.

Below the origin of the pyramidal bodies the floor of the fourth ventricle rapidly diminishes in width, the **restiform bodies** converge to form an acute angle, and the rhomboid fossa terminates in the **calamus scriptorius.** At its inferior angle, or **obex,** the ventricle occupies a deeper position in the substance of the medulla oblongata, and, disappearing altogether from the surface, merges in the **central canal,** which occupies the center of the spinal cord throughout its entire extent.

Shortly before their junction the restiform bodies separate into a mesial bundle, the **funiculus gracilis** (or funiculus of Goll), and a lateral bundle, the **funiculus cuneatus** (or funiculus of Burdach). These are apparently continued without interruption into the **posterior columns of the cord** (funiculus posterior). Ventrally the pyramids gradually become narrower and leave the surface to enter the substance of the medulla oblongata, emerging on the other side to form the *decussation of the pyramids*. Below the decussation the pyramids unite with the ventral portion of the restiform bodies, which does not form part of the posterior columns, to form the **lateral column** (funiculus lateralis) of the spinal cord. The **anterior columns** of the cord are formed from structures situated beneath the pyramids, which come to the surface below the point where the pyramids disappear **(funiculus anterior).**

In the spinal cord the gray matter is found in the center, grouped about the central canal, being the continuation of the gray matter of the rhomboid fossa. It constitutes the *anterior* and *posterior horns*. Thus in the cord the gray matter and the ventricular system occupy a deeper position and lie centrally, while the white matter occupies the periphery. The medulla oblongata thus gradually becomes converted into the **spinal cord**—more specifically, the cervical portion.

Let us now bestow a cursory glance on the base of the brain. In front of the broad prominence formed by the pons the crura are seen to diverge, having between them the posterior perforated space, and immediately anterior to the latter the two whitish eminences known as the corpora albicantia. In front of these is the continuation of the third ventricle, the infundibulum, capped by the pituitary body, occupying the angle of the optic chiasm, formed by the junction of the optic tracts, which unite at this point after sweeping around the crura.

The spinal marrow presents a cylindric, whitish cord about as thick as the little finger, and is surrounded by the meninges; it is contained in the spinal canal and extends to the upper border of the second lumbar vertebra. It gradually diminishes in diameter from above downward, and forms two enlargements: the cervical enlargement, at the level of the fifth or sixth cervical vertebra, and the lumbar enlargement, at the level of the twelfth thoracic vertebra. The enlargements are produced by an augmentation of the central gray substance contained in the anterior and posterior horns.[1] The portion between the two enlargements is known as the thoracic cord, and the terminal portion is designated the conus medullaris.

The two anterior columns of the cord are separated by a deep fissure, the anterior longitudinal sulcus, which conveys the blood-vessels. Between the posterior columns is the rudimentary posterior longitudinal sulcus, from which the septum dorsalis takes its origin and extends into the substance of the cord.

The three columns of the cord (anterior, lateral, and posterior) surround the gray matter in the anterior and posterior horns, as has been previously described. The columns and horns together terminate in the conus medullaris,

---

[1] The enlargements correspond to the situations where the nerves supplying the extremities make their exit from the spinal cord.

in which the lateral column is the largest and the anterior column is reduced to a narrow fasciculus. In the terminal portion of the cord the gray matter exceeds in amount the white matter, while the opposite condition prevails in the cervical enlargement.

At the surface of the brain-stem and spinal cord fibers from the white matter unite to form larger bundles, which make their exit as the **peripheral nerves.**

The nerves are divided into twelve pairs of cranial and thirty-one pairs of spinal.

With the exception of the fourth, the twelve pairs of cranial nerves emerge at the base of the brain in the following order:

1. **Olfactory Nerve.**—The nerve is formed by the union of the numerous small nervuli olfactorii which traverse the cribriform plate of the ethmoid bone. The fibers enter the **olfactory bulb,** which is lodged in the straight sulcus at the base of the frontal lobe. The olfactory bulb extends backward as the olfactory tract, and terminates in the tuber olfactorium, which is situated in front of and a little laterally from the chiasm. The olfactory tract in man represents a rudimentary portion of the brain, which in some animals develops into a lobe of considerable size and mass.[1]

2. **Optic Nerve.**—After leaving the eyeball the two nerves converge and enter the chiasm, where they undergo a partial decussation (the larger nasal bundles decussate). From the chiasm the optic tracts sweep backward over the cerebral peduncle and ascend to the lateral geniculate body, in which they apparently disappear.

3. **Oculomotor Nerve.**—It takes its origin beneath the corpora quadrigemina in numerous bundles of nerve-fibers which, after traversing the substance of the tegmentum, emerge at the superior border of the pons between the converging crura.

[1] It follows that, like the optic nerve, it differs from the other peripheral nerves.

4. **Trochlear Nerve.**—After emerging on the dorsal surface behind the posterior corpora quadrigemina, it undergoes total decussation in the medullary velum, from which point it descends toward the base of the brain and, sweeping over the crus, takes an anterior course.

5. **Trifacial Nerve.**—It is formed by an anterior motor and a posterior sensory root, and emerges at the lateral border of the pons. The posterior root forms the Gasserian ganglion, on the distal side of which the nerve subdivides into its three branches.

6. **Abducens Nerve.**—Its deep origin is in the floor of the fourth ventricle. The fibers traverse the medulla oblongata, and the two nerves emerge at the inferior border of the pons to the outer side of the pyramids.

7. **Facial Nerve.**—It emerges in common with the following nerve at the inferior border of the pons on the outer side of the olivary body.

8. **Auditory Nerve.**—The nerve arises by two roots, the vestibular nerve (anterior median root) and the cochlear nerve (posterior lateral root), and emerges from the base of the brain in company with the facial.

9. **Glossopharyngeal Nerve,** and—

10. **Pneumogastric Nerve.**—These nerves emerge together below the restiform body by numerous roots. The glossopharyngeal forms, besides other ganglia, the petrosal ganglion; the pneumogastric forms the jugular ganglion.

11. **Spinal Accessory Nerve.**—It arises by a number of roots from the upper portion of the cervical enlargement and medulla oblongata, and makes its appearance at the lateral column. Its internal branch joins the pneumogastric.

12. **Hypoglossus Nerve.**—It arises between the pyramids and olivary body by numerous fibers.

The spinal nerves are divided into eight cervical, twelve thoracic, five lumbar, five sacral, and one, or rarely two, coccygeal pairs. Their "roots" arise in the main from the corresponding segments of the cord—that is, from the eight cervical, twelve thoracic, five lumbar segments, etc. Each nerve arises by two roots, which leave the spinal cord separately. The **anterior motor roots** emerge between the anterior and lateral columns, while the **posterior sensory roots** leave the cord between the lateral column and the posterior column. Before the two roots become united in the nerve the posterior root forms a node-like enlargement — the **intervertebral ganglion** — which is lodged in the intervertebral foramen. The nerves for the neck and extremities form numerous anastomoses with each other, and thus produce the **nervous plexuses** (cervical, brachial, lumbar, sacral, etc.) before they are distributed to the soft parts. Strictly speaking, the peripheral nerves originate in these plexuses. From this arrangement it follows that the peripheral nerves contain mixed fibers from the anterior and posterior roots of several spinal segments. (See Plate 27.) The nerve-roots for the lower extremity, owing to their high origin at the level of the first lumbar vertebra (see Plate 27), continue their downward course through the intervertebral foramina for a certain distance before they make their exit, at first accompanying the conus medullaris, and lower down forming the cauda equina.

The **gangliated cord of the sympathetic** consists of a series of small ganglia arranged along the anterior surface of the vertebral column. The highest of these are the superior, middle, and inferior cervical ganglia, the ganglia being connected with one another by slender bundles of nerve-fibers. The ganglia are joined by numerous nerve-fibers derived from the cranial nerves and from the spinal plexuses. The main trunk of the sympathetic terminates on the coccyx in the **ganglion impar**. The sympathetic nerves, after emerging from the main trunk and its ganglia, either follow the blood-vessels or join the cranial and spinal nerves and are distributed to the organs which they supply—namely, all smooth muscle-fibers. Many of them first unite to form plexuses in the neighborhood of the viscera (cardiac, mesenteric, intestinal ganglia, etc.).

The **arteries** that supply the brain are derived from the **internal carotid** and **vertebral arteries** and the arterial **circle of Willis**, which is formed by their anastomoses. (See Plate 5.) The branches of the circle of Willis, which occupy the pia, are the following: Art. corp. callosi (corpus callosum, median surfaces of the hemispheres); art. fossæ Sylvii (tissues surrounding the fossa and basilar

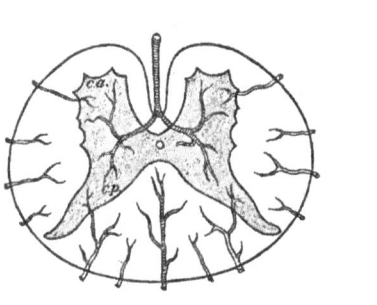 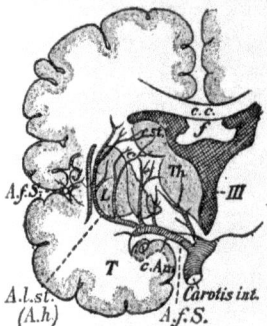

Fig. 4.   Fig. 5.

Figures 4 and 5 show the blood supply; figure 5 that of the art. fossæ Sylvii (A.f.S.), which supplies the basal ganglia and the inner capsule (a.l.st, art. lenticulostriata, a very important branch in pathologic lesions). Figure 4 represents a transverse section of the spinal cord with its blood-vessels. Note the manner in which the gray substance is supplied by the art. sulci anterior.

ganglia); art. choroidea (ventricles); art. profunda (occipital and temporal lobes), etc. The blood-vessels that supply the central white matter of the brain are so-called **end vessels**—that is to say, their anastomosis is not sufficient to permit neighboring vessels to establish collateral circulation. The cortical arteries, however, which enter from the pia anastomose freely with one another.

The arteries of the spinal cord are derived **partly from** the **vertebral arteries**—art. spinal., ant. and post.—and partly from the **intercostal arteries.** They enter the cord from all directions, but especially through the anterior longitudinal sulcus, and are also end vessels—that is, they end blindly.

The returning blood from the brain is carried by the **pial veins** into the **venous sinuses,** which empty into the **internal jugular vein.** The blood from the third ventricle is collected by the veins of Galen.

The veins of the spinal cord anastomose freely with one another and form **Breschet's venous plexus,** which surrounds the dura mater.

The lymphatic channels of the brain and spinal cord (the external coat of the vessel forms the "adventitious lymphatic sheath") communicate with the lymph-spaces formed by the meninges. The ventricles, therefore, are in direct communication with the subarachnoid space and contain the cerebrospinal fluid.

The **nerves** of the pia and dura are derived from the sympathetic system, with the exception of some in the dura which are branches of the sensory portion of the trifacial nerve.

PART II.

DEVELOPMENT AND STRUCTURE OF THE NERVOUS SYSTEM.

(Plates 15 to 53.)

THE central nervous system is derived from the ectoderm. In the center of the germinal area two ("medullary") folds of ectodermic tissue make their appearance, and as they approach each other dip down to form the **medullary groove.** This groove is later converted into the **medullary canal** by the union of the medullary folds along the dorsal line. The neuroglia, or sustentacular tissue of the nervous system, and the essential nerve substance are developed from the epithelial layers which form the lining of this neural canal. The meninges and bloodvessels are derived from the mesoderm.

Laterally and dorsally from the medullary groove a row of cells (the ganglionic cord) makes its appearance and later assumes a position by the side of the medullary canal along its entire extent. These masses of cells are the ancestors of the intervertebral ganglia and the homologous ganglia of the sensory cranial nerves (olfactory, Gasserian, cochlear, jugular, petrosal ganglia, etc.).

The nasal, club-like extremity of the medullary canal during the first embryonal month expands into three **primary brain vesicles,** the first and the third of which soon subdivide into two secondary compartments: The primary **forebrain** (subdividing into the *forebrain* and *interbrain*), the **midbrain,** and the **hindbrain** (the latter subdividing into the *hindbrain* and the *afterbrain*); from these three, or more correctly five, primary vesicles the entire brain is later developed. The cavity of the medullary canal becomes converted into the ventricular system, and the thickened walls of the canal and of the vesicles eventually form the structures of the spinal cord and brain.

By the ingrowth of the falciform process of the dura, invaginating the roof of the brain vesicle (pallium), the **forebrain** is divided into two lateral halves (primitive cerebral hemispheres), which, by virtue of their more rapid growth, soon overlap all the other portions of the brain. The thickening of the walls of the forebrain vesicle results in the formation of the cortex and cerebral medulla, while its primary cavity is converted into the lateral ventricle, into which the primitive corpus striatum projects. The latter eventually unites with the lateral wall at the external capsule, while the median surface remains free (caudate nucleus).

The derivatives of the *lateral wall* of the forebrain are the cortex and white matter of the convex surfaces, the outer capsule, the caudate nucleus, and the putamen of the lenticular nucleus. The derivatives of the *mesial wall* are the globus pallidus of the lenticular nucleus, the lamina cornea, fornix, septum lucidum, and nervi Lancisi. The internal capsule is formed later by union with the optic thalamus at the neural end plate.

At the median surface of the vesicles which form the hemispheres the corpus callosum makes its appearance, and, bridging over the median line, unites with the corresponding structure of the opposite side.

The earliest fissures and convolutions are formed between the second and third months by invaginations of the cortex, the fissure of Sylvius being the first to make its appearance. (See Plate 16.)

From the **interbrain** are derived the optic thalami and

24 MORPHOLOGY OF THE NERVOUS SYSTEM.

the other structures surrounding the cavity, which later becomes the third ventricle (pituitary body, conarium, olfactory tract, optic tract). The optic thalamus unites with the posterior segment of the corpus striatum ("stalk" of the optic thalamus), the union being effected by means of cells and their processes, which grow out from the optic thalamus at the end plate. Thus there is at this point a

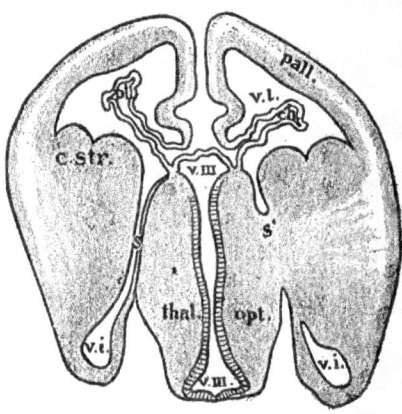

Fig. 6.—Section through the forebrain and midbrain (second month). On the left-hand side of the figure, at s, is the primary cavity of the cerebral vesicle; to the right, at s', is seen the union between the corpus striatum (c. str.) and optic thalamus (thal. opt), which forms the lateral ventricle (v. 1) and its descending cornu (v. i). pl. ch, Tela choroidea; v. III, third ventricle; pall, pallium (roof of the forebrain, which later develops into the cortex and white matter of the hemispheres).

direct communication between the forebrain and the interbrain.

From the **midbrain** are formed the corpora quadrigemina, tegmentum, and crusta, while the primitive cavity forms the aqueduct.

The **hindbrain** later becomes the cerebellum, and the **afterbrain** is eventually converted into the medulla oblongata.

Owing to the more rapid growth of the cerebral vesicles, especially of the forebrain, the following flexures are formed: In the afterbrain the cervical flexure (ventral); in the hindbrain the pontine, metencephalic, or frontal flexure (dorsal); and in the mid- and interbrain the ventral, posterior, and anterior cranial flexures.

Microscopic examination of the central nervous system shows that it is composed of two kinds of tissue, the sustentacular substance (neuroglia) and the nerve substance, consisting of cells and fibers embedded within it. Both tissues are derived from the ectodermal epithelial cells which line the neural canal. The spongioblasts proliferating within the central canal send out numerous fibrils in all directions which unite in a delicate network and thus form the glia cells (spindle cells, astrocytes). Another portion of the epithelial cells in the neural canal—the neuroblasts—develops into germ cells, which send out first a long, thick process, and later numerous smaller arborizations from which the ganglion cells and nerve-fibers are formed. Aggregations of these germ cells are found in certain regions of the central nervous system, as in the entire cortex of the cerebrum and cerebellum and in the basal ganglia, which must be regarded as modified portions of the cortex. They are also found in the optic thalamus, the corpora quadrigemina, etc., and, finally, below the midbrain, surrounding the central canal and extending down to the lower extremity of the spinal cord, where they are collectively termed the *central nuclear layer*.

The remaining portions of the central nervous system are formed chiefly by the long processes of these cells. Together these form the medullary or white matter, while the cell aggregations represent the ancestors of the gray matter.

The term neuron ($\tau\grave{o}$ $\nu\varepsilon\tilde{\upsilon}\rho o\nu$, nerve unit) comprises the *nerve-cell with its entire nerve process*, including all its connections.

The long processes from the ganglion cells in the cerebral cortex, basal ganglia, and optic thalami begin and end within the central organ—they are **central neurons.** The processes from the cells grouped about the central canal, however, in part leave the central organ and run toward the periphery of the body, or they originate in the peripheral spinal ganglia and grow into the central organ—they are **peripheral neurons.** The latter form the *motor cranial nerves*, which grow out from the mid- and hindbrain, and the *motor spinal nerves*, which originate in the ventral nuclear layer of the spinal cord and emerge from the anterior horn as the *anterior roots*. These last represent the long processes of the ganglion cells situated in the anterior horns.

The development of the peripheral sensory nerves is the exact reverse of this. They originate in the *cells of the spinal ganglia*, and enter the dorsal nuclear layer of the spinal cord in the posterior horn—**sensory spinal nerves.** In the same way the sensory cranial nerves originate in the Gasserian, cochlear, petrosal, and jugular ganglia, in the retina, and in the olfactory mucous membrane, which are the analogues of the spinal canal, and enter the substance of the brain (olfactory bulb, midbrain, afterbrain). At the same time another peripheral process grows out from each of these cells and runs to the skin as a **peripheral sensory nerve.** This neuron, therefore, has its cell approximately in the middle of its course.[1]

The neuroblasts gradually become converted into ganglion cells, and their processes may grow to a considerable length—in some cases to one meter. About the fifth month these processes become covered with a layer of delicate whitish medullary substance, which accompanies the process throughout its entire extent—in other words, *medullation* begins to take place. Every long process re-

[1] We learn from comparative anatomy that as we ascend in the animal scale the cell of the peripheral sensory neuron gradually descends more and more toward the spinal ganglia from its original position in the skin.

ceives such a covering or medullary sheath and thus becomes a functionating nerve-fiber.

Medullation occurs at different times in the different neuron plexuses. It begins during the fifth fetal month, as has been stated, and continues to adult life; successive portions of the process become covered with the medullary substance, which gives them their characteristic white color. The rule is that those nerve paths which first become functional first undergo medullation. Thus the peripheral reflex paths are the first to become medullated, the sensory central conduction paths before the motor, the peripheral paths before the central, the projection fibers before the association fibers, etc.

Medullation begins in the fifth embryonal month in certain portions of the spinal cord and brain, which are most important from a phylogenetic point of view. In the hemispheres medullation does not begin before the ninth month, the tegmental radiation connecting the superior parietal with the posterior central gyrus, and the optic radiation being the first to become medullated. The pyramidal tract and a part of the column of Goll in the spinal column are nonmedullated at birth. In the brain medullation begins at birth in the projection fibers and continues to the third month (central, occipital, temporal, hippocampal convolutions). In the frontal lobe and inferior portions of the parietal and temporal lobes medullation does not begin until later (from the fifth to the ninth month).

The fully formed neuroglia consists of numerous small cells (supporting cells, glia cells) the processes of which form a close, delicate network of innumerable fibrils, in which the ganglion cells and nerve-fibers are embedded. The original epithelial cells persist as the ependyma, which lines the walls of the central canal and ventricular system.

Fully matured *ganglion cells* consist in part of large cells, which may have various forms, but all possessing a distinctly marked nucleus, while their protoplasm may be variously modified and is often the seat of pigmentation: in part of small cranial cells consisting almost exclusively of nuclear substance. The cells send out processes in all directions, some of which form a rich arborization in the immediate neighborhood, thus increasing the sphere of action of the cell-body (**dendrons** or **protoplasmic processes**), and a single process which arises as the above-mentioned process of the neuroblast and later is known as the **axis=cylinder process**.

After its exit from the ganglion cell this axis-cylinder process becomes medullated, and is then known as a nerve-fiber. The nerve-fiber, therefore, consists of an axial filament, which in turn is composed of numerous single fibrillæ and an investing *medullary sheath* arranged in segments. At its point of exit from the central organ the nerve-fiber (peripheral nerve) becomes invested by an additional delicate envelope outside of the medullary sheath, which is known as the *sheath of Schwann*, *primitive sheath*, or *neurilemma*. The length of the axis-cylinder process varies greatly, but it always ends by splitting up into terminal fibrils, although it may, at various levels, give off lateral twigs, or *collaterals*, which also break up into terminal fibrils. Cells provided with a long process (Deiters' type) gradually preponderate over those whose processes are short and break up into their terminal fibrils in the immediate vicinity of the cell (Golgi's cells).

The ganglion cell with its dendrons and the axis-cylinder with its terminal fibrils together form an anatomic and physiologic unit—a neuron. Every nervous pathway is made up of a series of such neurons, communicating with one another. There does not appear to be any direct anatomic continuity in these neurons,[1] which communicate

---

[1] The doctrine of the neurons, especially the histologic conditions as we have just described them, has recently been attacked, with some show of reason. Some observers claim to have discovered anastomoses between the neurons, and axis-cylinders taking their origin in plexuses.

with one another very much like cog-wheels, the terminal fibrils of the axis-cylinder of one neuron inserting themselves between the arborizations of the cells (dendrons) of another neuron. The brain, spinal cord, peripheral nerves, and sympathetic system are composed exclusively of neurons of this character and their "articulations."

The transmission of an impulse from one neuron to another is probably effected by some form of movement in the terminal fibrils. The impulse is carried away from the cell in the axis-cylinder and toward the cell in the dendrons. Every neuron probably acts in relation with several others (intermediate neurons), the most extensive communication being made possible by the innumerable dendrons and collaterals.

The **gray matter** of the nervous system (cortex, ganglia, basal nuclei) is composed of the supporting neurogliar tissue, the ganglion cells with their dendrons, and more or less numerous nerve-fibers, both medullated and nonmedullated (pale or Remak's fibers).

The **white matter** (medulla of the hemispheres, corpus callosum, inner capsule, cerebral peduncle, columns of the spinal cord, and peripheral nerves) consists of medullated nerve-fibers only, the color and consistency of the substance depending on the presence of this medullary envelope.

A better idea of the minute microscopic structures of the various portions of the central nervous system than can be given by a mere description will be obtained from a study of plates 17 to 26 and their explanations and from the drawings in the text.

It now remains to give a short account of the internal connections between the various portions of the central nervous system.

The fibers which form the centrum semiovale begin and

This, however, has not been definitely proved in the case of man. The near future will undoubtedly bring forth many modifications of **the doctrine.**

end in *the cellular layers of the cortex*. They are divided into three systems.

I. The Commissural Fibers.—These form the greater part of the central white matter of the corpus callosum and connect symmetric areas of the convolutions of the two hemispheres with each other.[1] Those portions of the cortex that are not connected by the fibers of the corpus callosum—namely, the inferior, temporal, and occipital convolutions, and the olfactory lobe—communicate with one another by means of the deep *anterior commissure*.

II. Association Fibers.—These are composed of bundles of white fibers connecting the individual convolutions of the same hemisphere. The connection between adjacent convolutions and lobes is established by means of the *fibriæ propriæ*, while more remote convolutions and lobes communicate with each other by means of the *short and long association bundles*. These fibers pass from convolution to convolution within the hemisphere. As they enter the central medullary substance they are collected into larger bundles, which again subdivide in the more remote portions of the cortex. The most important association bundles are:

1. The *cingulum*, placed immediately above the corpus callosum and uniting the gyrus fornicatus with the gyrus hippocampi (association paths for the olfactory nerve).

2. *Fasciculus uncinatus*, between the inferior frontal convolution and the temporal lobe.

3. *Fasciculus longitudinalis inferior*, between the occipital and temporal lobes.

4. *Fasciculus longitudinalis superior* (arcuatus), connects the frontal lobe with the parietal and also with the temporal lobes.

5. *Fasciculus occipitofrontalis* (tapetum), connecting the

---

[1] It is probable that the corpus callosum, in addition to the commissural fibers, also contains association fibers connecting the two hemispheres. Many of the fibers of the corpus callosum are probably mere collaterals derived from the long bundles of association fibers.

frontal lobe with the occipital and temporal. In the frontal, parietal, and occipital lobes the association bundles connecting different parts of the same lobe and the other

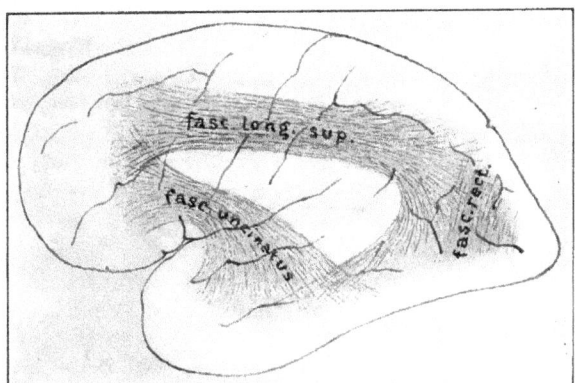

Fig. 7.

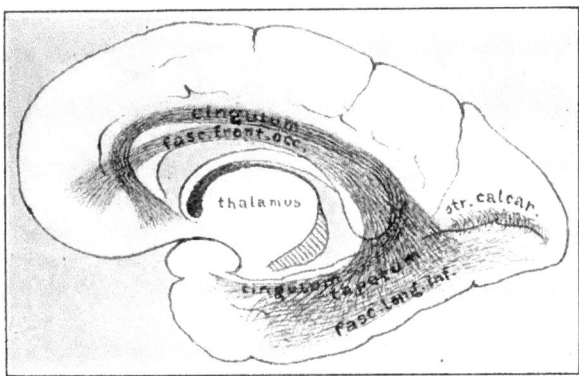

Fig. 8.

Figs. 7 and 8.—The long association fibers. Figure 7 shows the bundles contained in the lateral white substance of the hemispheres; figure 8, those in the mesial white matter. At the upper border a few short association bundles are shown diagrammatically.

portions of the cortex on the same side are especially numerous. The occipital lobe also contains the fasciculus rectus and fasciculus transversus.

III. The Projection Fibers.—These are the most important fiber tracts. They either originate or end in every portion of the cortex, especially in the convexity of the convolutions. After traversing the transverse commissural and longitudinal association fibers, they proceed to the deeper portions of the brain-stem and spinal cord, so as to establish a communication between them and the cortex. The term *corona radiata* is applied to the entire system of projection fibers.[1]

The tracts of the corona radiata are divided into *short* and *long* fibers, depending on the point at which their axis-cylinders subdivide into terminal fibrils. The fibers of the corona radiata are collected into a compact bundle in the internal capsule (anterior and posterior limb), and in their subsequent course downward they pass through the striate body.

1. Short Fibers of the Corona Radiata.—(a) One portion of the fibers of the corona radiata, originating in all the convolutions of the cortex and being contained in the internal capsule, enters the optic thalamus as the anterior, posterior, and inferior peduncles of the optic thalamus and is lost in the substance of that structure; others spread out over the surface of the optic thalamus before penetrating its substance (stratum zonale). In this way the optic thalamus receives *four* different peduncles: The anterior peduncle, from the frontal lobe; the superior peduncle, from the frontal, parietal, and temporal lobes; the posterior peduncle, from the temporal and occipital lobes; and the inferior peduncle, from the temporal lobe.

(b) Another tract of fibers leaves the anterior limb of the

---

[1] According to Flechsig, projection fibers originate only in the central convolutions, in the occipital and temporal lobes, while in the other lobes only association fibers have their beginning.

capsule and enters the caudate nucleus. (These must be regarded as association fibers.)

(c) Finally, a bundle of fibers derived from the cuneus and lingula of the occipital lobe enters the posterior segment of the posterior limb of the capsule, and thence proceeds to the primary optic centers, and to the pulvinar, lateral geniculate body, and anterior corpus quadrigeminum. These fibers are known as Gratiolet's optic radiation.

2. *The Long Fibers of the Corona Radiata.*—These are also derived from all parts of the cortex; they enter the internal capsule and proceed downward to the subthalamic region underneath the optic thalamus, and thence either into the tegmental or into the ventral portion of the cerebral peduncle.

(a) *Tegmental Fibers.*—Their exact course is not perfectly known. Some of them enter the tegmentum directly from the internal capsule (posterior limb), others after traversing the inner segments of the lenticular nucleus (lenticular loop, fillet from the globus pallidus) and breaking through that portion of the internal capsule which lies to the mesial side of these structures. The fibers either end at this point or continue downward as the *tract of the fillet* to the inferior extremity of the medulla oblongata. From recent investigations it appears probable that the fillet is interrupted in its course through the optic thalamus. We distinguish a mesial and a lateral tract of the fillet (central sensory pathway).

(b) *Tracts of the Crusta.*—All those fibers of the corona radiata which have not left the main body of the tract now pass from the internal capsule (anterior and posterior limbs) into the crusta, and thus leave the hemispheres in which they originate.

According to their origin, the fibers are divided into three groups:

a. *The Mesial Peduncular Fibers.*— These probably originate in the cortex of the frontal lobe, and, after traversing the anterior limb of the capsule, end in the mesial ganglia of the pons (frontal pontine tract).

β. *The Lateral Peduncular Fibers* (oval bundle— Türck's bundle).—These are derived from the temporal lobe. They pass through the posterior limb of the capsule

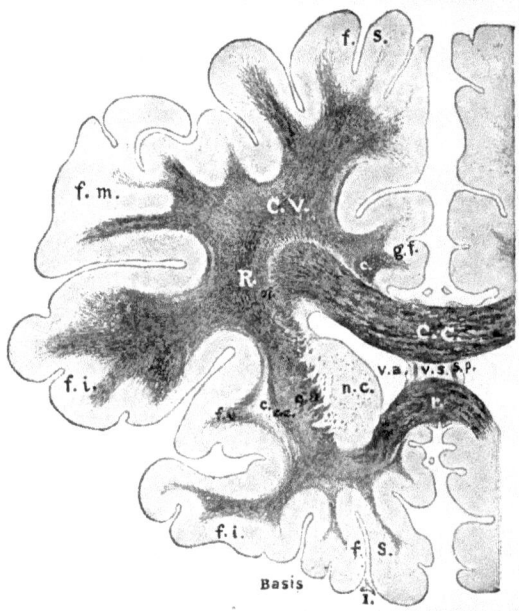

Fig. 9.—Section through the frontal lobe, showing the beginning of the most anterior bundles of the corona radiata, which contain the first fibers of the pyramidal tract (*R*): *c. c*, Corpus callosum; *C.V*, centrum semiovale Vieussenii; *c. a*, anterior limb of the internal capsule; *f. i*, inferior frontal convolution (base of the third frontal convolution—motor speech center). For the other letters consult Plate 28.

and end in the collateral ganglia of the pons (temporo-occipital pontine tract).

γ. *The Middle Peduncular Fibers.*

The Pyramidal Tract.—These fibers originate in the cortical cells of the central convolutions and their immediate neighborhood, and, after forming part of the corona radiata (Fig. 9), enter the internal capsule, where they are found in the knee and in the anterior third of the posterior limb. In the crusta they occupy a position between the bundles mentioned under *a* and *b*. (See Plate 68.)

This portion of the ventral peduncular fibers emerges at the posterior border of the pons in a compact bundle, known as the **pyramid**, and continues its way down the spinal cord as the **pyramidal tract**. Most of the fibers,

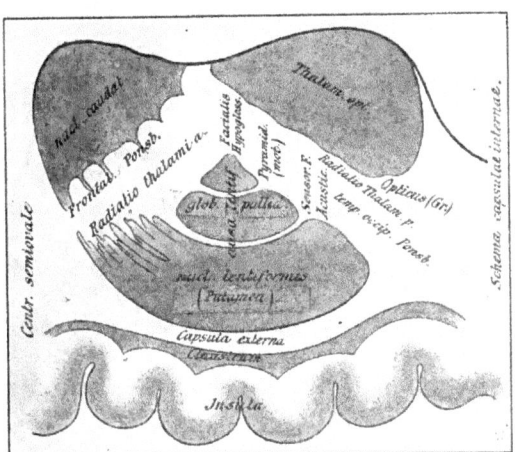

Fig. 10.—Schema of the internal capsule.

as has already been stated, undergo decussation and occupy the lateral column, while the smaller uncrossed portion remains in the anterior column. This tract contains the longest fibers of the corona radiata, and can be followed in the lateral column of either side as far down as the conus medullaris. From the cerebral peduncle onward fibers constantly leave the main tract and pass to the motor nuclei of the opposite side. This tract forms the **central motor pathway**.

The position of the various tracts is well shown in the accompanying schema of the capsule (Fig. 10), modified from Edinger.

The fibers of the corona radiata, which, as we have seen, are derived from the cortex, are later joined by other fibers from the **striate body** and **optic thalamus**, which continue downward as *short* tracts. The latter include:

1. The fibers running from the caudate nuclei and putamen to the optic thalamus (inner segment of the lenticular nucleus) and further downward to the substantia nigra in the crus (basal forebrain bundle).

2. Fibers beginning in the optic thalamus and ending in the tegmentum and corpus albicans. (See Fig. 11.) These contain the more important short tracts of the interbrain.

The following fibers take their origin in the tegmentum:

The **posterior longitudinal bundle**, situated immediately beneath the gray matter of the ventricle, which connects several cranial nerves and extends as far down as the cervical enlargement (see Fig. 11); a massive bundle of fibers which emerge from the *red nucleus* and, after decussating with a corresponding bundle from the opposite side, form the superior cerebellar peduncle, passing as such to the hemispheres of the cerebellum and ending in the corpus dentatum and cerebellar cortex.

In the cerebellum the following fibers are found:

The **middle cerebellar peduncle**, which passes to the pontine ganglia of the other side, where its fibers end, and the **inferior cerebellar peduncle**, going to the medulla oblongata (restiform body). These bundles contain fibers connecting the cerebellum with the olivary bodies and the posterior and lateral columns (direct cerebellar tract) of the spinal cord; some of these form long, and others short, tracts.

The white matter of the cerebellum also contains **commissural** and **association fibers** similar to those found in the cerebrum.

For the manner in which the white matter of the spinal cord is constructed from the projection fibers of the cere-

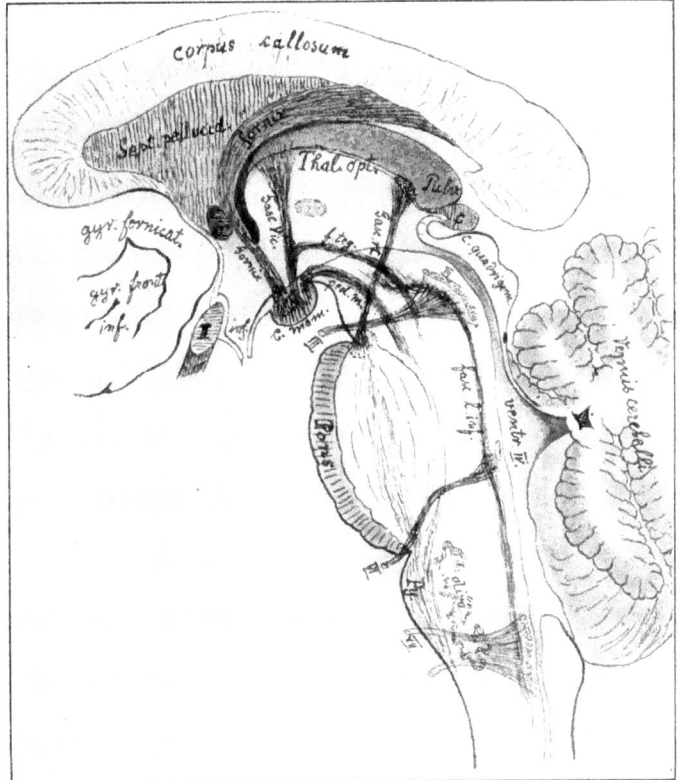

Fig. 11.—The short tracts in the brain-stem and interbrain. Sagittal section through the middle of the brain-stem: *inf*, Infundibulum; *c. mam*, corpus mammillare; *fasc. Vic*, bundles of Vicq d'Azyr; *f. teg*, tegmental bundle; *ped. m*, peduncle of corpus mammillare; *fasc. rt*, fasciculus retroflexus; *fasc. l. inf*, posterior longitudinal bundle; II, III, VI, XII, corresponding cranial nerves; *c*, pineal gland.

bral and cerebellar cortex, the pyramids, restiform bodies, etc., consult a former paragraph (p. 15).

In a section of the spinal cord we see the two halves separated in front by the anterior longitudinal fissure. Immediately behind this, in the median line, is the white anterior commissure, connecting one anterior column or, rather, anterior horn, with that of the other side. Ventrally from this is the central canal, which is for the most part obliterated, and behind the latter, the narrow posterior commissure.

The gray matter forms the anterior and posterior horns, and is surrounded by the anterior, lateral, and posterior columns of the cord.

1. The **anterior column** contains the uncrossed pyramidal tract and the anterior ground bundle (continuations of the constituent parts of the substantia reticularis in the tegmentum).

2. The **lateral column** contains the crossed pyramidal tract, the direct cerebellar tract (from the restiform body), the tract of Gowers (from the vermiform process of the cerebellum), the anterolateral ground bundle, and the mixed lateral zone (partly derived from the tegmentum).

3. The **posterior column** contains the columns of Goll and Burdach and the root-zones.

In addition to the fibers derived from the brain the spinal cord contains numerous fibers originating within its own substance (myelogenic, intramedullary fibers), and also fibers which come from the periphery (extraspinal fibers).

A more detailed description of the course and significance of the pathways that have been mentioned and of others will be found in Part III. The foregoing, it is hoped, will serve to explain the serial sections contained in Plates 28 to 52, which are intended as an introduction to the study of the topographic anatomy of the brain. The more complex relations between the gray matter of the cortex, basal ganglia, optic thalamus, and nuclei of the cranial nerves can only be studied from the illustrations, and the reader is therefore referred to the plates and to the explanatory notes which accompany them.

PART III.

ANATOMY AND PHYSIOLOGY OF THE MORE IMPORTANT NERVOUS PATHWAYS.
(Plates 54 to 57.)

WE understand by nervous pathway the anatomic basis for the transmission of a definite physiologic impulse from the ganglion cell to the end-organ which receives the impulse, including all the connections.

Every physiologic function requires for its completion a nervous pathway which is composed of a number of communicating neuron complexes, each individual neuron complex completely retaining its physiologic and anatomic independence. Thus there are pathways which consist of two, three, or even more successive neuron complexes. The more important of these belong to the projection system of the cerebral and cerebellar cortex. They are the following:

Nerve Tracts Associated with Known Functions.

1. The motor, corticomuscular, or centrifugal tract, consisting of two neuron complexes.

2. The sensory, centripetal tract, consisting of at least three, and probably more, neuron complexes.

These two tracts communicate with each other in two different divisions of their course:

(a) They have a lower connection, which forms the reflex tract and is not under the influence of the will. It is found in the subcortical nuclei (the basal ganglia; nuclei of pons, medulla, and cord).

(b) An upper connection in the cortex, the pathway of the reactions of conscious volition.

The course of the motor tract is much better known and much simpler than that of the sensory tract. We shall now proceed to consider these tracts and their communications, in the order named.

1. The Motor Pathway.

The pathway considered as a whole is composed of two successive neuron complexes, the *central*, or archineuron, and the *peripheral motor*, or teleneuron. The cells of the central neurons, situated in the central convolutions of the cerebral cortex,—pyramidal cells of the cortex,—send their nerve-fibers in a compact body, known as the *pyramidal tract*, by way of the corona radiata, through the knee and anterior third of the posterior limb of the internal capsule into the crusta. From there they are continued by way of the pons into the pyramids.

At the decussation of the pyramids the greater part of the fibers enter the lateral column of the cord, which is continued as the crossed *lateral pyramidal tract*. In the cervical enlargement these fibers are situated in the median portion of the lateral column, and as they proceed downward approach nearer and nearer to the periphery of the cord, terminating finally in the conus medullaris. A smaller number of the nerve-fibers are continued without decussation in the anterior pyramidal tract, and do not extend lower than the upper portion of the lumbar enlargement.

Along the entire extent of this tract, beginning at the crusta, certain nerve bundles leave the tract at various levels and, after undergoing decussation, pass to the other side. (See Fig. 14, which represents an anterior view of the pyramidal tract.) These nerve-fibers split up into

THE MOTOR PATHWAY.   41

terminal fibrils which end in the motor nuclei of the brain and spinal marrow. It follows, therefore, that the entire mass of fibers contained in the pyramidal tract gradually diminishes from above downward. In addition other collateral fibers are given off from the decussating fibers and

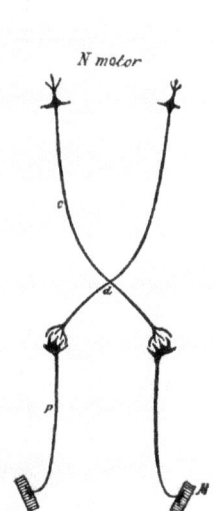
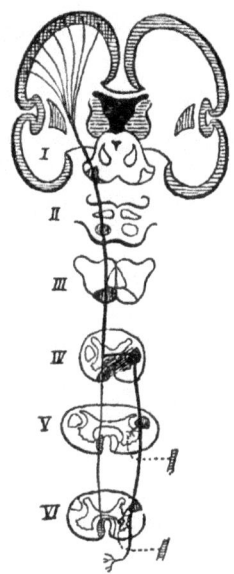

Fig. 12.—Schema of the motor pathway: *c*, Central, *p*, peripheral, neuron; *d*, decussation; *M*, muscle.

Fig. 13.—Schema showing the course of the pyramidal tract: *I*, In the cerebrum and crus; *II*, in the pons; *III*, in the medulla oblongata; *II'*, decussation of the pyramids—*V*, in the cervical enlargement; *VI*, in the lumbar enlargement.

pass to higher nuclei. Thus the entire central mass of neurons finally splits up in the substations which have been described as situated at various levels of the brain and spinal marrow. (See Fig. 13.)

These terminal nerve fibrils surround the dendrons of

the ganglion cells of the peripheral motor neurons which begin at this point—*i. e.*, at the substation just mentioned.

The nerve processes of these cells emerge as nerve-roots from the brain and anterior horn of the spinal cord of the same side, and are continued as motor fibers to the muscle, where they finally break up into their terminal fibrils among the individual muscle-fibers. The central motor neuron, therefore, undergoes decussation, while the peripheral does not. (See Fig. 12.) The impulses which originate in the cells of the cortex are transmitted to the muscle through the pathway formed of these two neurons, and from the decussation of the central neurons it follows that the cortex of each hemisphere controls the muscles of the opposite half of the body.

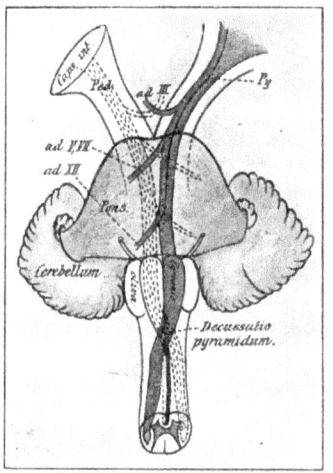

Fig. 14.—Schema showing the position of the pyramidal tract (*Py*) in the mesencephalon: *III, V, VII, XII*, Central motor pathways to the corresponding cranial nerves.

Every neuron cell exercises a trophic influence on its processes, including the long axis-cylinder process. If this influence is destroyed, the corresponding nerve-fiber undergoes degeneration, and the ganglion cell itself suffers degenerative changes if the continuity of the neuron is interrupted. The cell of the peripheral neuron in addition exercises a nutritive influence on the muscle-fibers to which it is distributed.

The most important constituents of the motor pathway, taken in the order in which the peripheral nerve tracts emerge from the brain from above downward, are the following:

1. Oculomotor Nerve.—The central neuron complex originates at some unknown point in the cortex (angular gyrus?), passes through the knee of the internal capsule, and leaves the pyramidal tract in the peduncle of the cere-

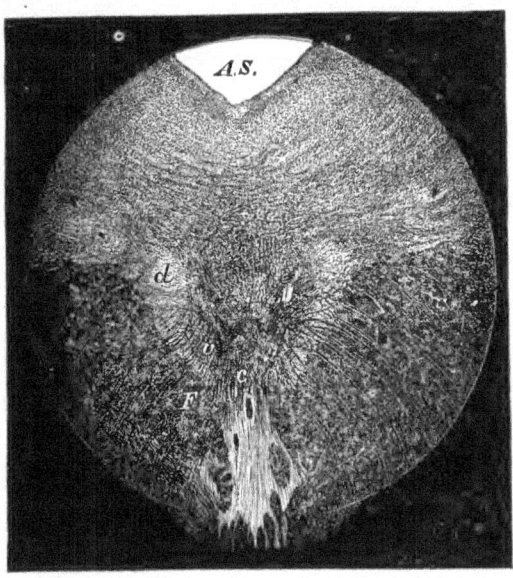

Fig. 15.—Oculomotor nucleus (medullary sheath stain; photograph, magnified 150 times): F, Fasc. long. post.; $A.S$, aqueduct of Sylvius; d, dorsal, r, ventral, c, central, nucleus. Note the decussation of the root-fibers from the ventral nucleus.

brum, perhaps forming a part of Spitzka's bundle or accessory fillet. (See Plate 42.) The latter arises from the mesial portion of the pyramidal region in the peduncle, and, after turning inward and upward and crossing the middle line, ends in the oculomotor nucleus of the opposite (and of the same?) side, which is situated in the central gray matter, underneath the aqueduct of Sylvius. The terminal fibers of the central neuron of the oculomotor surround the ganglion cells that are found in this region. These cells and their dendrites form the first portion of the peripheral neuron. The nerve-fibers emerge from the nucleus as the roots of the oculomotor nerve on the same and, to some extent, on the opposite side, and are continued in the trunk of the oculomotor nerve to the ocular muscles. (For a further description of their distribution and function see explanation to Plate 37.) The position and divisions of the oculomotor nucleus are seen in the accompanying Figure 15; see also Figure 29, on p. 184, and Figure 17. The latter also shows the probable relation of the divisions of the nucleus to the individual muscles.

2. **Trochlear Nerve.**—The course of the central neuron is the same as that of the oculomotor. After undergoing decussation the end-fibers break up in the trochlear nucleus of the opposite side, under the posterior corpora quadrigemina and behind the oculomotor nucleus. The peripheral neuron begins at this point, emerging as the trochlear nerve behind the quadrigemina, and crossing with all its fibers the nerve of the opposite side in the anterior medullary velum.

3. **Motor Portion of the Fifth Nerve.**—The central neuron originates at some unknown point in the cortex (inferior parietal gyrus?), traverses the knee of the internal capsule behind the fibers of the oculomotor, and leaves the peduncle in Spitzka's bundle (?). It undergoes decussation in the raphe of the tegmentum (accessory fillet), and surrounds with its end-fibers the cells of the motor nucleus of the fifth nerve, which is situated in the lateral portion of the tegmentum. From this point the peripheral neuron is continued as the motor root of the fifth nerve, emerging from the pons as the anterior root, after receiving some fibers from the motor nucleus of the opposite side. The nasal root of the fifth nerve (formerly

known as the ascending root) is also said to contain motor (trophic?) fibers. It originates in the lateral portion of the central gray matter of the aqueduct of Sylvius, from the large cells which are situated in the lower part of that region, and joins the anterior root of the fifth nerve at its exit from the brain.

4. Abducens.—The course of the *central* neuron is the same as for the oculomotor. After undergoing decussation the end-fibers split up in the abducens nucleus, underneath the floor of the fourth ventricle, near the median line. The *peripheral* neuron is given off from the cells of the abducens nucleus, and, after traversing the posterior portion of the pons, emerges as the abducens nerve.

5. Facial Nerve.—The *central* neuron complex originates in the cells of the lower third of the central convolutions. From here the tract proceeds in the posterior limb of the internal capsule, behind the knee, separates from the pyramidal tract in Spitzka's bundle, and, after decussating in the raphe of the tegmentum, joins the long facial nucleus of the opposite side, which is situated in the deeper portions of the medulla oblongata, laterally from the tegmentum. From this point the individual fibers of the facial nerve, forming the peripheral neuron, pass upward and inward to the genu of the facial, and arch outward and then downward until they finally emerge from the medulla oblongata as the facial nerve. This is the "*lower*" facial nerve (mouth and cheeks).

The *central* neuron for the "*upper*" facial nerve (brow) apparently follows some other course which is not known. The *peripheral* neuron is said to emerge from the posterior segment of the oculomotor nucleus and finally to reach the trunk of the facial.

The branch which supplies the orbicularis oris is said to contain fibers from the nucleus of the hypoglossus (?)

6. Motor Portion of the Glossopharyngeovagus.— The *central* neuron originates in some unknown portion of the cortex (middle frontal convolution?), descends in the pyramidal tract, and, after crossing in the raphe, reaches in some unknown way the nucleus ambiguus, which is assumed to be its motor nucleus. The latter is found in the prolongation of the facial nucleus within the posterior portion of the medulla oblongata. From this point the fibers of the *peripheral* neuron for the most part join the vagus.

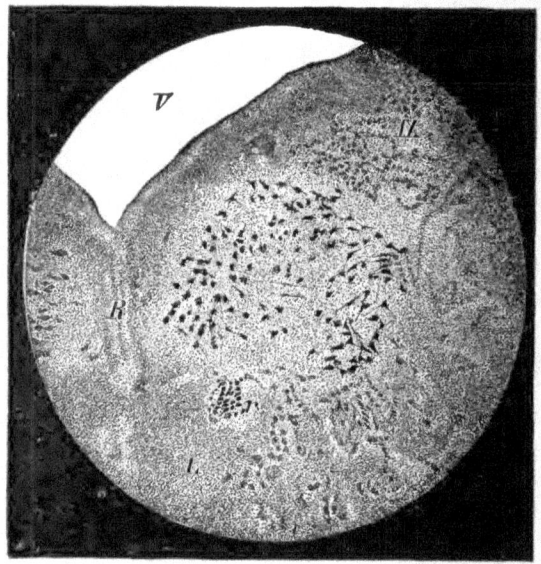

Fig. 16.—Nucleus of the right hypoglossus (stained with methylene-blue; photograph, magnified 150 times): *V*, Rhomboid fossa; *L*, post. long. bundle; *R*, raphe; *IX*, glossopharyngeovagus nucleus; *S*, Roller's accessory nucleus.

7. **Hypoglossus.**—The *central* neuron originates in the lower third of the central convolutions in front of the facial center, descends in the internal capsule behind the path of the facial, leaving the pyramidal tract in the accessory fillet. After crossing in the raphe of the teg-

mentum it enters the hypoglossus nucleus of the opposite side, among the cells of which it finally breaks up. (See Fig. 16.) At this point the *peripheral* neuron emerges from the medulla as the hypoglossus nerve.

The nerve paths described in **5, 6,** and **7**—that is, those which originate in the *left hemisphere*—are especially concerned in the act of speech. Their central neurons together form the *central speech path*, while their peripheral neurons form the *peripheral speech path*. The existence of a separate *speech path* has also been assumed but has never been proved.

8. Spinal Accessory Nerve.—The *central* neuron is said to originate in the base of the middle frontal convolution (?) and to follow the pyramidal tract. Its subsequent course is unknown, but it eventually enters the accessory nucleus of the opposite side, in the lower portion of the medulla and upper portion of the cervical enlargement. From this point the *peripheral neuron* proceeds as the spinal accessory nerve. A large part of the nerve—the internal branch—joins the pneumogastric.

9. The Motor Pathway of the Upper Extremity.—The *central* neuron complex originates in the cells of the middle third of the central convolutions, especially of the anterior convolution, passes down through the posterior limb of the internal capsule in its anterior third, and enters the pyramidal tract, which it accompanies through the ventral portion of the peduncle and pons into the pyramid. At the decussation of the pyramids the greater part passes to the lateral column of the opposite side, while a smaller portion descends, without decussating, in the anterior column of the cord (individual variations occur in this respect). At the level of the cervical enlargement the fibers are successively reflected at a right angle, and pass—those from the lateral pyramidal tract into the anterior horn of the same side, and those from the anterior pyramidal tract by way of the anterior commissure into the

48   *THE NERVOUS PATHWAYS.*

anterior horn of the opposite side.[1] Here the terminal fibers surround the cells of the anterior horn (especially the lateral groups) and their dendrons.

These cells form the beginning of the *peripheral* neuron of the motor tract. The nerve processes emerge as the anterior roots (fourth cervical to first dorsal), and reach the brachial plexus, from which they are continued into the various nerves of the arm. (For detailed description see the explanation of Plate 27.) The situation of the cells of the anterior horn and their relation to the individual muscles are best seen in Figure 17 on page 52.

The nerve tracts for the upper extremity are situated between those which supply the muscles of the neck above, and those which supply the muscles of the trunk below. The topography can readily be understood by a study of the plates mentioned; but little is known concerning the central course of the tract. The center for movements of the trunk is said to be situated in the superior frontal convolutions. It is probable that the pathway originates in the hemispheres both of the same and of the opposite side. In the same way other muscles whose functions are bilateral (eye, brow muscles, etc.) probably derive their innervation from the hemispheres both of the same and of the opposite side. But our knowledge of these uncrossed (or double crossed?) central pathways in man is very imperfect (uncrossed anterior pyramid?). (See foot-note.)

10. The Motor Pathway for the Lower Extremity.— The *central* neuron originates in the upper third of the central convolutions and in the paracentral lobule. It is continued in the pyramidal tract through the posterior limb of the internal capsule (in the center of the limb), and proceeds downward as described under **9**—that is to say, it undergoes a partial decussation at a lower level than that of the upper extremity. The great mass of the fibers

---

[1] This ultimate decussation of the anterior pyramidal tract has recently been disputed, with some reason, and it has been supposed that the tract ends in the anterior horn of the same side.

descend in the lateral pyramidal tract as far as the lumbar enlargement, where they are reflected into the anterior horn and break up into their terminal fibrils. From the cells of the anterior horn, especially those of the lateral groups, the *peripheral* neuron emerges as the anterior roots (five lumbar and five sacral), enters the lumbar and sacral plexuses, and is continued from these plexuses into the nerves of the lower extremities. (See Plate 27 and Fig. 17, in which the relations of the muscles to the various divisions of the peduncle and of the spinal cord on the right side of the body are shown.)

11. The motor pathway for the bladder, rectum, and sexual organs arises at some unknown point in the brain, the *central* neuron descending in the pyramidal lateral tract, probably in the anterolateral ground bundle, and terminating in the gray matter of the sacral cord. The *peripheral* neuron emerges as the second, third, and fourth sacral roots, and goes to the pudendal plexuses and finally to the muscles of the organs named. (See Plate 27.)

12. The sympathetic nerve receives *central* motor fibers of unknown cortical origin from the lateral columns. They appear to end in the anterior, and especially in the lateral, horn. At this point the *peripheral neuron* begins; it emerges in the anterior roots, and is finally distributed to the ganglions of the sympathetic nerves and their homologues. The cells in these ganglia form the beginning of the *motor sympathetic neuron*, the fibers of which are distributed to the various unstriped muscle-fibers in the vessels, intestines, heart (?), glands, etc. The vasomotor nerves also have their origin in the anterolateral ground bundle.

II. The Sensory Pathway.

Since the function of the sensory pathway is to transmit sensory impressions from the periphery to the center, we shall describe it in this direction, beginning, therefore, with the peripheral neuron.

The **peripheral sensory neuron complex** of the extremities and of the trunk is contained in the sensory fibers of the peripheral nerves, the cutaneous distribution of which is seen in Figures 23 to 25 and in Figure 17. It continues its course to the spine through the fibers of the various plexuses, and ends in the cells of the spinal ganglia (without directly entering the spinal cord). Each cell of the spinal ganglia gives off another fiber in the opposite direction. These fibers collectively form the **posterior roots,** and as such the sensory peripheral neuron finally reaches the spinal marrow, the posterior roots entering in two separate parts into the posterior columns that lie between the posterior horns. After its entrance into the spinal cord each root-fiber divides in the form of a T, and gives off an ascending and a descending branch. The two divisions of the posterior roots are:

1. The *lesser, lateral division* of the posterior root, which enters the tip of the posterior horn in the region known as Lissauer's tract, where each of its fibers divides into an ascending and a descending branch. The course of both branches is very short: after running a short distance within the cord, they are reflected at right angles into the posterior horn and there undergo division into their terminal fibrils around the cells of the posterior horn.

2. The *larger, mesial division* of the posterior root, which enters the lateral portion of the posterior column (Burdach's column), and is, therefore, known as the posterior root-zone. Here the fibers split up into an ascending and a descending branch.

The *descending* branches extend but a short distance, and are soon reflected at right angles into the posterior horn, where they undergo arborization; some of the *ascending* branches are also short; others have a longer course.

The short branches are soon reflected and pass partly into the posterior horn, partly into the anterior horn, and

THE SENSORY PATHWAY. 51

into the columns of Clarke, where they break up among the cells. The long fibers first continue their way in Burdach's column toward the brain, but as they are joined by other ascending root-fibers at higher levels they gradually approach nearer to the median line. The long fibers that enter the lumbar enlargement are, therefore, found in the column of Goll in the cervical region, while those that enter at a higher level, in the thoracic and cervical portion of the cord, occupy a more external position.

These long ascending fibers eventually break up into their terminal fibrils within the medulla oblongata, about the cells of the nucleus funiculus of Goll (f. gracilis) and the nucleus funiculus of Burdach (f. cuneatus).

All these fibers taken together form the *sensory peripheral neuron complex*. The cell of this neuron is, therefore, situated outside of the spinal cord, in the intervertebral ganglia; its dendritic processes are represented by the peripheral nerve and its principal cutaneous branches, while the nerve process corresponds to the posterior root-fiber and its terminal fibrils in the various portions and levels of the spinal cord.

These terminal divisions take place about the nerve-cells lying in the following regions:

1. In Goll's and Burdach's nuclei (funiculus gracilis and funiculus cuneatus) in the medulla oblongata.
2. In the various portions of the posterior horns.
3. In the so-called middle zones, between the anterior and the posterior horn.
4. In the columns of Clarke.
5. In the anterior horn.

The **central sensory neuron complex** begins in the regions included under 1 to 4. (For the nerve terminations under 5 see Reflex Paths.) Up to this point the distribution is fairly well settled, but the further course of the central sensory tract is still a matter of dispute, although it is very much better understood now than formerly. The points still under discussion will be referred to briefly

LOCATION OF THE SEGMENTS FOR
Sensibility. Motility.

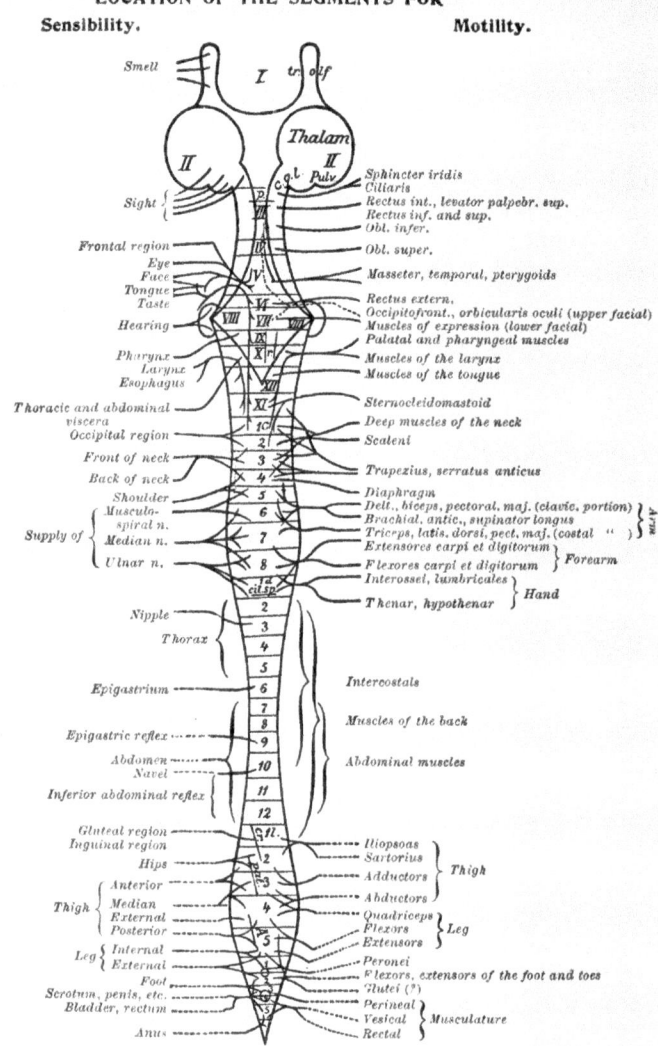

Fig. 17.—Explanation of abbreviations: *tr. olf*, Olfactory tract; *c. g. l*, lateral geniculate body; *p, r, cr, A*, indicate approximately the location of the reflex centers for the pupillary (*p*), the respiratory (*r*), cremasteric (*cr*), patellar (*pat*), and tendo Achillis (*A*) reflexes.

THE SENSORY PATHWAY. 53

in a subsequent paragraph; what follows is that description of the subsequent course of the neuron which harmonizes best with the postulates of pathology. The anatomic distribution in man is not absolutely known.

The beginning of the *central sensory neuron*, corresponding with the terminal divisions of the peripheral neuron, is found partly in the above-mentioned regions of the medulla oblongata, and partly in the gray matter of the posterior and anterior horns of the cord. We will discuss the separate portions in the order in which they are given above—1 to 4.

1. The central neuron has its origin in the cells of the funiculus gracilis and funiculus cuneatus in the medulla oblongata. From this point the fibers pass downward and toward the raphe, forming the *internal arcuate fibers*; at this point they cross the median line (decussation of the fillet, the beginning is seen in Plate 46, Fig. 1 (*fai*); it ends at the level shown in Plate 44, Fig. 2). Above this decussation the fibers, after being collected into a bundle, pass dorsally and above the pyramids (which have decussated at a

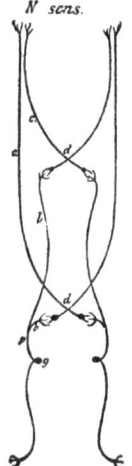

Fig. 18.—Schema of the sensory pathway: *c*, Central, *p*, peripheral, neuron; *g*, intervertebral ganglion cell; *b*, short, *l*, long, tract; *d*, decussation.

The vesical center lies in the third and fourth sacral segments; the anal center in the fourth and fifth (represented by circles); the centers for erection, ejaculation, labor pains (?) are probably also situated in this region.

In reality the divisions between the various segments are, of course, not so sharp as they are shown in the diagram, so that a given muscle or cutaneous region derives some of its controlling nerve-roots from the segments lying immediately above and below the principal segment. The sensory segment for any given region is regularly somewhat higher than the corresponding motor segment.

lower point), and lie next to the anterior ground bundle, where they are known as the **fillet** (laqueus superior). In its subsequent brainward course the fillet gradually increases in size and ranges itself between the superior and inferior olives that now make their appearance, forming the interolivary layer, still close to the median line. Higher up the fillet proceeds in the region of the tegmentum, where it broadens out and lies transversely beneath the tegmentum, being known at this point as the median fillet. In this way it passes through the dorsal portion of the pons. In the tegmentum it leaves the median line and assumes a position to the outer side of the red nucleus. From this point the superior fillet is continued to the subthalamic region, disappearing at a point slightly inferior to the level of the red nucleus. According to some authorities some of the fibers pass from this point directly through the internal capsule (peduncular fibers), while others form part of the ansa lentiformis, which passes transversely through the capsule. The fillet then breaks through the internal limb of the lenticular nucleus, and, ascending in the posterior limb of the capsule, reaches the cortex of the posterior central convolutions and of the parietal lobe. In this region the fibers of the neuron undergo their terminal divisions

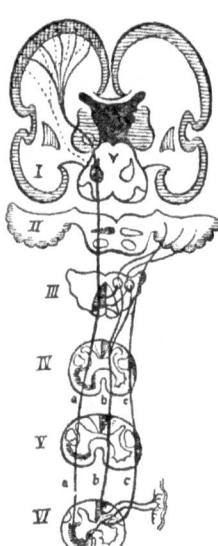

Fig. 19. — Schema showing the course of the sensory pathway: *I*, In the cerebrum and cerebral peduncles; *II*, pons and cerebellum; *III*, medulla oblongata; *IV*, upper portion of cervical cord; *V*, middle portion of cervical cord; *VI*, lumbar cord; *a*, fibers from the anterolateral columns and fillet; *b*, fibers in the posterior columns; *c*, fibers from cerebellum and lateral columns.

around cells situated in these portions of the cortex. It is probable that this portion is interrupted in some way in the globus pallidus.

Another portion of the *superior fillet* apparently passes directly from the subthalamic region to the internal capsule, and, ascending in the posterior limb behind the pyramidal tract, probably ends in the cortical area above referred to.

According to another description, the greater part or even all of the fibers of the superior fillet are interrupted in the ganglia of the subthalamic region, the globus pallidus, and especially the optic thalamus (in the lateral basal portion of the nucleus)—that is to say, the superior fillet ends here. According to this view, the final conduction to the cortex would necessitate a third or centrocortical neuron (in the corona radiata of the optic thalamus?), but our information on this point is very uncertain.

2. The central neurons which begin in the cells of the posterior horns for the most part form short nerve paths, most of which end within the spinal cord. Their fibers enter the lateral ground bundle of the same side (*fl* in the serial sections shown in Plate 47) and the ventral portion of the posterior column. After ascending or descending for a short distance they reenter the gray matter and break up into their terminal fibrils. These nerve paths are then joined by others of similar distribution, so that conduction is effected by relays, one short nerve path joining another.

The fibers enter the substantia reticularis of the tegmentum in the medulla and end in the nuclei situated in this region (nucl. lat. post. and ant. ?). From the cells of the substantia reticularis (nucleus magnocellularis) fibers are said to proceed brainward and join the *fillet*.

3. Three different kinds of fibers have their origin in the cells of the middle zone in the spinal cord, forming shorter and longer paths:

(*a*) Ascending fibers which enter the anterolateral tract of the same side. Some of these are short and end within the gray matter; others continue upward and reach the substantia reticularis of the tegmentum, where they join the fillet—*fal* in the serial sections.

(*b*) Ascending fibers which enter Gower's column of the same side, and continue upward as far as the medulla. All the longer nerve tracts give off collateral fibers which enter the gray matter at various levels.

Gower's column in part also enters the substantia reticularis in the medulla. Its termination within the mesencephalon, or vermiform process of the cerebellum (?), is still a matter of dispute.

(*c*) Fibers derived from the median groups of cells, especially in the anterior horn, so-called commissural cells, turn inward toward the median line, decussating in the anterior commissure. After entering the anterior horn of the opposite side they ascend on this side with the fibers mentioned under (*a*), forming long (?) nerve tracts. In the medulla they possibly join the fillet (probably after being interrupted in the cells of the substantia reticularis in the tegmentum), and accompany it in its subsequent course to the cortex.

4. From the cells in the columns of Clarke the fibers of the central pathway enter the direct cerebellar tract of the same side (*Cb* in the sections). In this they ascend and, joining the restiform body in the medulla at its ventral aspect, accompany this structure into the white matter of the cerebellum and terminate in the vermiform process (in the tegmental nucleus of the opposite side?).

Such, briefly described, is the course of the sensory central neurons for the trunk and extremities. It appears, therefore that a part of these neurons passes to the cortex directly through the fillet (decussating in the decussation of the fillet), while another part passes directly to the cerebellum through the direct cerebellar tract. A third portion, chiefly in the anterolateral tract, ascends only as far as the substantia reticularis of the tegmentum in the medulla oblongata (some of them undergoing decussation in the anterior commissure). From this point—that is, beginning in the nuclei of the substantia reticularis (?)—we must assume another centrocortical neuron for the conduction to the cortex. A part of these fibers (anterior ground bundle) are said to join the *superior fillet;* in this structure, therefore, the great mass of the central sensory neurons eventually passes to the cortex. The other part also ascends in the substantia reticularis of the tegmentum, at least as far as the optic thalamus.

A disputed point in this description is the part played by the *decussation in the anterior commissure.* Many authors deny that such a decussation exists, and maintain that there is only a direct conduction in the anterolateral tract. The posterior commissure also contains a few decussating fibers, but their significance is not well understood. The course of the fillet after leaving the subthalamic region, or, in other words, of that portion of the superior fillet which is interrupted in the thalamus, is also a matter of dispute, as is the part taken by the ansa lentiformis, as well as various other points. Compare the above-given description with the illustration of the sensory tracts in Figure 20.

As regards the conduction of the individual qualities of sensation, the following arrangement may be assumed as the probable one for man, judging from pathologic experience.

Sensory impressions received in the skin and deeper soft portions of the extremities and trunk are conducted in the peripheral neuron over the sensory nerves, spinal ganglion cells, and posterior roots, into the spinal cord. It is not yet definitely decided whether the various qualities of sensation have separate tracts in this part of their course, but it seems probable that they have. We know, for instance, that tactile impressions follow, or at least may follow, a different course than impressions of temperature and pain. The latter are conducted by the pathways that enter the posterior horn, and must continue in the anterolateral tract (central neuron). Part of them certainly undergo decussation (anterior commissure?) and reach the cortex, and hence the seat of consciousness, by way of the fillet.

The tactile sense and the muscle sense are said to reach the nuclei of Burdach and Goll through the long tracts in the posterior columns, and from there by the nerve path described (internal arcuate fibers), the fillet of the opposite side, by which they are conducted to the cortical center of consciousness. But it appears that for the tactile sense at least conduction is possible through other, shorter paths, those which have been described as consisting of successive relays. That the tactile sense is subsequently transmitted in the fillet is certain (for the most part, but not altogether, in the fillet of the opposite side).

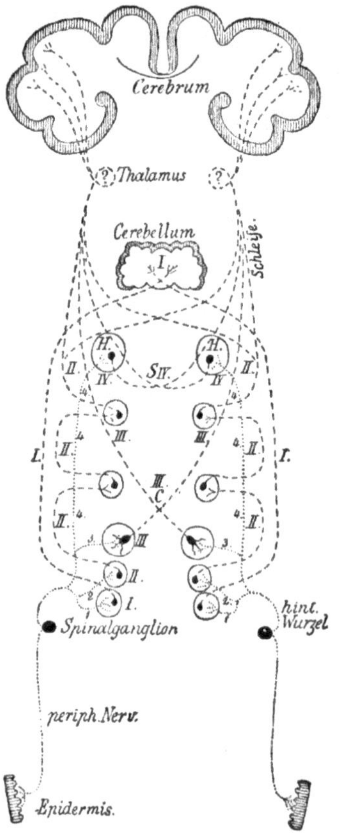

Fig. 20.—Schema of the sensory pathway: *Peripheral neuron* (dotted line): 1, 2, 3, Short, 4, long, tracts. The "switching stations" are indicated by small circles. *Central neuron* (broken line): *I*, Columns of Clarke (direct cerebellar tract); *II*, interrupted, *III*, long, anterolateral tracts. *H*, Nuclei of posterior column (f. gracilis and f. cuneatus); *SIV*, decussatio lemnisci; *Schleife*, fillet; *hint. Wurzel*, posterior root.

The **sensory nerves of the bladder, rectum, etc.**, enter the spinal cord by way of the third, fourth, and fifth posterior sacral roots, their peripheral neurons ending in the gray matter of the sacral cord. From this point, or perhaps higher up (long ascending fibers of the posterior roots?), the central conduction possibly begins in the long tracts of the posterior columns (columns of Goll?). Nothing definite is known of their further course to the higher centers.

Sensory fibers from the intestines (peritoneum, intestine, glands) also enter the **sympathetic plexuses,** especially the splanchnic plexus, and proceed to the spinal ganglia and the posterior roots. Their subsequent course appears to be through the lateral column (cerebellar lateral tract?).

The **tract of the fillet** in 'the tegmentum contains also the central neurons for the various **sensory cranial nerves** (except the olfactory and optic). We will describe them here in the order in which they enter from below upward.

1. The Sensory Portion of the Glossopharyngeo-vagus.—The *peripheral neuron fibers* run in two peripheral nerves to the cells of the petrosal and jugular ganglia, which are, therefore, the analogues of the intervertebral ganglion cells. Emerging from these in the corresponding nerve-roots, they pass through the medulla oblongata and enter the sensory glossopharyngeovagus nucleus in the posterior portion of the floor of the fourth ventricle, around the cells of which they undergo their terminal division. A part of them, instead of ending in this region, continue as the solitary bundle (fasciculus solitarius, or descending root of the glossopharyngeovagus) for a short distance downward, and end around cells in the neighborhood of this nucleus (posterior horn).

The *central neuron* originates in these cells and in the cells of the sensory nucleus. It runs toward the raphe, crosses to the other side at this point, and joins the median or superior *tract of the fillet* (described as the "scattered bundle" of the fillet). Together with the superior fillet the central neuron complex continues its way toward the cortex, lying behind the pyramidal fibers in the internal capsule, and undergoes its terminal division around the cortical cells near the termini of the fillet (posterior central convolution (?) for the fibers of taste in the base of the lower frontal convolution (?)).

2. Sensory Portion of the Trigeminus.—Its peripheral neuron fibers, after emerging from the three sensory branches of the fifth nerve, enter the cells of the Gasserian ganglion and emerge on the other side as the posterior root. After passing through the fibers of the pons they terminate around the cells of the *sensory nucleus of the trigeminus*. Some of the fibers descend for some distance to the upper portion of the cervical cord as the *descending (caudal Vc) root of the fifth nerve*, formerly erroneously called the ascending root, and are gradually lost. This descending root of the fifth nerve can be seen in any transverse section of the medulla oblongata, lying on the outer side of the remains of the posterior horn, the substantia reticularis of the tegmentum, the upper extremity of which forms the sensory nucleus of the trifacial. The "nasal root" of the fifth nerve, described above as a motor root, was formerly regarded as a sensory root; its significance is not quite clear. If, as seems probable, it is motor in character, it should also be designated *descending*. Finally, a third portion is said to pass directly from the sensory root of the trifacial nerve to the cerebellum (direct sensory cerebellar tract). On this supposition it should, therefore, be regarded as an analogue of the cerebellar lateral tract of the cord.

The *central neuron* originates in the cells of the sensory nucleus, situated in the immediate neighborhood of the descending root. The fibers, after decussating in the raphe of the tegmentum, join the superior fillet (scattered bundle) and accompany the latter toward the cortex (posterior central convolution), where they undergo their terminal division.

3. The Auditory Nerve.—The auditory nerve subdivides into two branches possessing distinct functions, the cochlear and the vestibular nerves.

(a) The *cochlear nerve* is the true nerve of hearing. The *peripheral neuron* begins in the organ of Corti in the cochlea, and enters the cells of the cochlear ganglion, an analogue of the intervertebral ganglia, also situated within the cochlea. [NOTE.—The peripheral neuron begins in the cells of the spiral ganglion, in the bony walls of the cochlea, and passes outward, terminating about the organ of Corti in the cochlear duct. The spiral ganglion is an analogue of the intervertebral ganglia.—E. D. F.] After emerging from the cochlear ganglia it enters the medulla as the cochlear nerve, and undergoes its terminal division about the cells of the ventral auditory nucleus, embracing the restiform body on each side. At this point the *central neuron* begins as the trapezoid body underneath the tegmentum and the striæ acustica above the tegmentum of the medulla, and runs to the raphe, where decussation takes place. It then continues in the *lateral inferior fillet of the corpora quadrigemina*, which is situated to the outer side of the mesial or superior fillet. Some of the fibers do not cross to the other side, but pass to the lateral fillet of the same side, and come into relation with the superior olive through fibers of the trapezoid body. The lateral fillet is continued to a point beneath the corpora quadrigemina at the region indicated, and ends partly in the posterior quadrigemina and partly, through the posterior brachium, in the median geniculate body; here it is joined by a third centrocortical tract (?). From this point it is supposed, on clinical grounds, that the central auditory pathway continues to the subthalamic region and thence to the posterior limb of the internal capsule, behind the above-described direct sensory (superior) fillet fibers of the internal capsule. From the capsule the fibers pass to the cortex of the superior temporal convolution, especially to its posterior third.

(b) *The Vestibular Nerve.*—The peripheral neuron originates where the neuron cells are situated, in the semicircular canals of the labyrinth, and undergoes its terminal division about the cells of the *dorsal auditory nucleus* and neighboring groups of cells (Deiters' nucleus), at the lateral margin of the floor of the fourth ventricle. [NOTE.—The peripheral neuron, which has its origin in the vestibular ganglion (intumescentia gangliformis of Scarpa) situated within the auditory meatus, is divided into two portions—an external and an internal portion. The external portion of the neuron passes from the ganglion and terminates about the fusiform cells in the semicircular canal. The internal portion passes dorsally, and terminates about the dorsal auditory nucleus and neighboring groups of cells (Deiters' nucleus) at the lateral margin of the floor of the fourth ventricle.] Part of the fibers unite to form the descending root of the eighth nerve, while others ascend to the cerebellum as the direct sensory cerebellar tract. From the sensory nucleus the central neuron (trapezoid body) passes up to the (mesial?) fillet, and so to the cortex, after undergoing decussation in the raphe. The cortical area is not known.

The course of the optic and olfactory nerves differs from that of the sensory nerves, which we have described so far. In fact they are not to be regarded as peripheral nerves, but as modified portions of the cerebrum, as appears from an examination of their structure and development.

4. Optic Nerve.—The *peripheral neuron* is situated entirely within the external layers of the retina. The *central neuron* begins in the internal ganglion layer of the retina, the neuron fiber in its centripetal course being contained in the optic nerve. A partial decussation takes place in the chiasm in such a way that the fibers from the left half of each retina come to lie within the left optic tract, and those from the right halves in the right optic tract. Thus the fibers from the nasal halves of both retinæ, comprising two-thirds of the entire optic nerve, undergo decussation.

It follows that each optic tract contains fibers from both optic nerves, representing both long and short nerve tracts. The long nerve tracts run within the optic tract to the lateral geniculate body, which they encircle, and pass directly to the adjoining posterior limb of the internal capsule, occupying its most posterior portion, and eventually terminate in the occipital lobe (Gratiolet's optic radiation). The existence of these *direct* fibers has been disputed, and not without good reason. The short nerve tracts, which are undoubtedly by far the more numerous, undergo their terminal division in the cells situated about the *primary* optic centers (lateral geniculate body, anterior corpus quadrigeminum, and pulvinar). From these cells a third centrocortical neuron, consisting of the nerve-fibers of these cells, joins the optic radiation in the posterior limb of the capsule, and passes to the cortex of the occipital lobe (cuneus). Here the fibers from both nerve tracts undergo their terminal division.

The optic tract also contains fibers derived from the anterior corpus quadrigeminum, which, for the most part, undergo decussation and pass centrifugally to the retina (descending optic fibers). Their significance is not clear.

5. Olfactory Nerve.—The *peripheral neuron* is represented by the olfactory nerves which begin in the specialized epithelial cells of the membrana olfactoria, the analogues of spinal ganglion cells. These nonmedullated fibers go to the olfactory bulb and terminate around the cells situated in that structure, which form the olfactory glomeruli. From this point the *central neuron* (mitral cells) continues within the olfactory tract. Some of the fibers undergo decussation in the anterior commissure, while others pass directly to the cortex in the gyrus fornicatus and gyrus hippocampi. (The fornix, corpora albicantia, and various bundles of fibers in the thalamencephalon also form part of the "olfactory fibrillation" and its association bundles.)

As in the case of the motor nerve tract, the *central neuron* for the most part undergoes decussation, while the *peripheral neuron* does not. (See Fig. 18.) Hence most impressions are conveyed to the cortex of the opposite hemisphere, and only a smaller part to the cortex of the same hemisphere, again resembling the conditions in the motor tract. However, the proportion of fibers going to the hemisphere of the same side is greater in the sensory than in the motor pathway.

We now turn to the discussion of the connections between the motor and the sensory pathways.

Both the peripheral motor and sensory neurons and the central motor and sensory neurons are physiologically connected with each other, the connection between the former being known as the *reflex path*, that between the latter as the *pathway of conscious volitional reaction*.

(a) **The Reflex Paths.** — By a reflex we mean a motor act performed automatically (nonvolitionally) in response to a sensory impression. The entire act is confined to the peripheral neurons,[1] which, therefore, form the reflex tract (reflex arc). The reflex arc is composed of a sensory portion contributed by the sensory peripheral neuron, a motor portion contributed by the motor peripheral neuron, and a connecting link formed by a branch of the sensory neuron after its entrance into the spinal cord or brain-stem. The latter is known as the *reflex collateral*, and has been described on page 51 as the short process of the posterior spinal roots passing to the motor cells in the anterior horn (under 5). The reflex tracts become medullated very early in fetal life, in accordance with the well-known fact that the first movements of the embryo are reflex in nature.

1. The Cutaneous and Tendon Reflex Arcs. — The course of these reflex arcs is better known than that of any other. The sensory portion is formed by the periph-

[1] It is still undecided whether any reflex paths exist in the sympathetic nerve (reflex center in the ganglia of the sympathetic).

eral sensory neuron, the connecting branch by the reflex collaterals which ramify among the cells of the anterior horn. It is probable that only a part of the cells in the anterior horn are concerned in this reflex. We distinguish a short and a long reflex arc.

(*a*) The *short reflex arc* consists of a collateral which passes directly from the posterior column through the posterior horn to the cell in the anterior horn (plantar reflex, patellar reflex, spinal reflexes).

(*b*) The *long reflex arc* is formed by the reflex collateral splitting up about a cell in the anterior horn. From this cell an ascending and a descending branch, with several collaterals, pass to one or more motor ganglion cells which may be situated at various levels of the anterior horn and brain-stem. This gives the possibility of reflex movements being transmitted to more remote muscle groups. The fibers of the posterior longitudinal bundle appear to be concerned in this function (reflex transmission of sensory impulses to the movements of the eye).

The localization of some of the reflexes belonging to this group is seen in Plate 13. (For more detailed description see Part IV, 3.)

2. The Complicated Reflex Arcs.—We have very little definite knowledge of the course of these reflexes. The *pharyngeal, nasal,* and *bronchial* reflex arc is composed of sensory fibers from the trifacial, glossopharyngeal, and pneumogastric nerves and the corresponding motor nerves, the pneumogastric and spinal accessory.

The *conjunctival reflex* is composed of fibers from the trigeminal and facial nerves.

The *pupillary reflex* is composed of fibers from the optic and oculomotor nerves (corpora quadrigemina—oculomotor nucleus?). The reflex collaterals evidently pass from the sensory nerves to the corresponding motor nuclei. It is supposed that the cortex is also included in some of these reflex arcs. We are still without any sufficient data for the localization of other important reflexes connected with the auditory, optic, and other nerves. (For a detailed description of these reflexes see Part IV, 4.)

The reflexes for the functions of the bladder and rectum are situated in the sacral cord. (See sensory and motor paths for these organs.)

(b) **The Volitional Pathways.**—Superimposed above the reflex arc, which is composed of the two peripheral neurons, there is a second arc, formed by the *central* sensory and motor neurons and their connecting fibers in the cerebral cortex. This arc effects the transmission of a conscious sensory impulse to a volitional motor act.

At the same time the central motor neuron exercises an inhibitory, and the sensory central neuron a controlling, influence on reflex processes.

All *conscious processes* are enacted in the cerebral cortex, in which the sensory nerve tracts end and the motor nerve tracts begin. The cerebral cortex also contains the connecting fibers between the motor and sensory portions of the cortex. It is improbable, although conceivable, that the sensory neuron fibers terminate directly about the motor ganglion cells; it is more likely that one or more neurons of another kind (transcortical) are interposed. (See the schema on Plate 17.)

A study of the development of the fetal and childish psychic activity affords an approximate idea of the character of conscious processes in the cerebellar cortex. Although it does not actually begin until after birth, yet a series of sensory and reflex processes are enacted even during intra-uterine life.

The first movements are undoubtedly reflex in character, since, as has been already stated, the reflex arcs early assume a medullary sheath. Since the fibers in the tegmentum (fillet) become medullated long before those in the central motor tracts, it is evident that there is a primary transmission of sensory impressions from the entire periphery of the body to the cerebral cortex, especially the posterior central convolution and the parietal lobe, forming

THE VOLITIONAL PATHWAYS—IDEATION.

the basis for the volitional activity that develops later. The neurons and neuron complexes situated in these areas possess the peculiar property of permanently preserving these sensory impressions as *memory pictures*, and reproducing them later under certain conditions. In this they are assisted by the *primary association processes* (connections with other cortical neurons, and corresponding chemic and physical processes in the structure of the neurons?).

After the child is born, another set of memory pictures, produced by the sound-waves that reach the upper temporal convolution through the lateral auditory fillet, are *stored up*. In like manner also are stored up the *visual impressions* which pass through the optic radiation and are deposited in the occipital lobe, especially in the cortex of the cuneus and in the gray matter surrounding the calcarine fissure. In addition there is a similar storing-up of olfactory and gustatory impressions.

These groups of memory pictures, which, as we have seen, are localized in different portions of the cortex, are connected by means of the *secondary association processes* with each other and with memory pictures in the hemispheres both of the same (association tracts in the stricter sense) and of the opposite side (commissural fibers). Thus each individual psychic process is associated with a distinct complex of specially trained neurons, belonging both to the projection and association fibrillation; these associated and cooperating neuron articulations may be designated as *neuron elements*.

It is by means of these association processes between the neuron elements that *ideation* takes place. Every idea or concept consists of a collection of associated memory pictures. The higher associations form the ideas, and the connection between these higher associations gives rise to logical mental processes. The reproduction of this association is called a *concept*. Only a part of all the associations is actively engaged at any definite time, the other part remaining dormant. The organ of the intellect is, therefore, the association fibrillation. The sum of the active associations plus the newly arrived sensory impressions make up the greater part of the *contents of consciousness*. Hence consciousness is subject to continual change.

It is probable that a considerable portion of the association fibers are concerned in what is known as subconsciousness (unconscious associations). In addition to the above-named sensory impressions there is another set of impressions which reach the cerebral cortex and which are worked up into *unconscious associations*. These include the muscular and articular impressions which are conducted toward the center in the early reflex processes. They are deposited in the central convolutions, probably in the immediate vicinity of the motor centers, and form the so-called *innervation feelings*, produced by the muscular activity of the various motor acts (kinesthetic memory pictures).

By the reproduction of these memory pictures of innervation—feelings which are deposited in postfetal life and connected with each other by unconscious associations—conscious volitional muscular activity is in some way made possible and subjected to the necessary control. A volitional movement is, therefore, merely the external expression of *certain concepts*. The path by which the impressions are transmitted from the endings of the sensory central neurons to those of the central motor neurons, which must be situated in the cortex, is the true analogue of the reflex collaterals of the peripheral neurons.

Perhaps an example will serve to illustrate the foregoing discussion. On Plate 17, Figure 3, we see the reflex arc: the sensory portion, *sp* (brown), the reflex portion, *r*, the motor portion, *mp* (blue). Above the reflex arc we see the central tract for conscious actions: the sensory portion (green), the connecting neuron (black), and the motor portion (red). The memory pictures of the special sense impressions and muscular sensations are deposited around the sensory (green) fibrillations in the cortex—that is to say, in the commissural and association neurons of the cortex (black) which go to, and come from, other areas in the cortex.

If the toe is irritated, there is a reflex twitching in the corresponding leg (reflex arc from the brown neuron to the blue, reflex transmission in the lumbar cord); at the same time the sensory irritation is transmitted by means of the green neuron to the cortex, where it becomes associated with various mental pictures and produces the well-known sensation of pain. As a second irritation is threatened (association with recent optic impressions), the painful sensation sends a message through the motor tracts (red-blue) necessary for the movement of the leg, by means of the corresponding *innervation* feelings (paracentral lobule), which convey the impulse to the muscles they supply.

Among the various cortical activities that are set in motion in this way we are chiefly interested in the act of speech. As the child learns to speak the sound pictures of the words that it hears are deposited in the superior temporal convolution of the left hemisphere (word-sound center, *sensory speech center*). In order to understand the meaning of the sound pictures (their interpretation) the associative activity by which they are encompassed is necessary.

The sensory speech center is connected by means of the fasciculus uncinatus with the *motor speech center*, which is situated at the base of the inferior frontal convolution on the left side (Broca's convolution). In this area, or at least in its immediate neighborhood, the innervation feelings (kinesthetic memory pictures) of all the muscular movements necessary for the act of speech (tongue, mouth, palate, larynx) are deposited by constant exercise and imitation. The production of these movements in response to an impulse from the sensory speech center ultimately leads to the complicated muscular acts necessary for the production of letters, words, and sentences. If by any accident the hearing of the child is destroyed, the power of learning to speak is necessarily lost and the child becomes a deaf mute. The processes that go on while the child is learning to speak are constantly accompanied by association processes with memory pictures in other centers, especially visual and tactile images. The greater the number of images stored up in the cortex, and the more effective the associations between them, the greater will be the intellectual capacity of the brain in question. The speech centers, like those which preside over reading and writing and which will be discussed below, are found only in one hemisphere—in the left hemisphere in right-handed people, usually in the right hemisphere in left-handed people. The motor speech center is probably identical with the centers of the facial, hypoglossus, etc. The speech tract (see p. 47) connects these centers in the left hemi-

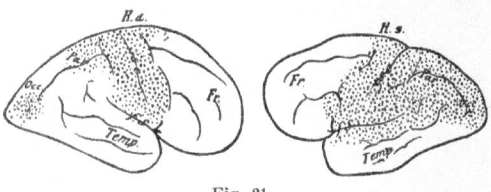

Fig. 21.

sphere with the nuclei of the seventh, twelfth, and other nerves on both sides of the brain.

When the child learns to read, the graphic memory pictures are deposited in the visual center in the occipital lobe (the interpretation of written speech is lodged principally in the angular gyrus). They reach the consciousness, however, only by association with the auditory center and with the motor speech center, because, in learning to read, the graphic image is always converted into an auditory image and into a motor speech image (reading aloud). In later life many people are more and more able to dispense with these association processes.

In learning to read, the graphic images are deposited as innervation feelings of the movements concerned in writ-

SPEECH, WRITING, ETC.

ing in the center for the right arm, and in the adjoining posterior third of the middle frontal convolution.[1] They become intimately associated with visual and auditory images on that side of the brain; therefore, the motor graphic images of the letters are produced before the visual images.

In some individuals the visual graphic associations are more prominent, while in others the kinesthetic associations are better developed. Hence the cortical areas in which these processes are enacted are the central convolutions, the superior temporal convolution, and the convolutions of the parietal and occipital lobe. The frontal lobe

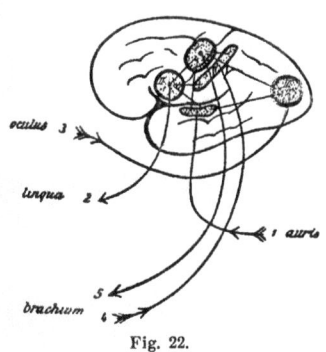

Fig. 22.

is regarded as the anatomic basis of the higher intellectual functions. But it is to be remembered that the complicated processes by which we are enabled to think necessitate very complex associations, the sum of which can not possibly be confined to the activity of a single lobe.

It is seen by Figure 21 that the left hemisphere is the more important as regards the distribution of the centers. The "*latent*" cortical areas are white. The dotted areas correspond with the psychosensory and psychomotor areas,

[1] Some authorities place the writing center in the inferior parietal lobule.

projection tracts and association tracts, while the other convolutions of the cortex (white) are said to contain exclusively association fibers. (For the details see Plate 21.)

Figure 22 is intended to illustrate the processes concerned in the acts of speech, writing, etc. The connections effected in speaking, writing, and reading are seen in the following scheme:

1. Sensory speech tract . . . . I center.
2. Motor speech tract . . . . II center.
3. Optic tract . . . . III center.
4. Kinesthetic tract for movements required in speaking and writing IV center.
5. Motor tract for writing . . . . . V center (center for the arm).

By x we will designate the ideation, which is not regarded as bound to a particular center, but rather as the effect of the entire associative activity. A part of the more important associations is added (as a).

Learning to speak: $1\ (a\ 3) - I \overset{x}{\overbrace{- II\ (a\ IV)}} - 2.$

Learning to read: $3 - \overset{x}{\overbrace{III - I\ (a\ IV)}} - II - 2.$

Learning to write: $3 - \overset{x}{\overbrace{III - I\ (a\ IV,\ a\ II)}} - V - 5.$
Spontaneous speech: $x - II\ (a\ IV,\ a\ I) - 2.$

Spontaneous reading: $3 - \overset{x}{\overbrace{III - I\ (a\ IV)}} - II - 2.$
Spontaneous writing: $x - I\ (II) - III - V\ (aIV) - 5.$
Imitative speech [1]: $1 - I - II\ (a\ IV) - 2.$
Imitative writing: $3 - III - V\ (a\ IV) - 5.$
Writing from dictation: $1 - I\ (a\ III) - V\ (a\ IV) - 5.$

To avoid repetition, any further important particulars in regard to the physiology of other portions of the brain will be referred to under the head of General Symptomatology, Part IV, 3, Topical Diagnosis.

A word in regard to the *coordination* of motor acts. Even the slightest motor act necessitates the cooperation

---

[1] If mechanical, without concept associations (x).

of several muscle groups. The regulation of the proper working of the various muscles concerned in any simple or complicated act is called *coordination*.

Even a very simple muscular act requires the coordination of antagonistic muscles; how much more then the complex motor processes made up of a succession of different single acts, such as walking, speaking, etc., where not only each individual motor act, but also the proper chronologic succession, requires careful regulation.

Cooperating muscle groups derive their peripheral and probably also their central neurons, or at least a part of them, from cells that are intimately connected with each other (coordination centers and coordination tracts of the brain and spinal cord). Thus the nuclei of the ocular muscles and the nuclei of the hypoglossus are very intimately connected. Even a single cell may send out through the collaterals motor impulses to various muscles, and thereby assist in the coordination of the muscular act.

The sensory impressions, especially impressions of muscular sense, play an important part in coordination, and it still remains to speak of this controlling influence and of the influence of the cerebellum on static coordination.

There is no doubt that the cerebellum exercises an influence on the static coordination and equilibrium of the body in the erect position and while walking. For this purpose it receives, through centripetal nerve tracts, the impressions of muscular sense, and optic, tactile, and other impressions from the periphery of the body. That portion of the posterior column which does not join the fillet makes its way from the nuclei in the posterior cord through the restiform bodies to the cerebellum. We further know that the cerebellum receives fibers through the cerebellar lateral tract (function unknown), from the vestibular nerve (semicircular canals—organ of equilibrium?), and from the trigeminus (direct sensory cerebellar tract). In the interpretation of the cerebellar influence on coordination, however, we are still in the speculative stage.

As the cerebellum possesses various connections with the cerebrum, it is quite conceivable that it may exert some controlling influence on the motor centers in the cortex, and, therefore, indirectly on muscular activity. But, unfortunately, it does not appear to be directly connected with these centers.

The fibers of the pons connect the cerebellum with the ganglia in the opposite side of the pons, where, as we have seen, both the frontal and the temporo-occipital pontal tract terminate. It appears, therefore, that each hemisphere of the cerebellum is in direct communication with the frontal, temporal, and occipital lobes of the opposite cerebral hemisphere.

In addition, there is a communication by means of the brachium between the red nucleus of the tegmentum (which in turn is connected with the optic thalamus, etc.) and the opposite hemisphere of the cerebellum. Although these connections between the cerebellum and cerebrum are well known, their functions are not understood; but it may be said that they appear to be in some way associated with coordination.

There is some anatomic basis for the theory that the muscles are directly influenced by the cerebellum. The cerebellum is connected, by means of the olivary fibers in the restiform body, with the olive of the opposite side, and from this point the central tegmental tract (mesial fillet) is continued upward, while the "olivary tracts" descend in the lateral column to cells in the anterior horn (?). When all is said, however, we must admit that we have no definite knowledge on this point.

It remains to be mentioned, in regard to the cerebellum, that it does not contain any separate centers like those in the cerebrum. Any one part of the cerebellum can be supplied by another. In general it may be said that it is credited with a *static*, *tonic*, and *sthenic* influence on muscular activity.

PART IV.

GENERAL PATHOLOGY AND TREATMENT OF DISEASES OF THE NERVOUS SYSTEM.

(Plates 58 to 72.)

1. The Causes of Diseases of the Nervous System.

THE diseases of the nervous system may be either primary affections of the nerve substance itself, or secondary to diseases of other tissues of the body, more particularly those in the immediate neighborhood of the brain (blood-vessels, membranes, bones, etc.). The most frequent causes of these secondary nervous diseases are:

(*a*) Degeneration of the vascular apparatus and its consequences (arteriosclerosis, thrombosis, embolism, rupture, aneurysm), giving rise to various nutritive disturbances or to mechanical compression and destruction of the nerve substance.

(*b*) Acute or chronic inflammatory processes in the cerebral and spinal meninges (acute tubercular, syphilitic meningitis, etc.) and in the bones of the skull and vertebral column (osteomyelitis, caries, gumma). These processes may lead to compression and nutritive disturbances, or they may spread by continuity to the nerve substance.

(*c*) Tumor formations of every kind in the tissues named (sarcoma, carcinoma, osteoma, solitary tubercle, gumma, cysticercus). These usually lead to compression of the adjacent nerve substance. Similar injuries may also be produced by cicatrization.

(d) Metastatic processes derived from purulent foci (pyemia, pulmonary abscess), tubercular foci, or malignant tumors in other organs.

(e) Intoxication in consequence of toxic materials being taken up or formed in the blood when diseased foci are present in other parts of the body (diphtheria, septicemia, erysipelas, typhoid, syphilis, nephritis, diabetes, etc.).

(f) General constitutional diseases (anemia, cachexia, chlorosis, etc.).

The diseases mentioned under (e) and (f) are frequently included among the **primary diseases** of the nervous system. In addition this group embraces a series of other toxic and infectious diseases which manifest themselves in the nervous system itself: poisoning by lead, arsenic, secale, and alcohol; acute poliomyelitis, acute myelitis, tabes dorsalis, acute neuritis, etc.

Here belong also the diseases due to embryonal predisposition (muscular atrophy, hereditary systemic diseases, etc.) and the group of **functional diseases** of the nervous system.

Diseases are termed functional when, with our present methods of examination, it is impossible to demonstrate any anatomic change in the nervous system to account for them. In such diseases we lack, therefore, an exact knowledge of the seat and character of the disease. They are considered, correctly or incorrectly, as disturbances in the transmission of the nervous function (due to molecular, chemic morbid processes). As our methods of examination are perfected their domain is constantly diminishing. They include at present hysteria, neurasthenia, genuine epilepsy, chorea, and a series of psychic disturbances, such as melancholia, mania, etc. In contradistinction to the functional diseases just mentioned, nervous diseases with demonstrable anatomic alterations are termed **organic and localizable diseases.**

Nervous diseases are also divided according to their etiology. Thus we speak of **endogenous diseases** when they are due to organic predisposition, and of **exogenous or acquired diseases** (toxic, infectious, etc.). But in view of our imperfect knowledge in regard to the etiology, and especially for didactic reasons, it is advisable in the classification to take account of the other principle as well.

In regard to endogenous diseases of the nervous system, or such as are due to faulty embryonal predisposition, it may be said that there is a group of diseases, one or the other of which may appear repeatedly, either in the same or in a similar form, in various members of the same family. How the defect, whatever it may be, originally entered the family we are unable to explain.

As in the case of most organs,—heart, kidney, liver,—the parenchymatous material used up in the function of the organ can not be completely replaced in old age, and a senile atrophy of the organ must therefore result, especially of its parenchymatous elements. We can readily understand, therefore, that in many individuals this senile exhaustion of individual organs or parts of organs may occur prematurely if those individuals have not originally been supplied with the necessary vital force. In such cases atrophy of the parts will take place as soon as the power of replacing the used-up material is lost (cirrhosis of the liver, contracted kidney, etc.). The same principle applies to various nerve tracts. Owing to some embryonal defect the nerve tract is gradually destroyed, often many years before the death of the individual, and nothing will avail to arrest the destructive process (involution diseases).

Recently the theory has been advanced that the choice of the nerve tracts which degenerate in this way is determined by the character of the function which they subserve. Moreover, that those tracts which are used most (reflex tracts, sensory tracts, pyramidal tracts) are most liable to undergo this degeneration, especially if any nutritive disturbances already exist in other parts of the body (cachexia, intoxication). This theory appears to be confirmed by some cases and disproved by others.

Even in the exogenous diseases of the nervous system, congenital or acquired, predisposition, the true nature of which is not well understood, undoubtedly plays an important rôle. In many diseases it is possible to demonstrate one or more concurrent exciting causes, such as undue mental exertion, excesses of all kinds, and a countless variety of constitutional diseases.

2. Pathologic Alterations in Nervous Diseases.

The disease may affect arbitrarily a certain portion of the nervous system and the nerve-cells and nerve-fibers which it may happen to contain (diffuse or focal diseases, in the spinal cord: transverse myelitis). Again, it may be confined to a combination of cells or fibers or even entire neurons which are anatomically and functionally related to each other; or, finally, it may involve an entire pathway (system diseases).

If two or more different combinations of neurons or tracts are attacked at the same time, we speak of a **combined system disease.** In focal diseases, for instance, the corresponding area of nervous substance is destroyed by an extravasation of blood. There results from this a defect on the surface of the organ, or a cavity within the substance of the organ, in which the remains of the coloring material of the blood can often be demonstrated long afterward, although the greater part of the contents may have undergone absorption.

In nutritive disturbances, such as arterial obstruction, compression, or inflammatory processes, softening or suppuration takes place if pyogenic micro-organisms are present. The cells and nerve-fibers involved undergo necrosis and degenerate completely. The products of decomposition, consisting of granules of fat and albumin,

SECONDARY DEGENERATIONS.

are carried off by the leukocytes (granule cells). In this case also a defect or a cyst finally results. The neuroglia surrounding a defect becomes greatly thickened, and forms an envelop which also partially fills the cavity of the cyst itself. This process of cicatrization eventually results in shrinking of the affected focus.

But in addition to these inflammatory consequences every focal disease gives rise secondarily to a number of other morbid processes. We have the so-called **secondary degenerations**, both ascending and descending, varying in the different nerve tracts and in part extending throughout the entire nervous system. The mechanism of these secondary degenerations is as follows:

Every neuron cell, as we have seen, exercises a nutritive influence on its component parts, the processes. Destruction of the cell or interruption of its connection with the corresponding cell-fiber is followed by secondary degeneration of the distal extremity of the fiber. The neuron cell itself also suffers secondary alterations if the fiber is divided in its continuity and the function is thus interfered with. After a solution of continuity has taken place, the degenerative process begins immediately in that part of the neuron which is nearest the periphery,—that is to say, its terminal divisions,—and eventually spreads to the entire course of the system affected. In other words, the degenerative process in any portion of a fiber separated from its cell begins at the periphery and works toward the controlling cell. If the solution of continuity is complete and sudden (trauma), the degeneration takes place in a few weeks or months, and an irreparable gap results at the site of the degenerated nerve tract. Regeneration, which takes place only in peripheral nerves, is effected by the proliferation of germinal cells from cells of the sheath of Schwann, which eventually succeed in reconstructing the nerve-fiber.

Secondary degeneration, or complete loss of the fiber, is to be distinguished from secondary atrophy or simple diminution in the bulk of fibers and cells. It occurs when the connection with the primary focus is only mediate, although the normal function is suspended.

Disease foci in the cerebral cortex give rise to secondary degeneration of the projection and association fibers which take their origin at that point. In the case of the latter degeneration is usually only partial, because function may still be carried on by means of collaterals which may have escaped. Secondary degeneration also occurs in the optic thalamus. Secondary atrophy develops in the various parts of the subthalamic region, the fillet, the red nucleus, and the brachium of the opposite side, while the remaining pathways and nuclei escape.

In lesions of the mesencephalon there is ascending and descending degeneration of the fillet and degeneration of the red nucleus and of the optic tract, while atrophy occurs in the ganglia of the pons, the brachia, the corpus dentatum of the cerebellum, etc. In lesions of the cerebellum degeneration takes place in the restiform body, inferior olive, middle peduncle of the cerebellum, etc., while atrophy takes place in the red nucleus of the opposite side, the brachia, etc. Lesions of the spinal cord are followed by ascending degeneration of the sensory pathways, especially the long pathways (columns of Goll, the cerebellar lateral tract), and descending degeneration of the motor pathways (pyramids, anterior and lateral columns of the cord, etc.). (For further details see Plates 65 to 72.)

Some pathways appear to possess the faculty of undergoing degeneration in both directions—as, for instance, the tract of the fillet. These nerve paths probably contain fibers of different origin.

Under the microscope the anatomic alterations appear to be practically the same in primary as in secondary degeneration of the nervous tissue. But it is to be remembered that, apart from coarse morphologic alterations, we know very little of the more delicate morbid processes in the nerve-cell and nerve-fiber. In the ganglion cells the protoplasm becomes cloudy, then degenerates, and finally shrinks. The cell becomes separated from its processes and the latter may eventually disappear entirely, or we may have the formation of vacuoles and abnormal pigmentation. The nerve-fibers swell up to five or even ten times their normal size, the medullary sheath breaks up into drops and finally undergoes absorption, while the axis-cylinder may disappear either before or after the degeneration of the sheath (degenerative process). The spaces left by the disappearance of the nerve-cells and fibers become filled with a close network of newly formed neuroglia containing numerous blood-vessels with thickened walls; frequently round-celled infiltration and granule cells may be seen. (See p. 79.) The final stage is a so-called sclerosis or substitution of cicatricial connective tissue for the degenerated nerve-fibers. (See Plate 63.)

3. Symptomatology and Topical Diagnosis of Nervous Diseases.

The nervous tissues may react to the various morbid processes in one of two ways: either they are stimulated to a morbid activity or the function is inhibited and finally abolished altogether. Frequently the two phenomena merge into one another, so that in the beginning of the disease the irritative symptoms will be more pronounced, and, as the disease progresses, the paretic phenomena or abolition of function become more conspicuous.

Disease of the motor corticomuscular pathway may give rise to irritative symptoms in the form of general convulsions, muscular spasms (tonic or persistent, and clonic or intermittent), coarse and fibrillar muscular twitchings, and to paralytic symptoms in the form of weakness (paresis or paralysis) of one or more groups of muscles, depending on the extent of the diseased area.

Disease of the sensory pathway may be followed by irritative symptoms in the form of violent neuralgic pains, morbidly increased sensibility (hyperesthesia, hyperalgesia), and by paralytic symptoms in the form of impairment or complete loss of sensibility or only of special kinds of sensation (anesthesia, analgesia, thermo-anesthesia). A disease of the pathways of coordination produces partial or complete loss of coordination in muscular movements (ataxia: motor ataxia, static ataxia).

The character of the symptoms depends less on the nature of the morbid process than on its localization and extent. In this connection it is important to distinguish between focal and system diseases. In the latter the symptoms are much more constant and logical than in the former, in which, of course, they vary according to the topography of the diseased focus. The interpretation of the symptoms of nervous diseases rests on the following principles:

A lesion of the **central motor neuron** is followed by paralysis of the muscles which it supplies, the muscular action being withdrawn from the control of the will power. Since the central neuron undergoes decussation, the paralysis must affect the opposite half of the body. The paralysis is spastic,—that is to say, the affected muscles offer a resistance to passive movements,—the muscular tone is heightened (hypertonia), and the muscles evince a tendency to undergo spontaneous shortening (contractures). Except for a moderate degree of "atrophy from disuse," there is, as a rule, no true degenerative muscular atrophy —that is, the amount of protoplasm in the muscle is not diminished. The reflex arc is not interrupted; on the contrary, the reflexes are heightened. If the lesion is in the vicinity of the cells of this neuron (cortex, central convolutions), the initial irritative symptoms may consist in involuntary twitchings of the muscle or muscles affected, motor irritative symptoms, tonic and clonic spasms, epileptiform convulsions (on one or both sides of the body), choreic movements, or slow involuntary incoordinate movements, athetosis, or involuntary excessive and unusual movements of the fingers, etc.

A lesion of the **peripheral motor neuron** is also followed by paralysis of the affected muscle, but as the lesion is situated below the decussation of the neuron, the paralysis will be found on the same side of the body. In this case the muscle is flaccid,—that is, there is no resistance to passive movement,—muscular tone is diminished (hypotonia, atonia), and there is no tendency to contractures. The rapidity with which the muscle undergoes degenerative atrophy depends on the character of the disease (the protoplasm of the muscle-fibers becomes cloudy, and then breaks up into granules and is absorbed). The muscle is finally converted into a fibrous mass after the protoplasm of the muscular fibers has completely disappeared. This change can be seen microscopically in a fresh section of muscle. The degenerated muscle tissue shows the atrophied fibers, which have a reddish color, while the sound tissue is dark red. (See also Electric Diagnosis in Part IV.)

The reflex arc is interrupted and the reflexes are therefore abolished. The fibrillary muscular twitchings, in which only very small fasciculi of the affected muscles participate, without producing any motion in the muscle, are often to be regarded as irritative symptoms; the muscle may be in a condition of constant undulatory vibration until this symptom also disappears.

In lesions of the *sensory pathway* sensation is affected on the opposite side of the body in disease of the *central*, on the same side in disease of the *peripheral*, neuron. The differences in the symptoms are, however, not so marked as in lesions of the motor pathway. The irritative symptoms, consisting of violent neuralgic attacks of pain, are referred to the posterior roots (peripheral neuron).[1]

Since the motor tract traverses the entire nervous sys-

[1] **Painful sensations** are also said to occur in central disease or focal disease in the last third of the posterior limb of the internal capsule.

tem, and in its course from the medulla downward the central portion successively gives off the peripheral parts, the motor symptoms observed in focal diseases affecting the central pathway are utilized, so to speak, as the abscissa, while the other focal symptoms correspond with the ordinates and thus indicate the level of the lesion.

We shall now proceed to a description of the symptoms of focal and system diseases.

I. SYMPTOMS OF FOCAL DISEASES.

A. Cerebral Diseases.

These are divided into direct or focal symptoms in the true sense of the term, and indirect or remote effects on neighboring portions of the brain, and, finally, into general symptoms depending on the nature and development of the lesion. The latter include fever, cachexia, vomiting, headache, and disturbances of the psychic activity. Extensive lesions are accompanied by disturbance of consciousness (coma, somnolence). The following description includes, of course, only the direct focal symptoms.

1. Symptoms of Cortical Lesions.—(a) **Frontal Lobe.**—A disease of the frontal lobe often runs its course without producing any symptoms. If the diseased focus is very extensive, there may be psychic disturbances (apathy, dementia, lack of concentration). If the posterior segment of the inferior frontal convolution on the left side is principally involved, there will be motor aphasia. If the lesion is even more extensive and includes the arm center in the central convolutions, there may be agraphia also (inability to write spontaneously). In lesions of both frontal lobes, especially tumors, disturbances of movement of the trunk (consisting of a kind of ataxia) and of phonation have been observed.

(b) **Central Convolutions.**—Disease of the upper third and of the paracentral lobule is followed by spastic paralysis of the entire lower extremity of the opposite side—*crural monoplegia;* irritative symptoms, if present, consist in clonic twitchings and choreic or athetoid movements of the leg.

Lesion of the middle third is followed by spastic *monoplegia brachialis* of the opposite side, and sometimes by irritative motor phenomena in that extremity.

Lesion of the lower third gives rise to facial monoplegia of the opposite side, and sometimes to twitchings in this portion of the territory of the facial nerve. Only the *lower* muscles supplied by the facial are involved.

Lesion in the area below and in front of the center for the face is followed by *lingual monoplegia*, or paralysis of the hypoglossus, on the opposite side; the tongue is turned toward the paralyzed side.

If the diseased area in the central convolutions is extensive and includes more than one center, it follows, of course, that more groups of muscles on the opposite side will be involved—partial or total hemiplegia (with total paralysis of the extremities, the facial and hypoglossus nerves, and of speech). The irritative symptoms in cortical lesions in this area, especially when due to trauma, consist in cortical, partial, or Jacksonian epilepsy. They are characterized by the successive irritation through the association bundles of all the motor centers in the order of their position, beginning with the one in the primary focus, so that the convulsions occur in the same order on the opposite side of the body (leg, arm, face, or in the inverse order). Moreover, they may even be conveyed to the other hemisphere by means of the commissural fibers. There is also a sensory Jacksonian epilepsy, similar to the motor variety, which manifests itself as an irritative condition in the sensory and speech centers.

In the case of focal disease situated in the central convolutions of both hemispheres there will be bilateral spastic paralysis, *diplegia facialis, brachialis,* etc. (or pseudobulbar paralysis).

The paralysis in these cases is spastic (see p. 82). The tendon reflexes on the paralyzed side, and frequently on the other side as well, are heightened, while the cutaneous reflexes on the other side are often diminished.

(c) **Parietal Lobe.**—A lesion of this lobe is sometimes followed by disturbances of sensation in the opposite half of the body (muscular and cutaneous sensations); the nature of this disturbance (hemianesthesia) is not very well understood. Lesion in the angular gyrus may be followed by disturbances in the oculomotor muscles, such as ptosis of the opposite eye and deviation of both eyeballs toward the side of the lesion (conjugate deviation). A lesion of the inferior parietal convolution (angular gyrus) on the left side is said to produce alexia, or inability to read, while the power of speech is not affected.

(d) **Occipital Lobe.**—Destruction of one occipital lobe is followed by the visual disturbance known as *hemianopsia*, or blindness of the temporal half of one retina and the nasal half of the other, or vice versâ. For instance, if the left lobe is destroyed, there will be blindness of the left half of each retina, or, in other words, loss of vision in the right half of the visual field—*right-sided hemianopsia*. If the lesion is more extensive, especially if situated in the left hemisphere, there may be loss of visual memory pictures and their associations, or *psychic blindness*—that is, inability to interpret or perhaps only to name an object seen (visual aphasia). If the lesion is unilateral, there may be total cortical blindness.

(e) **Temporal Lobe.**—Destruction of the superior temporal convolution in the left hemisphere is followed by loss of the auditory word-sound memory images and their associations, or *sensory aphasia*—that is, inability to understand the meanings of words, although the power of speech is retained.

In bilateral lesions there may be *cortical deafness* or sound-deafness.

(f) **Mesial Surface of the Hemispheres.**—The paracentral lobule belongs to the central convolutions; the cuneus to the occipital lobes. Destruction of the uncinate gyrus (gyrus hippocampi) is said to be followed by *central anosmia*, and a lesion of the posterior basal segment of the parietal lobe, by a *central ageusia;* the symptoms are pronounced only in bilateral lesions.

(g) **The Insula.**—A lesion of the left side of the insular region produces a disturbance in the associative activity between the speech centers (probably because of destruction of the fasciculus uncinatus). There is a partial inability to form words and sentences—*paraphasia*, etc. There is a want of control of the sensory speech center.

2. **Lesions of the Centrum Semiovale.**—These often produce no symptoms at all. If the lesion involves the destruction of nerve paths leading from the above-mentioned cortical areas (subcortical lesions), the same symptoms may be produced as in destruction of the cortex, except that there are usually no irritative phenomena. Thus there may be monoplegia, aphasia, hemianopsia (optic radiation), and hemianesthesia. As the central motor pathways tend to converge as they descend into the white matter, a great number of fibers are often involved in a comparatively small lesion. Whereas in cortical lesions monoplegia predominates, total or partial hemiplegia more frequently results from subcortical lesions.

Lesions of the corpus callosum usually produce no symptoms.

3. **Lesions of the Internal Capsule.**—(*a*) Destruction of the anterior limb usually does not give rise to any demonstrable symptoms.

(*b*) Destruction of the posterior limb, if the knee only is involved, produces paralysis of the facial (lower) and of the hypoglossus (if on the left side, aphasia) of the opposite side. If the lesion is bilateral, diplegia; if the central portion is involved, hemiplegia of the arm and leg of the opposite side; if the seat of the lesion is in the posterior portion, partial hemianesthesia of the opposite side of the body, hemianopsia, and sometimes impairment of hearing (?). As a rule, the lesion is so extensive that the greater part of the internal capsule is destroyed, and in that case all the phenomena mentioned are present together (total hemiplegia of the face, tongue, arm, and leg of the opposite side of the body, with hemianesthesia, hemianopsia, etc.).

The eye muscles, the muscles of mastication, the upper branches of the facial, and the muscles of the neck and trunk are paralyzed only in bilateral lesions, as they have an independent innervation on both sides of the body.

4. Lesions of the Corpus Striatum.—Lesions of the corpus striatum do not appear to be necessarily productive of any symptoms, and the phenomena that usually accompany them are to be attributed to involvement of the adjacent inner capsule (indirect symptoms).

5. Lesion of the optic thalamus, especially when bilateral, is followed by disturbances of the psychic reflexes, such as laughing, weeping, etc.

In addition to disturbances of coordination choreic irritative phenomena and muscular atrophy, developing with unusual rapidity on the other side of the body, have been referred to lesions in this area.

Destruction of the posterior section of the optic thalamus (pulvinar) is followed by partial hemianopsia.

6. Lesions in the subthalamic region are followed by crossed hemianesthesia (lesion of the fillet).

7. Lesions of the Corpora Quadrigemina.—The symptom produced is a peculiar disturbance of the gait—stumbling, uncertain gait, cerebellar ataxia, explained either by participation of the brachium or by remote effects on the adjoining cerebellum (?). This peculiar gait, however, can be utilized as a sign of disease in the corpora quadrigemina only when it is combined with other symptoms, as, for instance, ophthalmoplegia. This form of paralysis may be *nuclear*, or due to lesion in the oculomotor *fibers*, and may be either unilateral or bilateral, according to the situation; bilateral especially in the nuclear form (probably on account of the close proximity of the nuclei). Lesions in the more anterior nuclei situated in the lateral wall of the third ventricle appear to produce paralysis of the internal muscles of the eye (the ciliary muscles, sphincter pupillæ). If the lesion is situated beneath the anterior corpora quadrigemina, paralysis of the internal rectus, superior rectus, and levator palpebrarum superior is produced. The other nuclei of the ocular muscles are situated more posteriorly. The abducens escapes. If the lesion involves the tegmentum under the corpora quadrigemina (fillet), there will be incomplete hemianesthesia of the opposite side. Injury to the crusta produces hemiplegia of the arm and leg on the opposite side, and sometimes facial and lingual hemiplegia.

If the lesion is unilateral, there will be total hemiplegia of the opposite side, with oculomotor paralysis of the same side (peripheral neuron of the same side). This form of hemiplegia in which, in addition to the decussating central neurons, certain uncrossed peripheral neurons are involved in the lesion, is known as hemiplegia alternans (crossed hemiplegia). If the lesion is bilateral, the symptoms are modified in accordance with the extent of the lesion.

The paralyzed eye muscles, of course, undergo degenerative atrophy, while the paralysis in the extremities is spastic in character and is not accompanied by any marked degeneration of the muscle tissue. If the optic tract or the lateral geniculate body is involved in the lesion, there is total or partial hemianopsia. In destruction of the posterior corpus quadrigeminum and the median geniculate body the hearing is often disturbed, especially if the lesion is bilateral.

8. Lesions of the Pons.—Unilateral lesions may be followed by hemianesthesia (fillet), brachiocrural hemiplegia (pyramidal tract of the opposite side of the body); paralysis of the muscles of mastication on the same side (motor portion of trigeminus, peripheral neuron) or more posteriorly of the facial muscles of the same side (peripheral neuron, hemiplegia alternans). Destruction of the nucleus of the abducens is followed by combined oculomotor paralysis (rectus externus of the same, and rectus internus of the opposite, side). The sensory symptoms will be anesthesia in the region of the trigeminus of the same side, disturbances in the sense of taste, disturbances in the power of articulation (partial inability to form letters) on account of involvement of fibers from the facial and hypoglossus. Irritative symptoms in the form of vertigo, ataxia, and trismus may be present. Bilateral lesions produce corresponding symptoms.

9. **Lesions of the Medulla Oblongata.**—If the lesion is unilateral, there may be brachiocrural hemiplegia and hemianesthesia of the opposite side of the body. If the internal arcuate fibers in the posterior segment of the medulla are involved, there may even be bilateral hemianesthesia (the lesion is situated below the decussation of the fillet). In addition there may be paralysis of the hypoglossus of the same side (peripheral neuron, hemiplegia alternans).

The tongue is turned to the side of the lesion; the muscles on the corresponding side are degenerated. As a result, there will be defective articulation or bulbar speech, unaccompanied by disturbance of the speech center (dysarthria labiolingualis).

Among other symptoms may be mentioned paralysis of the muscles of deglutition, paralysis of the epiglottis (failure of the cartilage to close the larynx), dyspnea, aphonia (paralysis of the vocal cords), and circulatory disturbances, especially if the lesion is bilateral. Destruction of the inferior olives is said to be followed by disturbance of the equilibrium.

10. **Lesions of the Cerebellum.**—The symptoms produced are susceptible of many interpretations and are very indefinite. Disease of the vermiform process gives rise to disturbances of the equilibrium, attacks of vertigo, cere-

bellar gait (tottering gait), vomiting, and sometimes occipital headache.

A lesion in the middle cerebral peduncle is also followed by disturbance of the equilibrium, vertigo, and forced movements (rotation about the longitudinal axis).

Lesions of the hemispheres may be unproductive of symptoms.

11. Focal Diseases at the Base of the Brain.—They are characterized chiefly by simultaneous paralysis of several cranial nerves, either of the same or of both sides (oculomotor, abducens, facial, trigeminus, hypoglossus, etc.).

A lesion may at the same time involve the crusta (hemiplegia of the opposite side), the optic tract, and the chiasm.

It follows that there may be a great variety of symptoms, and their interpretation should not be difficult. (For further details see under Peripheral Nerves in this chapter.) The most frequent associations are the second and third, the sixth and seventh, and the tenth, twelfth, and eleventh (inferior, middle, and posterior fossæ of the skull).

To review briefly, a typical cerebral paralysis consists of spastic hemiplegia and hemianesthesia of the opposite side.

In cortical lesions monoplegia predominates; in lesions of the capsule, simple hemiplegia; in lesions of the corpora quadrigemina and crusta, hemiplegia with crossed oculomotor paralysis (hemiplegia alternans superior).

In lesions of the pons, hemiplegia with paralysis of the trigeminus and facial of the opposite side (hemiplegia alternans media).

In lesions of the medulla oblongata, hemiplegia with lesion of the hypoglossus, etc., of the opposite side (hemiplegia alternans inferior). This is, of course, on the supposition that the lesion is unilateral. As the projection fibers gradually approach each other more and more in their downward course to the cord, there is a correspondingly greater possibility of the lesion producing bilateral symptoms. This is even more the case in focal diseases of the spinal cord.

B. Focal Symptoms in Lesions of the Spinal Cord.

As hemiplegia is the typical cerebral lesion, so paraplegia, or paralysis of the extremities, not only of one, but of both sides, is the typical lesion of disease of the spinal cord. This is due to the fact that the motor paths for both sides of the body are situated comparatively near each other in the spinal cord, and are, therefore, very apt to be affected by the same lesion.

Unilateral injuries of the spinal cord may, however, occur from stab wounds or compression by a tumor, and present a very typical symptom-complex, known as Brown-Séquard's paralysis, which differs from the clinical picture seen in other diseases of the spinal cord.

Thus a unilateral lesion of the spinal cord is followed by paralysis of the extremities on the same side, varying more or less according to the seat of the lesion, while sensory disturbances are produced chiefly on the opposite side of the body. This distribution follows naturally from the fact that the motor paths decussate above the beginning of the spinal cord in the decussation of the pyramids, while the sensory paths enter the spinal cord for the most part uncrossed (anterolateral column, anterior commissure). There is, besides, a narrow zone of anesthesia on the paralyzed side, corresponding to the level of the lesion. This condition is due to injury of the uncrossed peripheral neurons of the same side at their entrance into the cord. Above this zone of anesthesia there is a narrow, girdle-like zone of hyperesthesia, due to irritation. The symptoms in a lesion of one half of the spinal cord are, however, not always so clearly marked as we have just described them. The following are the more important focal symptoms usually observed.

(a) **Lesions in the Cervical Enlargement.**—If the entire transverse section of the cord be involved, complete paralysis of both arms and legs—*paraplegia universalis*—with complete anesthesia of the trunk and extremities, results. The paralysis of the legs is spastic (central neuron), that of the arms flaccid, if the lesion is situated somewhere between the fifth cervical and first thoracic vertebræ (peripheral neuron, anterior horn). Those muscles of the upper extremity whose trophic centers in the anterior horn have been destroyed undergo a degenerative atrophy. The tendon reflexes in the upper extremities are abolished (interruption of reflex arc), while those in the lower extremities are heightened (degeneration of the central inhibitory fibers).[1] Sensation is disturbed as high up as the points of entrance of the posterior root-fibers into the diseased segments. There is also loss of sphincter control in the bladder and rectum, on account of the interruption in the central pathways of these organs. The intensity of the symptoms depends on the extent of the lesion.

The flaccid paralysis of the upper extremities affects either all or only certain groups of muscles, according to the seat of the lesion. (For further elucidation on this point see Fig. 17 on p. 52.) The most important segments of the cervical cord are the following:

α. Fourth segment: Paralysis of the diaphragm.

β. Fifth and sixth segments: Paralysis of the upper arm (deltoid, biceps, brachialis anticus, supinator longus) and possibly paralysis of the muscles about the shoulder.

γ. Seventh and eighth segments: Paralysis of the forearm (muscles of the forearm, triceps).

δ. Eighth cervical, first thoracic segments: Paralysis

---

[1] About ten cases have been reported in which complete division of the cord in the cervical region was followed by loss of the patellar reflex. Various explanations have been given for these exceptional cases,—degenerations in the lower reflex arc, interference with the reflexes by shock, or, according to others, degeneration of the cerebellar tracts to the reflex center,—but at all events the observations are not sufficiently numerous to affect the truth of the above statement in ordinary cases.

of the small muscles of the hand and occasionally pupillary symptoms. (See under C, 1.) In all these cases the muscles undergo degenerative atrophy.

(b) **Lesions in the Thoracic Region.**—The upper extremities are not affected unless the first thoracic segment is involved (small muscles of the hand).

The lower extremities are the seat of a spastic paralysis —*paraplegia inferior*—with heightened reflexes (patellar reflex and ankle-clonus, etc.). There is complete anesthesia (analgesia, thermotactile anesthesia, loss of muscular sense, etc.), extending to that region of the trunk the sensory fibers of which enter the posterior roots at the level of the spinal lesion.

There is also loss of control of the bladder and rectum. Those muscles of the trunk whose special segments are included in the lesion undergo degenerative atrophy, which, however, is usually very difficult to demonstrate (intercostal, lumbar, dorsal, abdominal muscles, etc.). (See Electric Diagnosis, p. 109.) If the paraplegia persists for a great length of time, the patellar reflexes may become faint, probably in consequence of the formation of contractures.

(c) **Lesions in the Lumbar Enlargement.**—Motion and sensation are affected in the lower extremities only. There is a *flaccid inferior paraplegia* (peripheral neuron), with complete anesthesia, the muscles of the legs undergoing degenerative atrophy and the reflexes being abolished. Also total paralysis of the bladder and rectum (sphincter reflex preserved, see p. 123).

If the lesion is situated in the upper portion of the lumbar enlargement, the muscles supplied by the crural nerves (quadriceps, psoas) degenerate; if in the lower portion, those supplied by the sciatic (glutei, peronei, muscles of the calf). (For more detailed information on the distribution of the paralysis see Fig. 17, p. 52.)

(d) **Lesions in the Sacral Region.**—The thigh in this case escapes, while some of the small muscles of the foot become paralyzed and atrophy. There is anesthesia in the outer border and toes of the foot and in the region of the anus. There are total vesical and rectal paralysis and loss of sphincter reflexes. The patellar reflex is preserved because the lesion is situated lower than the reflex arc.

(e) **Lesions in the Cauda Equina.**—The symptoms are, in the main, those of a lesion in the lumbosacral enlargement, as the cauda contains all the nerve tracts which begin at that point. If those fibers of the crural nerves that are the highest in situation escape, the paralysis will appear chiefly in the muscles supplied by the sciatic nerves —that is to say, there will be a flaccid paralysis of the peronei and other muscles of the leg and of the small muscles of the foot (sometimes also of the flexors of the thigh and of the glutei). Sensation is disturbed in the region supplied by the sciatic and sacral nerves. There is complete paralysis of the bladder and rectum if the nerves of these organs are involved. The patellar reflex will be preserved if the roots of the crural nerves are unaffected, otherwise it will be abolished. The Achilles tendon reflex and the sphincter reflex are abolished.

If the posterior roots at the corresponding levels are involved in the spinal lesion, violent neuralgic pains will appear in the region of their distribution; sometimes these pains correspond only to the highest roots affected by the disease. Not infrequently reflex muscular twitchings in the paralyzed limbs are observed in such cases.

C. Symptoms Observed in Lesions of the Peripheral Nerves.

Lesions of the peripheral nerves are followed by motor and sensory disturbances which correspond exactly to the region of their distribution; hence a knowledge of these symptoms is indispensable for an exact diagnosis. (See Plate 27.)

The paralysis is flaccid in character, and the muscle undergoes degenerative atrophy if the lesion is severe (peripheral neuron). The sensory disturbances are strictly confined to the distribution of the cutaneous nerve (in long-standing conditions the boundaries tend to become indistinct). Painful and abnormal sensations are often complained of (paresthesia, formication, pricking sensations, furry feeling, burning, etc.). The reflexes are diminished or lost if their corresponding arcs are included in the damaged nerves.

I. **Plexus Paralyses.**—The symptoms of plexus paralyses are made up of a mixture of the paralytic symptoms of all the nerves which compose them; the clinical picture, therefore, presents many variations. Some of the most typical and frequent lesions are the following:

(a) **Erb's Paralysis of the Brachial Plexus.**—This involves the fifth and sixth cervical roots, destruction of which is followed by paralysis and atrophy of the deltoid, biceps, brachialis anticus, supinator longus, supra- and infraspinatus. Accordingly, there is inability to raise and abduct the arm or to flex the forearm.

(b) **Paralysis of the Lower Portion of the Brachial Plexus.**—This involves the eighth cervical and first thoracic roots, and leads to paralysis and atrophy of the small muscles of the hand and anesthesia in the ulnar region. In addition there may be, if the first dorsal segment is involved, oculopupillary symptoms, as miosis, diminution in the palpebral fissure, retraction of the bulb. The lower extremities are not involved, the paralysis differing in this respect from that observed in lesions of the corresponding segments of the spinal cord.

II. **Lesions of the Cranial Nerves.**—The distribution of the sensory disturbance for the various nerve trunks is shown in Figures 23 to 25. The symptoms in lesions of the individual nerves are the following:

1. **Olfactory Nerve.**—Anosmia of the corresponding half of the nose and parosmia (disagreeable odors).

2. **Optic Nerve.**—Amaurosis of the corresponding eye and of the entire visual field, differing in this respect from

LESIONS OF THE CRANIAL NERVES.

disease of the optic tract, in which there is hemianopsia, or loss of vision in one half of the field. In some cases there is only impairment of the visual acuity—contraction of the visual field and atrophy of the optic nerve (white papilla), mydriasis, and reflex pupillary rigidity, while sensual reaction is preserved.

In *lesions of the chiasm* there is bitemporal hemianopsia (destruction of the internal retina bundles which decussate at this point).

3. Oculomotor Nerve.—Ptosis (paralysis of the levator palpebræ superioris); inability to rotate the eye inward and upward (internal rectus; superior and inferior oblique); crossed diplopia; fixation of the bulb in downward and outward rotation, owing to contracture of the intact external rectus. Further, there are pupillary rigidity and dilatation (mydriasis), due to interference with the action of the sphincter muscle, and loss of accommodation for near objects on account of paralysis of the ciliary muscle.

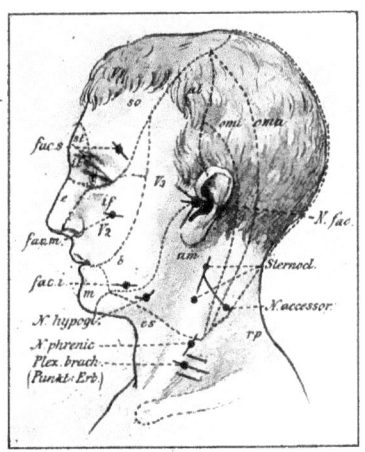

Fig. 23.—V_1, First division of trifacial: *so*, Supra-orbital; *st*, supratrochlear; *it*, infratrochlear; *e*, ethmoidal; laterally, the lacrimal. V_2, Second division of trifacial: *if*, Infra-orbital; labial. sup. V_3, Third division of trifacial: *at*, Auriculotemporal; lab. inf.; *m*, mental. *am*, Auricularis magnus; *omi*, occipitalis minor; *oma*, occipitalis major; *cs*, subcutaneus colli sup., med., inf. (cervical. ant.); *rp*, cervical. dorsal. The dots indicate where the electric current should be applied to the facial, phrenic, brachial plexus, etc.

4. Trochlear Nerve.—Diplopia in looking downward (superior oblique).

5. Trifacial Nerve.—(*a*) *Supra-orbital Branch.*—Anesthesia in the skin of the brow and bridge of the nose and of the conjunctiva. (See Fig. 23, V_1.)

(b) *Infra-orbital Branch.*—Anesthesia of the skin on the cheeks and alæ of the nose, anesthesia of the palate and disturbance of the sense of taste (Fig. 23, V_2).

(c) *Inferior Maxillary Division.*—Anesthesia of the skin over the lower jaw and of the mucous membrane of the

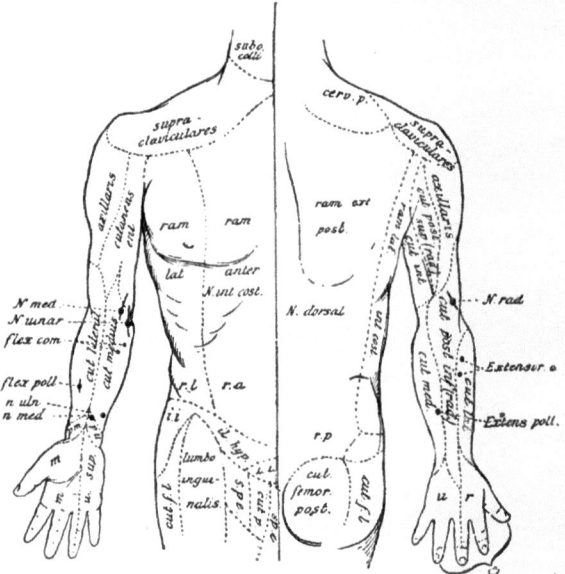

Fig. 24.—*m*, Median; *u*, ulnar; *r*, radial; *rp*, posterior root; *ii*, ilioinguinal; *sp.e*, external spermatic.

tongue and mouth (Fig. 23, V_3). Disturbance of the sense of taste in the anterior segment of the tongue; paralysis of the muscles of mastication and disturbance in salivary secretion; trismus (spasm of the muscles of mastication due to irritation). Irritation of the sensory branches gives rise to trifacial neuralgia of greater or less extent, according to the seat of the lesion; paresthesia also occurs.

6. Abducens Nerve.—Inability to rotate the eye outward (external rectus); deviation of the bulb inward, and diplopia on the same side when the glance is directed downward.

7. Facial Nerve.—Paralysis of the facial muscles of expression (upper and lower facial), of the mouth, the nose, the orbicularis oculi, and of the forehead. The lines of the face are obliterated; the palpebral fissure can not be closed (lagophthalmus); puckering of the lips, as in whistling, impossible; inability to retract the angles of the mouth, as in laughing.

Paralysis of the digastric (posterior belly), stylohyoid, etc., does not produce any symptoms.

If the lesion is situated within the Fallopian canal, the chorda tympani from the second (third?) branch of the trifacial may be involved and the sense of taste may be disturbed in the anterior segment of the tongue.

The irritative symptoms are: Convulsions of the muscles named, convulsion of the facial nerve, or tic convulsif, and blepharospasm. These symptoms may, however, be due to reflex or central irritation.

8. Auditory Nerve.—(*a*) *Cochlear Nerve.*—Deafness, paresthesia.

(*b*) *Vestibular Nerve.*—Disturbance of the equilibrium; attacks of vertigo and vomiting, with tinnitus aurium and whistling noises—Ménière's symptom-complex, especially in hemorrhage in the labyrinth.

9. Glossopharyngeal Nerve.—Partial disturbance of the sense of taste (posterior segment of the tongue); anesthesia of the nasopharynx.

10. Pneumogastric Nerve.—(*a*) *Sensory Branch* (*True Vagus*).—Anesthesia of the pharynx, larynx, esophagus, trachea, and bronchi.

(*b*) *Motor Branch* (*in part derived from the Spinal Accessory*).—Dysphagia (paralysis of the esophagus); disturbances of the gastric, cardiac, and respiratory functions. Paralysis of the recurrent (paralysis of the vocal cords); if bilateral, aphonia.

11. Spinal Accessory Nerve.—(*a*) *Pneumogastric Branch* (*Inferior Laryngeal*).—Paralysis of the recurrent, as above. Paralysis of the muscles of the palate and pharynx.

(*b*) *External Branch.*—Paralysis of the sternocleidomastoid and in part of the trapezius (difficulty in turning the head and raising the shoulder); irritative symptom, spasm of the spinal accessory or spastic torticollis (wryneck).

12. Hypoglossus.—Paralysis of one side of the tongue (when the tongue is protruded, it turns toward the paralyzed side), disturbances of the articulation (difficulty in forming the various letters).

III. Lesions of the more important Spinal Nerves.—For details, which can not be given here, see Plate 27 and text. The distribution of the anesthesia, which is not mentioned here, will be found in Figures 24 and 25.

1. Great Occipital Nerve.—Occipital neuralgia, anesthesia. (See Fig. 23.)

2. Phrenic Nerve.—Paralysis of the diaphragm; irritative symptoms, spasm of the diaphragm, singultus.

3. Axillary Nerve.—Paralysis of the deltoid (difficulty in raising and abducting the arm), anesthesia. (See Fig. 24.)

4. Posterior Thoracic Nerve.—Paralysis of the serratus magnus (the scapula projects from the thorax; inability to raise the arm beyond the horizontal).

5. Anterior Thoracic Nerves.—Paralysis of the pectoralis major, inability to abduct the arm.

6. Musculocutaneous Nerve.—Paralysis of the biceps and brachialis anticus (flexors of the forearm); anesthesia (see Fig. 24, *lateral cutaneous nerve*).

7. Radial Nerve.—Paralysis of the triceps (extension of the forearm); anconeus (absence of prominence of the anconeus in flexion of the forearm); paralysis of the extensors of the hand, of the first phalanges of the fingers, and of the extensors and abductors of the thumb. (For anesthesia see Fig. 24, *N. cut. post. sup.* and *inf, ram. dorsalis.*) The hand and fingers are paralyzed and limp (wrist-drop), and the grip is considerably weakened on account of paralysis of the antagonistic muscles.

8. Median Nerve.—Paralysis of the pronator muscles when the forearm is flexed, and of the radial flexors of the hand, distal phalanges of the fingers, and of the thumb (including the flexor carpi ulnaris and the ulnar portion of the flexor digitorum profundus). Inability to adduct the thumb and to extend the distal phalanges of the second, third, and, rarely, of the fourth fingers (lumbricales). (Anesthesia of the integument supplied by the volar branch of the median nerve, see Fig. 24, *m.*)

9. Ulnar Nerve.—Paralysis of the flexor carpi ulnaris and of the ulnar portion of the flexor digitorum profundus (distal phalanges of the fourth and fifth fingers); inability to flex the first phalanges (interossei) or to extend the distal phalanges of the fourth and fifth fingers (lumbricales). Inability to adduct the thumb and flex its first phalanx. Owing to the unopposed action of the antagonistic muscles, the so-called claw-hand (*main en griffe*) is produced. (Anesthesia, see Fig. 24, *uln. superfic* and *dorsalis.*)

In paralysis of the ulnar, median, and radial nerves the power of writing is much impaired, and the patient finds it impossible to seize and hold things. Complete paralysis of even one of these nerves materially affects the usefulness of the hand.

10. Intercostal Nerves.—Sensory irritative symptom, intercostal herpes zoster. Anesthesia.

11. Crural Nerve.—Paralysis of the psoas (elevator of the thigh) and the quadriceps (extensor of the leg); inability to walk or to assume a standing posture. Patellar reflex abolished. (For anesthesia see Fig. 25, *cruralis*, middle and infernal femoral cutaneous, and saphenous nerve.)

102   GENERAL PATHOLOGY AND TREATMENT.

12. Obturator Nerve.—Paralysis of the adductor muscles of the thigh. (Anesthesia, see Fig. 25.)

13. Sciatic Nerve.—Paralysis of the foot and toes and of the flexors of the leg. (Anesthesia, see Fig. 25, peroneal, anterior cutaneous, and plantar nerves.) Irritative symptom in the sensory fibers of the nerve, sciatica.

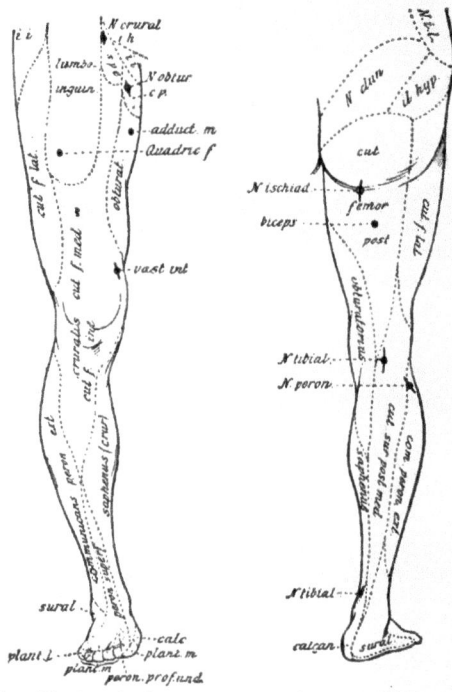

Fig. 25.—*ii,* Ilio-inguinal; *sp.e,* external spermatic; *ih,* iliohypogastric; *c.p,* posterior cutaneous.

14. Peroneal Nerve.—Paralysis of the peronei, tibialis anticus, extensores digitorum et hallucis. Inability to flex the foot on the leg (foot-drop). The outer border of the foot is lower than the inner border. Contractures in antagonistic muscles (muscles of the calf); talipes equinus or talipes varus (if the extensor digitorum only is involved) may be produced. (Anesthesia, see Fig. 25, *peroneus*.)

15. Tibial Nerve.—Paralysis of the muscles of the calf; plantar flexion impossible; inability to flex the toes. By contractures in the antagonistic muscles (peronei extensors) talipes calcaneus is produced. (For anesthesia see Fig. 25, plantar nerve.)

D. Symptoms of Disease of the Sympathetic Nerve.

The paralytic symptoms in lesions of the cervical portion are the following:

Miosis, diminution in the palpebral fissure, retraction of the bulb, oculopupillary symptoms (fibers from the first dorsal segment, see p. 94). Anomalies in the sweat secretion of the corresponding half of the body. Among the irritative symptoms have been mentioned dilatation of the pupil and disturbances in the circulation. Disease of the cardiac and splanchnic branches gives rise to disturbances in the cardiac, intestinal, and glandular functions, our knowledge of which is very imperfect. The nature of the disturbance appears to be chiefly motor, possibly also to some extent secretory.

II. THE SYMPTOMS OF SYSTEM DISEASES.

The term system diseases, as has been mentioned, is applied to symmetric processes affecting an entire nerve path, consisting of functionally and anatomically related fibers or neurons, or, at first, to processes affecting portions of neurons successively. In the end the disease rarely, if ever, confines itself to one portion of the neuron (cell or fiber), the entire neuron being eventually destroyed. The localization of the primary seat of the disease is often of the highest importance for the clinical course. Unfortunately, our knowledge of the direction in which the processes spread and their point of origin is in many particulars very incomplete.

1. **System Diseases of the Corticomuscular Motor Path.**—(a) **Of the Central Neuron (Simple Spastic Spinal Paralysis).**—Cases of this kind are rare. Anatomically we find a slowly progressing symmetric degeneration of the entire pyramidal tract (origin, the motor pyramidal cells in the cortex). Clinically we observe a slowly increasing spastic paralysis of the extremities, with heightened reflexes, but without muscular atrophy and without disturbances of sensation or of the bladder.

(b) **Of the Peripheral Neuron.**—This leads to flaccid muscular paralysis, with degenerative muscular atrophy. The reflexes are abolished. The primary seat may be in the neuron cell or in the neuron fiber.

a. **Primary Cell Diseases.**—The morbid process presents a great variety of symptoms, depending on the seat of the lesion.

Chronic and acute ophthalmoplegia, when the lesion is in the nuclei of the ocular muscles.

Bulbar Paralysis (Chronic and Acute).—The seat is in the bulbar nuclei of the facial, hypoglossus, and trifacial nerves.

Spinal Muscular Atrophy.—The lesion is in the gray matter of the anterior horn, particularly in the cervical portion of the cord.

Acute and Chronic Anterior Poliomyelitis.—Inflammatory processes in the gray matter of the anterior horn, affecting the ganglion cells.

β. **Primary (?) diseases of the fibers, neurotic muscular atrophy**, peroneal type of muscular atrophy (peroneal, ulnar, and median nerves). Participation of the ganglion cells can not be excluded with certainty.

The motor form of multiple neuritis may affect all the motor nerves.

γ. **Progressive Muscular Dystrophy.**—The disease is confined to the terminal portion of the neuron—*i. e.,* the muscle.

(c) Of the Entire Pathway.—In these cases there is degeneration of the pyramidal tract and of the peripheral nerves (ganglion cells and fiber, peripheral nerve)—that is, amyotrophic lateral sclerosis and possibly bulbar paralysis. The clinical symptoms are those of spastic paralysis of the extremities, with degenerative muscular atrophy.

It is probable that numerous intermediate forms between these distinct varieties occur.

2. System Diseases of the Centripetal Sensory Path.—We do not know of any isolated affections of the central path belonging to this category. There is, however, a degeneration of the peripheral neuron (so-called tabes dorsalis) of quite frequent occurrence, in which the neuron may be affected in its entire extent. In rare cases the central pathway may also be involved (lateral cerebral and anterolateral tract). The symptoms consist in painful sensations and disturbances of sensation and coordination; the reflexes are abolished. This category also includes the sensory form of multiple neuritis.

3. The Combined System Diseases.—These include degenerative processes affecting simultaneously both the motor and the sensory paths.

(a) **Hereditary or Friedreich's Ataxia.**—The central motor neuron (pyramidal tract) and the peripheral and central sensory neuron (posterior columns, cerebral lateral tracts) are diseased. (For symptoms see Special Pathology.)

(b) **Tabes combiné,** or true tabes, with participation of the lateral pyramidal tracts, frequently with participation of other neurons—for instance, peripheral motor neurons (oculomotor, abducens, etc.).

(c) Another class of morbid diseases, better known anatomically than clinically (posterior columns, lateral cerebellar tract, pyramidal tract). Whether other cerebral tracts may become the primary seat of system disease is not known.

4. General Considerations on Methods of Examination and Diagnosis.

1. Before proceeding with the examination, the history should be carefully taken, as it is often of the greatest assistance in the diagnosis. Among others, the following points should be carefully determined:

(*a*) Heredity (nervous diseases, consanguinity of the parents, psychosis, alcoholism, suicide, tuberculosis, and syphilis).

(*b*) The previous history of the patient in regard to mode of life and habits (education, temperament, alcohol, tobacco, morphin, excesses of every kind); occupation (overexertion, manual work, lead, arsenic); former diseases (psychic and bodily injuries, acute infectious diseases, tuberculosis, and syphilis).

(*c*) The history of the present disease, its cause, mode of origin, and course.

2. The examination of the nervous system should in every instance be preceded by a careful examination of the general condition and of the state of the more important internal organs (nutrition and vigor, lung, heart, abdominal functions, pulse, urine). Particular attention should be paid to symptoms of syphilis, tuberculosis, purulent foci, malignant tumors, bone diseases, diabetes, aural and ocular diseases.

I. The Examination of the Motor Sphere.

This includes: **1. The external condition of the muscles** (atrophy, hypertrophy, folds in the muscles), to determine which, by inspection, the examiner's eye must be trained by constant study of the normal body. Atrophy in the muscles of the hand, peroneal atrophy, facial paralysis, atrophy of the shoulder-girdle, abnormal position of the extremities, etc., can be seen at the first glance. This part of the examination should include measurement of the atrophied extremities with a tape-measure and comparison with the sound side.

2. Examination for Motor Irritative Symptoms.—These include tremors of the extremities (alcoholism, morphinism, neurasthenia, Basedow's disease); we distinguish fine tremors, up to twenty a second, and slow tremors, up to six vibrations a second. Special forms are the tremor of paralysis agitans, the intention tremor in multiple sclerosis, which is rather a disturbance of coordination, and nystagmus of the eye muscles. Spasms of individual muscles or muscle groups, either clonic (interrupted) or tonic (uninterrupted), and tetanoid or tonic spasm of all the muscles of the body. A contracture is a permanent tonic condition of spasm. A convulsion is a form of extensive tonic or clonic spasm; epileptiform convulsions are periodic convulsions (also hysteric convulsions). *Choreic* movements are involuntary, but not brusque, like true convulsions; the movements are irregular and occur in the quiescent state. *Athetoid* movements are similar, but extraordinarily exaggerated movements, occurring especially in the fingers and toes. These conditions may be present in cortical lesions or after apoplexies, but may also occur without apparent cause.

Fibrillary muscular contractions have been referred to on page 83.

3. The Examination of Motor Power.—The power of each of the more important muscles should be tested separately. For estimating the power of some of the muscles, as those used in gripping, we have the dynamometer, but in most cases the strength of the muscle is determined by comparing it with that of the other side and by the resistance offered to the hand of the examiner. Proficiency in this respect can only be acquired by long practice.

The functions of all the muscles are tested in the order of the motor nerves, beginning with the eye muscles. (See Plate 27.) The extent and force of both active and passive movements should be determined, the attention being specially directed to the joints.

It is exceedingly important to examine the gait: whether it is paretic or laborious, as a result of muscular weakness; spastic, on account of abnormal muscular stiffness; ataxic, from disturbance of the coordination; hemiplegic, the patient dragging one of his legs and advancing the other by a movement of adduction instead of raising the foot (in central paralysis); or, finally, peroneal, the tips of the toes dragging on the ground because the peronei are paralyzed.

4. Examination of the Power of Coordination.—This is done by requiring the patient to carry out complicated movements of the arms, such as bringing the tips of the fingers together, and various movements of the legs. If the nicety of the movements is impaired, the condition is termed *ataxia*. It occurs in multiple sclerosis, tabes dorsalis, hereditary ataxia, multiple neuritis, etc. *Static* coordination (attitude of the trunk) is tested by requiring the patient to stand with his eyes closed; swaying under these conditions is known as Romberg's sign. In cerebellar ataxia the gait resembles that of a drunken man and is very characteristic.

5. Examination of the Electric Condition of the Muscles.

Electric Diagnosis.—This is a diagnostic procedure of the greatest value. In the electric examination we utilize the galvanic, primary, or constant current; or the faradic, induced, secondary, or interrupted current. The galvanic is the more important.

(a) **Galvanic Examination.**—The usual apparatus contains:

1. Cells containing two fluids.	Bunsen's cell	Zinc in H_2SO_4. Carbon in HNO_3.
	Grove's cell	Zinc in H_2SO_4. Platinum in HNO_3.
2. Cells with only one fluid.	Leclanché's cell	Zinc Carbon (Braunstein) in HCl_4.
	Bunsen's cell	Zinc Carbon in $KMnO_4 + H_2SO_4$,

with the addition of sulphid of mercury to replace the used-up zinc amalgam.

The chemic processes (formation of a salt) that are set up in these cells produce a difference in the electric potential between the two poles, the zinc pole (negative pole, oxygen pole) and the carbon pole (positive pole, hydrogen pole), and the neutralization of this difference by wire connections produces the galvanic electric current.

The current flows from the positive pole (anode) to the negative pole (cathode)—that is to say, from the carbon to the zinc. To assist the memory it may be remembered that C comes before Z. The electromotive force depends on two conditions: the internal resistance offered by the cells and the external resistance that the current has to overcome. The dry skin of a human being at first offers a very great resistance when it is included in the circuit. After a time the resistance diminishes and is finally overcome, the current passing without interruption.

The strength of the current is measured by means of the galvanometer, and is expressed in milliamperes, an arbitrary unit which has now come into general use.

The strength of the current can be graduated by means of rheostats (the addition of resistance coils).

The healthy muscle, when irritated with the galvanic current, reacts with a rapid and lightning-like contraction, both on opening and closing the current, the contractions taking place in the following order as the strength of the current is increased:

On cathodal closing, CCl; anodal closing, ACl; anodal opening, AO; and, finally, on cathodal opening, CO.

If the current is still further increased, a tetanic contraction takes place (CClTe before AClTe).

When the muscle is degenerating the electric reactions are somewhat different. The contraction does not take place abruptly and like a flash of lightning, but slowly, sluggishly, and in distinct, visible waves. In addition, anodal closing contraction takes place before the cathodal contraction. This morbid condition is designated as the *reaction of degeneration* (RD).

As degenerative muscular atrophy only occurs in lesions of the peripheral motor neuron (see p. 83), the presence of pronounced reaction of degeneration affords a sure means of distinguishing central disease from disease of the peripheral motor neuron. Reaction of degeneration takes place whether it is the cell or the fiber of the peripheral neuron that is the first to become diseased.

We distinguish between complete and partial reaction of degeneration. In *complete* reaction of degeneration the muscle can not be stimulated through the nerve (indirect stimulation), and if the muscle is stimulated directly, the reactions of degeneration ensue. If the degenerative atrophy has run its course and the muscle is completely converted into connective tissue (sclerosis), even the reactions of degeneration disappear in direct stimulation. If the muscle recovers, however, the reactions of degeneration disappear, the contractions become normal, and the muscle responds to stimulation of the nerve (indirect stimulation), even before the reaction of degeneration disappears.

In *partial* reaction of degeneration the muscle can still be stimulated through the nerve, and the reaction of degeneration ensues when the muscle is stimulated directly. This form occurs in milder lesions. Thus, the examination with a galvanic current enables us not only to localize the disturbance (peripheral neuron), but also to determine the *severity of the lesion*—in other words, the prognosis.

If in any case of muscular paralysis due to a lesion of the peripheral neuron the reactions of degeneration do not make their appearance within a few days, a complete cure may be expected in the course of a few days or weeks (mild form). If partial reactions of degeneration take place, the paralysis will last not less than several months (medium form). If complete reactions of degeneration occur, recovery may take place after several months (four to nine). On the other hand, the paralysis may be permanent (disappearance of the reactions of degeneration—severe form). The last-named result can not be predicted with certainty. The reactions of degeneration occur in conjunction with fibrillary muscular contractions and an atrophy in all nuclear lesions of the peripheral neuron (spinal muscular atrophy, anterior poliomyelitis, amyotrophic lateral sclerosis, myelitis, etc.); in all severe lesions of the anterior roots and of the peripheral nerves (neuritis, compression, traumatism). In addition to the qualitative alteration there may also be a quantitative change, in the form of either a morbid diminution or heightening of the excitability of the muscle. This quantitative difference, however, has not the same significance as the qualitative changes. Before we proceed with the explanation of this alteration we will describe briefly—

(b) **Examination with the Faradic Current.** — The faradic or induction apparatus in common use contains, in addition to the galvanic cells that produce the necessary primary current (usually the modified Leclanché and Bunsen), a DuBois Reymond induction coil consisting of two movable wire coils. The primary current is produced in the primary coil and generates by induction a secondary current in the secondary coil, placed above the primary coil, the induced current flowing in the opposite direction to the primary.

By means of an interrupter (Wagner hammer) the primary current is constantly interrupted, and its direction changed by means of an electromagnet. In this way a series of secondary currents are induced in the induction coil, always in the opposite direction and also alternating, the strength of the current being regulated by the distance between the secondary and the primary coils. The strength of the current is read in centimeters of the distance between the coils; the greater the distance, the weaker the current. When the reactions of degeneration are present under stimulation with the galvanic current, the muscle fails to respond either to nervous or to muscular irritation with the faradic current. If recovery takes place, the muscle responds somewhat earlier to indirect than to direct stimulation.

In regard to the quantitative changes in the irritability, it is to be remembered that the various nerves and muscles require varying strengths of current for their stimulation, depending on their position and composition. Hence one must know the average strength required to stimulate the normal muscle in order to be able to determine whether there is any morbid quantitative alteration in the excitability. The necessary current strength for the various nerves and muscles is determined at definite points,—the motor points,—and for electrodes of a definite size (normal electrode, 3 sq. cm.). The most important figures in milliamperes for the normal galvanic, and in centimeters for the distance between the coils for faradic, irritability of the nerves are the following, taken from Stintzing (the figures for the muscles are comparatively unimportant):

	Galvanic.	Faradic.
Facial nerve	1.75 ma.	121 cm.
Frontal branch	1.45 "	128 "
Mental branch	0.95 "	132 "
Spinal accessory nerve	0.27 "	137 "
Median nerve (in the arm)	0.9 "	122 "
Ulnar nerve	0.55 "	130 "
Radial nerve	1.8 "	105 "
Crural nerve	1.05 "	111 "
Peroneal nerve	1.1 "	115 "

Morbid increase in the galvanic excitability occurs especially in conjunction with the reactions of degeneration, and without the reactions of degeneration in tetany, myelitis, etc. (also of faradic excitability). Diminution in the electric excitability accompanies all the forms of simple atrophy (central palsies). Morbid diminution in the resistance of the skin occurs in Basedow's disease, in which the skin is abnormally moist.

II. Examination of the Sensory Sphere.

1. Subjective Symptoms.—These include all the statements of the patient, either spontaneous or in answer to inquiry, of painful sensations of every kind, their localization, character, and duration. We distinguish genuine pain (cause, mechanical, inflammatory, or toxic irritation of the sensory nerves) and indefinite pain of longer duration, such as headache and cardiac and gastric distress. Different from either of these varieties is the central psychic pain that occurs in neuroses and psychoses and can not be localized.

In this category belong also paresthesias or abnormal sensations, such as burning, furry feeling, formication, occurring in neurasthenia, neuritis, tabes, myelitis, etc. Insomnia occurs when the nervous system is either exhausted or abnormally excited. Vertigo is observed chiefly in circulatory disturbances of the brain (hyperemia, anemia, arteriosclerosis, epilepsy), in neurasthenia, and in diseases of the eye and ear.

2. Objective Examination of the Various Modes of Sensation in the Skin.—(a) **Tactile Sense.**—The same examination serves to determine both the tactile and the pressure sense of the skin.[1] The patient is asked to distinguish between contact with the point and the head of a pin, or with a cotton pellet or the examiner's fingers. He should be told to answer "now" whenever he feels the test-object. In order to test the patient's attention it is well to make occasional "blind tests," taking care not to fatigue the patient unduly. The examination should be repeated frequently at different times. If possible, the diseased side should be compared with the sound side of the body by going over all the various regions of the skin.

---

[1] The skin contains various sensory points or areas, where sensation for the different modes of sensation is concentrated. Thus, we speak of thermic areas, pressure areas, and pain areas; the last-named are the most numerous.

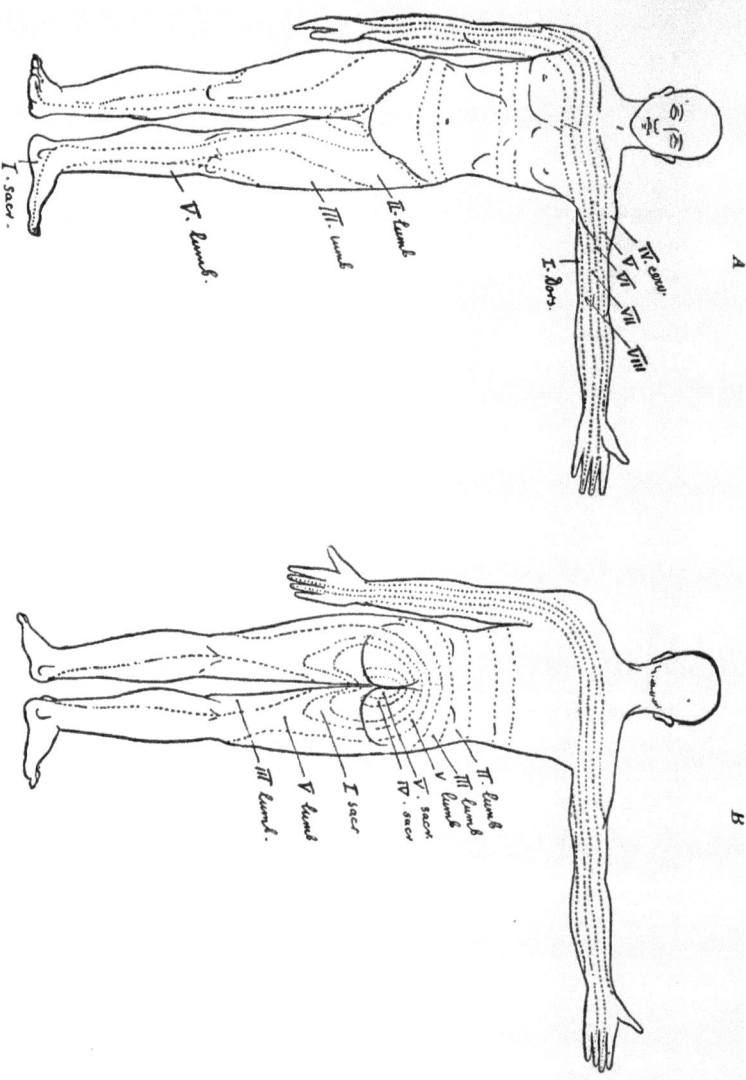

Fig. 26.—Cutaneous areas corresponding to the sensory segments of the spinal cord : *A*, Anterior, *B*, posterior, surface (after Sticker, "Münch. med. Wochenschr.," 1896, p. 194). See also Fig. 17.

It may be useful, also, to test the sensitiveness of the skin to faradic stimulation, the strength of current being indicated by the number of centimeters measuring the distance between the coils. There may be anesthesia, or total abolition of the tactile sense, when there is complete interruption of the sensory pathway, especially in focal diseases (see 3 in this chapter) and in hysteria of central origin. Hypesthesia, or diminution in the tactile sense, when there is a partial interruption of the sensory path, as in neuritis, tabes, etc.; hyperesthesia, or morbid exaggeration of sensation. (See under Pain Sense.) The extent of the anesthetic areas should be carefully outlined. In lesion of a peripheral nerve it will be found to correspond to the distribution of the nerve. (See Figs. 23, 24, and 25.) In diseases of the spinal cord the anesthetic area will be found to extend as high up as the cutaneous area supplied by the uppermost segment involved. (See Fig. 26 and under **b.**)

(b) **Localization of Sensations (Topographic Sense).**—This is tested at the same time as the tactile sense. The patient, having been blindfolded, is asked to indicate the precise spot where he feels the sensation.

The power of feeling two contact points on the skin at a given distance from each other is tested by means of a pair of compasses. The following table, taken from Weber, indicates the distances in millimeters at which the points of the compass are felt as two distinct points in different parts of the body:

Tip of the tongue	1 mm.		Arm	65	mm.
Lips (muc. mem.)	4 "		Forearm	39	"
Tip of the nose	6.5 "		Hand { volar	11	"
Cheeks	11 "		{ dorsal	28	"
Forehead	30 "		Tip of finger	2	"
Chest	44 "		Thigh	65	"
Middle of back	65 "		Leg	39	"
Buttocks	39 "		Tip of toe	11	"

The lower the number, the greater the sensitiveness of the corresponding region. In *polyesthesia* the patient mistakes a single contact for several (tabes).

(c) **Pain Sense.**—The pain sense in the individual regions of the body is tested by inserting a needle to various depths. The sense can be accurately measured with the faradic current, the strength of the current being increased up to the point of painfulness. It is only called for, however, in very delicate clinical examination. The pain sense may be diminished (*hypalgesia*) or abolished altogether (*analgesia*).

Analgesia occurs in association with loss of the tactile sense in focal diseases, hysteria, tabes dorsalis, and, by tumors, in syringomyelia.

The pain sense may be delayed—that is, it may require for its perception a summation of protracted stimuli (in tabes, myelitis, and neuritis). When this is the case, the patient first announces that he feels the contact of the object, and later expresses the painful sensation by an exclamation, as "Now!" "Ouch!" Abnormally protracted pain sense occurs in tabes and neuritis.

Hyperalgesia, or abnormal sensitiveness to contact and thermic stimuli, occurs as an irritative symptom in focal diseases, in hysteroneurasthenia, in lesions of one side of the cord, and in neuritis.

(d) **Temperature Sense.**—Cold and heat perception is to be tested separately, with test-tubes filled with iced water and with warm water (not hot). The temperature sense may be blunted or abolished. Thermo-anesthesia for both hot and cold, or for either alone, occurs in focal diseases, tabes, syringomyelia, myelitis, and neuritis. The two sensations may be mistaken for one another—perverted temperature sense (tabes, myelitis, neuritis).

3. **Sensation in the Deeper Parts of the Body.**—(a) **The sense of weight** is tested by applying different weights wrapped up in cloths and comparing the results with those obtained in a normal subject.

(b) **The power of perceiving passive motions** is tested by performing some slight passive movement and requiring the patient, who has been blindfolded, to indicate whether the limb has been flexed, extended, raised, abducted, etc.

(c) **The sense of position** is tested by placing an arm or a leg in a certain position, and, after blindfolding the patient, asking him to imitate it with the other extremity.

These disturbances, together with others that are difficult to test, such as sensations in the limbs and muscles, are designated as disturbances of the *muscle sense;* they occur in tabes, hereditary ataxia, hysteria, and in focal diseases.

4. **Methods of Testing the Special Senses.**—(a) **The Sense of Sight.**—Each eye and the homologous halves of the retina are to be tested separately. In some cases it is necessary to determine the visual acuity and the extent of the visual field by means of the perimeter. For this the reader is referred to text-books on ophthalmology. An approximate idea of the size of the visual field can be obtained by gradually bringing the hand or test-card into the visual field, while the patient keeps his eyes fixed. If, for instance, when the hand is approached from the left side of the patient toward the median line and is not perceived with both eyes before it reaches the middle line, while on the right side the hand is perceived before it reaches the middle line, there exists left-sided bilateral homonymous hemianopsia (the lesion is located in the optic tract of the right side, the primary optic centers, the optic radiation, or the occipital lobe of the right side). In the same way concentric contraction of the visual field or central defects (scotomata) may be roughly determined. Failure to perceive a visual impression in both temporal halves of the visual field (bitemporal hemianopsia) points to an affection of the chiasm. In injury of the optic nerve there is more or less amblyopia or amaurosis of the corresponding eye. (In regard to diplopia see under Paralysis of the Ocular Muscles.)

Examination of the eye-ground by means of the ophthalmoscope is indispensable in any grave disease of the nervous system. It may elicit the important sign of choked disc. This phenomenon is due to obstruction of the lymphatic flow in the sheath of the optic nerve, which occurs when the intracranial tension is increased, as by tumors. A similar condition, known as optic neuritis, in which the exudation is less profuse, may also occur in intracranial tumors and in multiple neuritis, brain syphilis, meningitis, etc. It may end in atrophy of the optic nerve, manifesting itself in pallor of the papilla, which is sharply outlined.

Atrophy of the optic nerve also occurs primarily in tabes, multiple sclerosis, and paralytic dementia.

(b) **The Sense of Hearing.**—Each ear is to be tested separately with a watch (normal distance, 3 meters and over) or by the patient's ability to hear whispering at even greater distances.

To determine whether the deafness is due to disease of the labyrinth or of the sound-conducting organs (middle ear), the tuning-fork test is employed. If a tuning-fork be first placed on the head, and as soon as it ceases to be heard by bone conduction be held before the patient's ear, one of the two following results will be obtained: (1) either the sound will again be heard (positive Rinné), in which case the disease is situated in the labyrinth (meningitis, disease of the auditory nerve), or (2) the tuning-fork will not be heard (negative Rinné)—a sign of middle-ear involvement.

In severe grades of nervous deafness bone conduction disappears entirely.

Paresthesias of the sense of hearing occur in the form of buzzing and ringing sounds in otitis, Ménière's symptom-complex, anemia, etc.; auditory hyperesthesia, in which sound perception is accompanied by pain, occurs in hysteria, hemicrania, etc.

(c) **The Sense of Smell.**—The two halves of the nose are tested separately by means of some odoriferous substances, care being taken to avoid any substance, such as

EXAMINATION OF THE REFLEXES.

ammonia, which would irritate the trifacial nerve. Oil of peppermint, balsam of Peru, oil of almond, and asafetida may be used. Excluding for the present diseases of the nasal mucous membrane, anosmia occurs in peripheral lesions (tumors, injury of the anterior fossa of the skull, atrophy of the olfactory nerve); central disturbances are rarely seen except in hysteria.

(d) **The Sense of Taste.**—The two halves of the tongue should be tested separately in the anterior two-thirds (trifacial) and posterior third (glossopharyngeal) by applying sapid substances, such as solutions of common salt, sugar, vinegar, or quinin. Ageusia, or loss of the sense of taste, occurs in lesions of the peripheral nerves (facial in the Fallopian canal; trifacial), in hysteria, and rarely in central lesions.

III. Examination of the Reflexes.

The reflexes may be heightened, diminished, or abolished.

Increase in the reflexes depends either on failure of the inhibition through the central pathways, as in exhaustion, neurasthenia, or disease of the inhibitory pathway, or on abnormal irritability within the reflex arc, as in neuritis, meningitis, tetanus. *Diminution* or *abolition* of the reflexes occurs when the reflex arc is interrupted, whether in the sensory or motor portion or in the connecting link formed by the reflex collaterals; reflexes are also absent in deep coma and in intoxications. In marked exaggeration of the tendon reflexes continuous stimulation produces a rapid succession of reflex contractions (patellar clonus, ankle-clonus). The most important reflexes to examine are the following:

1. Cutaneous Reflexes and Reflexes of the Mucous Membrane.—The plantar reflex and the reflex sensibility of the tips of the fingers are tested with a needle, by contact with heat or cold, or by tickling the part (summated impulses).

The pathway of these reflexes is imperfectly known; the sensory branch appears to communicate by means of collateral and reflex neurons (long reflex arc) with the entire motor sphere.

In unilateral lesions interrupting the pyramidal tract the cutaneous reflexes are frequently diminished, while the tendon reflexes are exaggerated.

The cremaster reflex, or contraction of the cremaster muscle following irritation of the inner surface of the thigh, and the abdominal reflex, contraction of the abdominal muscles at various levels (upper and lower reflex), elicited by stroking the skin of the abdomen, are of very little clinical significance, so far as we know. Both reflexes appear to be absent in focal cerebral lesions on the side opposite to that of the diseased focus, while in multiple sclerosis they are often absent on both sides.

The conjunctival reflex consists in closure of the lids when the conjunctiva is touched. It is absent in paralysis of the trifacial and facial nerves.

The palpebral reflex consists in closure of the lids when an object is suddenly brought close to the eye; it is absent in lesions of the optic nerve and in facial paralysis.

The pharyngeal reflex consists in a choking movement following irritation of the mucous membrane with a brush; it is absent in paralysis of the vagus and spinal accessory. The palatal reflex effects contraction of the palate after contact.

2. The Periosteum and Tendon Reflexes.—(*a*) The patellar tendon reflex is the most important. By tapping the patellar tendon while the muscles of the legs are relaxed, a contraction of the quadriceps is induced, the patient's attention being diverted by pressing his hand or separating his folded hands. If the contractions are vigorous, the leg is jerked forcibly upward. The patient should sit on the edge of a chair, with the entire sole of the foot on the floor and the leg slightly extended.

The intensity of the reflex varies widely within physiologic limits in various individuals. Exaggeration of the reflex occurs in neurasthenia, in lesions of the central motor neuron (inhibitory fibers in the pyramidal lateral tract), in irritation of the reflex arc (meningitis, tetanus, neuritis), and in exhausting diseases. The reflex is abolished when the reflex arc is interrupted (tabes, crural neuritis, anterior poliomyelitis, myelitis in the lumbar enlargement), in coma, in epileptic attacks, and in recent injuries of the spinal cord, probably as a result of irritation of the inhibitory fibers. (See foot-note, p. 93.)

The Achilles tendon reflex is subject to the same variations as the knee-jerk. It consists in twitching of the muscles of the calf when the Achilles tendon is tapped. When this reflex is exaggerated, it produces the not unusual phenomenon of ankle-clonus, elicited by forcible flexion of the foot on the leg. The more important of the periosteal and tendon reflexes in the arm are the following:

Radial and ulnar periosteal reflex, elicited by striking the styloid process of the radius or ulna; and the triceps tendon reflex, elicited by striking the tendon above the olecranon.

In addition to the reflexes mentioned, the masseter reflex should be tested. It consists in a movement of the lower jaw, elicited by striking against a piece of wood applied to the lower jaw. The clinical significance of this reflex is not very great. The pathologic alterations that occur are subject in general to the above-mentioned principles.

3. The Pupillary Reflex.—The following varieties are distinguished:

(*a*) Reaction to light, or contraction of the pupil by the action of the sphincter muscle when the same eye is illuminated (irritation of the optic nerve).

(*b*) Consensual reaction to light, which follows illumination of the other eye.

(*c*) Reaction of accommodation or contraction of the pupil in accommodating the eye to near objects; really a secondary movement.

(*d*) Converging reaction; of little clinical significance. The contraction is proportionate to the tension of the rect. med.

The reaction to light should be tested for each eye separately, so as to exclude consensual reaction. If hemianopsia is present, each half of the retina should be tested separately. It is best to use the ophthalmoscope, but for ordinary purposes it is enough to cover the eyes with both hands and then to remove one hand quickly.

Before examining the eyes it is well to determine whether the pupil is abnormally dilated or contracted. Dilatation (mydriasis) occurs in atropin and cocain poisoning, blindness, coma, epileptic convulsions, paralysis of the oculomotor, and other conditions. Contraction (miosis) occurs in morphin poisoning, tabes, paralytic dementia, meningitis, affection of the first dorsal segment, iritis, etc. Inequality in the pupils, which occurs in paralysis, tabes, meningitis, and other conditions, should not be overlooked.

The reaction to light may be abnormally sluggish or altogether lost when the reflex arc is interrupted, as in blindness due to disease of the optic nerve, in oculomotor paralysis, or in lesions of the reflex collaterals (tabes, paralytic dementia) in the corpora quadrigemina. It is also observed in coma, narcosis, and during epileptic convulsions, but not in hysteria.

In lesions of the optic tract there is *hemianopic pupillary rigidity* when the blind half of the retina is illuminated.

IV. Examination of the Functions of the Bladder and Rectum.

(a) Lesion of the Central Pathways (Myelitis Dorsalis, Focal Diseases).—In lesion of the *motor* path there is retention of the urine and of the alvine discharges; voluntary evacuation is interfered with. If the bladder is distended, there is dribbling of urine.

Lesion of the *sensory* paths destroys sensation in the bladder, and hence the desire to urinate, retention resulting.

(b) **Lesion of the peripheral pathways** and of the bladder center (reflex collaterals in the sacral portion of the cord) produces incontinence of urine and of the alvine discharges; also sphincter paralysis (lesion in the lumbar and sacral region or chorda equina), and constant dribbling of urine. The reflex contraction of the sphincter ani, which can be felt with the finger and which is present in central disturbances, is absent.

In addition to these paralytic phenomena there may be irritative symptoms of a reflex or central character, such as constant desire to urinate, tenesmus, strangury.

Vesical disturbances are very likely to result in cystitis (secondary inflammation, polionephritis, and pyemia, conditions which always threaten a patient suffering from spinal disease).

V. Examination of Trophic and Vasomotor Disturbances.

Trophic disturbances occur in lesions of the anterior horn, in neuritic processes, and in diseases of the blood-vessels, etc. The most important symptoms are redness, swelling, cyanosis, abnormal pallor, urticaria-like eruptions of the skin, erythromelalgia (painful swelling of the hands and feet occurring in paroxysms), and multiple cutaneous edema. Atrophy of the skin or glossy skin, scleroderma, atrophy of the skin on one side of the face (hemiatrophia facialis); anomalies in the sweat secretion (hyperhidrosis, unilateral sweating in hysteria and neurasthenia).

Idiopathic gangrene of the extremities occurs in Raynaud's disease, syringomyelia, and in Morvan's disease; bed-sores (in paraplegia) are only indirectly due to nervous influences. Perforating ulcer in tabes (chronic ulcer in the toes); alterations in the joints, arthropathies; swelling, thickening, and hypertrophy in tabes, etc.

VI. The Examination of the Psychic Functions.

1. Speech and Writing (Aphasia and Agraphia).—
(a) **Disturbances of the Articulation (Dysarthria).**— By this term is meant a disturbance of the speech in the peripheral pathway. There may be inability to pronounce the individual letters clearly, the pronunciation may be nasal or guttural and altogether unintelligible, accompanied with great straining of the muscles of the mouth and tongue. This occurs in bulbar diseases, in lesions of the hypoglossus and facial nerve, in malformation of the muscles used in speech, absence of palate, etc. Among special varieties are the typical *bulbar speech*, nasal speech (*rhinolalia*), and slow speech (*bradylalia*). Scanning speech occurs in multiple sclerosis. Halting speech, or *dysarthria literalis*, includes various defects in the speech, especially in the power of forming letters.

Stammering is due to abnormal spastic contractions of the muscles of speech, of central origin. Stammering is aggravated in moments of psychic emotion, while halting speech is improved. In disturbances of the articulation the labial, dental, palatal, and nasal sounds are tested separately.

(b) **Aphasia.**—Aphasia is always due to a central lesion. It may be cortical (the focus is in the cortex), transcortical (destruction of the association fibers), or subcortical (interruption in the motor pathway from the center to the periphery).

a. In *motor or ataxic aphasia* the patient is unable to say anything, but understands everything that is said to him (lesion at *II*, Fig. 13, consult p. 41).

If the patient is unable to say a single word of his own accord, there is *total motor aphasia*. If he is still able to say a few words, such as "yes" and "no," the condition is known as *monophasia* β. In *sensory aphasia*, or word-deafness (lesion at I), the patient no longer understands spoken language, but there is no disturbance of the speech-forming apparatus. The speech, however, is always impaired, because the necessary association fibers, the fasciculus uncinatus between I and II, are destroyed. The patient either misplaces his words or uses improper words to express his ideas, or the power of forming sentences is lost—*paraphasia*. One form of this is the so-called *literal paraphasia*, or stumbling over syllables, in which letters and syllables are misplaced (paralytic dementia). When the memory for words is impaired so that the patient is suddenly unable to think of a certain name of a person or object, without any impairment of the power of understanding spoken language, the condition is termed *amnesial aphasia*.

γ. Motor aphasia occasionally, and sensory aphasia very frequently, is associated with inability to write, *agraphia* (destruction of V or the association fibers connecting I and II with V; see Paragraphia).

δ. A person who may or may not be the subject of sensory aphasia may be unable to read, although there is no actual visual disturbance. This condition is termed *alexia*. The lesion is in the inferior parietal lobe (supramarginal convolution ?).

If the lesion is very extensive, these phenomena may be associated and there may be *total motor and sensory aphasia*.

ε. *Mind-blindness* is a condition in which a patient is unable to recognize the meaning of objects which he sees (lesion at III), or he is unable to find the right word for an object seen, although there is no motor aphasia. This condition is designated as *optic aphasia* (interruption of the association tracts uniting III with I and II, inferior longitudinal bundle).

Interruptions of the association tracts uniting I, III, and V produce *paragraphia* (similar to paraphasia), while interruptions of the tracts between I, II, and the supramarginal convolution produce *paralexia*. These two conditions are seen chiefly in paralytic dementia in conjunction with defective speech (stumbling over syllables).

The term *dysgraphia* is applied to disturbances in the power of writing when they are of peripheral origin, analogous to dysarthria. They include *tremulous writing* (tremor senilis, alcoholicus, etc.) and *ataxic writing* (hereditary ataxia, multiple sclerosis).

Dyslexia is a functional disturbance in the power of reading, with marked loss of endurance.

The presence of these central disturbances of the speech and other functions may be determined in the following manner: The examiner engages the patient in conversation, thus: He asks him, "How long have you been ill?" If the patient fails to answer, there may be, after excluding deafness and psychosis:

(*a*) *Deaf-mutism.*—This will be at once recognized by the patient beginning to gesticulate.

(*b*) *Total motor and sensory aphasia*, which can only be determined by inquiry of a third person.

If the patient nods, and answers other questions which can be answered by "yes" or "no" in the same way, and is evidently unable to utter a word, it is usually a sign of *motor aphasia*. If the question makes no impression on him and he does not comply with the examiner's request to close his eyes or perform other acts of this nature, there is *sensory aphasia;* but if he promptly responds by doing everything that he is asked to do, sensory aphasia can be excluded with certainty.

If the patient answers every question with the same word, such as "no, no," there is *monophasia*. If, instead of answering correctly, he misplaces his words, syllables, or letters, there is *paraphasia*. It is well to apply a rigorous test by asking the patient to pronounce difficult words and phrases, such as "electricity," "third mounted artillery brigade," and similar long words or phrases. The patient is then shown various objects, such as

AGRAPHIA. 127

a match or a lead-pencil, and is asked what they are used for. If he is unable to indicate their use, either by word or gesture, sensory aphasia and peripheral visual disturbances being excluded, there is *mind-blindness*. If the patient understands the use of the object but is unable to give its right name when asked to do so, there is *optic aphasia*.

The above-mentioned disturbances having been excluded, the patient is now asked to repeat words, sentences, and numbers. If he fails to do this correctly because his recollection of the examiner's words is imperfect, there is *amnesic aphasia*.

The next step in the examination consists in testing the power of writing. The patient is asked to write down words and numbers from dictation. If he does not write at all, sensory aphasia being excluded, there is *agraphia*, or if he is able to write only one word, such as "no," there is *monographia*. If the writing is full of mistakes and syllables and letters are transposed or omitted, there is *paragraphia*. If the patient is unable to remember for more than an instant or two what has been dictated, there is *amnesic agraphia*. In the same way the power of spontaneous writing and copying should be tested, and if the patient is able to write, he should be examined, to determine whether he understands what he has written.

To test the power of reading the patient is asked to read written or printed words and numbers. If he is unable to do so, motor aphasia and visual disturbances being excluded, there is *alexia, monolexia*, or *paralexia*. Again, the examiner should note whether the patient understands what he reads. If there is inability to remember for any length of time the letters or numbers read, it is a sign of *amnesic alexia*. A more rigorous test may be made by asking the patient to form words and numbers from certain given letters and figures.

2. Testing the Memory.—The disturbances of the memory associated with the power of speaking, reading, and writing have already been described under the head of amnesic aphasia, alexia, and agraphia.

In addition, the memory should be tested in regard to impressions acquired in early life and to more recent events, which are obtained from the history.

The examination of recent impressions includes both simple and complicated associations, single words or numbers, or rows of figures. Disturbances of the memory are designated *amnesia*. They occur in injuries to the skull, contusions, focal disease in the brain, and in dementia. The examination should include a rigorous test of all the various associations,—auditory, visual, tactile, etc.,—the details of which can not be given here.

3. **Other Psychic Disturbances.**—The examiner should determine whether there is any **disturbance of consciousness** (coma, somnolence, torpor), whether the intelligence is normal or impaired (dementia, idiocy), whether there is any morbid motor or sensory **emotional condition** (delirium, emotional disturbance with impaired consciousness, hallucinations, morbid sensory illusions of central origin, visions, morbid misapprehension of sensory impressions), and whether there are any delusions (systematized, fixed or transient flight of ideas).

The presence of **melancholia** (morbid depression), **mania** (morbid exaltation), or **hypochondria** must not be overlooked. The finding of these symptoms does not by any means justify the examiner in making a diagnosis of the psychosis of which these symptoms are supposed to be typical.

Diagnosis.

The diagnosis can be made only after a complete examination and careful review of the history. The examiner should satisfy himself in regard to the following questions:

1. Is there actually a disease of the nervous system, or is it merely simulated by anemia, tuberculosis, tenia, etc.?

2. Granted that there is a nervous affection, is it possible that some other bodily disease may be responsible for it (arteriosclerosis, tumors, diseases of the heart, lungs, stomach, kidneys, blood, etc., diabetes)?

3. Is the nervous disease functional or organic in character? This question can often be answered at once, but in many cases it requires much thought and a long course of observation. Thus, choked disc, degenerative muscular atrophy (RD), loss of the patellar and pupillary reflexes, are always due to an organic lesion. The mode of origin of the disease must be carefully considered.

4. Granted that the disease is organic, where is the lesion situated? (See General Symptomatology, Part IV, 3.) *Is it a focal disease or a system degeneration?*

5. What is the nature of the disease? The answering of this question will necessitate a careful consideration of the mode of origin of the disease, its possible connection with other diseases (infections, tumors), the site of the lesion, and the bearing of other symptoms that may be present (fever, cachexia). In many cases a single examination is not sufficient, and not rarely the course of the disease must be followed for some time before a diagnosis can be arrived at. If, as in many cases, a positive diagnosis is out of the question, the examiner must content himself with making a provisional one. It is well not to make such a diagnosis as paralytic dementia, brain-tumor, or tabes dorsalis without due deliberation, certainly never after the first examination, without very strong reasons.

5. General Remarks on the Treatment of Nervous Diseases.

The treatment of nervous diseases, more than that of any other bodily affections, demands that the attending physician should both act and think according to the dictates of psychology. Unfortunately, this part of our medical education still leaves much to be desired. But it is none the less true that a knowledge of the anatomic and clinical facts is far from being all that is required. The treatment includes:

1. **The Prophylaxis.**—No other field of medicine presents greater possibilities for the exercise of judgment in forestalling disaster, as there is no other in which so much mischief is caused by negligence on the part of the attending physician. For the guidance of the latter the following points may be emphasized. A physician should withhold his consent to matrimonial alliances between persons suffering from mental or nervous diseases, or between persons with any inherited taint (hereditary system diseases). The feeding and care of children in regard to proper hygienic measures should be under medical supervision. Patients should be carefully informed concerning the evil effects of an improper mode of life (alcohol, tea, tobacco, excesses of all kinds, morphin, the latter especially in the case of doctors) and of certain trades and professions (overexertion, working at irregular times, hygiene of factories, etc.).

Careful directions should be given in regard to such matters as personal cleanliness, bathing, clothing, exercise, etc.

2. **Curative Treatment.**—Unfortunately, this is possible in only a few diseases.

(*a*) **Intoxications.**—Cases of poisoning by lead and arsenic can be guarded against, or at least very much improved, by forbidding the patient to engage in certain kinds of work and by insisting on his observing proper precautions. Alcoholism and the morphin and cocain habits are best treated in institutions. In almost every case alcohol, morphin, and cocain can be withdrawn at once. In alcoholism sudden withdrawal is not followed by any distinct symptoms, in spite of anything that may have been said to the contrary, and, while it is true that sudden withdrawal of cocain or morphin may produce severe symptoms,—although these have often been very

CURATIVE TREATMENT.

much exaggerated,—nevertheless, if there is any hope for a patient at all, it is not likely that he will succumb to them. Hence the so-called cures without coercing and tormenting the patient are to be condemned, as they rarely produce any permanent results. The practice of compensating the patient for the loss of morphin by large doses of alcohol is apt to prove dangerous in the end.

I do not wish to say that in very severe cases morphin should be withheld altogether during the first three or four days, but it should not be given after that period, and then only when there are unmistakable objective signs of collapse.

(b) All **syphilitic** cases where the diagnosis is absolutely certain, and all suspected cases, should be subjected as early as possible to a course of mercurial inunctions (3 to 5 gm., 45 grains to 1½ drams). This may be supplemented either from the beginning or later on by potassium iodid in doses of forty-five minims a day. Potassium iodid should never be tried alone.

In malarial neuralgia give quinin (8 to 24 grains).

(c) The third class of diseases that are amenable to direct treatment are those which admit of **surgical operations.** The number of these diseases has been constantly growing. Without counting direct injury to the nervous system, we have in this category:

a. Brain diseases in which the lesion can be accurately located (spicules of bone, purulent foci), if they are situated near the cortex ; in purulent foci exploratory trephining and puncture are perfectly justifiable.

In conditions of increased intracranial pressure, such as hydrocephalus, at least a temporary improvement may be effected by trephining or paracentesis of the ventricular system (the central canal has even been successfully tapped in the lumbar enlargement [1]). Suppurations due to caries in bones and joints exerting an injurious influ-

[1] It is to be stated, however, that puncture has been followed by sudden death, especially in cases of cerebellar tumor.

ence on the nervous system can, of course, be reached by surgical treatment. Whether Jacksonian epilepsy can always be successfully treated by surgical measures must still be regarded as an unsettled question. In genuine epilepsy it is better not to operate.

As regards tumors, experience shows that only very few are operable; but the opening of brain abscesses, on the other hand, has been followed by excellent results.

β. *Diseases of the Spinal Cord.*—Operative treatment has in the past been resorted to chiefly in myelitis due to compression by tumors or caries, and in diseases caused by injury. The results, however, have not been very encouraging. The difficulty of the operation depends on several factors, such as the uncertainty of the diagnosis, both as regards the character of the disease and its exact localization, and the difficulty experienced by the surgeon in finding his bearings in the operative field. Nevertheless, we may hope for better results in the future, especially in cases which present themselves for operation early, before the graver irreparable lesions in the nervous substance have made their appearance (secondary degenerations).

If secondary degeneration has already set in, all that can be hoped for is palliation of the pain.

γ. *Peripheral Nerves.*—The best results have been obtained in this portion of the nervous system, because the power of regeneration is far greater in the nerves themselves than in the tissues of the brain and spinal cord. Complete repair is possible even when some time has elapsed after a solution of continuity has taken place. Cicatricial processes and tumors giving rise to pressure symptoms have always been treated by operative means and with very good success.

The repair of a nerve that has been divided in its continuity can often be hastened by means of a plastic operation. The success of a surgical operation, as has been said, depends chiefly on an early and exact localization of the lesion.

δ. In regard to the many successful operations for the transplantation of tendons to healthy muscles, consult the paragraph on Anterior Poliomyelitis.

3. Symptomatic Treatment.—This will be entirely successful in all cases in which no grave degenerative process has made its appearance. With the present means at our command the prognosis is quite unfavorable in degenerative affections of the cell, fiber, and muscle, especially when they are of central origin. Individual symptoms can sometimes be treated and may even be temporarily improved.

(a) **Psychic Treatment (Moral Treatment).**—Much may be accomplished by judicious encouragement, by rational explanation, and by showing the patient that he is alarming himself unnecessarily; a certain dictatorial severity even may be of great service. The importance of some systematic occupation should be emphasized. Thus, a schedule of hours may be suggested for the day's work, and the patient may be encouraged to engage in outdoor occupations, such as horticulture, etc. This can not be insisted on too strongly, especially in the case of neuroses.

It is of the highest importance that the physician should have the patient's entire confidence, and the best way to obtain this is by accurate examination and careful diagnosis. A careful examination in itself often has a decided moral effect, and may be said to be one of the most important therapeutic measures.

Hypnotism should be resorted to only in cases which ought to be treated by psychic means and in which the above-mentioned measures have failed. There is no doubt that the treatment is often effective, but in many cases the results are not permanent and in not a few the ultimate effect is even harmful. No one who does not possess special qualifications and is not perfectly familiar with all the details of hypnotism has any right to resort to this mode of treatment. (For particulars in this respect consult the paragraph on Hysteria.)

(b) **Physical (Hygienic) Treatment.**—The diet, the hours of sleep and rest, and other matters of that kind should be regulated according to general therapeutic principles. If possible, all artificial measures should be dispensed with. The use of alcoholic beverages should be restricted or, better, forbidden altogether, and the physician should do everything in his power to combat the senseless doctrine of the nerve-strengthening power of wine, which is still held by the laity and by many apothecaries and physicians. Fruit, cocoa, tea, mild coffee, even cider and beer in moderation, may be recommended.

Hydrotherapy.—Sponging with moderately cold water, douches, cool (77° to 86° F.) and warm (90° to 100° F.) baths, hot and cold packs, and hot-water compresses may be employed. After a warm bath the patient should always be sponged with cold water.

It is often very advantageous to send the patient to the various baths, especially the smaller places, or to the seashore or the mountains.

Massage, gymnastic exercise, and *Weir Mitchell's treatment* (" *Mastkuren* ") are often useful if carried out according to the physician's orders.

Electricity is often the last resort. The question as to how it acts, whether indirectly, by psychic impression, or directly, is still a matter of dispute. Both the galvanic and the faradic currents are used. According to the general opinion, the galvanic current acts on deeper structures than does the faradic. The galvanic current is to be employed in painful affections and in affections of central origin; the anode has a quieting effect, while the cathode is irritating; hence the anode should be applied to the painful spot. The faradic current is indicated in peripheral diseases, especially in muscular paralyses. As it is very important not to have the current too strong, the instrument should always be provided with a galvanometer.

(c) **Medicinal Treatment.**—This should not be the first, but the last, remedy to be tried, unless there are special indications. The ruling principle should always be *nil nocere*, for in any case drugs are of little value, and the risk is great in proportion to the possible benefit. Hence the patient should not be subjected to unnecessary expense. There are certain drugs, however, which unquestionably influence the nutrition, such as arsenic (arsenious acid, $\frac{1}{12}$ to $\frac{1}{5}$ grain; Fowler's solution, 5 to 10 drops a day; iron, Blaud's pills; iron and quinin; iron and arsenic pills).

As sedatives, the bromids are to be recommended (the potassium, sodium, or ammonium bromid, or combinations of them, 1 to 4 drams a day). Antipyrin may also be given, 15 to 30 grains, etc. To allay the pain, such remedies as opium, morphin (contraindicated in neurosis), codein, and heroin are found indispensable. In neuralgia the following remedies have been recommended: Antipyrin, 15 to 30 grains; quinin, 8 to 24 grains; the salicylates (sodium salicylate, 45 grains to 3 drams; salicylic acid, $\frac{1}{2}$ to 1 dram); phenacetin, 8 to 24 grains; antinervin, 8 to 24 grains; salophen, 8 to 24 grains; analgen, 15 to 30 grains; salipyrin, 15 to 24 grains; pyramidon, 8 grains, etc.

The following hypnotics are the most commonly used: Sulphonal, 15 to 30 grains; hypnal, 8 to 30 grains; trional, 8 to 24 grains; chloral, 15 to 30 grains; and chloralamid, 30 to 45 grains. Other remedies are often employed on theoretic grounds; they are: Ergotin, $\frac{3}{4}$ to $4\frac{1}{2}$ grains; silver nitrate, $\frac{1}{8}$ to $\frac{3}{4}$ grain; strychnin, $\frac{1}{60}$ to $\frac{1}{15}$ grain; atropin, $\frac{1}{140}$ to $\frac{1}{70}$ grain per diem; etc. Some of these are very dangerous poisons and should be used guardedly, as their value in any case is very doubtful. Ointments and cutaneous irritants often have a good sedative effect.

PART V.

SPECIAL PATHOLOGY AND TREATMENT.

(Plates 75 to 84 and preceding Plates.)

I. DISEASES OF THE MEMBRANES AND BLOOD-VESSELS OF THE BRAIN.

ON the surface of the brain, diseases of these structures act on the cortical substance; at the base of the brain, on the cranial nerves at their point of exit; in the spinal cord, on the nerve-roots—the symptoms being thus dependent on the seat of the morbid process.

1. Internal Hemorrhagic Pachymeningitis (Hematoma of the Dura Mater).

Morbid Anatomy.—An inflammatory membranous exudate forms on the inner surface of the dura, with development (secondary?) of interstitial hemorrhages. The cause is unknown.

The disease occurs in adults in association with alcoholism, senility, or paralytic dementia, and may be idiopathic.

The **symptoms**, which come on successively as the hemorrhages develop, consist of headache and irritative and paralytic cortical phenomena (convulsions limited to one side of the body, hemiplegia, fever).

The **diagnosis** must be made from brain-tumor, which is steadily progressive; cerebral hemorrhage, which rarely gives rise to irritative symptoms; meningitis (different course and the presence of symptoms referable to the base); uremic coma (examination of urine, course); and cerebral syphilis (concomitant symptoms).

Treatment.—Rest, ice-bag, venesection, calomel (gr. iv, t. i. d.), drastics, and relief of symptoms as they arise (hypnotics and morphin).

2. Acute Leptomeningitis (Meningitis of the Convex Surface).—(a) Epidemic Cerebrospinal Meningitis. —An epidemic infectious disease, occurring also sporadically, caused by the diplococcus intracellularis.

Morbid Anatomy.—The presence and development of the diplococcus (which enters through the nose, through excoriations, or through the lymphatic and vascular channels (?)) set up an inflammation in the soft membranes of the spinal cord. The meshes of the pia, especially on the convex surface of the cerebral hemispheres, become filled with an exudate, at first serous and later purulent.

Course.—The onset of the disease is quite abrupt; it occurs most frequently in young individuals, and begins with a general feeling of malaise, followed by violent headache, vomiting (cerebral), and chills. The condition rapidly becomes worse. Herpes labialis, persistent high temperature, and marked leukocytosis are characteristic. The occurrence of rigor and pains in the muscles of the neck on movement of the head (irritation of the upper cervical roots) and clouding of the consciousness practically determine the diagnosis. Later on there are delirium and symptoms of cortical irritation (convulsions, palsies, monoplegia and hemiplegia, and hyperesthesia); finally, coma, trismus, opisthotonos, retention of urine and feces, and Cheyne-Stokes breathing. In the severest cases death occurs before the eighth day (meningitis siderans): moderately severe cases may be protracted to eight weeks and longer, although recovery is possible even when the disease is very severe.

Sequelæ.— Deafness (lesion of the auditory nerve), blindness, cephalalgia, paralyses, brain abscess.

The **diagnosis** must be made from typhus (gradual onset, absence of herpes, and leukocytosis), pneumonia (sputum, pulmonary symptoms), pyemia (purulent foci, absence of rigidity of the neck), tubercular meningitis (basal symptoms, signs of constitutional tuberculosis), purulent meningitis (primary purulent focus), and ulcerative endocarditis (not epidemic).

Treatment.—Rest; cold packs; baths are too severe, although warm baths have lately been much lauded; icebag; leeching (mastoid process); calomel (four grains twice repeated); blister to the occiput; inunctions with blue ointment; antipyretics; narcotics.

(**b**) **Purulent Meningitis.**—This follows suppurative processes in the ear (otitis media, caries of the petrous portion of the temporal bone), erysipelas, pyemia, and other acute infectious diseases. Accordingly, various micro-organisms are found: streptococcus pyogenes, streptococcus erysipelatis, staphylococcus aureus and albus.

The **morbid anatomy** is the same as in the foregoing variety. The most extensive purulent foci are found on the convex surface, but may also occur elsewhere.

Course.—The onset and course are the same as in the foregoing variety. There is, perhaps, a somewhat greater liability to paralysis of the cranial nerves that make their exit at the base of the brain; optic neuritis and pupillary changes occur.

For **diagnosis** see under (**a**). It is particularly important to determine the original cause of the disease.

Treatment as under (**a**). Surgical interference.

3. **Tubercular Meningitis (Basilar Meningitis).**— It follows primary tuberculosis of the lungs, lymphatic glands, or bones, particularly in children.

Morbid Anatomy.—The tubercle bacilli are carried by the circulation to the soft membranes; here they lead to the formation of miliary tubercles and the deposition of a fibrinous, gelatinous exudate on the base of the brain, in the meshes of which are imbedded miliary nodules. The nodules may spread to the brain substance and form tumor-like solitary tubercles.

Course.—The disease begins gradually, with malaise, headache, and vomiting. After a time the symptoms of cortical irritation become more marked, with delirium and convulsions (cri hydrencéphalique in children), trismus, and irregular heart action. There are somnolence, temperature up to 102.2° F., irregular fever, rigidity of the neck, coma.

Later, paralysis of individual cranial (oculomotor, facial, abducens) nerves, monoplegia, aphasia, death.

Diagnosis.—The disease must be differentiated from purulent meningitis, q. v. Diagnosis is confirmed by finding tubercle bacilli in the sputum or in the cerebrospinal fluid withdrawn by lumbar puncture.

Tubercles on the choroid.

Treatment as under 2.

4. **Syphilitic or Gummatous Meningitis and Brain Syphilis.**—It makes its appearance in the secondary and tertiary periods of syphilis, never until several months after the infection. The characteristic syphilitic neoplasms (gumma, infiltration, caseation) make their appearance in the soft membranes, especially on the base of the skull, and in close relation with the blood-vessels in that region. Three forms of brain syphilis are distinguished:

(a) The true diffuse, **basilar syphilitic meningitis**, characterized by the formation of thickened plates, in some cases circumscribed to definite localities. The symptoms are in the main the same as those of tubercular basal meningitis.

(b) Formation of **isolated gummata** in the membranes, rarely in the substance of the brain. The symptoms are those of brain-tumor.

(c) A form associated with peculiar **alterations in the blood-vessels (syphilitic endarteritis)**, with or without diffuse or circumscribed gummatous meningitis. The intima of the vessels at the base of the brain undergoes proliferation, so that the lumen is narrowed. This is apt to be followed by thrombosis and resulting necrosis. (See Embolism.) The individual varieties often occur in combination, so that the clinical picture of brain syphilis presents numerous variations. The symptoms vary much in intensity, exacerbations alternating with temporary remissions.

Course.—The disease begins with meningitic symptoms (headache, vomiting), which are followed by attacks of partial unconsciousness, palsies in the extremities, convolutions, dementia, and apathy, together with lesions of the basal nerves (optic atrophy and neuritis, oculomotor, facial paralysis, etc.); polyuria and polydipsia occur. The softening process gives rise to successive attacks of hemiplegia, and the picture is further complicated by aphasia and epileptic seizures. Recovery is possible, but more or less paralysis usually remains.

Diagnosis.—The signs of a former infection play the most important part in the diagnosis (abortions, scars, glandular enlargement); in doubtful cases the diagnosis may later be reached *ex juvantibus*. Syphilis should be thought of in any case of meningitis which presents an unusual course.

Treatment.—Inunctions, potassium iodid (see General Treatment); symptomatic.

5. **Thrombosis of the Sinuses.**—Thrombosis in the venous sinuses is usually secondary to other disease localized in their immediate neighborhood, especially if of an inflammatory character, the process extending to the wall of the sinus (phlebitis). It may occur in caries and osteomyelitis of the petrous portion of the temporal bone and mastoid process, in purulent meningitis, brain abscess, phlegmon; or spontaneously, in old age (marantic thrombosis, chlorosis, cachexia).

Marantic thrombosis is frequently localized in the superior longitudinal and in the transverse sinuses. In aural affections the thrombosis commonly forms in the transverse sinus. The thrombus breaks down as the result of secondary infection and leads to metastatic pyemia, the emboli making their way through the jugular vein and right heart into the lung.

The **symptoms** vary according to the seat of the thrombus. Meningitic symptoms (headache, vomiting, convulsions, coma) are usually present; also paralysis and rigor of the muscles of the neck. Thrombosis of the transverse sinus produces edema over the mastoid process (venous stasis). The internal jugular vein on the same side is flaccid, and the external jugular vein empties itself more rapidly. In thrombosis of the cavernous sinus the ophthalmic veins are engorged, the lids are edematous, the conjunctivæ are chemotic; protrusion of the eyeball and ocular palsies are present (the oculomotor and abducens occupy compartments in the wall of the sinus). Thrombosis of the superior longitudinal sinus betrays itself by venous stasis in the veins of the nose (epistaxis).

A positive **diagnosis** is not always possible, because the condition is often masked by the symptoms of the primary disease (abscess, meningitis). It can be made with certainty only after the above-mentioned hypostatic phenomena have made their appearance.

Treatment.—Either surgical (opening of the sinus and packing with gauze) or symptomatic.

6. **For diseases of the arteries** and their consequences see Hemorrhage, Embolism and Aneurysm in the following section.

II. THE DISEASES OF THE BRAIN SUBSTANCE.

A. ORGANIC DISEASES.

1. Circulatory Disturbances and their Consequences.

(a) **Anemia and Hyperemia.**—These two conditions occur as temporary or lasting symptoms in a great number of conditions, as in exhaustion, fever, and the various forms of anemia.

Temporary cerebral (especially cortical) **anemia** gives rise to attacks of syncope. Persistent anemia after hemorrhages or in secondary and primary anemia due to other causes shows itself in impairment of the general condition, somnolence, fatigue, tinnitus aurium, vertigo, nausea, and fits of yawning.

Treatment.—Infusion of salt solution; horizontal position; enemata; cutaneous irritation in acute anemia; rubefacients; egg and milk diet; iron and arsenic and other symptomatic remedies in chronic anemia. Alcohol in the form of red wine is quite superfluous and rather injurious than beneficial in the treatment of anemia.

Hyperemic conditions, such as sudden attacks of heat, palpitation, vertigo, a feeling of oppression in the head, occur in plethoric individuals and those of the so-called epileptic habit. It is probable that arteriosclerosis is largely responsible for these symptoms, although this is difficult to demonstrate.

Treatment.—Regulation of the diet; restriction in the use of alcohol and tobacco; baths (Marienbad); exercise, and regulation of the cardiac and renal functions.

(b) **Cerebral Hemorrhage.**—The arteries of the brain are characterized by an unusual tendency to the formation of miliary and larger aneurysms, rupture of which is responsible for a great variety of cerebral lesions. The bursting of even a very small aneurysm may lead to the gravest consequences if an important pathway or nerve center is destroyed by the hemorrhage. Miliary aneurysms of this character may occur in any arteries of the brain, but are found most frequently in the branches of the artery of the fissure of Sylvius, the most important branch of which, the lenticulostriate artery (shown in Fig. 5, p. 20), is involved more often than any other. The resulting extravasation of blood produces more or less extensive destruction of the surrounding brain substance. If a thrombus is formed, the hemorrhage becomes arrested and the extravasated blood is absorbed and partly converted into connective tissue. On the surface of the brain this process leaves a defect, while in the interior a cyst remains at the site of the hemorrhage.

The **causes** that may lead to the formation of such an aneurysm are arteriosclerosis due to chronic alcoholism, syphilis, gout, chronic nephritis, old age, and other unknown causes.

A hemorrhage occurring in the region of the basal ganglia and adjacent portions of white matter—the internal capsule—is followed by the gravest consequences. This region is supplied principally by the above-mentioned branch of the artery of the fissure of Sylvius, which, from its great liability to hemorrhage, has been named by Charcot the "*artère d'hémorrhagie.*"

The hemorrhage is attended by the phenomena of cerebral apoplexy, the so-called apoplectic stroke. After the phenomena of the initial injury have run their course, a permanent hemiplegia remains as a residuum. The occurrence of an apoplexy may be preceded by certain prodromal symptoms affecting the circulation, such as headache, vertigo, tinnitus aurium, and fatigue on the slightest exertion. In many cases, however, the apoplectic stroke occurs without any warning and without any ascertainable cause, or it may come on suddenly after bodily exertion or mental excitement. The patient is suddenly seized with nausea, his head swims, he becomes confused and falls to the ground unconscious. This is known as the *insult.* It may last only a few minutes or several days, depending on the severity of the case.

During the period of insult the patient remains in a state of complete unconsciousness and fails to react to stimuli. The respiration is slow and stertorous (snoring), often intermittent, pupillary reaction is uncertain, the extremities are motionless, and when the arm is released, it falls lifeless by the patient's side. In some cases mild spastic phenomena are observed. There is retention of the urine and feces, and sometimes conjugate deviation of the eyeballs. The temperature may be subnormal or normal, or hyperpyrexia may even be present, especially toward the end. If death does not occur during this period,—and this will depend on the extent and location of the injury,—the patient gradually recovers from his stupor, regains consciousness, and the exact nature of the paralysis is now first discovered.

The paralysis is usually much more extensive immediately after the hemorrhage, and the condition gradually improves more or less in the course of a few weeks. The initial symptoms, which tend to disappear partially during the first weeks, are known as *indirect focal symptoms*. They depend on the pressure exerted by the diseased focus on neighboring portions, and therefore disappear when the corresponding regions of the brain recover themselves.

The *direct focal symptoms*, on the contrary, are irremediable and permanent, as they are due to the destruction of definite nerve paths and centers. They vary greatly with the localization and extent of the hemorrhage, ranging from slight transient (passagère) hemiparesis to total hemiplegia, with hemianesthesia and hemianopsia. The muscular paralysis in cerebral hemorrhages usually affects an entire *muscle mechanism*—that is, a group of muscles functionally associated. If the hemorrhage is located in the left hemisphere, it follows that the paralysis will in most cases be accompanied by some form of aphasia. Hemorrhages in the white matter may exist without producing any symptoms, while a hemorrhage in the brain-stem may produce crossed hemiplegia. (Consult Part IV, 3.)

The affected muscles show spastic paralysis, with a tendency to the formation of contractures, but without degenerative atrophy. The tendon reflexes are exaggerated; the cutaneous reflexes on the paralyzed side are frequently diminished (see p. 82). In rare cases a form of atrophy developing with unusual rapidity has been observed (lesion of the optic thalamus?); cerebral atrophy. The hemiplegic gait has been referred to on page 108. The following movements are often permanently lost: opening of the hand and supination of the arm, while the power of closing the hand and pronating the arm is often retained.

Choreic and athetoid irritative phenomena may occur on the side of the hemiplegia (posthemiplegic hemichorea, hemiathetosis). In extensive or in repeated hemorrhages (which are quite common), the intelligence of the individual suffers; he becomes morbidly irritable or total dementia may develop secondarily.

Diagnosis.—Cerebral hemorrhage is to be differentiated from uremic coma (urine), diabetic coma (acetone odor, sugar), extrameningeal hemorrhage from the middle meningeal artery in fracture of the skull (history, typical course of the increasing brain pressure), cerebral embolus (early age, heart diseases, symptoms less severe, pachymeningitis, *q. v.*). (For the topical diagnosis consult Part IV, 3, I.)

Treatment.—Prophylaxis. (See under Hyperemia.) During the period of insult ice-bag, rest, evacuation of the bladder and rectum, venesection, stimulants. After the period of insult reassurance of the patient, gymnastic exercise, electricity, massage, baths (salt and mud); symptomatic.

(c) **Brain Embolism and Thrombosis.**—Embolism occurs when fibrin clots are swept into the arteries of the brain and lodge in one of the smaller branches. The embolism is usually derived from the left heart (endocarditis of the mitral valve or of the aorta). It traverses the internal carotid and becomes arrested in a vessel of the first, second, or third order, according to its size, frequently in the artery of the fissure of Sylvius on the left side. As the arteries of the brain are end arteries and the collateral circulation can not, therefore, be reestablished, the area supplied by the occluded vessel undergoes necrosis. Softening takes place (see under General Pathology), the contents of the softening focus are absorbed, and a defect (yellow plate) remains at the site of the lesion if situated on the surface, or a cyst if the necrotic area was in the substance of the brain.

Sometimes occlusion of the vessels and its consequences may occur by primary thrombus formation in the brain arteries, without any embolic process having taken place (syphilitic obliterating endarteritis, arteriosclerosis). Foci of softening are often multiple.

Course.—The clinical symptoms vary according to the individual artery occluded; in the main they are the same as in cerebral hemorrhage.

Symptoms.—Embolism produces a primary apoplectic insult similar to that observed after hemorrhage, but the coma does not last so long and is not so deep as in the former condition. On the other hand, prodromal symptoms may be more numerous and more marked in embolism, and especially in primary thrombus formation. There is the same appearance of direct and indirect focal symptoms, but the indirect symptoms disappear more rapidly, as some anastomosis always takes place at the boundary of the necrotic area. Symptoms that fail to disappear after a few days are irremediable and persist permanently as direct focal symptoms. According to the seat of the embolus, there may be rapidly disappearing hemiparesis, and lasting and more or less extensive hemiplegia; aphasia is more frequent than in hemorrhage; alternating palsies, hemianopsia, etc., occur.

For **diagnosis** and **treatment** see under Hemorrhage.

(d) **Aneurysms.**—The larger aneurysms occur most frequently in the arteries at the base of the brain, the artery of the fissure of Sylvius, carotid, anterior communicating artery, basilar and vertebral arteries. Owing to the pressure on the brain substance, cranial nerves, and pyramidal tract in the pons and medulla oblongata, alternating hemiplegias make their appearance. Aneurysm of the internal carotid gives rise to pulsating **exophthalmos.**

(e) **Arteriosclerosis of the Arteries of the Brain.**
—The **symptoms,** in addition to a tendency to hemorrhage, thrombosis (softening foci and aneurysm), are such as have been mentioned under Cerebral Hyperemia: milder grades of hemiparesis, transient attacks of vertigo, visual disturbances, etc., depending on various circulatory disturbances.

For the **treatment** see under Hyperemia.

2. Inflammatory Diseases of the Brain-Substance.

(a) **Brain Abscess.**—This occurs after injury to the skull or in connection with other inflammatory processes, such as purulent meningitis, caries, otitis media, osteomyelitis, pyemia, and abscess of the lungs. An abscess is called idiopathic when no primary affection can be discovered.

Abscesses are most frequently found in the temporal lobe and in the cerebellum, especially when they are secondary to disease of the ear.

The following organisms have been found: Staphylococcus aureus; the diplococcus of Fränkel; streptococcus pyogenes; oïdium albicans; tubercle bacilli; bacillus proteus, and others.

Course.—A brain abscess may become encapsulated and thus remain latent for a long period (as long as ten years in some cases), and then, without any discoverable cause, suddenly produce violent focal symptoms complicated by symptoms of meningitis (rupture into a ventricle from without).

The **symptoms** of brain abscess are partly paralytic (the focal symptoms) and partly irritative. *(1) General symptoms:* Persistent, dull headache; vomiting; vertigo; irregular low fever; at times comatose conditions; retardation of the pulse-rate and convulsions. *(2) Focal symptoms,* including a great variety of paralytic and irritative phenomena, as hemiplegia, hemianopsia, epileptic attacks; in cerebellar abscess, cerebellar ataxia; when the abscess is in the temporal lobe, sensory aphasia. The last-named symptom may be absent. Impending rupture (extrameningeal) is heralded by exacerbation of the symptoms. Not infrequently there are marked cachexia and apathy.

Diagnosis.—Brain-tumor, in which there is almost always choked disc and in which fever is absent, must be excluded. The diagnosis rests on the demonstration of a primary purulent focus, the history of a previous injury, meningitis (rapid course, hyperesthesia, high fever, rigidity of the neck), thrombosis of a sinus (pyemic fever), local edema.

Treatment.—Exclusively surgical; trephining, puncture with a probe, opening.

(b) **Acute Nonsuppurative Encephalitis.**—This includes various processes, the exact nature of which is not known.

α. A **hemorrhagic** form, characterized by the appearance of acute inflammatory phenomena and the formation of great numbers of minute inflammatory hemorrhagic foci in the cortex and basal ganglia (infectious? toxic?).

The **symptoms** are both meningitic and focal, the latter varying according to the seat of the affection.

The **prognosis** is not always unfavorable.

β. A similar form, which is observed chiefly in chronic alcoholism, is characterized by numerous small hemorrhages in the brain-stem, especially in the region of the aqueduct, underneath the corpora quadrigemina. It leads to palsies of the ocular muscles (acute ophthalmoplegia).

γ. An obscure process that forms the basis of so-called **cerebral paralysis of children.** This form of infantile paralysis is either congenital or acquired in earliest infancy (various processes?).[1]

Course.—During the first months of life the infant is

---

[1] Other forms of cerebral infantile palsy are due to injuries to the skull during forceps deliveries, intra-uterine circulatory disturbances (endarteritis, phlebitis), and various forms of arrested development.

suddenly seized with severe meningitic symptoms, which, however, soon disappear. They depend on certain inflammatory processes in the central convolutions which have run their course and been followed by a formation of scars, cysts, atrophied areas, and defects (porencephalia) in the affected parts of the brain. Accordingly, certain cerebral palsies, always spastic in character, remain after the initial symptoms have disappeared. If the lesion is bilateral, there will be spastic paraplegia. The growth in the paralyzed portion of the body (an arm or a leg, or one side) is much retarded compared with that of the other side, and one entire half of the body may remain atrophic (hemiatrophia spastica). The irritation of the scar in the cortex frequently leads to epileptic seizures and athetosis, while psychic defects—idiocy, deaf-mutism, and defects in the speech—are often present.

The **treatment** is symptomatic. (See Meningitis.)

3. Brain-tumor.

Tumors may develop in the interior of the brain after traumatism, as metastatic growths derived from other tumors in the body, or they may develop spontaneously.

They may grow:

From the bone (sarcoma, carcinoma, osteoma, gumma).

From the meninges (sarcoma, carcinoma, fibroma, solitary tubercle, gumma).

From the blood-vessels (gumma, aneurysm).

In the brain substance (glioma, sarcoma, metastatic and primary carcinoma, cysticerci, echinococci).

The most frequent tumors in the adult are the glioma, gumma, and sarcoma; in the child, the solitary tubercle.

The **symptoms** vary according to the size, the rate of growth, the number, and the seat of the tumors. All tumors have certain symptoms in common, depending on the presence of a growing foreign body within the limited space of the cranial cavity. They are known as general tumor symptoms. The other symptoms depend chiefly on the seat, and to some extent on the variety, of the tumor present.

Course.—The *general symptoms* of brain-tumor are caused by their encroachment on the cranial cavity, and the resulting increase in the intracranial pressure, which exerts an injurious influence both on the brain as a whole and on the vascular and lymphatic circulation. These symptoms are : (*a*) Headache, persistent, diffuse, dull, and of progressive intensity, throbbing in character ("Schettern"); (*b*) cerebral vomiting, not depending on the ingestion of food and occurring paroxysmally ; (*c*) vertigo, feeling of oppression, somnolence ; (*d*) slowing of the pulse ; (*e*) epileptiform and apoplectiform seizures ; (*f*) *choked disc*, or optic neuritis, the cardinal symptom of brain-tumor. (See Part IV, p. 118.)

The *focal symptoms* are divided into *direct*, or focal, and *indirect*, or remote, symptoms. They vary according to the seat of the growth, and consist of monoplegia, hemiplegia, sometimes with paralysis of the cranial nerves of the opposite side, hemianesthesia, hemianopsia, cerebellar ataxia (corpora quadrigemina, cerebellum), aphasia, and basal symptoms. (For a detailed account see under Focal Diseases, Part IV, 3.) Jacksonian epilepsy is common. Tonic and later clonic convulsive attacks of gradually increasing extent also occur.

The focal symptoms may, however, be absent or, at least, very indistinct. Tumors of the corpora quadrigemina may produce acute internal hydrocephalus by pressure on the veins of Galen in the third ventricle, thus obstructing the flow of the cerebrospinal fluid. (See Hydrocephalus, p. 151.)

Diagnosis.—First of all, the presence of a brain-tumor is diagnosticated from the general symptoms.

The following conditions are to be excluded : Abscess and hydrocephalus, *q. v.* Next, the seat of the tumor is determined by attention to the focal symptoms, as explained in Part IV, 3, whether at the base of the skull (anterior middle or posterior fossa), in one of the lobes of the cerebral hemispheres, in the brain-stem (corpora quadrigemina or pons), or in the cerebellum. Only the direct focal symptoms which are persistent and progressive can be utilized in the topical diagnosis; the indirect symptoms, or those that are transient and of varying intensity, are useless for this purpose. It is, however, not always possible to distinguish between the two kinds of symptoms. Finally, an attempt should be made to determine the nature of the tumor by looking for signs of tuberculosis or lues, or for the presence of a primary tumor in other parts of the body. Many kinds of tumors have characteristic seats; thus, a tumor at the base of the brain is either a gumma or a sarcoma; gliomata are found in the brain substance. Cerebellar and pontine tumors are usually solitary tubercles or gliomata. The growth of a sarcoma is rapid; that of a glioma, slow.

Treatment.—If there is the faintest suspicion of lues, inunctions and potassium iodid. If the tumor is in the cortex, an attempt at operative removal is justifiable (see General Treatment); otherwise the treatment is merely symptomatic—narcotics, bromids.

4. Internal Hydrocephalus.

By this term is meant a pathologic increase in the amount of cerebrospinal fluid in the lateral and third ventricles. The term external hydrocephalus is applied to a collection of fluid in the subarachnoid space, which communicates with the ventricles. Internal hydrocephalus may be congenital or acquired. The cause is supposed to be either an inflammatory disease of the ependyma of the ventricles and of the choroid plexus, or an obstruction to the outflow from the third ventricle by some inflammatory change.

In marked grades of hydrocephalus the cerebral convolutions are flattened and the brain substance is much diminished in quantity and atrophied on account of the pressure. The circumference of the skull may reach fifty to sixty centimeters, the normal being less than fifty in children. The collection of fluid in the third ventricle produces a bulging of the floor and pressure on the structures lying beneath it: optic nerve, chiasm (bitemporal hemianopsia), oculomotor, and abducens nerves.

Course.—Hydrocephalus, when congenital or acquired in early childhood, is associated with idiocy, bilateral spastic palsies, and epileptiform attacks. Early death is the rule. In adults the development of hydrocephalus is accompanied by meningitic phenomena: headache, vomiting, coma, optic neuritis—but no fever. The course is marked by exacerbations and remissions; choked disc may be present.

The **diagnosis** from brain-tumor can not always be made with certainty (absence of the increase in the circumference of the skull, more rapid development, and remissions not so frequent).

Treatment.—Operative: puncture of the ventricle or of the central canal at the lumbar enlargement between the third and fourth lumbar vertebræ. The needle should be inserted to a depth of from seven to eight centimeters in an adult. Manometric pressure in the lateral decubitus is normally from forty to sixty millimeters of water; a rise above 150 mm. is pathologic. The value of these surgical measures is, however, very doubtful. Externally, blue ointment; unguent. tartari stibiatis, applied after shaving the occiput. Calomel.

5. Paralytic Dementia (Progressive Paralysis).

Progressive paralysis is due to a degenerative process in the brain. Numerous minute, medullated and non-medullated nerve-fibers and possibly some cells are primarily destroyed, especially in the cortex. The alterations are said to be most marked in the frontal lobe. Owing to the destruction of the nerve-fibers the thickness of the cortex gradually diminishes, and ultimately the entire

PARALYTIC DEMENTIA.

brain becomes atrophied. In addition to this degenerative process chronic inflammatory changes in the vessels, the neuroglia, and the meninges, and internal hydrocephalus, etc., are constantly present.

The disease is particularly common in men. It shows a remarkable tendency to follow syphilis, and shares with tabes the appellation *metasyphilis*. It is also known to follow traumatism.

Course.—The degeneration of the nervous elements in the cortex is attended with progressive deterioration of the mental functions, the intelligence, the character, the memory, and the power of speech (associative functions).

Symptoms.—The change in the character is often the first prominent symptom: Dullness, irritability, tendency to commit excesses, inability to do any mental work, depravity. If the patient presents himself during this period, the following characteristic symptoms are to be specially looked for.

1. Rigidity of the pupils, either unilateral or bilateral; unequal pupils.

2. Paralytic disturbances of speech (literal paraphasia): negligent, incorrect manner of speaking, omission or transposition of letters and syllables. (See under Disturbances of Speech, Part IV, 4.) Or agraphia and alexia may be present—letters, syllables, or words may be omitted or punctuation marks put in the wrong places.

3. Loss of Patellar Reflex.—Paralytic dementia may occur in connection with tabetic symptoms; or it may be associated with disease of the lateral tracts, in which case the reflexes will be exaggerated.

4. Tremor of the hands, and of the tongue and lips while speaking.

The *paralytic attacks* occur later in the disease. There may be apoplectiform disturbances of consciousness, with or without epileptiform seizures. The concomitant paralytic symptoms usually disappear as the attack passes off.

The psychic deterioration goes steadily on, and finally

leads to delusions of grandeur and attacks of mania. The disease is marked by long periods of remission, during which the patient appears to regain his normal condition, but the malady soon breaks out again with renewed intensity. In the final stages the subject becomes totally demented and sinks into a brutish state. Death occurs from exhaustion or inspiration pneumonia after a period varying from a few months to two or three years.

Diagnosis.—Paralytic dementia must be differentiated from severe neurasthenia (persistent absence of the objective symptoms); multiple sclerosis, *q. v.*; brain syphilis (pronounced focal symptoms).

The **treatment** is best carried out in an institution; it is purely symptomatic. Antisyphilitic treatment is rather harmful than beneficial.

6. Ophthalmoplegia.

Bilateral paralysis of the ocular muscles from disease situated in the nuclei of the oculomotor nerve, beneath the corpora quadrigemina, occurs in a variety of diseases.

(a) **Acute Ophthalmoplegia.**—Among the causes other than the above-mentioned hemorrhagic encephalitis are other hemorrhagic embolic processes following heart disease, syphilis, alcoholism, arteriosclerosis, etc., and tumors.

(b) **Chronic Progressive Ophthalmoplegia.**—Like bulbar paralysis, which will be discussed in the following section, this belongs to the system diseases of neuron cells. (See Part IV, 3.) There is a slowly progressive atrophy in the cells of the oculomotor nucleus, which in the course of years leads to total paralysis of all the external, and rarely of the internal, muscles of the eyeball. The oculomotor fibers, of course, disappear also.

The disease occurs either by itself or as a concomitant of tabes, paralytic dementia, bulbar palsy, and multiple sclerosis.

Treatment.—Antisyphilitic, if indicated.

7. Bulbar Paralysis.

(a) The acute form may be due to thrombosis, embolism, or to inflammatory or hemorrhagic processes.

Symptoms.—The onset of the symptoms is usually sudden, as in apoplexy. They consist in paralysis of the muscles of the tongue and pharynx, disturbances of phonation and respiration, and paralysis of the facial, abducens, and trifacial nerves. Bulbar speech, paralysis of the extremities, and sudden death from failure of heart and respiration.

(b) Chronic Progressive Bulbar Paralysis.—**Morbid Anatomy.**—The anatomic basis is a slowly progressive destruction of the cells of the nuclei situated in the medulla oblongata, especially in the motor nuclei (peripheral neuron cells) of the hypoglossus, facial, vagus, spinal accessory, and trifacial nerves. The pyramidal tract and the anterior horns of the spinal cord are frequently involved, hence any intermediate form between simple bulbar paralysis and amyotrophic sclerosis with bulbar symptoms may occur. (See under System Diseases.)

Concerning the **etiology**, very little is known.

Course.—The clinical phenomena develop very gradually. First certain bulbar disturbances of the speech are noticed, the letters r, s, and l being less distinctly pronounced. Later, there develop a bilateral atrophy (RD) and paresis of the lips, tongue (fibrillary contractions), the muscles concerned in deglutition and phonation, and, rarely, of the muscles of mastication. Finally, complete rigidity of the muscles of expression (the lower facial only is, as a rule, involved), salivation, and inability to swallow or articulate (anarthria) occur. There are no sensory disturbances.

There may be psychic alterations, such as constant tendency to weep, etc.; and if other systems, as the pyramids, are involved, spastic paralysis of the extremities and atrophy of the muscles of the hand may occur. (See Amyotrophic Lateral Sclerosis.) The patients die of asthenia or inspiration pneumonia.

Treatment.—Symptomatic; electricity, baths, tubal feeding. Arsenic, strychnin, potassium iodid, and atropin are without effect. It is impossible either to replace the ganglion cells that have been destroyed or to arrest the progress of the disease.

Bulbar paralysis may be simulated by other diseases.

(a) **Pseudobulbar paralysis** is due to softening foci from embolus or hemorrhage in corresponding regions of the two cerebral hemispheres. If the centers for the facial, hypoglossus, etc., are injured, the symptoms of bulbar paralysis without muscular atrophy may be produced. It is to be remembered, however, that other diseased foci may be present in the medulla at the same time.

(b) **Bulbar Paralysis Without any Pathologic Changes.**— The disease is a combination of bulbar symptoms with paretic conditions of other extremities, etc. The muscles readily become fatigued; paresis may be present, but without atrophy. Up to the present time no anatomic basis has been discovered for the disease.

It is not always possible to exclude these forms, especially in the diagnosis of an acute disease. Hysteria and multiple sclerosis under certain conditions may produce a similar clinical picture. The above-mentioned points in the diagnosis should, therefore, receive the most careful attention. The most characteristic feature of the symptom-complex is its gradually progressive development.

8. Diseases of the Cerebellum.

These have been discussed under Tumor and Abscess. Other diseases of the cerebellum, such as atrophy and sclerosis, are rare.

9. Multiple Cerebrospinal Sclerosis.

See under Diseases of the Spinal Cord.

B. CEREBRAL DISEASES OF UNKNOWN CHARACTER AND LOCALIZATION.

Cerebral Neuroses.

This term embraces all those diseases of the brain the exact nature and seat of which are unknown.

1. Neurasthenia.—Neurasthenia, with hysteria and hypochondria, represents the transition to grave psychic diseases (psychoses). Neurasthenia is a chronic condition of morbid asthenia and irritability of various psychic and bodily functions, due to improper training and bringing-up, to overexertion and excesses of all kinds, and is, in many cases, dependent on hereditary predisposition.

Symptoms.—The patient is depressed or anxious and irritable; the will power and the capacity for work are impaired, particularly such work as requires mental concentration. Among other symptoms may be mentioned: fatigue after the slightest exertion; a morbid tendency to introspection (nosophobia, syphilophobia); insomnia; feeling of oppression in the head; tremors and palpitation.

The clinical picture may be in addition complicated by a long array of other physical symptoms; abnormal sensations of every kind; pains; disturbances of the gastric and intestinal functions (hyperacidity, nervous dyspepsia) and of the sexual power. (Consult, in this connection, the paragraph on Occupation Neuroses, p. 189.)

In severe grades of neurasthenia the patient is harassed by uncontrollable thoughts and metaphysical mania, but the condition does not develop into any other psychic affection. The typical course of neurasthenia is intermittent: the patient may feel quite well for a long time, when suddenly the distressing symptoms again make their appearance in full force.

Diagnosis.—Exclude other bodily diseases, such as paralytic dementia, multiple sclerosis, and hysteria, by repeated careful examination (urine, lungs, heart, stomach).

The differential diagnosis from these three diseases will be found under the respective headings.

Treatment.—Allay the patient's fears and forebodings as much as possible and give him moral encouragement. A neurasthenic patient should always be carefully examined; it is a great mistake, both from a therapeutic and diagnostic point of view, to send him away without a minute objective examination, for such a patient is really ill. Give abundant and nutritious diet; cold baths or change of air, either at the seashore or at the mountains; Weir Mitchell's treatment (four weeks in bed on a diet of milk, eggs, and large quantities of meat); electricity; gymnastic exercise; arsenic, iron, quinin. Do not give too much medicine—no morphin.

2. **Hypochondria.**—This affection shares with neurasthenia the symptom of morbid introspection; but whereas in neurasthenia the patient's complaints as to the location and intensity of the pain vary from time to time, the sensations complained of in hypochondria are more constant and localized. As a rule, the patient complains of some disturbances of the abdominal functions. The effect of these sensations on the psychic condition is more lasting and more systematized; in fact the depression of hypochondria is much deeper seated than that of neurasthenia. A neurasthenic discusses his symptoms with the greatest frankness, while the hypochondriac broods over his troubles in sullen taciturnity.

Gastro-intestinal disease (latent carcinoma, tapeworm) is to be excluded. Hypochondria can be distinguished from beginning paranoia and the systemic delusions characteristic of that condition only by careful observance of the progress of the disease.

The **treatment** is the same as for neurasthenia.

3. **Hysteria.**—**Definition.**—Hysteria is a psychosis due to some morbid disturbance of volition and psychic representation, manifesting itself in an endless variety of functional anomalies of the motor and sensory spheres, for

which it is impossible to discover any organic basis. The manifestations of the disease are all purely psychogenic in origin.

Course.—Hysteria occurs most frequently in young individuals. The most important factors in the etiology are heredity, education, and emotional disturbances.

The psychic condition in hysteria undergoes a morbid change, so that the patients, either by suggestion or auto-suggestion, exhibit a variety of psychic and bodily reactions. They are irritable, capricious, absent-minded, and very uncertain in their actions (explosive actions); the intelligence is not affected.

The bodily symptoms are (1) *stigmata*, which are permanent, but may be absent, and (2) paroxysmal *hysteric attacks*.

1. Stigmata.—(*a*) *Hemianesthesia*, or total loss of sensation of one half the body or of individual regions, including all the qualities of sensation, pain, heat, etc. The sense of taste, smell, and hearing may be lost on the same side and the color-sense may be impaired (achromatopsia). The visual field may be contracted or there may be an unusual tendency to ocular fatigue. The hemianesthesia is due to loss of a part of the associations necessary for conscious sensation.

(*b*) *Hyperesthesia* of one half, or part of one half, of the body, pain elicited by pressure on the ovaries, the groin, the patella, and vertebral pain.[1] Hysteric attacks can be produced by irritation of these points (hysterogenic zones—loss of central associative inhibition).

Pains and abnormal sensations of various kinds, such as globus hystericus, etc., are often complained of.

(*c*) *Hysteric palsies*, which may simulate almost any form of disease. They are due to a central paralysis of the will power (paralysis of certain movements, not of

---

[1] This tenderness on pressure, however, is often present in healthy individuals and may also be suggested by the physician's repeated examinations.

individual muscles), and may disappear as rapidly as they came.

The most common forms are hysteric aphonia, agraphia, aphasia, aphagia, hysteric hemiplegia (without involvement of the facial and hypoglossus), hysteric astasia (inability to stand), and abasia (inability to walk); forced movements of various kinds; retention of urine.

(*d*) *Hysteric Contractures.*—These are due to central irritation of a purely functional character. The greatest variety of contractures, either of the flexors or of the extensors, is observed, involving either the head or the extremities.

2. Hysteric Attacks.—Central irritative phenomena, manifesting themselves in a great variety of different forms and combinations and occurring either spontaneously or as the result of a kind of reflex excitation (fright, emotion, sensation, etc.). Clonic and tonic convulsions of the extremities and of the trunk follow each other in rapid succession. There is gasping respiration or dyspnea; consciousness is rarely affected to any marked degree, although the patient does not remember anything about the attacks (amnesia). During the convulsions the patient may assume a number of grotesque attitudes in rapid succession (clownism, "*arc de cercle*"), while the limbs execute the most peculiar movements (grand hysteria). Trismus, choking fits, and hysteric attacks of laughing and weeping may be more or less pronounced. During the attacks the patient often has pleasant or unpleasant hallucinations, which impel her to shout or call names or to gesticulate wildly and make faces.

Coma, such as is observed in epileptic attacks, never occurs; the reflexes are preserved. In ordinary attacks the patient can be roused by sprinkling the face with water, and even if the attack is severe, a painful prick in the sole of the foot with a needle will almost always suffice to rouse her.

Characteristic features of hysteric attacks are the exaggerated effect and changeable nature of the convulsions and the fact that the attacks can be induced and prevented by appropriately influencing the patient by suggestion.

A number of diseases, some of which are known by separate names, are included in the category of *psychogenic conditions:* Akinesia algera, or pain on motion, without any recognizable cause, and hence inability to move a part; chorea electrica, or forced spasmodic movements of the body; paramyoclonus multiplex, clonic muscular contractions occurring alternately in various parts of the body (biceps, quadriceps, supinator longus, trapezius, etc.); astasia and abasia (*q. v.*).

The **diagnosis** can be arrived at only by keeping the entire clinical picture of hysteria in mind—a single symptom does not suffice; by a careful examination the presence of stigmata and the occurrence of attacks can usually be discovered. It is not always possible to distinguish hysteria from neurasthenia, but in most cases some one symptom will decide between the two conditions. In severer forms psychic disturbances may be more pronounced (moral defects).

Treatment.—The treatment for the most part must be psychic; the patient should be encouraged to follow some regular occupation. An attempt should be made to restore her confidence in her own will power; if possible, she should be removed to an institution, where she will be away from nervous and overanxious members of her family. The attacks should be made light of; the diet, of course, should be regulated, and baths and douches should be ordered. In some cases iron and bromid are indicated, but their usefulness bears no proportion to that of the moral treatment. Morphin should never be given.

Hypnotic treatment, as a rule, only removes individual symptoms and rarely brings about complete cure of the malady. In many cases it is the means of bringing new symptoms into existence. It is much better to depend on a rational and not directly hypnotic, but merely psychic, suggestion. (Slight deceptions are permissible and, indeed, very useful—so-called suggestions during the waking state.)

4. Traumatic Neuroses.—The cases belong in part to neurasthenia, in part to hypochondria and hysteria. They have this in common that they are produced by some psychic or physical injury, usually in patients predisposed by heredity or alcoholism.

In view of the possibility of exploiting the disease as a means of revenue from accident-insurance policies, patients of this kind are very difficult to treat. It is often exceedingly difficult to draw the line between intentional exaggeration and morbid psychic inhibition. For therapeutic reasons it is well to be guarded at first in determining the degree of disability. A definite opinion should be given only in exceptional cases; as a rule, it should be withheld until the patient has been examined repeatedly. In this class belong the neuroses after railway accidents—railway spines and other conditions.

For the **treatment** see under Neurasthenia and Hysteria.

5. Hemicrania and Migraine.—This consists in periodic attacks of violent headache, confined to one side of the head and associated with nausea and vomiting. It may occur by itself, but is more frequently associated with other nervous symptoms and is often dependent on hereditary predisposition. The attacks may be produced by reflex irritation (diseases of the nose, stomach, or genitalia). The frequency and duration of the attacks are subject to wide variations. The attack may be preceded or accompanied by visual disturbances, such as flashes, scotomata, diminution in the visual field. Hyperacidity is often present (toxic effect?).

Treatment.—Carlsbad or other baths, iron, arsenic, and removal of the exciting cause. Symptomatic. Antinervin, citrophen, antipyrin, caffein, or combinations of these; mustard foot-baths; compresses; rest. Never give morphin.

6. Cephalalgia (Habitual Headache).—Headache is frequently only a concomitant symptom of other disease (fever, circulatory disturbance, intoxications, tumors); it may, however, in nervous individuals constitute the most prominent symptom.

In the **diagnosis** we must exclude, in addition to the above-named conditions, disease of the nasal and frontal cavities and diseases of the eyes (myopia, astheriopia, etc.).

For the **treatment**, antinervin; see also Neurasthenia.

7. True Epilepsy.—By the term epilepsy is meant the periodic appearance of the so-called epileptic convulsions. True epilepsy is to be distinguished from the symptomatic form, or Jacksonian epilepsy, which has been referred to repeatedly in the section on Focal Diseases of the Brain.

The epileptic attacks are thought to originate in the cortex, particularly in the central convolutions; their cortical origin is, however, not generally admitted. The attacks are originally excited by the irritation of an injured spot in the cortex (scar, spicule of bone, inflammatory process); this is at least very probable in the symptomatic form, and is supposed to be the case also in true epilepsy. From the original focus the irritation is transmitted, through the association tracts, to neighboring centers, and thus produces the epileptic convulsion.

The **etiologic factors** in the production of true epilepsy are heredity, traumatism, and infectious diseases. The disease often appears in childhood, and may vary greatly in respect to duration and intensity. The epileptic attacks may be severe or mild in character (*grand mal—petit mal*) or the attack may take the form of a stuporous condition.

Attack.—A typical attack begins with an *aura* (headache, nausea, vertigo, visual and auditory sensations), which is immediately followed by the seizure. The patient falls to the ground unconscious, and is thrown into a tonic convulsion affecting chiefly the extensor and, to some extent, the flexor muscles of the entire body. All the reflexes are abolished, and the pupils are dilated. After a time (about half a minute) this condition is succeeded by the clonic stage, characterized by violent forced contractions of the extremities and muscles in other parts of the body. The patient bites his tongue and foams at the mouth.

After a few minutes the force of the convulsion spends itself, and the patient falls into a comatose condition, from which he awakes after a variable interval of time. Headache, nausea, and fatigue may persist for some time after the attack. The patient does not remember anything that occurs during the attack. In the milder attacks the tonic and clonic stages are not so well marked, and in the equivalents there is, instead of an attack, a momentary dazed condition ("Dämmerzustand"), which may be accompanied by maniacal seizures, delirium, and hallucinations. The attacks occur most frequently during the night (epilepsia nocturna). When they occur with great frequency, the condition is not without danger and is known as *état de mal* (status epilepticus). In some, but not by any means in all, cases the attacks, if they persist for a number of years, eventually lead to a psychic degeneration.

In the **diagnosis** we must exclude hysteric attacks (*q. v.*), Jacksonian epilepsy (focal symptoms during the intervals of attack), uremic attacks (examination of urine), simulation (reflexes not abolished—prick the patient in the sole of the foot), and attacks of paralytic dementia (history, attacks are of longer duration).

Treatment.—Potassium bromid (one to four drams per diem); opium, $1\frac{1}{2}$ to 15 grains per diem, given some time before, is often of service when the attacks are frequent. Cold baths. No alcohol. Vegetable diet. If the focal symptoms are very marked, operative interference may be considered.

8. Eclampsia Infantum.—During the first years of life general convulsions may make their appearance in the course of a great variety of diseases (gastro-intestinal diseases, dentition, fever, rickets). Their occurrence is explained by deficiency of the reflex inhibitory apparatus in the infantile nervous system.

The convulsions consist in alternate tonic and clonic contractions of the entire body. The children often cry out convulsively. In rare cases the condition is later followed by epilepsy.

Diagnosis.—Exclude tubercular meningitis (basal symptoms, fever).

Treatment.—Correct the primary condition (worms, improper feeding); pack with wet cloths; cutaneous irritation; douches; cold sponging.

9. Chorea Minor (St. Vitus' Dance; Sydenham's Chorea).—This is a disease of youth. Nothing is known either of its origin or of its seat (cortex? optic thalamus?); it is usually thought to be of infectious origin. Its frequent occurrence in acute rheumatic polyarthritis and rheumatic endocarditis is, to say the least, suggestive. It not infrequently occurs during pregnancy, when it is likely to be unusually violent.

Course.—The chorea consists in involuntary, incessant, and irregular movements of the fingers, hands, arms, legs, head, facial muscles, etc. All the muscles that are usually under the control of the will exhibit a constant restlessness, so that it is impossible for the child to maintain the body or the extremities in the same position for any length of time.

The **symptoms** in individual cases vary from scarcely perceptible choreic movements of the fingers, often mistaken for wilful misbehavior in the school-room, to pronounced muscular mania (*folie musculaire*). In severe cases of this kind the child may be unable to speak, walk, or eat. Chorea is sometimes unilateral (hemichorea, also called transitory hemiparesis). The restlessness disappears during the night. The disease may last from a few months to several years; relapses are common; in the end, however, almost all cases recover.

Treatment.—Arsenic, antipyrin (eight to sixteen grains three times a day), salol, massage, diet. The child should be kept out of school.

10. **Chronic Hereditary Chorea (Huntingdon's Chorea).**—This is an entirely different disease from chorea minor. Its true nature is still unknown. It occurs later in life in individuals predisposed by heredity, and is characterized by motor irritative phenomena and isolated contractions, which in the course of years increase in extent and intensity. *Pari passu* there is progressive decay of the mental faculties. As far as known, recovery has never occurred.

11. **Paralysis Agitans (Parkinson's Disease).**—The disease usually makes its appearance in advanced age. Nothing is known of its nature. It is supposed to be caused by emotions and mental worry.

The affection begins with a peculiar slow, rhythmic tremor (five to six beats a minute) of the arm and hands, similar to the motion made in rolling pills. The tremor persists when the patient is at rest. It is aggravated by excitement. As the years go on the tremors become more extensive. All the extremities, the head, and the lips become involved, and the patient assumes a characteristic attitude, with the head bent forward, the back bowed, and the arms slightly flexed at the elbows. During sleep the tremors usually subside. Eventually paralytic symptoms make their appearance. The disease is incurable.

Treatment.—Rest, good food, bromids.

12. **Congenital Myotonia (Thomsen's Disease).**—This is a rare affection, hereditary in character. All the voluntary movements, especially walking, are impeded by spastic contractions, occurring spontaneously. The rigidity of the muscles is increased by mental emotion (resembles stammering).

Treatment.—Baths ; gymnastic exercise.

13. **Idiopathic Tremor.**—A tremor is not infrequently observed in the head and extremities in healthy individuals

with perhaps a slight neurasthenic taint. The condition is not rarely hereditary and is aggravated by excitement.

Treatment.—See Neurasthenia. The extremities may be tied fast; massage.

III. DISEASES OF THE SPINAL CORD.

A. DISEASES CAUSED BY FOCAL LESIONS INVOLVING A CROSS-SECTION OF THE CORD.

Diseases of the Spinal Meninges.

Disease of the spinal meninges is usually associated with inflammatory processes in the cerebral portion of these structures; it is rarely isolated. The meninges are involved most frequently in cerebrospinal meningitis and in purulent meningitis; more rarely they are the seat of tubercular lesions. The anatomic changes are the same as in the cerebrum.

The clinical symptoms are often quite overshadowed by those which are due to the cerebral condition. The following symptoms are thought to be due to irritation of the spinal roots (reflex through the posterior or direct from the anterior?): Rigidity of the nuchal muscles (roots of the upper portion of the cervical enlargement), opisthotonos (thoracic portion), hyperalgesia (radiating pains), paralysis of the bladder. The spinal origin of these symptoms is not quite definitely settled. In many instances it is not possible to exclude the influence of cerebral disease. Among the idiopathic forms we have:

1. **Hypertrophic Cervical Pachymeningitis.**—This consists in a marked inflammatory thickening of the dura, especially in the region of the cervical cord, forming adhesions with the pia-arachnoid, and leading to compression of the cervical nerve-roots and cord. The cause is unknown (syphilis?).

The **symptoms** are those of a focal disease in the cervical enlargement (see Part IV, 3), the symptoms of irritation of the nerve-roots being particularly marked:

Violent neuralgic pains in the back of the neck and scapular region, paralysis, and muscular atrophy, most pronounced in the muscles supplied by the ulnar and median nerves—*i. e.*, the small muscles of the hand and the flexor muscles. The contraction of the antagonistic groups of radial muscles produces the so-called *preacher's hand*. In rare cases the gait is spastic and the bladder function is impaired. Improvement is possible.

Treatment.—Antisyphilitic. Electricity. Symptomatic. Cauterization of the back of the neck.

2. Syphilitic Spinal Meningomyelitis.—The soft membranes of the spinal cord become the seat of superficial gummatous neoplasms, seen with the naked eye as a thick, jelly-like deposit, similar in appearance to those seen in brain syphilis, with which the disease may or may not be associated. These deposits may compress the spinal cord by surrounding it in its entire circumference, as seen in Figure 27, or they may extend into the cord substance. The disease attacks most frequently the thoracic portion of the cord. The arteries exhibit the same changes as in syphilitic endarteritis in the cerebrum. The neoplasm extends into the nerve-roots, and in some cases true gummatous tumors are observed. According as one or the other feature is most marked the disease is designated as syphilitic meningomyelitis, meningoneuritis, or meningo-arteritis.

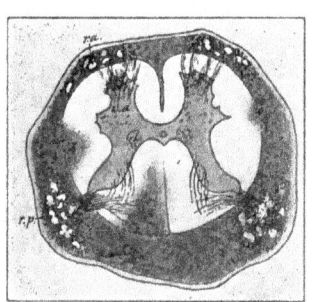
Fig. 27.

The **symptoms** are due either to compression or directly to the diseased condition of the nervous elements, and vary both in extent and intensity, according to the nature and severity of the primary disease: Violent paroxysms of pain; spastic paraparesis of the legs, not infrequently more pronounced on one side, thus pointing to a unilateral lesion, with exaggerated tendon reflex; vesical and rectal disturbances (retention) and slight sensory disturbances (paresthesia).

Diagnosis.—The intermittence of the symptoms and the occurrence of temporary improvement, followed by relapses, are characteristic of the disease. In some cases the presence of brain symptoms may assist the diagnosis (basal palsies). The essential point in the diagnosis is the demonstration of a previous infection. A special form of this disease is Erb's syphilitic spinal paralysis. This is characterized by the gradual development of spastic paresis in the legs, with slight muscular spasms, increased reflexes, mild sensory disturbances, and the absence of ataxia and of pupillary anomalies.

Treatment.—Antisyphilitic treatment is indicated when there is the slightest suspicion of syphilis—inunctions, injections, potassium iodid. If, as is frequently the case, degenerative processes have already made their appearance, partial improvement is all that can be expected, and the treatment is then merely symptomatic—baths, etc.

3. **Compression of the Spinal Cord (Compression Myelitis).**—Although this may be due to a variety of processes, it seems advisable to discuss it in this connection. In many cases the most definite diagnosis that can be made is that of the existence of compression from some unknown cause.

Compression of the spinal cord may be due to:

1. Diseases of the bone—caries of the vertebræ, compression by a purulent focus, exuberant granulations pressing on the meninges (tubercular meningitis), sequestra, fractures of the bone due to angulation of the vertebral column, carcinoma beginning in the vertebra, and traumatic fractures and luxations of the vertebral column.

2. Diseases of the meninges—pachymeningitis, syphi-

litic meningitis, tubercular meningitis, sarcoma, lipoma, fibroma, echinococcus.

3. Diseases of the spinal cord—glioma, sarcoma, gumma, tubercle.

By far the most common causes of compression are caries and carcinoma. As a result of the compression the integrity of the nerve-fibers and nerve-cells which make up the corresponding segment is seriously impaired. The first effect is edema in the segment pressed upon (obstruction of the lymph-channels); during this stage there is a possibility of regeneration. If, however, the pressure continues and increases in intensity, the nervous elements become swollen and soften and are finally completely destroyed. In most cases, therefore, there is no true myelitis.

Course.—The most important symptoms of compression are the violent radiating pains, due probably to irritation of the nerve-roots, which frequently follow the distribution of the peripheral nerves (neuralgic form), and either surround the trunk like a girdle, *girdle pains*, or radiate into the extremities. They frequently produce reflex contractions in the muscles of the extremities, as these are no longer under the control of the will. Hyperesthesia and paresthesia may also be produced. The rigidity in the muscles of the back of the neck and back must also be attributed to irritation of the nerve-roots. The remaining symptoms vary according as the lesion is situated in the cervical, thoracic, lumbar, or sacral portion of the cord or in the cauda equina. (See Part IV, 3.) They consist, therefore, of palsies, either spastic or flaccid, muscular atrophies, and disturbances of the bladder and of sensibility. The compression usually affects the thoracic portion of the cord (spastic paraplegia of the legs, disturbances of the bladder and of sensation; the arms escape). Death is caused by the primary disease, cystitis, asthenia, or decubitus.

Diagnosis.—The existence of compression must first

be diagnosticated and then its level (see Part IV, 3), and to do this it is best to proceed in the following manner :

First determine which extremities are paralyzed—if the legs alone, investigate the condition of the knee-jerk. If this is lost, the lesion is usually situated in the lumbar enlargement, or possibly in the nerve-roots contained in the cauda equina (?) ; if fibers of the sciatic only are compressed, the patellar reflex is preserved. If the knee-jerk is exaggerated, the lesion must be situated above the reflex arc—that is, either in the thoracic or in the cervical portion of the cord.

If the arms are free from symptoms, especially if the muscles of the hands are not atrophied, the lesion is situated in the thoracic portion of the cord.

Tumors in the cauda equina produce deep sacral pain, at first often mistaken for sciatica, vesical and rectal paralysis, disturbances in erection and ejaculation, paraplegia dolorosa inferior, muscular atrophies, anesthesia of the legs (especially the posterior surface), of the anal region, and of the scrotum ; decubitus. The lesion may be more accurately located by noting which muscles are atrophied (RD), as shown in Figure 17, and by noting the level at which the sensory disturbance begins. Usually the lesion is located too low, because we are not as yet sufficiently informed as to the exact localization in the individual segments. Tumors especially are usually found to be situated two or three segments higher than would appear to be indicated by the level of the highest sensory disturbance.

After the level of the lesion has been determined as accurately as possible by a process of exclusion from below upward, and from above downward, we determine, by means of Plate 27, which spinal process or processes correspond to the level found. The vertebral column is then examined with special care in this region, especially in regard to its mobility.

In determining the nature of the compressing process

172   SPECIAL PATHOLOGY AND TREATMENT.

the following possibilities must be taken into consideration :

Caries.—Age ; changes in the vertebral column (acute-angled kyphosis) ; tenderness on pressure ; deep abscesses ; fever (cystitis being excluded) ; tuberculosis in other parts of the body ; long duration.

Carcinoma.—Advanced age ; cachexia ; metastasis, rapid course ; most intense pain.

Glioma Medullare.—Slow development, the symptoms at first unilateral.

Even after the most careful study it is not infrequently impossible to arrive at a definite diagnosis ; compression may be absent, even in spite of the most pronounced symptoms.

Treatment.—In caries, extension and plaster-of-Paris jacket ; arsenic (operative (?) : resection of the vertebral arches). In tumors, surgical treatment. Tumors in the cauda equina give the best prospects of success. (See General Treatment.) In most cases the treatment is symptomatic—cleanliness, care of the skin, catheterization, morphin.

4. Acute and Chronic Myelitis.—A number of affections differing both in their etiology and morbid anatomy are included under the term **myelitis.**

They are all characterized by a diffuse circumscribed or cylindric degeneration of nerve-fibers and cells contained in a certain region of the spinal cord, by the formation of neurogliar tissue, and by more or less round-celled infiltration and alteration of the pia-arachnoid. They are usually of toxic origin, and follow in the wake of infectious diseases (typhoid, influenza, gonorrhea, erysipelas, syphilis, etc.) ; some forms are due to direct infection.

They are classified, according to their clinical course, into acute, lasting several weeks ; subacute, lasting two or three months ; and chronic forms. The commonest seat of myelitis is the thoracic portion of the cord. The most frequent form is that due to syphilitic infection.

The **symptoms** vary greatly according to the seat of the disease. (See Part IV, 3.)

Thoracic myelitis, the most frequent form, is characterized by spastic paraplegia of the legs, without very marked paroxysms of pain, although such may be present; disturbances of sensation and of the bladder; paresthesia and ataxic conditions in the legs.

In **lumbar myelitis** we have flaccid paraplegia of the legs, loss of reflexes, paralysis of the bladder, etc.

In **cervical myelitis** there are spastic paraplegia of the legs, atrophy of the muscles of the arms, etc.

Decubitus and cystitis frequently mark the beginning of the end.

This disease must be differentiated from compression myelitis (*q. v.*) and combined system diseases (slow course).

The method of determining the level of the lesion and the **treatment** will be found under Compression Myelitis.

If syphilis is present, inunctions are indicated. As the degenerative process has already begun, the treatment is only partially successful.

Among special forms should be mentioned:

(*a*) *Acute disseminated myelitis* (the sudden appearance of multiple foci of degeneration in the white substance), which is again subdivided into an ataxic and a paraplegic form. The ataxia is not accompanied by nystagmus, thus differentiating the disease from sclerosis. Disturbance of the speech and psychic disturbances are often present. This form often occurs in association with optic neuritis, resembling in this respect multiple sclerosis, which runs a more chronic course. The condition is then termed disseminated encephalomyelitis. When it occurs in association with multiple neuritis, we speak of disseminated neuromyelitis.

(*b*) In *severe anemias* numerous foci of degeneration are found, especially in the posterior and lateral columns. The condition is probably secondary to disease of the blood-vessels, as are also, in some instances, some of the above-mentioned forms.

The symptoms are mild ataxia and sensory disturbances and loss of patellar reflex.

5. Syringomyelia.—This term is applied to focal diseases characterized by abnormal cavity formations in the interior of the white substance. The condition may be due to various causes; it may be congenital or may develop later in life in predisposed individuals (hydromyelia). It may be due to the breaking-down of central proliferations of neurogliar tissue (central gliosis), or may occur from some unknown cause after trauma, hemorrhages, etc.

The excavations may include the entire length of the spinal cord, and may even extend into the medulla oblongata. The favorite seat is the cervical enlargement, so that the principal symptoms are those produced by a lesion of this portion of the cord.

The cavity usually begins in the vicinity of the central canal, and leads to gradual destruction of the central gray substance in the anterior and posterior horns, and of the nerve-fibers and ganglion cells situated in those regions.

The individual **symptoms** taken by themselves are not characteristic, but taken altogether they are practically pathognomonic of syringomyelia. They are:

1. Progressive muscular atrophy and *paralysis*, affecting chiefly the upper extremities, more pronounced on one side, sometimes more bilateral in character. The small muscles of the hand and the triceps are most frequently attacked; the atrophied muscles are the seat of fibrillar contractions and give the reactions of degenerations (degenerative atrophy, disease of the peripheral neuron cells).

2. Disturbances of sensation in the arms, especially analgesia and thermo-anesthesia, with integrity of the tactile sense (dissociation of the anesthesia).

3. Trophic disturbances in the fingers and joints, such as necrosis, suppuration, subluxations, hypertrophies.

In addition there may be spastic paraparesis of the legs

or bulbar symptoms (paralysis of the spinal accessory, hypoglossus, etc.). Atypical cases resembling tabes, spastic spinal paralysis, etc., are not infrequently observed.

The process is slowly progressive.

Diagnosis.—Spinal muscular atrophy, in which sensation is normal, must be excluded. Atypical cases are very difficult to recognize.

Treatment.—Symptomatic; electricity, baths, etc.

6. Hemorrhages in the Central Canal.—Hemorrhage may be either extramedullary and between the meninges (intrameningeal apoplexies, hematorrhachis), or in the substance of the spinal cord itself (hematomyelia). They are usually due to traumatism. In intrameningeal hemorrhage the symptoms are similar to those produced by spinal meningitis, except that the phenomenon occurs suddenly after trauma (symptoms of irritation of the roots, paraplegia, disturbances of the bladder and of sensation).

The **symptoms** of hematomyelia present the same combinations as those in syringomyelia; the localization is the same, but they appear suddenly after trauma and vary somewhat according to the seat and extent of the lesion. The seat of the hemorrhage is determined by the principles laid down on page 171.

The condition is not infrequently improved by **treatment,** which consists of rest and, later, warm baths.

7. Multiple Cerebrospinal Sclerosis (Sclerose en plaques).—Focal sclerosis is a disease of the most enigmatic character. It is characterized by the appearance of a number of small, irregularly scattered foci in the brain and spinal cord (primarily encephalitic or myelitic?), with destruction of the medullary sheath of the nerve-fibers situated in those foci. The axis-cylinder, however, persists and continues to functionate for some time longer, so that the fibers are not completely destroyed. The disease frequently occurs in young subjects in the wake of infectious diseases (?).

The **symptoms** are progressive and develop very gradually. In the beginning the patient experiences difficulty in performing certain movements. There are weakness and want of control of the arms and legs, tremors appear when the patient takes hold of an object (intention tremor), and the gait becomes stiff and uncertain (spastic and ataxic).

In addition nystagmus, scanning speech, slight vesical disturbances, and occasionally optic atrophy develop. The knee-jerks are exaggerated. From time to time there are apoplectiform attacks; sensory disturbances are usually slight; paresthesia may be present.

While this description applies to typical cases, there are many variations, depending on the site of the focus, and these *formes frustes* (spurious forms) of multiple sclerosis are frequently mistaken for other diseases. Many of the above-named symptoms may be absent. In some cases ataxia is more marked, in others the spastic paralysis of the legs; a third group is characterized by the presence of bulbar symptoms.

Course.—The course of the disease is extremely chronic and occasionally interrupted by temporary improvement. The intelligence may eventually be affected.

Diagnosis.—We must exclude neurasthenia, hysteria (occasional presence of different clinical pictures), paralytic dementia (pupils, history). Other diseases of the spinal cord, such as myelitis, spastic spinal paralysis, etc., can not always be excluded with certainty.

Treatment.—Gymnastic exercises, massage, baths, symptomatic.

B. SYSTEM DISEASES.

For a description of their general characters see Part IV, 3, page 104. They are for the most part very chronic, progressive, and incurable, because when cells and fibers once degenerate in the brain and spinal cord, they can never recover.

8. **Spastic Spinal Paralysis.**—This is a rare disease.

The anatomic basis is a symmetric primary degeneration of the pyramidal tract (central motor neuron complex).

Course.—The disease begins in adults (children ?) with a slowly progressive spastic paralysis of the legs, arms, and facial muscles, without muscular atrophy or disturbance of the bladder or of sensation. The knee-jerks and ankle-clonus are exaggerated.

There are also other forms of spastic bilateral palsies; the *cerebral spastic paralysis of children*, the form occurring in *multiple sclerosis, hydrocephalus, myelitis*, etc. In most, but not all, of these cases other symptoms are superadded to those mentioned above (impure cases).

9. Amyotrophic Lateral Sclerosis.—In addition to the pyramidal tract the motor cells in the anterior horn (peripheral neuron), especially in the lumbar enlargement and possibly also in the nerve nuclei of the bulb, are included in the morbid process. (See Part IV, 3.)

Course.—The disease begins in adults with the appearance of muscular weakness and atrophy in the hands (interossei, thenar muscles), accompanied or followed later by the development of a spastic paretic gait. The atrophy of the muscles of the arm slowly progresses (see under Spinal Muscular Atrophy), the muscles present fibrillary contractions and the reactions of degeneration. Eventually the muscles of the arm and shoulder atrophy completely. The reflexes are preserved or even exaggerated; the legs are completely paralyzed and spastic; the knee-jerks are exaggerated; ankle-clonus is present; bladder and sensation are normal; pain is present, especially in the muscles of the arm. In many instances the symptoms of chronic progressive bulbar paralysis are superadded early in the course of the disease.

Treatment.—Symptomatic; electricity, baths, arsenic, strychnin, feeding by means of esophageal tube.

10. Progressive Spinal Muscular Atrophy.—In this affection the motor ganglion cells in the anterior horn of the spinal cord, especially in the cervical enlargement, are destroyed by a slowly progressive degeneration. The pyramidal tract is not involved. The alterations in the muscle consist in a slow, degenerative atrophy of the individual fibrils. There is an increase in the number of nuclei in the sheath of the fibrils and the protoplasm shrinks, although even very much attenuated fibers may show a distinct transverse striation. Eventually the sheath disappears along with the remains of the protoplasm, and nothing remains but the connective-tissue portion of the fiber.

Course.—The clinical symptoms are those of amyotrophic lateral sclerosis without spastic phenomena: A very slowly developing and gradually extending atrophy and paralysis of the small muscles of the hand and later of all the muscles of the arm and shoulder, with fibrillary contractions and the reactions of degeneration; the legs often escape; sensation and bladder function are not affected. Duration, one to several years. Owing to the atrophy of the thenar muscles adduction of the thumb is impossible—Simian hand. The deltoid muscle often atrophies before the other muscles of the arm and forearm. Even the nuchal muscles and the intercostals, or rarely the diaphragm, may be involved. Bulbar paralysis may follow or may develop simultaneously.

Diagnosis.—See under Progressive Muscular Dystrophy.

Treatment.—See Amyotrophic Lateral Sclerosis.

There is another form of muscular atrophy, the so-called *peroneal type* of progressive muscular atrophy. This form may occur in several members of the same family, and is characterized by atrophy of the peronei and tibialis anticus, etc., in addition to the small muscles of the hand. The condition leads to paralytic club-foot and peroneal gait, in which the patient raises the thighs unusually high, while the tip of the foot drags on the ground. The patellar reflexes are abolished. Slight disturbances of sensibility are present in the toes and fingers. The atrophy in the muscles of the arms and legs gradually increases. Anatomically, we find degenerative changes in the peroneal, median, and thenar nerves and in the lumbar and cervical enlargement, where the cells of the anterior horns appear to be involved.

11. **Progressive Muscular Dystrophy (Primary Myopathy).**—Whether this disease is of spinal origin is still an open question, as up to the present time the changes found have been confined to the muscles. It is to be regarded as the last link in the chain of motor system diseases.

The muscle-fibers undergo an extremely gradual, non-degenerative atrophy. The individual fibers shrink and eventually disappear; the transverse striations persist for a long time; the muscular nuclei become multiplied, fat is deposited between the fibers, and hypertrophic fibers are not uncommon. Their thickness measures from 150 to 200 μ. The disease is often hereditary and makes its appearance in early life. The atrophied muscles present the phenomenon of simple atrophy only; fibrillary contractions and the reactions of degeneration are absent; the atrophy is slowly progressive. Recovery does not occur, but the process is sometimes brought to a standstill.

Depending on the period when the disease first makes its appearance, various forms are distinguished, which in their subsequent course merge into one another. They are:

(a) **Pseudohypertrophy.**—This begins in early childhood, with weakness in the muscles of the back, gradually extending to the lumbar and femoral muscles. The muscles show no alteration in shape. They appear rather hypertrophic on account of the deposition of fat (lipomatosis). The children are unable to get up from the floor without supporting themselves with their hands; the gait becomes waddling, and finally walking is impossible. Later curvature of the spine develops (lordosis).

(b) **The Infantile Variety.**—This begins in children, frequently with atrophy and paralysis of the facial muscles (expressionless countenance — "facies myopathique"). Later the muscular atrophies of the extremities belonging to the next form are superadded.

(c) **Juvenile Form.**—This appears during or after puberty. We distinguish a *shoulder-girdle type*, affecting the pectoral muscles, trapezius, latissimus dorsi, serratus anticus, triceps, and biceps, which undergo atrophy in the order named. The small muscles of the hand, the deltoid, and the sternocleidomastoid escape (the opposite condition obtains in spinal muscular atrophy). The other is a *pelvic girdle type*, in which the quadriceps, glutei, and peronei are affected. The calf muscles escape. The two forms merge into one another or exist side by side.

The **diagnosis** of muscular atrophies requires a familiarity with the normal configuration of the extremities. A practised eye will recognize at the first glance atrophy of the lumbricales by the depressions between the first phalanges, of the thenar and hypothenar groups by abnormal dimples, of the pectoral muscles by deep depression below the clavicle, which is very prominent, of the deltoid by flattening of the shoulder, of the trapezius by diminution in the size of the neck, of the rhomboid muscles by the presence of abnormal depressions where normally elevations should exist, of the quadriceps by a flattening of the upper surface of the thighs, or of the peronei by the absence of normal prominence outward from the crest of the tibia, etc.

The differential diagnosis between the individual forms is very simple. It is based purely on the beginning of the disease.

Treatment.—Symptomatic and orthopedic.

12. **Anterior Poliomyelitis.**—The inflammatory diseases of the gray substance in the anterior horn of the spinal cord are either acute or chronic, and exert their malign influence on the motor ganglion cells situated in the region. Accordingly they lead to degenerative muscular atrophies and paralyses.

(a) **Acute Anterior Poliomyelitis.**—This affection makes its appearance during the first years of life, rarely in adult age, as an acute infectious disease, the bacterial origin of which is unknown. It manifests itself in an inflammation of the substance of the anterior horns, the inflammation beginning in the blood-vessels. The disease is ushered in by fever, vomiting, and delirium. This is followed by moderately deep coma, lasting several days, after which the patient improves, but there is found to be

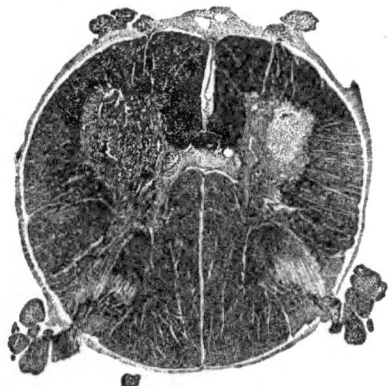

Fig. 28.—Transverse section of the lumbar enlargement in anterior poliomyelitis. The diseased focus is readily seen in the anterior horn, especially in the lateral cell-groups. The entire right half of the cord is shrunken.

a flaccid paralysis of the arms and legs (rarely of the face, etc.) and of the bladder, with loss of reflexes, but without pain or sensory disturbances. Some of the paralytic phenomena disappear after a time; others are permanent, but are usually confined to one side. The affected muscles undergo a rapid degenerative process.

The remains of this disease which persist in later life are termed *infantile spinal paralysis*. Their anatomic basis consists in a shrinking of the affected anterior horn. (See

Fig. 28, anterior horn on the right side.) Contractures result from the action of the antagonistic muscles; the development of the affected members is retarded.

The most frequent palsies that result are paralysis of the peronei and extensors (talipes equinovarus), paralysis of the upper-arm type (deltoid, biceps, brachialis anticus, supinator longus), and of the forearm type (triceps, extensors of the hand).

Treatment.—In the beginning, rest, baths, leeches to the back, purgatives, and sweat cures; later, gymnastic exercises and orthopedic treatment.

An important orthopedic measure consists in transferring the action of an adjoining sound muscle to the tendon of the paralyzed muscle. In talipes valgus the extensor hallucis is sutured to the tendon of the tibialis anticus; in talipes varus the hallucis is attached to the extensor digitorum communis; in pes equinus the peroneus and flexor digitorum to the tendo Achilles, etc. Good results have also been achieved by dividing the muscles. In the forearm the thenar and radial muscles can be advantageously utilized to supply the function of the paralyzed flexors and extensors of the fingers.

(b) **Chronic Poliomyelitis.**—So-called *chronic atrophic spinal paralysis* is a rare disease, occurring in adults, characterized by the more or less rapid development of flaccid paralysis, first in the lower, and later in the upper, extremity, followed by degenerative atrophy. The reflexes are abolished; sensation and bladder function are normal. Many muscles may escape; improvement is possible.

Diagnosis.—Lumbar myelitis, sensory disturbances, and multiple neuritis (*q. v.*) must be excluded.

Treatment.—Baths, electricity, symptomatic.

13. **Tabes Dorsalis.**—The anatomic basis of tabes dorsalis consists in a chronic progressive degeneration of the peripheral sensory neuron complex, especially of the lower extremities. The degeneration affects most extensively that portion of the neuron complex which begins in the

spinal ganglia, enters the substance of the spinal cord through the posterior roots, and continues within the cord (the long tracts in the posterior columns; the short tracts enter the posterior horns, Clarke's columns, and anterior horns; see p. 51). The peripheral portions of the neuron, consisting of the sensory cutaneous nerves, are, however, attacked by degenerative processes. But in addition to these tracts the tabetic process frequently attacks other pathways, both sensory (central) and motor (peripheral and central neuron complexes), producing combined forms. In typical cases certain definite reflex arcs (reflex collaterals) —namely, those concerned in the patellar and pupillary reflexes—are first destroyed. It is not as yet definitely known at what point the disease takes its origin. (For further details of the morbid anatomy the student is referred to Plates 77 and 78.)

As has been stated, the peripheral neuron complex of the lower extremities is most frequently attacked, more rarely that of the upper extremity only is affected (high tabes), either alone or in combination with the peripheral neuron of the fifth nerve, especially the descending root of the glossopharyngeal, etc. These forms are all to be regarded as different varieties of the same disease.

In a large proportion of cases a former syphilitic infection is shown by statistics to be the cause of the degenerative process.

The symptoms develop slowly and may be divided into three stages:

1. The Neuralgic Stage.—This is characterized by violent, fulminating attacks of pain, with occasional exacerbations, radiating into the legs (lancinating pains, symptoms of irritation of the posterior roots?), and not infrequently by paresthesias and painful, oppressive sensations in the epigastric region (girdle pain). If the patient presents himself at this time, the examiner, as a rule, finds the two symptoms, which, when present together, are pathognomonic of tabes; they are:

184 SPECIAL PATHOLOGY AND TREATMENT.

1. Reflex pupillary rigidity, or failure to react to light with accommodation preserved; contracted pupil.

2. Loss of the patellar reflex (Westphal's sign).

2. The Ataxic Stage.—This may make its appearance after a variable interval (sometimes lasting many years) has elapsed since the appearance of the first symptoms. The most characteristic feature is the tabetic gait or

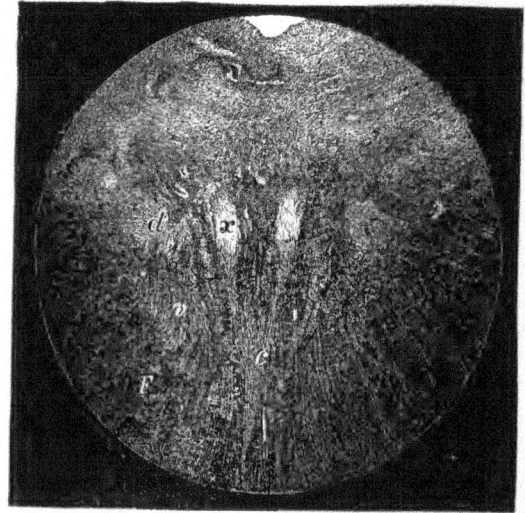

Fig. 29.—Oculomotor nucleus in tabes dorsalis (medullary sheath stain, photograph, magnified 80 times): *F*, Posterior longitudinal bundle; *d*, dorsal, *v*, ventral, *c*, central, *x*, Westphal's, nucleus, which in this illustration appears unusually pale, owing to a marked degeneration of the fibers (connected with loss of the pupillary reflex?).

ataxia. The patient throws his feet about and brings them to the ground with a stamp; the gait is uncertain, but not paretic. The ataxia is considerably increased when the patient closes his eyes (Romberg's phenomenon).

In addition there are slight disturbances of the bladder

function, the sensitiveness to painful and thermic stimuli is blunted, and optic atrophy may make its appearance.

3. Paralytic Stage.—The interval between this and the preceding stage is also variable. The ataxia gradually increases, and can even be noticed as the patient moves about in bed, the gait becomes more and more paretic-ataxic, and finally walking becomes impossible. As a rule, there is never a true paralysis.

The disturbances of sensation and of the bladder function increase.

The lancinating pains are constantly present and periodically culminate in the so-called tabetic crises, consisting in intensely painful attacks of colic, vomiting, cough, and dyspnea (abdominal, gastric, laryngeal crises, etc.).

Effusions into the joints, arthropathies (trophic?), and ulcerations (*mal perforant*) are common. Not infrequently paralysis of the eye muscles and of the trifacial nerve and hemicrania-like conditions occur early in the disease.

The **diagnosis** of tabes presents no difficulty in ordinary cases. It may, however, be obscured by an atypical mode of onset and by the absence of important symptoms, such as the pupillary reflex, and the abolition of the patellar reflex. Alcoholic and diabetic neuritis and hereditary ataxia must be excluded. The differential diagnosis from these conditions will be discussed under their respective heads.

Treatment.—The value of antisyphilitic treatment is doubtful. Baths, rest, massage, gymnastic exercises to correct the muscular incoordination, attention to diet, electricity, suspension; nitrate of silver, potassium iodid, secale cornutum, antinervin, narcotics.

14. Hereditary Ataxia (Friedreich's Disease).— This is a combined system disease. The degeneration in the posterior columns of the spinal cord is accompanied by a similar process in the direct cerebellar tract and pyramidal tract. The cerebellum is probably also involved. The disease often appears in families.

It begins in early life, with a gradually increasing disturbance of the coordination in the movements and attitude of the extremities, trunk, and head; ataxia of the legs and arms—Romberg's phenomenon. The incoordination manifests itself in the trunk, both on motion and during rest, as when the patient is seated. The gait is vacillating, resembling the cerebellar gait, and the paresis is usually more prominent. In addition there are nystagmus, slight disturbances of speech, and some disturbance of sensibility and of the bladder function.

Diagnosis.—The knee-jerk is abolished, but the pupillary reflex is normal—a differential point in the diagnosis from tabes. The neuralgic pains of tabes are also absent. The disease slowly progresses to a complete paralysis; contractures in the fingers are common. It lasts many years. Recovery has never been reported.

Treatment.—Symptomatic.

Other forms of **combined system diseases** similar to hereditary ataxia also occur, presenting in the main the symptoms of a spastic spinal paralysis with some disturbance of sensation and bladder function, combined with ataxia. This class includes a hereditary form of spastic spinal paralysis affecting the pyramidal tract, posterior columns, and lateral cerebellar tract, besides other varieties concerning which but little is known.

IV. DISEASES OF THE PERIPHERAL NERVES.

A. DISEASES OF SINGLE NERVES.

A great variety of causes may produce lesions of the peripheral nerves: Traumatism, tumors of all kinds (tumors in the soft parts, small exostoses in the bony canals, neuromata), cicatricial processes, chemic changes produced by the formation of toxic substances during the course of, or subsequent to, acute infectious diseases in which individual nerves may be injured—toxic neuritis. A spontaneous (inflammatory?) affection of single nerves—

rheumatic neuritis—is also quite common, especially facial neuritis.

In severe neuritic processes the nerve-fiber is completely destroyed and replaced by sclerotic connective tissue. In milder grades of the degenerative processes the nerves may be completely regenerated (parenchymatous neuritis), the nerve tissue differing in this respect from the tissues of the spinal cord. We distinguish various forms according to their severity.

1. **The Diseases of the Motor Nerves.**—Any of the above-mentioned lesions affecting a purely motor or mixed nerve may give rise to paralytic and irritative symptoms (localized muscular spasms) in the domain of the affected nerve. We distinguish three forms of paralysis: A severe, a moderately severe, and a mild form, depending on the duration, which in turn depends on the severity of the neuritic process.

For the details in the **diagnosis** the student is referred to the paragraph on Electric Diagnosis, Part IV, page 108.

The most frequent forms of paralysis are: Facial paralysis—usually rheumatic—in middle-ear disease, due to a compression neuritis of the nerve in its course through the bony canal. Paralysis of the radial nerve, usually due to compression and occurring especially in narcosis, in paralysis of the fifth and sixth roots of the brachial plexus, by compression between the clavicle and the first rib during sleep, and in lead-poisoning; oculomotor paralysis—postdiphtheric; recurrens paralysis, due to compression by aneurysms or tumors; paralysis of the spinal accessory; paralysis of the brachial plexus during labor; paralysis of the median and thenar nerves from injuries.

For a detailed account of the **symptoms** of these and other possible paralyses consult Part IV, 3, page 97.

Of the localized muscular spasms produced by disease of individual peripheral nerves the more frequent are the following:

Spasm of the facial nerve, clonic convulsions of the entire musculature of one side of the face (*tic convulsif*). A partial form is represented by blepharospasm, or tonic and clonic convulsions of the eyelids.

Spasm of the muscles of mastication, or trismus, a tonic spasm usually central in origin.

Spasm of the spinal accessory,—spastic torticollis,—a severe tonic and clonic convulsion, frequently involving, in addition to the trapezius and sternocleidomastoid, the other nuchal muscles innervated by the cervical plexus (splenius, etc.). The latter group may also be attacked separately.

Clonic spasm of the diaphragm, singultus, spasm of the calf muscles (crampus sensu strictiori), and others.

The cause of these cramps is not by any means always a lesion of the peripheral motor nerves. In many cases they are reflex in character, as, for instance, in violent neuralgia, etc.

It is often very difficult to distinguish convulsions of central (psychogenic) origin from those due to peripheral irritation. The two causes may be at work at the same time and together produce the convulsions (predisposition due to central disease and peripheral exciting cause). The spasms that are to be interpreted in this way include fits of yawning, laughing, weeping, and shouting (see Hysteria), the saltatory reflex spasm (muscular contractions when the patient attempts to walk), multiple paramyoclonus (see Hysteria), also the so-called occupation neuroses which occasionally attack neurasthenic individuals and consist in disturbances of the coordination of certain muscles required for definite movements performed in the course of the patient's ordinary occupation, especially in manual work (reading, sewing, violin- and piano-playing, etc.).

Writer's cramp—mogigraphia—consists in uncontrollable spasms in the muscles of the hand and fingers, accompanied by tremors and weakness and, occasionally, painful sensations. Continuous writing becomes utterly impossible (spastic paralytic tremor-like neuralgic form). The disability is increased by psychic emotion and fear, greatly as in stammering.

Treatment.—The patient must stop writing at stated intervals and use a thick penholder (Nussbaum's holder). Cold sponging, massage, gymnastic exercises, electric treatment, bending of the arms, writing machine.

Note.—Occupation palsies similar to the occupation spasms and also associated with muscular atrophy are sometimes observed. Blacksmiths are attacked in this way in the small muscles of the hand; drummers in the extensor and flexor longus of the thumb; dairymen suffer a paralysis of the ulnar nerve, etc. Other forms of paralysis and spasms, as a rule, require no treatment in mild cases, although electricity and massage may be employed.

In the severe forms treatment is usually of very little value. Removal of the cause, gymnastic exercises, massage, baths, cutaneous irritation, actual cautery for spasms. (For psychic treatment see under Hysteria and Neurasthenia.)

2. **Diseases of the Sensory Nerves.**—The same causes acting on sensory nerves produce either anesthesia in the area of distribution, representing the paralytic symptom, or violent radiating pains, representing the irritative symptom. The latter are more important than the former. These neuralgic pains, which occur in paroxysms, are not infrequently accompanied by paresthesia and by some disturbance of the sensibility in the affected portion of the skin. They develop most frequently after severe infectious diseases (malaria, influenza), or in other toxic diseases, such as diabetes, syphilis, gout, nephritis; in arteriosclerosis (sciatic nerve); as a result of mechanical injury (tumors, scars, neuromata). Acute spontaneous forms (neuritis?) may be accompanied by cutaneous affections, such as herpes zoster, urticaria, and erythema.

For the **diagnosis** of neuralgia it is necessary that the pain should correspond exactly to the area of distribution of the affected nerve or nerve-trunk, and that the nerve should be sensitive to pressure, especially at its point of exit from the bony canal. A neuralgic attack can often be provoked by pressure on these so-called painful points (*points douloureux*). The most important forms of neuralgia are:

Trifacial Neuralgia (Tic Douloureux; Reflex Facial Spasm).—It is usually confined to one division of the nerve (supra-orbital, infra-orbital, inframaxillary) and sometimes to neuralgia of the tongue. Painful points correspond to the exit of the nerves from the cranium (supra-orbital notch, infra-orbital, and mental foramina).

Occipital Neuralgia (*Occipitalis Major*); **Intercostal Neuralgia** (*Intercostal Nerves*); **Sciatic Neuralgia or Sciatica** (*Sciatic Nerve*).—In the last-mentioned form, which is extremely refractory to treatment, the pains radiate from the hip to the knee, and in some cases to the outer border of the foot (regions supplied by the sciatic nerve). Painful points are found at the sciatic foramina, in the middle line of the posterior surface of the thigh, in the gluteal fold, and in the popliteal space. The pain is aggravated by flexing the thigh on the abdomen, with the leg extended, owing to the stretching of the nerve. The muscles of the thigh sometimes atrophy, and curvature of the spine may result (scoliosis).

Diagnosis.—Carcinoma of the rectum, coxalgia, and tabes dorsalis must be excluded. It is of the greatest importance to examine the urine for sugar and albumin. Other forms of neuralgia are spermatic neuralgia, irritable testes, coccygodynia, and joint neuralgias.

Treatment.—Removal of the primary diseases (syphilis!); galvanic current, using a low current strength; counterirritation (mustard-plaster blisters, cupping); sweat cures, hot baths, hot compresses (often better than ice), friction, and massage. Antineuralgic drugs, such as salicylic acid, antipyrin, analgen, etc. Arsenic, potassium iodid. In severe cases the use of morphin and cocain may be justifiable. Operative: resection of the nerve and, in sciatica, stretching.

B. MULTIPLE NEURITIS.

Multiple neuritis or simultaneous disease of several nerves is almost exclusively due to toxic or infectious causes. It occurs as a sequel to diphtheria, tuberculosis, typhoid, influenza, and erysipelas; during the puerperium and pregnancy; in syphilis, gonorrhea, diabetes, alcoholism, and lead and arsenic poisoning, etc.

Anatomically we find a parenchymatous degeneration (primary disintegration of the medullated nerve-fibers), with interstitial changes, probably secondary in character (round-celled infiltration, sclerosis). This is the so-called *parenchymatous neuritis* and is the most common form, but there is also one which begins as a perineuritis and interstitial neuritis. It is probable that in most cases the ganglion cells in the anterior horn are also affected, although it can not always be demonstrated, but whether this is primary or secondary is still an open question.

Course.—The onset of multiple neuritis is usually acute, with general febrile symptoms, pain, and paresthesia. This is soon followed by muscular paralysis, which in severe cases is later accompanied by degenerative atrophy, exhibiting in most cases a definite symmetric distribution. In other cases ataxic symptoms are more prominent, combined with muscular paresis. The muscles most frequently affected are the extensors of the arms and legs (extensores digitorum et carpi, quadriceps), the psoas, the peronei; any muscle may, however, be affected.

The reflexes in the affected region are abolished; in mild cases they may also be increased. Disturbances of sensation are present (hyperesthesia, paresthesia, anesthesia), and the muscles may present the various reactions of degeneration. (See Part IV, p. 108.) Both the nerve-trunks and the muscles are exquisitely painful on pressure.

After a variable interval (weeks to months—acute, subacute, and chronic forms, see Electric Diagnosis) improvement gradually begins and in most cases goes on to complete cure. Severe cases may terminate fatally in a very short time when the pneumogastric or phrenic nerves are involved.

We distinguish a motor, a sensory, and an ataxic form, according as the motor, sensory, or coordinating disturbances are more prominent. It is difficult, however, to draw a sharp dividing-line, as some of the symptoms of all three forms are usually present. The ataxic form, on account of its resemblance to tabes, is called *pseudotabes*. The most important forms are:

(a) **Alcoholic Neuritis.**—**Motor Form.**—Flaccid bilateral paralysis of the peronei, quadriceps, glutei, extensores carpi et digitorum communis, extensores pollicis, etc.

Knee-jerks abolished; sensory disturbances; paresthesia. In other cases the radiating pains, paresthesia, and tenderness of the affected nerves and muscles are more prominent; while in a third group the ataxic gait, muscular paralyses, or atrophies, with preservation of the pupillary reflex (in contradistinction to tabes), form the principal features (diabetic polyneuritis is a similar form). At the same time other phenomena of alcoholism, such as psychic disturbances, delirium, maniacal conditions, and mental confusion may be present.

(b) **Diphtheric Neuritis.**—This affects chiefly the motor nerves. Dysphagia (spinal accessory and vagus) and ocular palsies (diplopia and loss of accommodation) are the commonest manifestations. In severe cases the knee-jerk is abolished and a flaccid paralysis of the extremities develops. The vagus may be paralyzed.

(c) **Saturnine Neuritis.**—This occurs in compositors, dyers, etc. The muscles most commonly affected are the extensors of the hand and fingers supplied by the radial nerve (except the supinator longus). In addition there are sensory irritative phenomena: lead colic, **paresthesia**, slight disturbances of sensation.

(d) **Arsenical Neuritis.**—This is characterized especially by severe sensory phenomena: paresthesia in the fingers, pain, disturbances of sensibility. Paralytic symptoms are also present. (Compare Mercurial Neuritis.)

Note.—Acroparesthesia (painful paresthesia in the tips of the fingers) without motor disturbances is a disease that more or less closely resembles arsenical neuritis. Its true nature is unknown.

(e) **Multiple Neuritis of Pregnancy and the Puerperium.**—The thenar, median, sciatic, and crural nerves are specially liable to be affected. An entire extremity may be involved. The symptoms are chiefly motor; the reflexes are abolished.

(f) **Infectious Multiple Neuritis.**—Its origin is unknown, but is almost certainly infectious. It begins with general febrile symptoms and with violent neuralgic pain, both spontaneous and elicited by pressure; muscular weakness rapidly develops and goes on to a flaccid paralysis affecting first the legs and then the arms (ascending form). The tendon reflexes are abolished; disturbances of sensation, edema, acceleration of the pulse, and dyspnea (implication of the vagus) make their appearance. The duration is variable; most cases recover. Death is due to paralysis of the pneumogastric.

This form was formerly known as "Landry's paralysis." Alterations in the spinal cord, probably secondary in character, may be present in the form of certain definite degenerations. Cases also occur in which there is a focal myelitis (myeloneuritis). A positive diagnosis is difficult. The prognosis is unfavorable.

Note.—A similar clinical picture is observed in *acute polymyositis*, which is no doubt etiologically related to infectious polyneuritis. It differs from the latter in the more pronounced tenderness in the muscles on pressure and the comparative mildness of the neuritic pains. Sensory disturbances and the reactions of degeneration are absent. On the other hand, there are febrile constitutional symptoms, marked paralytic conditions, edema, and cutaneous eruptions (trichinosis must be excluded).

Anatomically we find inflammatory alterations in the muscles (round-celled infiltrations, etc.). Myositic changes are also quite frequently found in primary neuritis.

In the **diagnosis** of the various forms of neuritis we must exclude the following conditions: Tabes dorsalis (pupillary rigidity, bladder disturbances, paralysis of the eye muscles, prominence of the ataxic symptoms, comparative insignificance of the muscular paresis in the initial stage, history); lumbar myelitis (bladder disturbances, the nerves are not painful on pressure); anterior poliomyelitis (absence of sensory disturbances, of tenderness on pressure, and of spontaneous pains). The examination of the urine for albumin, sugar, and lead is very important.

Treatment. — Removal of the cause—alcohol, lead; antisyphilitic, if indicated. Rest, salicylates, antipyrin. Later, electricity, gymnastic exercises, massage, and baths.

V. OTHER DISEASES OF THE NERVOUS SYSTEM THE NATURE AND SEAT OF WHICH ARE NOT KNOWN.

1. **Basedow's disease** is the term applied to a group of symptoms consisting of exophthalmos, struma (vascular), tachycardia,—paroxysmal, pulse 100 to 160,—associated with other nervous phenomena. The latter include tremor of the extremities, hyperidrosis, feeling of heat, attacks of vomiting, and irritability. The eyeballs are prominent, and winking occurs only at long intervals (Stellwag's sign). There is lagging of the upper lid when the eyeball is rotated downward (Graefe's sign) and the internal recti are often insufficient (Moebius' symptom). The disease is supposed by some to be due to a morbid activity of the thyroid gland (toxic); according to others the seat of the lesion is in the medulla oblongata.

The **symptoms** may be more or less pronounced; in some cases they are barely perceptible (atypical forms). The disease lasts many years.

Treatment.—Bromids, arsenic, phosphate of sodium ($\frac{1}{2}$

to 3 drams per diem). Digitalis has no effect. Good food, electricity, friction and massage, baths.

2. Myxedema.—As the development of myxedema is accompanied by atrophy of the thyroid gland, there appears to be no doubt that the disease has some connection with this structure. The immediate cause appears to be the absence of its secretion (the opposite condition to that which obtains in Basedow's disease?). Total extirpation of the thyroid gland is followed by a similar condition (cachexia strumipriva).

The chief **symptom** of myxedema consists in a disfiguring edema in the skin of the face and hands. The skin becomes thick and dry, and its upper layers desquamate. The movements are clumsy and uncertain. The mental condition is affected: the subject becomes apathetic and finally demented.

Treatment.—Good results are obtained by the administration of thyroid gland in substance, by subcutaneous injection of the juice, and by the use of glycerin extract, thyroid gland tablets, and thyreoidinum siccum internally.

3. Acromegaly.—In this mysterious disease there is slow, abnormal growth of the fingers, hands, feet, nose, lips, and jaws (the "points," "akra," of the body), leading to permanent disfigurement. Optic-nerve atrophy and ocular palsies frequently result from the pressure of the enlarged pituitary body in the sella turcica. Glycosuria is often present.

Other processes belonging under this head have been discussed in Part IV, 4 (hemiatrophia facialis, edema cutis circumscriptum, erythromelalgia, symmetric gangrene).

4. Tetany.—This consists in paroxysmal attacks of painful tonic spasms, affecting especially the flexor muscles of the fingers ("Pfötchenstellung"; main en griffe), arms, and toes. The spasms are symmetric and can be provoked by pressure on the nerve-trunks (Trousseau's phenomenon). The attacks may occur at intervals for several weeks or more.

SPECIAL PATHOLOGY AND TREATMENT.

Note.—Tetanic spasms, especially of the flexors of the fingers and muscles of the calf, are frequently seen in neuritis, in alcoholic subjects, and in persons suffering from gastric disturbances. They may, however, also occur in otherwise healthy persons (manual workers, etc.).

Tetanus is a septic disease following wounds and is caused by the toxins of the tetanus bacillus. It is a secondary infection which may occur after slight injuries, manifesting itself in tonic convulsions affecting all the muscles of the body.

PART VI.

GENERAL REMARKS ON AUTOPSY TECHNIC AND THE MICROSCOPIC EXAMINATION OF THE NERVOUS SYSTEM.

In opening the cavity of the skull and spinal column it must always be borne in mind that a microscopic examination of the central organs may eventually be necessary. In many cases the exact anatomic condition can not be determined without this examination, as the macroscopic appearances, while they may explain a coarse focal lesion, do not suffice to determine which of the different forms of degenerative disease is present. This cardinal rule is often violated.

The autopsy in such cases should be performed as soon after death as possible, never later than twenty-four hours. In diseases of the spinal cord the body should be laid on its face, to avoid the confusing effects of postmortem gravitation.

The greatest mistake made in autopsies which may in other respects be correctly performed consists in carelessly cutting, compressing, and distorting the brain and cord, often rendering it impossible subsequently to make a proper microscopic examination.

The first point is the removal of the brain. If the membranes (tentorium, etc.) are not completely loosened and the cervical cord and cranial nerves carefully divided, the brain can not be removed without an undue amount of pulling, which may destroy parts of the brain that have undergone softening. In the next place an unnecessary number of incisions are too often made in the central ganglia, the corpora quadrigemina, etc., so that it is very difficult later to recognize the parts in serial sections.

It is customary to make these incisions obliquely through the central ganglia, thus disturbing the relations of the soft tissue of the brain to such an extent that it is impossible afterward to orient one's self in a microscopic section. The incisions in such cases should always be made exactly horizontal or exactly frontal; it is best to avoid cutting the fresh brain altogether.

The brain must never come in contact with water, as this gives rise to misleading appearances when the brain is hardened.

After opening a diseased focus by a superficial horizontal cut, it is much better not to attempt any fresh investigation of the details. It is not likely that any more will be learned, no matter how many incisions are made. The minute examination should be deferred until the brain has been hardened in formalin (aqueous solution, 20 to 30%) from six to eight days and then in Müller's fluid.[1] If the brain is kept at a temperature of 30° C., and if the lateral ventricles are opened and the corpus callosum detached, the examination can be made after a few weeks without doing any damage. It will then be much easier to recognize the relations of the parts, and degenerations which could not be seen in the recent condition are recognized at the first glance.

The spinal cord is often injured by careless use of the chisel and forceps; mere tugging and squeezing may lacerate a softened area. In the case of the cord also the caution against making too many incisions should be remembered. In dividing the posterior roots it is well to cut as far out as possible, so as to obtain a part, at least, of the spinal ganglia along with the posterior roots. This is always possible in the lumbar enlargement.

After carefully considering the course of the disease, the examiner should make up his mind before the autopsy what nerves or muscles are probably diseased and ought

---

[1] Bichromate of potassium 2 gm., sulphate of sodium 1 gm., distilled water 100 c c.

to be taken out. The nerves are secured to small pieces of wood, and, like the muscles, carefully labeled with the name, side of the body, and level at which they were removed. The report of the autopsy should be as minute as possible. The condition of the bones of the skull and spinal column and of the meninges and bloodvessels should be accurately described and the contents of the ventricles noted. The latter point should be determined before the brain is removed; all measurements must be made on the fresh preparation.

In some cases, especially in recent focal diseases, the microscopic examination can be made at once without hardening the tissue. A small piece is excised with the scissors, placed on a slide, and teased. In this way granule cells, degenerated nerve-cells and fibers, and degenerated muscle-fibers can be recognized. To bring the parts out more clearly the slide may be rapidly stained with a drop of 1 per cent. methylene-blue solution or with hematoxylin.

Degenerated portions of tissue are cut into small pieces and immediately placed in a 1 per cent. solution of osmic acid, which is to be kept in the dark. After twenty-four hours the products of degeneration (fat granules) will be stained black. This proceeding (Marchi's method) is even more successful in tissue hardened in Müller's fluid (not in alcohol).

Whenever it is desired to make a systematic examination, hardening is absolutely indispensable. The best results are obtained with Müller's fluid or alcohol, depending on the particular tissue it is desired to examine. For the examination of nerve-fiber (degenerations) Müller's fluid must be used; if the condition of the ganglion cells (inflammatory degenerative processes) is to be investigated, the tissue must be hardened in alcohol. In other cases the tissue may be first hardened in formalin.

It is often desired to examine both fibers and ganglion cells. In such a case the cells can be fairly well stained when the tissue is hardened in Müller's fluid. It is much better, on the whole, to put the greater part of the brain, spinal cord, nerves, and muscles into Müller's fluid after it has been hardened in formalin, and to harden some of the more important smaller pieces in absolute alcohol immediately after removal from the body. Such preparations can also be stained for bacteria.

It requires several months to harden a brain in Müller's fluid. The time can, however, be considerably shortened by keeping the jar in a temperature of about 30° C.

The solution must be constantly renewed; during the first six days, if the jar is kept in a warm place, the solution should be renewed every day, later at longer intervals. As the hardening process goes on additional incisions, either horizontal or frontal, should be made from time to time to allow the chrome salts to penetrate the tissue more easily. The tissues should never be examined until they are completely hardened; the pieces must be brown, not yellow. If the hardening is incomplete, unpleasant artifacts will be produced when the tissue is stained.

Hardening in absolute alcohol requires only a few days. The alcohol should be changed several times. After a tissue has been hardened in Müller's fluid it is to be cut in thin slices and hardened again in alcohol, but without dehydrating, if it is intended to use a medullary sheath stain. The tissue is then placed first in thin and then in thick celloidin for the purpose of imbedding. After an interval varying from five to twenty days, or even longer, depending on the size of the pieces, the tissues are mounted on blocks and laid in 70 per cent. alcohol; after a few hours they are ready to cut.

The cutting is done with a microtome, and the sections need not be very thin. If an uninterrupted series of sections is desired, a piece of firm medicated toilet-paper, which has been previously labeled, is moistened with a sugar solution, placed on a plate, and covered with a layer of thin celloidin. The sections are then laid in order on the paper, to which they immediately adhere. This is kept in 70 per cent. alcohol. When the sections are to be examined, they are easily loosened from the paper by placing the latter in water. To stain the nerve-fiber, Weigert-Pal's hematoxylin stain for medullary sheaths is used. To stain the cells carmin or double carmin stain is used for tissues hardened in Müller's fluid, and Nissl's methylene-blue for tissues hardened in alcohol. (For further directions the student is referred to the text-books of Kahldon, Friedländer-Eberth, and others.)

With the medullary sheath stain all the medullated nerve-fibers are stained black; hence if such fibers are normally absent, or if they are degenerated or destroyed, the corresponding areas are not stained and appear pale instead of black. The fatty constituents of the medullary sheath enter into a firm chemic union with the pigment of the hematoxylin, and this produces the black color.

The most modern method, Golgi's impregnation with silver (Cajal), can be used in pathologic cases only under certain restrictions, as it does not work uniformly well.

Our knowledge of the structure of the nervous system has been gained chiefly by means of the following methods of investigation:

1. By reconstruction of serial sections through a normal, fully developed human brain (Stilling, Meynert, etc.), various methods of staining or impregnation being used (Weigert, Golgi, Cajal, and Nissl).

2. By the examination of pathologic cases, especially of secondary degenerations (Türck, Waller).

3. By comparative anatomy and comparative embryology (Meynert, Edinger, and others).

4. By a study of the development (medullation, etc. Kölliker, Kupffer, His, Flechsig, and others).

5. By the examination of degenerations produced experimentally (Gudden, Monakow, and others).

These methods have been used as much as possible in the preparation of the plates contained in this atlas.

BIBLIOGRAPHY.

The following works, which have been utilized by the author in the preparation of this epitome, are recommended as admirable reference books for students of neurology:

1. Anatomy.

The text-books of Koelliker (Gewebelehre), Henle, Hoffmann-Schalbe, Raube, Gegenbaur. Monographs: von Flechsig (Leitungsbahnen, Plan des menschlichen Gehirns), Lenhossek (minute structure), Edinger (twelve lectures), v. Gehuchten (Gehirnanatomie), Bechterew (Leitungsbahnen), Obersteiner (Anleitung zum Studium der nervösen Organe). The works of Meynert, Gudden, His, Golgi, Cayal, and others.

2. Physiology and Pathology.

Charcot (lectures), Erb (Electrotherapie, Rückenmarkskrankheiten in "Ziemssen's Handbuch," vol. xi), v. Strümpell (text-book), Leyden (clinical lectures), Wernicke (Gehirnkrankheiten), Gowers ("Diseases of the Nervous System"), Seeligmüller (text-book), P. Marie (lectures), Liebermeister (lectures), Eulenburg (article on "Nervous Diseases" in the Encyclopedia), Mendel (ibid., article on the "Brain"), Oppenheim (text-book), Hirt (text-book), Déjerine ("Centres Nerveux"). Leube (diagnosis); the works of Westphal, Kussmaul, Nothnagel, Munk, Hitzig, Lichtheim, Ferrier, and many others.

ABBREVIATIONS USED IN THE FIGURES.

a. . . . Anterior.
A. b. . Basilar artery.
A. c. c. . Artery of corpus callosum (commissural artery).
a. l. . . Ansa lentiformis.
a. d. . . Descending root of auditory nerve.
A. S. . Aqueduct of Sylvius.
A. f. s. . Sylvian artery, middle cerebral artery.
A. v. . Vertebral artery.
a. v. . . Arch of vertebra.
B. . . . Brachium (superior peduncle of cerebellum).
Bulb.olf. Olfactory bulb.
c. . . . Conarium, pineal body.
C. a. . Anterior horn of spinal cord.
c. a. . . Anterior commissure (brain and cord).
c. a. . . Anterior horn of lateral ventricle.
c. Am. . Cornu Ammonis.
Cb. . . . Cerebellum and direct cerebellar tract in cord and medulla.
c. c. . . Corpus callosum.
c. c. . . Corpus candicans or albicans.
c. e. . . External capsule.
cerv. . Cervical.
c. g. l. . External geniculate body.
c. g. m. Internal geniculate body.
Ch. . . . Optic chiasm.
C. i. . . Internal carotid.
c. i. a. . Anterior limb of internal capsule.
c. i. p. . Posterior limb of internal capsule.
c. L. . . Luys' body, subthalamic body.
Cl. . . Column of Clarke.
Cl. . . Claustrum (brain).
c. m. . Middle commissure.
C. p. . Posterior horn of spinal cord.
c. p. . . Posterior horn of lateral ventricle.
c. p. . . Posterior commissure.
c. q. a. . Anterior corpus quadrigeminum.
c. q. p. . Posterior corpus quadrigeminum.
c. r. . . Restiform body.
c. sbth. Subthalamic body.
c. st. . Corpus striatum.
c. t. . . Central tegmental tract (fillet).
c. tr. . Corpus trapezoides.
cun. . . Cuneus.
C. V. . Centrum semiovale of Vieussens.
d. . . . Dura mater.
D. Br. . Decussation of brachia.
Dec. Pyr. Decussation of pyramids.
Ea. R. . Reactions of degeneration.
f. . . . Fornix.
f. a. . . Anterior ground bundle.
f. a. e. . External arciform fibers.
f. a. i. . Internal arciform fibers.

ABBREVIATIONS USED IN THE FIGURES.

f. al. . . Anterolateral ground bundle (mixed lateral zone).
f. B. . . Funiculus cuneatus.
f. c. . . Calcarine fissure.
f. d. . . Descending fornix.
f. G. . . Funiculus gracilis.
Fl. . . Flocculus.
fl. . . . Lateral ground bundle.
f. l. . . } Posterior longitudinal
f. l. p. } bundle.
f. p. . . Posterior column.
F. rhomb. Rhomboid fossa.
f. S. . . Fissure of Sylvius.
G. . . . Gowers' tract.
g. ang. Angular gyrus.
g. cent. Central convolutions.
g. fr. . Frontal convolution.
g. H. Hippocampal convolution.
gl. p. Globus pallidus (middle and inner zones of lenticular nucleus).
g. l. . . External geniculate body.
g. m. . Internal geniculate body.
g. o. . . Occipital convolution.
G. o. . Gratiolet's optic radiation.
g. sm. . Supramarginal gyrus.
g. t. . . Temporal convolution.
K. . . Raphé of the tegmentum.
L. . . . Boundary zone of Lissauer.
L. . . . Lenticular nucleus.
L. . . . Lateral.
l. pc. . Paracentral lobule.
m. . . Mesial.
M. ob. . Medulla oblongata.
n. . . . Nodulus.
N. am. . Amygdaloid nucleus.
N. B. . Nucleus of Burdach, cuneate nucleus.
n. c. . . Caudate nucleus.
n. f. a. . Arciform nucleus.
N. G. . Nucleus of Goll, nucleus of the clava.

n. VIII.
d. . . . Dorsal nucleus of auditory nerve.
n. VIII v. Ventral nucleus of auditory nerve.
n. v. . . Red nucleus.
O. . . . Olive (inferior, greater).
ol. m. . Mesial accessory olive.
ol. p. . Posterior accessory olive.
ol. s. . Superior olive.
p. . . . Pia.
p. . . . Posterior.
Ped. . . Cerebral peduncle, pes, crusta pedunculi.
Pl. ch. . Choroid plexus.
Pulv. . Pulvinar.
Put. . . Putamen.
Py. . . Pyramidal tract.
q. a. . . Anterior corpus quadrigeminum.
q. p. . . Posterior corpus quadrigeminum.
R. . . Raphé of the tegmentum and pons.
r. a. . . Anterior root.
R. c. . Ramus arteriosus communicans.
r. p. . . Posterior root.
R. subth. Subthalamic region.
S. a. . . Anterior longitudinal sulcus.
S. . . . Solitary bundle (descending root of IX and X).
S. g. . . Substantia gelatinosa, posterior horn.
S. n. . . Substantia nigra.
S. p. . . Posterior longitudinal sulcus.
s. p. . . Septum lucidum.
S. r. t. . Substantia reticularis of tegmentum.
str. s.
m., i. . Superior, middle, and inferior layer.
st. a. . Striæ acusticæ.
t. . . . Tænia thalami.
T. teg. . Tegmentum.
Th. . . Optic thalamus.
tr. o. . Optic tract.

ABBREVIATIONS USED IN THE FIGURES.

trig. olf. Trigonum olfactorium.
U. . . Uvula (vermiform process of cerebellum).
unc. . . U n c u s (Hippocampal gyrus).
V. . . Ventricle (lat., med., III).
v. IV. . Fourth ventricle.
V. s. . Superior vermiform process of cerebellum.
V. i. . . Inferior vermiform process of cerebellum.
v. . . . Vertebra.
v. m. a. Anterior medullary velum (with lingula).
z. v. . . Root-zone.
V. c. . . Caudal, descending root of trigeminus.
V. m. . Motor nucleus of trigeminus.
V. n. . Nasal descending root of trigeminus.
V. s. . Sensory nucleus of trigeminus.
VIII c.
N. . . Cochlear nerve.
VIII v.
N. . . Vestibular nerve.

INDEX.

ABDUCENS nerve, 18
   lesions of, symptoms, 99
   motor pathway in, 45
Abscess, brain, 147; Pl. 60, Fig. 1
Achilles tendon reflex, 121
Acquired diseases, 77
Acromegaly, 195
Afterbrain, 23
Ageusia, central, 87
Akinesia algera, 161
Alcoholic neuritis, 192
Alexia, 125, 127
Amnesia, 128
Amnesial aphasia, 125
Amygdaloid nucleus, 10
Amyotrophic lateral sclerosis, 177; Pl. 63, Fig. 3
   section of cord in, Pl. 78
Analgesia, 116
Anemia of brain, 141
Aneurysm of brain, 146; Pl. 59, Fig. 1
Anode, 109
Anosmia, central, 87
Anterior columns of cord, 15, 38
   commissure, 11
   poliomyelitis, 180
Aphasia, 124
   amnesial, 125, 127
   motor, 124, 125
   optic, 125
   sensory, 86, 125
   visual, 86
Apoplectic stroke, 143
Apoplexy, Pl. 65
Aqueduct of Sylvius, 12
Arachnoid, 2
Arc de cercle, 160
Archineuron, 40

Arcuatus, 30
Arsenical neuritis, 193
Arteries of brain, 20
   of spinal cord, 20
Arteriosclerosis of brain, 147
Articulation, disturbances of, 124
Ascending degeneration of spinal cord, Pl. 73
Association fibers, 30
Astrocytes, 25
Ataxia, 108
   Friedreich's, 105
   hereditary, 105, 185
Ataxic gait, 108
   writing, 126
Athetoid movements, 107
Atrophy, neurotic muscular, Pl. 64, Fig. 5
   spinal muscular, 104
Auditory nerve, 18
   lesions of, symptoms, 99
   sensory pathway of, 61
Autopsy technic of nervous system, 197
Axillary nerve, lesions of, symptoms, 100
Axis-cylinder process, 28

BASAL forebrain bundle, 36
   ganglia, horizontal section of, Pl. 9
Base of brain, disease of, symptoms, 91
Basedow's disease, 194
Basilar meningitis, 138
Bladder, examination of functions of, 122
   motor pathway of, 49
   sensory nerves of, 59

Blindness, psychic, 86
Blood-vessels of brain, diseases of, 136
Brachial monoplegia, 85
  plexus, Erb's paralysis of, 96
Bradylalia, 124
Brain, anatomy of, 1
  anemia of, 141
  aneurysm of, 146; Pl. 59, Fig. 1
  arteriosclerosis of, 147
  base of, Pl. 5
  circulatory disturbances, 141
  development of, Pl. 16
  embolic softening, Pl. 62, Fig. 2
  horizontal section of, Pl. 6
  hyperemia of, 141
  in situ, Pl. 1
  mesial surface, Pl. 4
  of dog, four coronal sections through, Pl. 11
  outer surface of, Pl. 3
  tumor of, Pl. 59, Fig. 3
  ventricular system of, Pl. 7
  vesicles, primary, 22
  with meninges removed, Pl. 2
Brain-abscess, 147; Pl. 60, Fig. 1
Brain-embolism, 145
Brain-stem, Pl. 10
  coronal section through, Pl. 12, 13
Brain-substance, diseases of, 141
Brain-syphilis, 139
Brain-thrombosis, 145
Brain-tumor, 149
Breschet's venous plexus, 21
Bulbar paralysis, 104, 155
  speech, 124
Burdach, funiculus of, 15

CALAMUS scriptorius, 15
Calf muscles, spasm of, 188
Capsula Reilii, 10
Capsule, external, 10
Caries of vertebra, Pl. 59, Fig. 2
Cathode, 109
Cauda equina, lesions of, symptoms, 95
Caudate nucleus, 5
  development of, 23

Causes of diseases of nervous system, 75
Cella media, 6
Cells, galvanic, 108
Central convolutions, 3
  disease of, symptoms, 84
  motor neuron, 40
    symptoms of lesion of, 82
    pathway, 35
  neuron, system disease of, symptoms, 104
  neurons, 26
  nuclear layer, 25
  sensory neuron complex, 51
    pathway, 33
  sulcus, 3
Centripetal sensory path, system disease of, symptoms, 105
Centrum semiovale, disease of, symptoms, 87
  Vieussenii, 5
Cephalalgia, 163
Cerebellar convolution, Pl. 20
  cortex, Pl. 19
Cerebellum, 12
  development of, 24
  influence of, in coordination, 73
  lesions of, symptoms, 90
Cerebral convolutions, Pl. 20 and 21
  hemorrhage, 142
  neuroses, 157
  paralysis, characters of, 91
Cerebrospinal meningitis, epidemic, Pl. 58
  sclerosis, multiple, Pl. 77
Cervical enlargement, lesions of, symptoms, 93
Chiasm, lesions of, symptoms, 97
Chorea, chronic hereditary, 166
  Huntingdon's, 166
  minor, 165
  Sydenham's, 165
Choreic movements, 107
Choroid plexuses, 9
Cingulum, 30
Circle of Willis, 20
Claustrum, 10

Clonic spasm, 107
Cochlear nerve, lesions of, symptoms, 99
  sensory pathway of, 61
Collaterals, 28
Columns of spinal cord, 38
Combined system disease, 78; Pl. 82, 105
Commissural fibers, 30
Compression myelitis, 169; Pl. 75, Fig. 3
  of spinal cord, 169
Conarium, 11
Concept, 67
Congenital myotonia, 166
Conjunctival reflex, 120
  arc, 65
Conscious processes, 66
Consciousness, disturbances of, 128
Contents of consciousness, 68
Contracture, 107
Contractures, hysteric, 160
Convolution, central, 3
  cerebral, development of, 23
  inferior marginal, 4
    temporal, 4
  occipitotemporal, 4
  supramarginal, 4
Convulsion, 107
Coordination, 72
  centers, 73
  examination of, 108
Cord, compression of, 169
  diseases of, 167
  posterior columns of, 15
Cornu ammonis, 6
Corona radiata, 32
Corpora quadrigemina, 12
  lesions of, symptoms, 88
Corpus callosum, 5
  disease of, symptoms, 87
  dentatum cerebelli, 14
  striatum, 5, 8
    disease of, symptoms, 88
  subthalamicum, 11
Cortex cerebri, 3
Cortical lesions, symptoms of, 84
Corticomuscular motor path, symptoms of disease of, 104

Cranial nerves, 17
  development of, 26
  distribution of, Pl. 27
  lesions of, symptoms, 96
Cremaster reflex, 120
Crural monoplegia, 85
  nerve, lesions of, symptoms, 101
Crus ascendens fornicis, 7
Crusta, 5
  secondary degenerations of, Pl. 67, 68
Cuneiform lobe, 14
Cuneus, 4
Cutaneous reflex arc, 64
  reflexes, 119

DECUSSATION of pyramids, 15
Degeneration of nerve-cells and fibers, products of, Pl. 63, Fig. a-f
  reaction of, 110
Deiters' cells, 28
  nucleus, 62
Dementia, paralytic, 152
Dendrites, Pl. 17
Dendrons, 28
Descending degeneration in spinal cord, Pl. 72
Development of nervous system, 22
Diagnosis, 128
  electric, 108
  methods of, 106
Diaphragm, spasm of, 188
Digitationes cornu ammonis, 6
Diphtheric neuritis, 192
Diplegia, 85
Dura mater, 1
Dysarthria, 124
Dysgraphia, 126
Dyslexia, 126
Dystrophy, progressive muscular, 104, 179; Pl. 64, Fig. 4

ECLAMPSIA infantum, 164
Electric diagnosis, 108
  treatment, 134
Electromotive force, 109
Embolic softening of brain, Pl. 62, Fig. 2

Embolism, brain, 145
Embolus, 14
Embryonal area, Pl. 15
Encephalitis, acute hemorrhagic, Pl. 61, Fig. 2
  nonsuppurative, 148
Endogenous diseases, 76
Epilepsy, 163
Epileptiform convulsions, 107
Epiphysis, 11
Erb's paralysis of brachial plexus, 96
État de mal, 164
Examination, methods of, 106
  of bladder function, 122
  of coordination, 108
  of external condition of muscles, 106
  of memory, 127
  of motor irritative symptoms, 107
    power, 107
    sphere, 106
  of pain sense, 116
  of reflexes, 119
  of sense of hearing, 118
    of smell, 118
    of taste, 119
    of weight, 116
  of sensory sphere, 113
  of sight, 117
  of speech, 124
  of tactile sense, 113
  of temperature sense, 116
  of topographic sense, 115
  of trophic disturbances, 123
  of vasomotor disturbances, 123
  of writing power, 127
  with faradic current, 111
Exogenous diseases, 77
External capsule, 10
Extraspinal fibers, 38

FACIAL monoplegia, 85
  nerve, 18
    lesions of, symptoms, 99
    motor pathway in, 45
    spasm of, 188
    spasm, reflex, 190
Falx cerebri, 2

Faradic current, examination with, 111
Fascia dentata, 6
  tarini, 6
Fasciculus longitudinalis inferior, 30
  superior, 30
  occipitofrontalis, 30
  uncinatus, 30
Fibers, association, 30
  commissural, 30
  extraspinal, 38
  intramedullary, 38
  lateral peduncular, 34
  mesial peduncular, 33
  microscopic examination of, 199
  myelogenic, 38
  projection, 32
Fibriæ propriæ, 30
Fibrillary muscular contractions, 83
Fifth nerve, motor pathway in, 44
  ventricle, 8
Fillet, 54
  atrophy of, Pl. 70, Fig. 3
  tract of, 33
Fimbria, 6
Fissure of Rolando, 3
  of Sylvius, 4
    development of, 23
  parieto-occipital, 4
  Simian, 3
  triradiate, 5
Fissures, cerebral, development of, 23
Flocculus, 14
Focal disease, 78
  symptoms of, 84
Folia cacuminis, 13
Foot-drop, 102
Foramen of Monro, 9
Forebrain, 22
Fornix, pillars of, 7
Fourth ventricle, 13
Friedreich's ataxia, 105
  disease, 185
Frontal lobe, 3
  disease of, symptoms, 84
  pontine tract, 34

INDEX.

Functional diseases, 76
Funiculus anterior, 15
  cuneatus, 15
  gracilis, 15

GAIT, 108
Galvanic examination of muscles, 108
Gangliated cord of sympathetic, 19
Ganglion habenulæ, 11
  impar, 19
  intervertebral, 19
Ganglion-cells, 27 ; Pl. 18
  development of, 26
Ganglionic cord, 22
Genu of corpus callosum, 5
Girdle pains, 170
Glia cells, 25; Pl. 18
Globus pallidus, 10
Glossopharyngeal nerve, 18
  lesions of, symptoms, 99
Glossopharyngeovagus, motor pathway in, 45
  sensory pathway of, 59
Golgi's cells, 28
Goll, funiculus of, 15
Graefe's sign, 194
Gratiolet's optic radiation, 33
Gray commissure, 11
  matter of cord, Pl. 52
  structure of, 29
Gyrus fornicatus, 5
  hippocampi, 5

HARDENING, technic of, 200
Headache, habitual, 163
Hearing, testing of, 118
Hematoma of dura mater, 136
Hematomyelia, 175
Hematorrhachis, 175
Hemianesthesia, 159
Hemianopic pupillary rigidity, 122
Hemianopsia, 86, 117
Hemicrania, 102
Hemiplegia alternans, Pl. 65, Fig. 2
Hemispheres, disease of mesial surface of, symptoms, 86

Hemorrhage, cerebral, 142 ; Pl. 62, Fig. 1
  in central canal of cord, 175
Hereditary ataxia, 105, 185
Hindbrain, 23
Huntingdon's chorea, 166
Hydrocephalus, chronic, Pl. 61, Fig. 1
  internal, 151
Hydrotherapy, 134
Hygienic treatment, 134
Hypalgesia, 116
Hyperemia of brain, 141
Hyperesthesia, 115
  in hysteria, 159
Hyperhidrosis, 123
Hypertrophic cervical pachymeningitis, 167
Hypesthesia, 115
Hypnotics, 135
Hypnotism, 133
Hypochondria, 158
Hypoglossal nerve, 18
  lesions of, symptoms, 100
  motor pathway of, 46
Hysteria, 158
  attacks of, 160
Hysteric contractures, 160
  palsies, 159

IDEATION, 67
Idiopathic tremor, 166
Infantile spinal paralysis, 181
Infectious multiple neuritis, 193
Inferior cerebellar peduncle, 36
Infundibulum, 11
Innervation feelings, 68
Insula, disease of, symptoms, 87
Interbrain, 23
Intercostal arteries, 21
  nerves, lesions of, symptoms, 101
  neuralgia, 190
Intermediate neurons, 29
Internal capsule, development of, 23
  disease of, symptoms, 87
  hydrocephalus, 151
Intervetebal ganglion, 19
Intestines, sensory fibers of, 59

Intoxications, treatment of, 130
Intramedullary fibers, 38
Island of Reil, 4

KINESTHETIC memory pictures, 69

LAGOPHTHALMOS, 99
Lamina cornea, 9
Landry's paralysis, 193
Laqueus superior, 54
Lateral columns of cord, 15, 38
　peduncular fibers, 34
　ventricle, 6
Lenticular loop, 33
　nucleus, 5, 10
Leptomeningitis, acute, 137
Lingual monoplegia, 85
Literal paraphasia, 125, 127
Lobe, frontal, 3
　occipital, 3
　parietal, 3
　temporal, 4
Lobus lingualis, 4
Localization of sensations, 115
Lower extremity, motor pathway of, 48
Lumbar enlargement of cord, lesions of, symptoms, 94

MAIN en griffe, 101, 195
Marchi's method, 199
Massage, 134
Masseter reflex, 121
Median nerve, lesions of, symptoms, 100
Medical treatment, 135
Medulla oblongata, 14
　development of, 24
　lesions of, symptoms, 90
　positions of nuclei and course of cranial nerves in, Pl. 23
　secondary degenerations in, Pl. 70
Medullary canal, 22
　folds, 22
　groove, 22
　sheath, 28
Medullation, 26

Medullation, process of, Pl. 53
Membranes, cerebral, diseases of, 136
Memory pictures, 67
　testing, 127
Meninges, spinal, diseases of, 167
Meningitis, basilar, 138
　epidemic cerebrospinal, 137; Pl. 58
　purulent, 138
　syphilitic, 139
　tubercular, 138; Pl. 58
Meningomyelitis, syphilitic spinal, 168
Mesial peduncular fibers, 33
Microscopic examination of nervous system, 197
Midbrain, 23
Middle cerebellar peduncle, 36
Migraine, 162
Mind-blindness, 125, 127
Miosis, 103, 122
Moebius' symptom, 194
Mogigraphia, 188
Monolexia, 127
Monophasia, 124, 126
Monoplegia, brachial, 85
　crural, 85
　facial, 85
　lingual, 85
Monro, foramen of, 9
Monticulus, 13
Moral treatment, 133
Morphology of nervous system, 1
Motor aphasia, 124
　irritative symptoms, examination of, 107
　nerves, diseases of, 187
　pathway, 40
　　of abducens, 45
　　of bladder, 49
　　of facial nerve, 45
　　of fifth nerve, 44
　　of glossopharyngeovagus, 45
　　of hypoglossus, 46
　　of lower extremity, 48
　　of oculomotor nerve, 43
　　of rectum, 49
　　of sexual organs, 49
　　of spinal accessory nerve, 47

Motor pathway of sympathetic nerve, 49
  of trochlear nerve, 44
  of upper extremity, 47
  symptoms of disease of, 81
  peripheral neurons, nuclei of, Pl. 24
  power, examination of, 107
  speech center, 69
  sphere, examination of, 106
Multiple cerebrospinal sclerosis, 175
  neuritis, 191; Pl. 84
    infectious, 193
    of pregnancy, 193
Muscle sense, 117
  pathway of, 58
Muscles, examination of, 106
Muscular atrophy, spinal, Pl. 64, Fig. 1
Musculocutaneous nerve, lesions of, symptoms, 100
Mydriasis, 97, 122
Myelitis, 172; Pl. 63, Fig. 1
  acute disseminated, 173
  chronic, Pl. 63, Fig. 4
  compression, 169
  dorsalis, 122
  various forms of, Pl. 75
Myelogenic fibers, 38
Myeloneuritis, 193
Myopathy, primary, 179
Myotonia congenita, 166
Myxedema, 195

NERVE, abducens, 18
  auditory, 18
  facial, 18
  glossopharyngeal, 18
  hypoglossal, 18
  oculomotor, 17
  olfactory, 17
  optic, 17
  pneumogastric, 18
  spinal accessory, 18
  tracts with known functions, 39
    schema of, Pl. 54–56
  trifacial, 18
  trochlear, 18
Nerve-cell, 25

Nerve-fiber, 28
Nerves, cranial, 17
  of pia and dura, 21
  peripheral, 17
  spinal, 18
Nervous diseases, causes of, 75
  pathologic alterations in, 78
  symptomatology of, 81
  topical diagnosis of, 81
  treatment of, 129
  plexuses, 19
  system, development of, 22
    morphology of, 1
Neuralgia, 189
  trifacial, 190
Neurasthenia, 157
Neurilemma, 28
Neuritis, acute, Pl. 63, Fig. 2
  alcoholic, 192
  arsenical, 193
  diphtheric, 192
  multiple, 191; Pl. 84
  parenchymatous, 191
  postdiphtheric, Pl. 84, Fig. 3
  saturnine, 192
Neuroblasts, 25
Neuroglia, development of, 22, 25
  structure of, 27
Neuron, 25, 28
  central motor, 40
    sensory, 51
  elements, 67
  peripheral motor, 40
    sensory, 50
Neurons, arrangement of, Pl. 17
Neuroses, cerebral, 157
  occupation, 188
  traumatic, 162
Nucleus, amygdaloid, 10
  caudate, 5
  globosus, 14
  lenticular, 5, 10
  red, 11
  ruber, 11

OBEX, 15
Obturator nerve, lesions of, symptoms, 102
Occipital lobe, 3
  disease of, symptoms, 86

Occipital nerve, lesions of, symptoms, 100
  neuralgia, 190
Occipitotemporal convolution, 4
Occupation neuroses, 188
  palsies, 189
  spasms, 188
Oculomotor nerve, 17
  lesions of, symptoms, 97
  motor pathway in, 43
Olfactory bulb, 17
  fibrillation, 63
  nerve, 17
    lesions of, symptoms, 96
    sensory pathway of, 63
  sulcus, 5
  tract, 17
Olivary bodies, 15
Operative treatment, 131
Operculum, 4
Ophthalmoplegia, 104, 154
  chronic progressive, Pl. 66, Fig. 3
Optic aphasia, 125
  nerve, 17
    lesions of, symptoms, 96
    sensory pathway of, 62
  thalamus, 11
    disease of, symptoms, 88
  tract, 12
Organic diseases, 76
Oval bundle, 34

PACCHIONIAN bodies, 2
Pachymeningitis, hypertrophic cervical, 167
  internal hemorrhagic, 136
Pain sense, examination of, 116
Palpebral reflex, 120
Paracentral lobule, 4
Paragraphia, 127
Paralexia, 126, 127
Paralysis agitans, 166
  bulbar, 155
  cerebral, character of, 91
  chronic atrophic spinal, 182
    bulbar, Pl. 78, Fig. 1
  Erb's, 96
  infantile cerebral, medulla oblongata in, Pl. 70, Fig. 2

Paralysis, infantile spinal, 181
  Landry's, 193
  of lower portion of brachial plexus, 96
  plexus, symptoms of, 96
  progressive, 152
  pseudobulbar, 156
  simple spastic spinal, 104
  spastic, Pl. 65, Fig. 1
  spinal, 176 ; Pl. 81
Paralytic dementia, 152
Paramyoclonus multiplex, 161
Paraphasia, 87, 125
Paraplegia, flaccid inferior, 94
  inferior, 85
  universalis, 93
Parenchymatous neuritis, 191
Paresthesias, 113
Paretic gait, 108
Parietal lobe, 3
  disease of, symptoms, 86
Parieto-occipital fissure, 4
Parkinson's disease, 166
Passive motions, perception of, 116
Patellar tendon reflex, 120
Pathology, special, 136
Pathway, nervous, 39
Peduncles, cerebellar, 14
Pedunculus conarii, 11
Perforated space, posterior, 16
Periosteum reflex, 120
Peripheral motor neuron, 40
  symptom of lesion of, 83
  nerves, 17
    degeneration of, Pl. 83
    diseases of, 186
    lesions of, symptoms, 95
    neurons, 26
  sensory neuron complex, 50
Peroneal gait, 108
  nerve, lesions of, symptoms, 102
Pes, 5
Pharyngeal reflex, 120
Phrenic nerve, lesions of, symptoms, 100
Physical treatment, 134
Pia mater, 2
Pial veins, 21

INDEX.

Pineal gland, 11
Pituitary body, 12
  development of, 24
Plexus, choroid, 9
  paralyses, symptoms of, 96
Plexuses, nervous, 19
Pli courbè, 4
Pneumogastric nerve, 18
  lesions of, symptoms, 99
Poliomyelitis, anterior, 104, 180
  chronic, 182
Polyesthesia, 11
Polymyositis, acute, 193
Polyneuritis, alcoholic, Pl. 84, Figs. 1 and 2
Pons, lesions of, symptoms, 89
  secondary degenerations of, Pl. 69
  Varolii, 14
Position, sense of, 117
Postdiphtheric neuritis, Pl. 84, Fig. 4
Posterior columns of cord, 15, 38
  commissures, 11
  longitudinal bundle, 36
Precuneus, 4
Primary cell diseases, symptoms of, 104
  diseases, 76
  myopathy, 179
Primitive sheath, 28
Progressive muscular dystrophy, 104, 179; Pl. 64, Fig. 4
  paralysis, 152
  spinal muscular atrophy, 177
Projection fibers, 32
Prophylaxis, 130
Protoplasmic processes, 28
Pseudobulbar paralysis, 156
Pseudohypertrophy, 179
Psychic blindness, 86
  functions, examination of, 124
  treatment, 133
Psychoses, 157
Ptosis, 20, 97
Pulvinar, 11
Pupillary reflex, 121
  arc, 65
Purulent meningitis, 138
Putamen, 10

Pyramid, 33
Pyramidal bodies, 14
  tract, 34, 40
  descending degenerations of, Pl. 71
Pyramids, decussation of, 15

RADIAL nerve, lesions of, symptoms, 100
  reflex, 121
Reaction of degeneration, 110
Rectum, examination of function of, 122
Red nucleus, 11
Reflex, Achilles tendon, 121
  arc, 64
  conjunctival, 65
  cutaneous, 64
  pupillary, 65
  tendon, 64
  collateral, 64
  conjunctival, 120
  cremaster, 120
  facial spasm, 190
  masseter, 121
  palpebral, 120
  patellar tendon, 120
  paths, 64
  periosteum, 120
  pharyngeal, 120
  pupillary, 121
  radial, 121
  tendon, 120
  triceps tendon, 121
  ulnar, 121
Reflexes, cutaneous, 119
  examination of, 119
  of mucous membranes, 119
Reil, island of, 4
Restiform bodies, 14, 15
Rhinolalia, 124
Rhomboid fossa, 13; Pl. 10
Rinné's test, 118
Rolando, fissure of, 3
Romberg's phenomenon, 184
  sign, 108
Roots of spinal nerves, 19

SACRAL region of cord, lesions of, symptoms, 94

Saturnine neuritis, 192
Scattered bundle, 59
Sciatic nerve, lesions of, symptoms, 102
Sciatica, 190
Sclerose en plaques, 175
Sclerosis, amyotrophic lateral, 177 ; Pl. 63, Fig. 3
  section of cord in, Pl. 78, Fig. 3
  multiple cerebrospinal, 175 ; Pl. 77
Secondary association processes, 67
  atrophy, 79
  degenerations, 79
    in medulla oblongata, Pl. 70
    of crusta, Pl. 67, 68
    of pons, Pl. 69
Sedatives, 135
Sensations, localization of, 115
Sense of weight, examination of, 116
Sensory aphasia, 86, 125
  impressions, pathway of, 57
  nerves, diseases of, 189
  pathway, 49
    of auditory nerve, 61
    of glossopharyngeovagus, 59
    of olfactory nerve, 63
    of optic nerve, 62
    of trigeminus, 60
    of vestibular nerve, 62
  symptoms of disease of, 81, 83
  speech center, 69
  sphere, examination of, 113
Serial sections of brain and cord, Pl. 28-50
Sheath of Schwann, 28
Sight, testing of, 117
Simian fissure, 3
Singultus, 188
Sinuses of dura mater, 1
Sinus-thrombosis, 140
Smell, testing of, 118
Spasm of diaphragm, 188
  of facial nerve, 188
  of mastication, 188
  of spinal accessory, 188
  reflex facial, 190

Spastic gait, 108
  spinal paralysis, 176 ; Pl. 81
  torticollis, 188
Special pathology, 136
Speech, examination of, 124
  path, 47
Spinal accessory nerve, 18
  lesions of, symptoms, 100
  motor pathway in, 47
  spasm of, 188
  cord, anatomy of, 15
  arteries of, 20
  ascending degeneration of, Pl. 73
  columns of, 15, 16, 38
  compression of, 169
  course of fibers in, Pl. 57
  descending degeneration of, Pl. 72
  diseases of, 167
    symptoms, 92
  gray matter of, Pl. 52
  hemorrhages in central canal of, 175
  sections of, Pl. 14
  meninges, diseases of, 167
  meningomyelitis, 168
  muscular atrophy, 104
    progressive, 177
  nerves, 18
    development of, 26
    distribution of, Pl. 27
    paralysis, simple spastic, 104
    spastic, 176
Spindle cells, 25
Splenium, 5
Stammering, 124
Static coordination, 108
Status epilepticus, 164
Stigmata, hysteric, 158
Stratum zonale, 32
Stria pinealis, 11
Striæ acusticæ, 14
St. Vitus dance, 165
Subarachnoid space, 2
Subjective symptoms, examination of, 113
Substantia nigra, 12
Subthalamic region, lesion of, symptoms, 88

Sulci, cerebral, 3
Sulcus, central, 3
　olfactory, 5
　rectus, 5
Supramarginal convolution, 4
Surgical operations, 131
Sydenham's chorea, 165
Sylvius, aqueduct of, 12
　fissure of, 4
Sympathetic nerve, lesions of, symptoms, 103
　motor pathway of, 49
Symptomatic treatment, 133
Symptomatology of nervous diseases, 81
Symptoms of cortical lesions, 84
　of focal diseases, 84
　of system diseases, 103
Syphilis, brain, 139
Syphilitic cases, treatment, 131
　meningitis, 139
　spinal meningomyelitis, 168
Syringomyelia, 174 ; Pl. 76
System disease, 78
　　centripetal sensory path, symptoms, 105
　　combined, symptoms, 105
　　corticomuscular motor path, 104
　　spinal cord, 176
　　symptoms of, 103

Tabes combiné, 105
　dorsalis, 105, 182 ; Pl. 79, 80
　olfactorum, 17
Tactile sense, examination of, 113
　pathway of, 58
Tænia medullaris, 11
Tapetum, 30
Taste, examination of, 119
Tegmental fibers of corona radiata, 33
Tegmentum, 12
　ventriculorum, 6
Tela choroidea inferior, 2
　superior, 9
Teleneuron, 40
Temperature sense, examination of, 116
Temporal lobe, 4

Tendon reflex arc, 64
　reflexes, 120
Tentorium, 2
Tetanus, 196
Tetany, 195
Thalamus, optic, 11
Thermo-anesthesia, 116
Third ventricle, 9
Thomsen's disease, 166
Thoracic nerve, lesions of, symptoms, 100
　region of cord, lesions of, symptoms, 94
Thrombosis, brain, 145
　of sinuses, 140
Tibial nerve, lesions of, symptoms, 103
Tic convulsif, 188
　douloureux, 190
Tonic spasm, 107
Tonsilla, 14
Topographic sense, examination of, 115
Torticollis, spastic, 188
Tract of crusta, 33
　of fillet, 33
　pyramidal, 34
Traumatic neuroses, 162
Treatment, 129
　hygienic, 134
　medical, 135
　moral, 133
　physical, 134
　psychic, 133
　special, 136
　symptomatic, 133
Tremor, examination of, 107
　idiopathic, 166
Triceps tendon reflex, 121
Trifacial nerve, 18
　lesions of, symptoms, 97
　neuralgia, 190
Trigeminus, sensory pathway of, 60
Trigonum habenulæ, 11
Triradiate fissure, 5
Trismus, 188
Trochlear nerve, 18
　lesions of, symptoms, 97
　motor pathway in, 44

Trophic disturbances, examination of, 123
Trousseau's phenomenon, 195
Tubercular meningitis, 138; Pl. 58
Tumor of brain, 149; Pl. 59, Fig. 3
of pons, Pl. 60, Fig. 2; Pl. 66, Fig. 2
Türck's bundle, 34

ULNAR nerve, lesions of, symptoms, 101
reflex, 121
Unconscious associations, 68
Upper extremity, motor pathway of, 47

VASOMOTOR disturbances, examination of, 123
Velum interpositum, 9
Venous sinuses, 1
Ventricle, fifth, 8
fourth, 13
lateral, 6
Ventricle, third, 9
Ventricles, cerebral, 6
Ventricular system of brain, schema of, Pl. 8
Vermiform process, 12
Vermis, 12
Vertebral arteries, 20
Vestibular nerve, lesions of, symptoms, 99
sensory pathway of, 62
Visual aphasia, 86
impressions, storing up of, 67
Volitional pathways, 66

WAGNER hammer, 111
Westphal's sign, 184
White matter, structure of, 29
Willis, circle of, 20
Word-deafness, 125
Word-sound center, 69
Wrist-drop, 101
Writer's cramp, 188
Writing, examination of, 127
Wry neck, 100

Catalogue of the Medical Publications
OF
W. B. SAUNDERS & COMPANY
PHILADELPHIA   LONDON
925 Walnut Street   161 Strand, W. C.

Arranged Alphabetically and Classified under Subjects
See page 18 for a List of Contents classified according to subjects

THE books advertised in this Catalogue as being *sold by subscription* are usually to be obtained from travelling solicitors, but they will be sent direct from the office of publication (charges of shipment prepaid) upon receipt of the prices given. All the other books advertised are commonly for sale by booksellers in all parts of the United States; but books will be sent to any address, carriage prepaid, on receipt of the published price.

Money may be sent at the risk of the publisher in either of the following ways: A postal money order, an express money order, a bank check, and in a registered letter. Money sent in any other way is at the risk of the sender.

SPECIAL OFFER To physicians of approved credit books will be sent, post-paid, on the following terms: $5.00 cash upon delivery of books, and monthly payments of $5.00 thereafter until full amount is paid. Physicians not known to the house will be expected to furnish the names of satisfactory references. Any one or two volumes will be sent on thirty days' time to those who do not care to make a larger purchase.

AN AMERICAN TEXT-BOOK OF APPLIED THERAPEUTICS.

Edited by JAMES C. WILSON, M. D., Professor of Practice of Medicine and of Clinical Medicine, Jefferson Medical College, Philadelphia. Handsome imperial octavo volume of 1326 pages. Illustrated. Cloth, $7.00 net; Sheep or Half Morocco, $8.00 net. *Sold by Subscription.*

AN AMERICAN TEXT-BOOK OF THE DISEASES OF CHILDREN. Second Edition, Revised.

Edited by LOUIS STARR, M. D., Consulting Pediatrist to the Maternity Hospital, etc.; assisted by THOMPSON S. WESTCOTT, M. D., Attending Physician to the Dispensary for Diseases of Children, Hospital of the University of Pennsylvania. Handsome imperial octavo volume of 1244 pages, profusely illustrated. Cloth, $7.00 net; Sheep or Half Morocco, $8.00 net. *Sold by Subscription.*

AN AMERICAN TEXT-BOOK OF DISEASES OF THE EYE, EAR, NOSE, AND THROAT.

Edited by G. E. DE SCHWEINITZ, M. D., Professor of Ophthalmology, Jefferson Medical College, Philadelphia; and B. ALEXANDER RANDALL, M. D., Professor of Diseases of the Ear, University of Pennsylvania. Imperial octavo, 1251 pages; 766 illustrations, 59 of them in colors. Cloth, $7.00 net; Sheep or Half Morocco, $8.00 net. *Sold by Subscription.*

AN AMERICAN TEXT-BOOK OF GENITO-URINARY AND SKIN DISEASES.

Edited by L. BOLTON BANGS, M. D., Professor of Genito-Urinary Surgery, University and Bellevue Hospital Medical College, New York; and W. A. HARDAWAY, M. D., Professor of Diseases of the Skin, Missouri Medical College. Imperial octavo volume of 1229 pages, with 300 engravings and 20 full-page colored plates. Cloth, $7.00 net; Sheep or Half Morocco, $8.00 net. *Sold by Subscription.*

AN AMERICAN TEXT-BOOK OF GYNECOLOGY, MEDICAL AND SURGICAL. Second Edition, Revised.

Edited by J. M. BALDY, M. D., Professor of Gynecology, Philadelphia Polyclinic, etc. Handsome imperial octavo volume of 718 pages; 341 illustrations in the text, and 38 colored and half-tone plates. Cloth, $6.00 net; Sheep or Half Morocco, $7.00 net. *Sold by Subscription.*

AN AMERICAN TEXT-BOOK OF LEGAL MEDICINE AND TOXICOLOGY.

Edited by FREDERICK PETERSON, M. D., Chief of Clinic, Nervous Department, College of Physicians and Surgeons, New York; and WALTER S. HAINES, M. D., Professor of Chemistry, Pharmacy, and Toxicology, Rush Medical College, Chicago. *In Preparation.*

AN AMERICAN TEXT-BOOK OF OBSTETRICS.

Edited by RICHARD C. NORRIS, M. D.; Art Editor, ROBERT L. DICKINSON, M. D. Handsome imperial octavo volume of 1014 pages; nearly 900 beautiful colored and half-tone illustrations. Cloth, $7.00 net; Sheep or Half Morocco, $8.00 net. *Sold by Subscription.*

AN AMERICAN TEXT-BOOK OF PATHOLOGY.

Edited by LUDWIG HEKTOEN, M. D., Professor of Pathology in Rush Medical College, Chicago; and DAVID RIESMAN, M. D., Demonstrator of Pathologic Histology in the University of Pennsylvania. *In Press, Ready Shortly.*

AN AMERICAN TEXT-BOOK OF PHYSIOLOGY. Second Edition, Revised, in Two Volumes.

Edited by WILLIAM H. HOWELL, PH. D., M. D., Professor of Physiology, Johns Hopkins University, Baltimore, Md. Two royal octavo volumes of about 600 pages each. Fully illustrated. Per volume: Cloth, $3.00 net; Sheep or Half Morocco, $3.75 net.

AN AMERICAN TEXT-BOOK OF SURGERY. Third Edition.

Edited by WILLIAM W. KEEN, M. D., LL.D., F. R. C. S. (Hon.); and J. WILLIAM WHITE, M. D., PH. D. Handsome octavo volume of 1230 pages; 496 wood-cuts and 37 colored and half-tone plates. Thoroughly revised and enlarged, with a section devoted to "The Use of the Röntgen Rays in Surgery." Cloth, $7.00 net; Sheep or Half Morocco, $8.00 net,

THE NEW STANDARD   **THE NEW STANDARD**

THE AMERICAN ILLUSTRATED MEDICAL DICTIONARY.

For Practitioners and Students. A Complete Dictionary of the Terms used in Medicine, Surgery, Dentistry, Pharmacy, Chemistry, and the kindred branches, including much collateral information of an encyclopedic character, together with new and elaborate tables of Arteries, Muscles, Nerves, Veins, etc.; of Bacilli, Bacteria, Micrococci, Streptococci; Eponymic Tables of Diseases, Operations, Signs and Symptoms, Stains, Tests, Methods of Treatment, etc., etc. By W. A. NEWMAN DORLAND, A. M., M. D., Editor of the "American Pocket Medical Dictionary." Handsome large octavo, nearly 800 pages, bound in full flexible leather. Price, $4.50 net; with thumb index, $5.00 net.

Gives a Maximum Amount of Matter in a Minimum Space and at the Lowest Possible Cost.

This is an entirely new and unique work, intended to meet the need of practitioners and students for a complete up-to-date dictionary of moderate price. It contains more than twice the material in the ordinary students' dictionary, and yet, by the use of a clear, condensed type and thin paper of the finest quality, it forms an extremely handy volume only 1¾ inches in thickness. It is a beautiful specimen of the bookmaker's art. It is bound in full flexible leather, and is just the kind of book that a man will want to keep on his desk for constant reference. The book makes a special feature of the newer words, and defines hundreds of important terms not to be found in any other dictionary. It is especially full in the matter of tables, containing more than a hundred of great practical value. An important feature of the book is its handsome illustrations and colored plates drawn especially for the work, including new colored plates of Arteries, Nerves, Veins, Bacteria, Blood, etc.—twenty-four in all. This new work has been aptly termed by a competent critic "The New Standard."

THE AMERICAN POCKET MEDICAL DICTIONARY. Third Edition, Revised.

Edited by W. A. NEWMAN DORLAND., M. D., Assistant Obstetrician to the Hospital of the University of Pennsylvania; Fellow of the American Academy of Medicine. Containing the pronunciation and definition of the principal words used in medicine and kindred sciences, with 64 extensive tables. Handsomely bound in flexible leather, with gold edges. Price $1.00 net; with thumb index, $1.25 net.

THE AMERICAN YEAR-BOOK OF MEDICINE AND SURGERY.

A Yearly Digest of Scientific Progress and Authoritative Opinion in all branches of Medicine and Surgery, drawn from journals, monographs, and text-books of the leading American and Foreign authors and investigators. Arranged with editorial comments, by eminent American specialists, under the editorial charge of GEORGE M. GOULD, M. D. Year-Book of 1901 in two volumes—Vol. I. including *General Medicine;* Vol. II., *General Surgery.* Per volume: Cloth, $3.00 net; Half Morocco, $3.75 net. *Sold by Subscription.*

ABBOTT ON TRANSMISSIBLE DISEASES.

The Hygiene of Transmissible Diseases: their Causation, Modes of Dissemination, and Methods of Prevention. By A. C. ABBOTT, M. D., Professor of Hygiene and Bacteriology, University of Pennsylvania. Octavo, 311 pages, with numerous illustrations. Cloth, $2.00 net.

ANDERS' PRACTICE OF MEDICINE. Fourth Revised Edition.

A Text-Book of the Practice of Medicine. By JAMES M. ANDERS, M. D., PH. D., LL. D., Professor of the Practice of Medicine and of Clinical Medicine, Medico-Chirurgical College, Philadelphia. Handsome octavo volume of 1292 pages, fully illustrated. Cloth, $5.50 net; Sheep or Half Morocco, $6.50 net.

BASTIN'S BOTANY.

Laboratory Exercises in Botany. By EDSON S. BASTIN, M. A., late Professor of Materia Medica and Botany, Philadelphia College of Pharmacy. Octavo, 536 pages, with 87 plates. Cloth, $2.00 net.

BECK ON FRACTURES.

Fractures. By CARL BECK, M. D., Surgeon to St. Mark's Hospital and the New York German Poliklinik, etc. With an appendix on the Practical Use of the Röntgen Rays. 335 pages, 170 illustrations. Cloth, $3.50 net.

BECK'S SURGICAL ASEPSIS.

A Manual of Surgical Asepsis. By CARL BECK, M. D., Surgeon to St. Mark's Hospital and the New York German Poliklinik, etc. 306 pages; 65 text-illustrations and 12 full-page plates. Cloth, $1.25 net.

BOISLINIÈRE'S OBSTETRIC ACCIDENTS, EMERGENCIES, AND OPERATIONS.

Obstetric Accidents, Emergencies, and Operations. By L. CH. BOISLINIÈRE, M. D., late Emeritus Professor of Obstetrics, St. Louis Medical College. 381 pages, handsomely illustrated. Cloth, $2.00 net.

BÖHM, DAVIDOFF, AND HUBER'S HISTOLOGY.

A Text-Book of Human Histology. Including Microscopic Technic. By DR. A. A. BOHM and DR. M. VON DAVIDOFF, of Munich, and G. CARL HUBER, M. D., Junior Professor of Anatomy and Director of Histological Laboratory, University of Michigan. Handsome octavo of 501 pages, with 351 beautiful original illustrations. Cloth, $3.50 net.

BUTLER'S MATERIA MEDICA, THERAPEUTICS, AND PHARMACOLOGY. Third Edition, Revised.

A Text-Book of Materia Medica, Therapeutics, and Pharmacology. By GEORGE F. BUTLER, PH. G., M. D., Professor of Materia Medica and of Clinical Medicine, College of Physicians and Surgeons, Chicago. Octavo, 874 pages, illustrated. Cloth, $4.00 net; Sheep or Half Morocco, $5.00 net.

CERNA ON THE NEWER REMEDIES. Second Edition, Revised.

Notes on the Newer Remedies, their Therapeutic Applications and Modes of Administration. By DAVID CERNA, M. D., PH. D., Demonstrator of Physiology, Medical Department, University of Texas. Rewritten and greatly enlarged. Post-octavo, 253 pages. Cloth, $1.00 net.

CHAPIN ON INSANITY.

A Compendium of Insanity. By JOHN B. CHAPIN, M. D., LL.D., Physician-in-Chief, Pennsylvania Hospital for the Insane; Honorary Member of the Medico-Psychological Society of Great Britain, of the Society of Mental Medicine of Belgium, etc. 12mo, 234 pages, illustrated. Cloth, $1.25 net.

CHAPMAN'S MEDICAL JURISPRUDENCE AND TOXICOLOGY. Second Edition, Revised.

Medical Jurisprudence and Toxicology. By HENRY C. CHAPMAN, M. D., Professor of Institutes of Medicine and Medical Jurisprudence, Jefferson Medical College of Philadelphia. 254 pages, with 55 illustrations and 3 full-page plates in colors. Cloth, $1.50 net.

CHURCH AND PETERSON'S NERVOUS AND MENTAL DIS= EASES. Second Edition.

Nervous and Mental Diseases. By ARCHIBALD CHURCH, M. D., Professor of Nervous and Mental Diseases, and Head of the Neurological Department, Northwestern University Medical School, Chicago; and FREDERICK PETERSON, M. D., Chief of Clinic, Nervous Department, College of Physicians and Surgeons, New York. Handsome octavo volume of 843 pages, profusely illustrated. Cloth, $5.00 net; Sheep or Half Morocco, $6.00 net.

CLARKSON'S HISTOLOGY.

A Text-Book of Histology, Descriptive and Practical. By ARTHUR CLARKSON, M. B., C. M. Edin., formerly Demonstrator of Physiology in the Owen's College, Manchester; late Demonstrator of Physiology in Yorkshire College, Leeds. Large octavo, 554 pages; 22 engravings and 174 beautifully colored original illustrations. Cloth, $4.00 net.

CORWIN'S PHYSICAL DIAGNOSIS. Third Edition, Revised.

Essentials of Physical Diagnosis of the Thorax. By ARTHUR M. CORWIN, A. M., M. D., Instructor in Physical Diagnosis in Rush Medical College, Chicago. 219 pages, illustrated. Cloth, $1.25 net.

CROOKSHANK'S BACTERIOLOGY. Fourth Edition, Revised.

A Text-Book of Bacteriology. By EDGAR M. CROOKSHANK, M. B., Professor of Comparative Pathology and Bacteriology, King's College, London. Octavo, 700 pages, 273 engravings and 22 original colored plates. Cloth, $6.50 net; Half Morocco, $7.50 net.

DACOSTA'S SURGERY. Third Edition, Revised.

Modern Surgery, General and Operative. By JOHN CHALMERS DACOSTA, M. D., Professor of Principles of Surgery and Clinical Surgery, Jefferson Medical College, Philadelphia; Surgeon to the Philadelphia Hospital, etc. Handsome octavo volume of 1117 pages, profusely illustrated. Cloth, $5.00 net; Sheep or Half Morocco, $6.00 net.

Enlarged by over 200 Pages, with more than 100 New Illus= trations.

DAVIS'S OBSTETRIC NURSING.

Obstetric and Gynecologic Nursing. By EDWARD P. DAVIS, A. M., M. D., Professor of Obstetrics in Jefferson Medical College and the Philadelphia Polyclinic; Obstetrician and Gynecologist to the Philadelphia Hospital. 12mo volume of 400 pages, fully illustrated. Crushed buckram, $1.75 net.

DESCHWEINITZ ON DISEASES OF THE EYE. Third Edition, Revised.

Diseases of the Eye. A Handbook of Ophthalmic Practice. By G. E. DE SCHWEINITZ, M. D., Professor of Ophthalmology, Jefferson Medical College, Philadelphia, etc. Handsome royal octavo volume of 696 pages; 256 fine illustrations and 2 chromo-lithographic plates. Cloth, $4.00 net; Sheep or Half Morocco, $5.00 net.

DORLAND'S DICTIONARIES.

[See *American Illustrated Medical Dictionary* and *American Pocket Medical Dictionary* on page 3.]

DORLAND'S OBSTETRICS.

A Manual of Obstetrics. By W. A. NEWMAN DORLAND, M. D., Assistant Demonstrator of Obstetrics, University of Pennsylvania; Associate in Gynecology, Philadelphia Polyclinic. 760 pages; 163 illustrations in the text and 6 full-page plates. Cloth, $2.50 net.

EICHHORST'S PRACTICE OF MEDICINE.

A Text-Book of the Practice of Medicine. By DR. HERMAN EICHHORST, Professor of Special Pathology and Therapeutics and Director of the Medical Clinic, University of Zurich. Translated and edited by AUGUSTUS A. ESHNER, M. D., Professor of Clinical Medicine, Philadelphia Polyclinic. *In Press. Ready Soon.*

FRIEDRICH AND CURTIS ON THE NOSE, THROAT, AND EAR.

Rhinology, Laryngology, and Otology, and their Significance in General Medicine. By DR. E. P. FRIEDRICH, of Leipzig. Edited by H. HOLBROOK CURTIS, M. D., Consulting Surgeon to the New York Nose and Throat Hospital. Octavo, 348 pages. Cloth, $2.50 net.

FROTHINGHAM'S GUIDE FOR THE BACTERIOLOGIST.

Laboratory Guide for the Bacteriologist. By LANGDON FROTHINGHAM, M. D. V., Assistant in Bacteriology and Veterinary Science, Sheffield Scientific School, Yale University. Illustrated. Cloth, 75 cts. net.

GARRIGUES' DISEASES OF WOMEN. Third Edition, Revised.

Diseases of Women. By HENRY J. GARRIGUES, A. M., M. D., Gynecologist to St. Mark's Hospital and to the German Dispensary, New York City. Octavo, 756 pages, with 367 engravings and colored plates. Cloth, $4.50 net; Sheep or Half Morocco, $5.50 net.

GOULD AND PYLE'S CURIOSITIES OF MEDICINE.

Anomalies and Curiosities of Medicine. By GEORGE M. GOULD, M. D., and WALTER L. PYLE, M. D. An encyclopedic collection of rare and extraordinary cases and of the most striking instances of abnormality in all branches of Medicine and Surgery, derived from an exhaustive research of medical literature from its origin to the present day, abstracted, classified, annotated, and indexed. Handsome octavo volume of 968 pages; 295 engravings and 12 full-page plates. Popular Edition. Cloth, $3.00 net; Sheep or Half Morocco, $4.00 net.

GRAFSTROM'S MECHANO-THERAPY.

A Text-Book of Mechano-Therapy (Massage and Medical Gymnastics). By AXEL V. GRAFSTROM, B. SC., M. D., late House Physician, City Hospital, Blackwell's Island, New York. 12mo, 139 pages, illustrated. Cloth, $1.00 net.

GRIFFITH ON THE BABY. Second Edition, Revised.

The Care of the Baby. By J. P. CROZER GRIFFITH, M. D., Clinical Professor of Diseases of Children, University of Pennsylvania; Physician to the Children's Hospital, Philadelphia, etc. 12mo, 404 pages, 67 illustrations and 5 plates. Cloth, $1.50 net.

GRIFFITH'S WEIGHT CHART.

Infant's Weight Chart. Designed by J. P. CROZER GRIFFITH, M. D., Clinical Professor of Diseases of Children, University of Pennsylvania. 25 charts in each pad. Per pad, 50 cts. net.

HART'S DIET IN SICKNESS AND IN HEALTH.

Diet in Sickness and Health. By MRS. ERNEST HART, formerly Student of the Faculty of Medicine of Paris and of the London School of Medicine for Women; with an Introduction by SIR HENRY THOMPSON, F. R. C. S., M. D., London. 220 pages. Cloth, $1.50 net.

HAYNES' ANATOMY.

A Manual of Anatomy. By IRVING S. HAYNES, M. D., Professor of Practical Anatomy in Cornell University Medical College. 680 pages; 42 diagrams and 134 full-page half-tone illustrations from original photographs of the author's dissections. Cloth, $2.50 net.

HEISLER'S EMBRYOLOGY.

A Text-Book of Embryology. By JOHN C. HEISLER, M. D., Professor of Anatomy, Medico-Chirurgical College, Philadelphia. Octavo volume of 405 pages, handsomely illustrated. Cloth, $2.50 net.

HIRST'S OBSTETRICS. Second Edition.

A Text-Book of Obstetrics. By BARTON COOKE HIRST, M. D., Professor of Obstetrics, University of Pennsylvania. Handsome octavo volume of 848 pages; 618 illustrations and 7 colored plates. Cloth, $5.00 net; Sheep or Half Morocco, $6.00 net.

HYDE & MONTGOMERY ON SYPHILIS AND THE VENEREAL DISEASES. 2d Edition, Revised and Greatly Enlarged.

Syphilis and the Venereal Diseases. By JAMES NEVINS HYDE, M. D., Professor of Skin and Venereal Diseases, and FRANK H. MONTGOMERY, M. D., Associate Professor of Skin, Genito-Urinary, and Venereal Diseases in Rush Medical College, Chicago, Ill. Octavo, 594 pages, profusely illustrated. Cloth, $4.00 net.

THE INTERNATIONAL TEXT-BOOK OF SURGERY. In Two Volumes.

By American and British Authors. Edited by J. COLLINS WARREN, M. D., LL. D., F. R. C. S. (Hon.), Professor of Surgery, Harvard Medical School, Boston; and A. PEARCE GOULD, M. S., F. R. C. S., Lecturer on Practical Surgery and Teacher of Operative Surgery, Middlesex Hospital Medical School, London, Eng. Vol. I. *General Surgery.*—Handsome octavo, 947 pages, with 458 beautiful illustrations and 9 lithographic plates. Vol. II. *Special or Regional Surgery.*—Handsome octavo, 1072 pages, with 471 beautiful illustrations and 8 lithographic plates. *Sold by Subscription.* Prices per volume: Cloth, $5.00 net: Sheep or Half Morocco, $6.00 net.

"It is the most valuable work on the subject that has appeared in some years. The clinician and the pathologist have joined hands in its production, and the result must be a satisfaction to the editors as it is a gratification to the conscientious reader."—*Annals of Surgery.*

"This is a work which comes to us on its own intrinsic merits. Of the latter it has very many. The arrangement of subjects is excellent, and their treatment by the different authors is equally so. What is especially to be recommended is the painstaking endeavor of each writer to make his subject clear and to the point. To this end particularly is the technique of operations lucidly described in all necessary detail. And withal the work is up to date in a very remarkable degree, many of the latest operations in the different regional parts of the body being given in full details. There is not a chapter in the work from which the reader may not learn something new."—*Medical Record*, New York.

JACKSON'S DISEASES OF THE EYE.

A Manual of Diseases of the Eye. By EDWARD JACKSON, A. M., M. D., Emeritus Professor of Diseases of the Eye, Philadelphia Polyclinic and College for Graduates in Medicine. 12mo, volume of 535 pages, with 178 illustrations, mostly from drawings by the author. Cloth, $2.50 net.

KEATING'S LIFE INSURANCE.

How to Examine for Life Insurance. By JOHN M. KEATING, M. D., Fellow of the College of Physicians of Philadelphia; Ex-President of the Association of Life Insurance Medical Directors. Royal octavo, 211 pages. With numerous illustrations. Cloth, $2.00 net.

KEEN ON THE SURGERY OF TYPHOID FEVER.

The Surgical Complications and Sequels of Typhoid Fever. By WM. W. KEEN, M. D., LL. D., F, R. C. S. (Hon.), Professor of the Principles of Surgery and of Clinical Surgery, Jefferson Medical College, Philadelphia, etc. Octavo volume of 386 pages, illustrated. Cloth, $3.00 net.

KEEN'S OPERATION BLANK. Second Edition, Revised Form.

An Operation Blank, with Lists of Instruments, etc. Required in Various Operations. Prepared by W. W. KEEN, M. D., LL.D., F. R. C. S. (Hon.), Professor of the Principles of Surgery and of Clinical Surgery, Jefferson Medical College, Philadelphia. Price per pad, of 50 blanks, 50 cts. net.

KYLE ON THE NOSE AND THROAT. Second Edition.
Diseases of the Nose and Throat. By D. BRADEN KYLE, M. D., Clinical Professor of Laryngology and Rhinology, Jefferson Medical College, Philadelphia. Octavo, 646 pages; over 150 illustrations and 6 lithographic plates. Cloth, $4.00 net; Sheep or Half Morocco, $5.00 net.

LAINÉ'S TEMPERATURE CHART.
Temperature Chart. Prepared by D. T. LAINÉ, M. D. Size 8 x 13½ inches. A conveniently arranged Chart for recording Temperature, with columns for daily amounts of Urinary and Fecal Excretions, Food, Remarks, etc. On the back of each chart is given the Brand treatment of Typhoid Fever. Price, per pad of 25 charts, 50 cts. net.

LEVY, KLEMPERER, AND ESHNER'S CLINICAL BACTERIOLOGY.
The Elements of Clinical Bacteriology. By DR. ERNST LEVY, Professor in the University of Strasburg, and DR. FELIX KLEMPERER, Privatdocent in the University of Strasburg. Translated and edited by AUGUSTUS A. ESHNER, M. D., Professor of Clinical Medicine, Philadelphia Polyclinic. Octavo, 440 pages, fully illustrated. Cloth, $2.50 net.

LOCKWOOD'S PRACTICE OF MEDICINE.
A Manual of the Practice of Medicine. By GEORGE ROE LOCKWOOD, M. D., Professor of Practice in the Women's Medical College of the New York Infirmary, etc. 935 pages, with 75 illustrations in the text, and 22 full-page plates. Cloth, $2.50 net.

LONG'S SYLLABUS OF GYNECOLOGY.
A Syllabus of Gynecology, arranged in Conformity with "An American Text-Book of Gynecology." By J. W. LONG, M. D., Professor of Diseases of Women and Children, Medical College of Virginia, etc. Cloth, interleaved, $1.00 net.

MACDONALD'S SURGICAL DIAGNOSIS AND TREATMENT.
Surgical Diagnosis and Treatment. By J. W. MACDONALD, M. D. Edin., F. R. C. S. Edin., Professor of Practice of Surgery and Clinical Surgery, Hamline University. Handsome octavo, 800 pages, fully illustrated. Cloth, $5.00 net; Sheep or Half Morocco, $6.00 net.

MALLORY AND WRIGHT'S PATHOLOGICAL TECHNIQUE.
Pathological Technique. A Practical Manual for Laboratory Work in Pathology, Bacteriology, and Morbid Anatomy, with chapters on Post-Mortem Technique and the Performance of Autopsies. By FRANK B. MALLORY, A. M., M. D., Assistant Professor of Pathology, Harvard University Medical School, Boston; and JAMES H. WRIGHT, A. M., M. D., Instructor in Pathology, Harvard University Medical School, Boston. Octavo, 396 pages, handsomely illustrated. Cloth, $2.50 net.

McFARLAND'S PATHOGENIC BACTERIA. Third Edition, increased in size by over 100 Pages.
Text-Book upon the Pathogenic Bacteria. By JOSEPH McFARLAND, M. D., Professor of Pathology and Bacteriology, Medico-Chirurgical College of Philadelphia, etc. Octavo volume of 621 pages, finely illustrated. Cloth, $3.25 net.

MEIGS ON FEEDING IN INFANCY.

Feeding in Early Infancy. By ARTHUR V. MEIGS, M. D. Bound in limp cloth, flush edges, 25 cts. net.

MOORE'S ORTHOPEDIC SURGERY.

A Manual of Orthopedic Surgery. By JAMES E. MOORE, M. D., Professor of Orthopedics and Adjunct Professor of Clinical Surgery, University of Minnesota, College of Medicine and Surgery. Octavo volume of 356 pages, handsomely illustrated. Cloth, $2.50 net.

MORTEN'S NURSES' DICTIONARY.

Nurses' Dictionary of Medical Terms and Nursing Treatment. Containing Definitions of the Principal Medical and Nursing Terms and Abbreviations; of the Instruments, Drugs, Diseases, Accidents, Treatments, Operations, Foods, Appliances, etc. encountered in the ward or in the sick-room. By HONNOR MORTEN, author of "How to Become a Nurse," etc. 16mo, 140 pages. Cloth, $1.00 net.

NANCREDE'S ANATOMY AND DISSECTION. Fourth Edition.

Essentials of Anatomy and Manual of Practical Dissection. By CHARLES B. NANCREDE, M. D., LL.D., Professor of Surgery and of Clinical Surgery, University of Michigan, Ann Arbor. Post-octavo, 500 pages, with full-page lithographic plates in colors and nearly 200 illustrations. Extra Cloth (or Oilcloth for dissection-room), $2.00 net.

NANCREDE'S PRINCIPLES OF SURGERY.

Lectures on the Principles of Surgery. By CHARLES B. NANCREDE, M. D., LL.D., Professor of Surgery and of Clinical Surgery, University of Michigan, Ann Arbor. Octavo, 398 pages, illustrated. Cloth, $2.50 net.

NORRIS'S SYLLABUS OF OBSTETRICS. Third Edition, Revised.

Syllabus of Obstetrical Lectures in the Medical Department of the University of Pennsylvania. By RICHARD C. NORRIS, A. M., M. D., Instructor in Obstetrics and Lecturer on Clinical and Operative Obstetrics, University of Pennsylvania. Crown octavo, 222 pages. Cloth, interleaved for notes, $2.00 net.

OGDEN ON THE URINE.

Clinical Examination of the Urine and Urinary Diagnosis. A Clinical Guide for the Use of Practitioners and Students of Medicine and Surgery. By J. BERGEN OGDEN, M. D., Instructor in Chemistry, Harvard University Medical School. Handsome octavo, 416 pages, with 54 illustrations, and a number of colored plates. Cloth, $3.00 net.

PENROSE'S DISEASES OF WOMEN. Third Edition, Revised.

A Text-Book of Diseases of Women. By CHARLES B. PENROSE, M. D., PH. D., formerly Professor of Gynecology in the University of Pennsylvania. Octavo volume of 531 pages, handsomely illustrated. Cloth, $3.75 net.

PRYOR—PELVIC INFLAMMATIONS.
The Treatment of Pelvic Inflammations through the Vagina. By W. R. PRYOR, M. D., Professor of Gynecology, New York Polyclinic. 12mo, 248 pages, handsomely illustrated. Cloth, $2.00 net.

PYE'S BANDAGING.
Elementary Bandaging and Surgical Dressing. With Directions concerning the Immediate Treatment of Cases of Emergency. By WALTER PYE, F. R. C. S., late Surgeon to St. Mary's Hospital, London. Small 12mo, over 80 illustrations. Cloth, flexible covers, 75 cts. net.

PYLE'S PERSONAL HYGIENE.
A Manual of Personal Hygiene. Proper Living upon a Physiologic Basis. Edited by WALTER L. PYLE, M. D., Assistant Surgeon to the Wills Eye Hospital, Philadelphia. Octavo volume of 344 pages, fully illustrated. Cloth, $1.50 net.

RAYMOND'S PHYSIOLOGY.
A Manual of Physiology. By JOSEPH H. RAYMOND, A. M., M. D., Professor of Physiology and Hygiene and Lecturer on Gynecology in the Long Island College Hospital. 382 pages, 102 illustrations, and 4 full-page colored plates. Cloth, $1.25 net.

SALINGER AND KALTEYER'S MODERN MEDICINE.
Modern Medicine. By JULIUS L. SALINGER, M. D., Demonstrator of Clinical Medicine, Jefferson Medical College ; and F. J. KALTEYER, M. D., Assistant Demonstrator of Clinical Medicine, Jefferson Medical College. Handsome octavo, 801 pages, illustrated. Cloth, $4.00 net.

SAUNDBY'S RENAL AND URINARY DISEASES.
Lectures on Renal and Urinary Diseases. By ROBERT SAUNDBY, M. D. Edin., Fellow of the Royal College of Physicians, London, and of the Royal Medico-Chirurgical Society ; Professor of Medicine in Mason College, Birmingham, etc. Octavo, 434 pages, with numerous illustrations and 4 colored plates. Cloth, $2.50 net.

SAUNDERS' MEDICAL HAND-ATLASES. See pp. 16 and 17.

SAUNDERS' POCKET MEDICAL FORMULARY. Sixth Edition, Revised.
By WILLIAM M. POWELL, M. D., author of "Essentials of Diseases of Children"; Member of Philadelphia Pathological Society. Containing 1844 formulæ from the best-known authorities. With an Appendix containing Posological Table, Formulæ and Doses for Hypodermic Medication, Poisons and their Antidotes, Diameters of the Female Pelvis and Fetal Head, Obstetrical Table, Diet List for Various Diseases, Materials and Drugs used in Antiseptic Surgery, Treatment of Asphyxia from Drowning, Surgical Remembrancer, Tables of Incompatibles, Eruptive Fevers, etc., etc. Handsomely bound in flexible morocco, with side index, wallet, and flap. $2.00 net.

SAUNDERS' QUESTION-COMPENDS. See pages 14 and 15.

SCUDDER'S FRACTURES. Second Edition, Revised.
The Treatment of Fractures. By CHAS L. SCUDDER, M. D., Assistant in Clinical and Operative Surgery, Harvard University Medical School. Octavo, 433 pages, with nearly 600 original illustrations. Polished Buckram, $4.50 net; Half Morocco, $5.50 net.

SENN'S GENITO-URINARY TUBERCULOSIS.
Tuberculosis of the Genito-Urinary Organs, Male and Female. By NICHOLAS SENN, M. D., PH. D., LL.D., Professor of the Practice of Surgery and of Clinical Surgery, Rush Medical College, Chicago. Handsome octavo volume of 320 pages, illustrated. Cloth, $3.00 net.

SENN'S PRACTICAL SURGERY.
Practical Surgery. By NICHOLAS SENN, M. D., PH. D., LL.D., Professor of the Practice of Surgery and of Clinical Surgery, Rush Medical College, Chicago. Handsome octavo volume of over 1000 pages, profusely illustrated. *In Press.*

SENN'S SYLLABUS OF SURGERY.
A Syllabus of Lectures on the Practice of Surgery, arranged in conformity with "An American Text-Book of Surgery." By NICHOLAS SENN, M. D., PH.D., LL.D., Professor of the Practice of Surgery and of Clinical Surgery. Rush Medical College, Chicago. Cloth, $1.50 net.

SENN'S TUMORS. Second Edition, Revised.
Pathology and Surgical Treatment of Tumors. By NICHOLAS SENN, M. D., PH.D., LL.D., Professor of the Practice of Surgery and of Clinical Surgery, Rush Medical College, Chicago. Octavo volume of 718 pages, with 478 illustrations, includidg 12 full-page plates in colors. Cloth, $5.00 net; Sheep or Half Morocco, $6.00 net.

STARR'S DIETS FOR INFANTS AND CHILDREN.
Diets for Infants and Children in Health and in Disease. By LOUIS STARR, M. D., Editor of "An American Text-Book of the Diseases of Children." 230 blanks (pocket-book size), perforated and neatly bound in flexible morocco. $1.25 net.

STENGEL'S PATHOLOGY. Third Edition, Thoroughly Revised.
A Text-Book of Pathology. By ALFRED STENGEL. M. D., Professor of Clinical Medicine, University of Pennsylvania; Visiting Physician to the Pennsylvania Hospital. Handsome octavo, 873 pages, nearly 400 illustrations, many of them in colors. Cloth, $5.00 net; Sheep or Half Morocco, $6.00 net.

STENGEL AND WHITE ON THE BLOOD.
The Blood in its Clinical and Pathological Relations. By ALFRED STENGEL. M. D., Professor of Clinical Medicine, University of Pennsylvania; and C. Y. WHITE, JR., M. D., Instructor in Clinical Medicine, University of Pennsylvania. *In Press.*

STEVENS' MATERIA MEDICA AND THERAPEUTICS. Second Edition, Revised.
A Manual of Materia Medica and Therapeutics. By A. A. STEVENS, A. M., M. D., Lecturer on Physical Diagnosis in the University of Pennsylvania. Post-octavo, 445 pages. Flexible Leather, $2.00 net.

STEVENS' PRACTICE OF MEDICINE. Fifth Edition, Revised.
A Manual of the Practice of Medicine. By A. A. STEVENS, A. M., M. D., Lecturer on Physical Diagnosis in the University of Pennsylvania. Specially intended for students preparing for graduation and hospital examinations. Post-octavo, 519 pages; illustrated. Flexible Leather, $2.00 net.

STEWART'S PHYSIOLOGY. Fourth Edition, Revised.
A Manual of Physiology, with Practical Exercises. For Students and Practitioners. By G. N. STEWART, M. A., M. D., D. Sc., Professor of Physiology in the Western Reserve University, Cleveland, Ohio. Octavo volume of 894 pages; 336 illustrations and 5 colored plates. Cloth, $3.75 net.

STONEY'S MATERIA MEDICA FOR NURSES.
Materia Medica for Nurses. By EMILY A. M. STONEY, late Superintendent of the Training-School for Nurses, Carney Hospital, South Boston, Mass. Handsome octavo volume of 306 pages. Cloth, $1.50 net.

STONEY'S NURSING. Second Edition, Revised.
Practical Points in Nursing. For Nurses in Private Practice. By EMILY A. M. STONEY, late Superintendent of the Training-School for Nurses, Carney Hospital, South Boston, Mass. 456 pages, with 73 engravings and 8 colored and half-tone plates. Cloth, $1.75 net.

STONEY'S SURGICAL TECHNIC FOR NURSES.
Bacteriology and Surgical Technic for Nurses. By EMILY A. M. STONEY, late Superintendent of the Training-School for Nurses, Carney Hospital, South Boston, Mass. 12mo volume, fully illustrated. Cloth, $1.25 net.

THOMAS'S DIET LISTS. Second Edition, Revised.
Diet Lists and Sick-Room Dietary. By JEROME B. THOMAS, M. D., Instructor in Materia Medica, Long Island Hospital; Assistant Bacteriologist to the Hoagland Laboratory. Cloth, $1.25 net. Send for sample sheet.

THORNTON'S DOSE-BOOK AND PRESCRIPTION-WRITING.
Dose-Book and Manual of Prescription-Writing. By E. Q. THORNTON, M. D., Demonstrator of Therapeutics, Jefferson Medical College, Philadelphia. 334 pages, illustrated. Cloth, $1.25 net.

VAN VALZAH AND NISBET'S DISEASES OF THE STOMACH.
Diseases of the Stomach. By WILLIAM W. VAN VALZAH, M. D., Professor of General Medicine and Diseases of the Digestive System and the Blood, New York Polyclinic; and J. DOUGLAS NISBET, M. D., Adjunct Professor of General Medicine and Diseases of the Digestive System and the Blood, New York Polyclinic. Octavo volume of 674 pages, illustrated. Cloth, $3.50 net.

VECKI'S SEXUAL IMPOTENCE.
The Pathology and Treatment of Sexual Impotence. By VICTOR G. VECKI, M. D. From the second German edition, revised and enlarged. Demi-octavo, 291 pages. Cloth, $2.00 net.

VIERORDT'S MEDICAL DIAGNOSIS. Fourth Edition, Revised.
Medical Diagnosis. By DR. OSWALD VIERORDT, Professor of Medicine, University of Heidelberg. Translated, with additions, from the fifth enlarged German edition, with the author's permission, by FRANCIS H. STUART, A. M., M. D. Handsome octavo volume, 603 pages; 194 woodcuts, many of them in colors. Cloth, 4.00 net; Sheep or Half-Morocco, $5.00 net.

WATSON'S HANDBOOK FOR NURSES.
A Handbook for Nurses. By J. K. WATSON, M. D. Edin. American Edition, under supervision of A. A. STEVENS, A. M., M. D., Lecturer on Physical Diagnosis, University of Pennsylvania. 12mo, 413 pages, 73 illustrations. Cloth, $1.50 net.

WARREN'S SURGICAL PATHOLOGY. Second Edition.
Surgical Pathology and Therapeutics. By JOHN COLLINS WARREN, M. D., LL.D., F. R. C. S. (Hon.), Professor of Surgery, Harvard Medical School. Handsome octavo, 873 pages; 136 relief and lithographic illustrations, 33 in colors. With an Appendix on Scientific Aids to Surgical Diagnosis, and a series of articles on Regional Bacteriology. Cloth. $5.00 net; Sheep or Half Morocco, $6.00 net.

SAUNDERS'
QUESTION=COMPENDS.

ARRANGED IN QUESTION AND ANSWER FORM.

The Most Complete and Best Illustrated Series of Compends Ever Issued.

NOW THE STANDARD AUTHORITIES IN MEDICAL LITERATURE
WITH

Students and Practitioners in every City of the United States and Canada.

Since the issue of the first volume of the Saunders Question-Compends,

OVER 175,000 COPIES

of these unrivalled publications have been sold. This enormous sale is indisputable evidence of the value of these self-helps to students and physicians.

SEE NEXT PAGE FOR LIST.

Saunders' Question=Compend Series.

Price, Cloth, $1.00 net per copy, except when otherwise noted.

"Where the work of preparing students' manuals is to end we cannot say, but the Saunders Series, in our opinion, bears off the palm at present."—*New York Medical Record.*

1. **Essentials of Physiology.** A new work in preparation.
2. **Essentials of Surgery.** By EDWARD MARTIN, M. D. Seventh edition, revised, with an Appendix and a chapter on Appendicitis.
3. **Essentials of Anatomy.** By CHARLES B. NANCREDE, M. D. Sixth edition, thoroughly revised and enlarged.
4. **Essentials of Medical Chemistry, Organic and Inorganic.** By LAWRENCE WOLFF, M. D. Fifth edition, revised.
5. **Essentials of Obstetrics.** By W. EASTERLY ASHTON, M. D. Fourth edition, revised and enlarged.
6. **Essentials of Pathology and Morbid Anatomy.** By F. J. KALTEYER, M. D. *In preparation.*
7. **Essentials of Materia Medica, Therapeutics, and Prescription-Writing.** By HENRY MORRIS, M. D. Fifth edition, revised.
8, 9. **Essentials of Practice of Medicine.** By HENRY MORRIS, M. D. An Appendix on URINE EXAMINATION. By LAWRENCE WOLFF, M. D. Third edition, enlarged by some 300 Essential Formulæ, selected from eminent authorities, by WM. M. POWELL, M. D. (Double number, $1.50 net.)
10. **Essentials of Gynecology.** By EDWIN B. CRAGIN, M. D. Fourth edition, revised.
11. **Essentials of Diseases of the Skin.** By HENRY W. STELWAGON, M. D. Fourth edition, revised and enlarged.
12. **Essentials of Minor Surgery, Bandaging, and Venereal Diseases.** By EDWARD MARTIN, M. D. Second edition, revised and enlarged.
13. **Essentials of Legal Medicine, Toxicology, and Hygiene.** This volume is at present out of print.
14. **Essentials of Diseases of the Eye, Nose, and Throat.** By EDWARD JACKSON, M. D., and E. B. GLEASON, M. D. Second edition, revised.
15. **Essentials of Diseases of Children.** By WILLIAM M. POWELL, M. D. Second edition.
16. **Essentials of Examination of Urine.** By LAWRENCE WOLFF, M. D. Colored "VOGEL SCALE." (75 cents net.)
17. **Essentials of Diagnosis.** By S. SOLIS-COHEN, M. D., and A. A. ESHNER, M. D. Second edition, thoroughly revised.
18. **Essentials of Practice of Pharmacy.** By LUCIUS E. SAYRE. Second edition, revised and enlarged.
20. **Essentials of Bacteriology.** By M. V. BALL, M. D. Fourth edition, revised.
21. **Essentials of Nervous Diseases and Insanity.** By JOHN C. SHAW, M. D. Third edition, revised.
22. **Essentials of Medical Physics.** By FRED J. BROCKWAY, M. D. Second edition, revised.
23. **Essentials of Medical Electricity.** By DAVID D. STEWART, M. D., and EDWARD S. LAWRANCE, M. D.
24. **Essentials of Diseases of the Ear.** By E. B. GLEASON, M. D. Second edition, revised and greatly enlarged.

A NEW VOLUME.

25. **Essentials of Histology.** By LOUIS LEROY, M. D. With 73 original illustrations.

Pamphlet containing specimen pages, etc., sent free upon application.

Saunders' Medical Hand=Atlases.

VOLUMES NOW READY.

ATLAS AND EPITOME OF INTERNAL MEDICINE AND CLINICAL DIAGNOSIS.

By DR. CHR. JAKOB, of Erlangen. Edited by AUGUSTUS A. ESHNER, M. D., Professor of Clinical Medicine, Philadelphia Polyclinic. With 179 colored figures on 68 plates, 64 text-illustrations, 259 pages of text. Cloth, $3.00 net.

ATLAS OF LEGAL MEDICINE.

By DR. E. R. VON HOFFMAN, of Vienna. Edited by FREDERICK PETERSON, M. D., Chief of Clinic, Nervous Department, College of Physicians and Surgeons, New York. With 120 colored figures on 56 plates and 193 beautiful half-tone illustrations. Cloth, $3.50 net.

ATLAS AND EPITOME OF DISEASES OF THE LARYNX.

By DR. L. GRUNWALD, of Munich. Edited by CHARLES P. GRAYSON, M. D., Physician-in-Charge, Throat and Nose Department, Hospital of the University of Pennsylvania. With 107 colored figures on 44 plates, 25 text-illustrations, and 103 pages of text. Cloth, $2.50 net.

ATLAS AND EPITOME OF OPERATIVE SURGERY.

By DR. O. ZUCKERKANDL, of Vienna. Edited by J. CHALMERS DACOSTA, M. D., Professor of Principles of Surgery and Clinical Surgery, Jefferson Medical College, Philadelphia. With 24 colored plates, 214 text-illustrations, and 395 pages of text. Cloth, $3.00 net.

ATLAS AND EPITOME OF SYPHILIS AND THE VENEREAL DISEASES.

By PROF. DR. FRANZ MRACEK, of Vienna. Edited by L. BOLTON BANGS, M. D., Professor of Genito-Urinary Surgery, University and Bellevue Hospital Medical College, New York. With 71 colored plates, 16 illustrations, and 122 pages of text. Cloth, $3.50 net.

ATLAS AND EPITOME OF EXTERNAL DISEASES OF THE EYE.

By DR. O. HAAB, of Zurich. Edited by G. E. DE SCHWEINITZ, M. D., Professor of Ophthalmology, Jefferson Medical College, Philadelphia. With 76 colored illustrations on 40 plates and 228 pages of text. Cloth, $3.00 net.

ATLAS AND EPITOME OF SKIN DISEASES.

By PROF. DR. FRANZ MRACEK, of Vienna. Edited by HENRY W. STELWAGON. M. D., Clinical Professor of Dermatology, Jefferson Medical College, Philadelphia. With 63 colored plates, 39 half-tone illustrations, and 200 pages of text. Cloth, $3.50 net.

ATLAS AND EPITOME OF SPECIAL PATHOLOGICAL HISTOLOGY.

By DR. H. DURCK, of Munich. Edited by LUDWIG HEKTOEN, M. D., Professor of Pathology, Rush Medical College, Chicago. In Two Parts. Part I. *Ready*, including Circulatory, Respiratory, and Gastro-intestinal Tract, 120 colored figures on 62 plates, 158 pages of text. Part II. *Ready Shortly.* Price of Part I., $3.00 net.

Saunders' Medical Hand=Atlases.

VOLUMES JUST ISSUED.

ATLAS AND EPITOME OF DISEASES CAUSED BY ACCIDENTS.

By DR. ED. GOLEBIEWSKI, of Berlin. Translated and edited with additions by PEARCE BAILEY, M. D., Attending Physician to the Department of Corrections and to the Almshouse and Incurable Hospitals, New York. With 40 colored plates, 143 text-illustrations, and 600 pages of text. Cloth, $4.00 net.

ATLAS AND EPITOME OF GYNECOLOGY.

By DR. O. SHAEFFER, of Heidelberg. *From the Second Revised German Edition.* Edited by RICHARD C. NORRIS, A. M., M. D., Gynecologist to the Methodist Episcopal and the Philadelphia Hospitals; Surgeon-in-Charge of Preston Retreat, Philadelphia. With 90 colored plates, 65 text-illustrations, and 308 pages of text. Cloth, $3.50 net.

ATLAS AND EPITOME OF THE NERVOUS SYSTEM AND ITS DISEASES.

By PROFESSOR DR. CHR. JAKOB, of Erlangen. *From the Second Revised German Edition.* Edited by EDWARD D. FISHER, M. D., Professor of Diseases of the Nervous System, University and Bellevue Hospital Medical College, New York. With 83 plates and a copious text. $3.50 net.

ATLAS AND EPITOME OF LABOR AND OPERATIVE OBSTETRICS.

By DR. O. SHAEFFER, of Heidelberg. *From the Fifth Revised German Edition.* Edited by J. CLIFTON EDGAR, M. D., Professor of Obstetrics and Clinical Midwifery, Cornell University Medical School. With 126 colored illustrations. $2.00 net.

ATLAS AND EPITOME OF OBSTETRICAL DIAGNOSIS AND TREATMENT.

By DR. O. SHAEFFER, of Heidelberg. *From the Second Revised German Edition.* Edited by J. CLIFTON EDGAR, M. D., Professor of Obstetrics and Clinical Midwifery, Cornell University Medical School. 72 colored plates, numerous text-illustrations, and copious text. $3.00 net.

IN PRESS FOR EARLY PUBLICATION.

ATLAS AND EPITOME OF OPHTHALMOSCOPY AND OPHTHALMOSCOPIC DIAGNOSIS.

By DR. O. HAAB, of Zürich. *From the Third Revised and Enlarged German Edition.* Edited by G. E. DE SCHWEINITZ, M. D., Professor of Ophthalmology, Jefferson Medical College, Philadelphia. With 149 colored figures and 82 pages of text.

ADDITIONAL VOLUMES IN PREPARATION.

CLASSIFIED LIST
OF THE
MEDICAL PUBLICATIONS
OF
W. B. SAUNDERS & COMPANY

ANATOMY, EMBRYOLOGY, HISTOLOGY.
Bohm, Davidoff, and Huber—A Text-Book of Histology, ... 4
Clarkson—A Text-Book of Histology, . . 5
Haynes—A Manual of Anatomy, . . . 7
Heisler—A Text-Book of Embryology, . 7
Leroy—Essentials of Histology, ... 15
Nancrede—Essentials of Anatomy, . . . 15
Nancrede—Essentials of Anatomy and Manual of Practical Dissection, ... 10

BACTERIOLOGY.
Ball—Essentials of Bacteriology, ... 15
Crookshank—Bacteriology, ... 5
Frothingham—Laboratory Guide, . . . 6
Levy and Klemperer's Clinical Bacteriology, ... 9
Mallory and Wright—Pathological Technique, ... 9
McFarland—Pathogenic Bacteria, . . . 9

CHARTS, DIET-LISTS, ETC.
Griffith—Infant's Weight Chart, ... 7
Hart—Diet in Sickness and in Health, . 7
Keen—Operation Blank, ... 8
Laine—Temperature Chart, ... 9
Meigs—Feeding in Early Infancy, . . . 10
Starr—Diets for Infants and Children, . 12
Thomas—Diet-Lists, ... 13

CHEMISTRY AND PHYSICS.
Brockway—Essentials of Medical Physics, ... 15
Wolff—Essentials of Medical Chemistry, 15

CHILDREN.
An American Text-Book of Diseases of Children, ... 1
Griffith—Care of the Baby, ... 7
Griffith—Infant's Weight Chart, ... 7
Meigs—Feeding in Early Infancy, . . . 10
Powell—Essentials of Diseases of Children, ... 15
Starr—Diets for Infants and Children, . 12

DIAGNOSIS.
Cohen and Eshner—Essentials of Diagnosis, ... 15
Corwin—Physical Diagnosis, ... 5
Macdonald—Surgical Diagnosis and Treatment, ... 9
Vierordt—Medical Diagnosis, ... 14

DICTIONARIES.
The American Illustrated Medical Dictionary, ... 3
The American Pocket Medical Dictionary, ... 3
Morton—Nurses' Dictionary, ... 10

EYE, EAR, NOSE, AND THROAT.
An American Text-Book of Diseases of the Eye, Ear, Nose, and Throat, . . 1
De Schweinitz—Diseases of the Eye, . 6
Friedrich and Curtis—Rhinology, Laryngology, and Otology, ... 6
Gleason—Essentials of Diseases of the Ear, ... 15
Grunwald and Grayson—Atlas of Diseases of the Larynx, ... 16
Haab and De Schweinitz—Atlas of External Diseases of the Eye, ... 16
Jackson—Manual of Diseases of the Eye, 8
Jackson and Gleason—Essentials of Diseases of the Eye, Nose, and Throat, 15
Kyle—Diseases of the Nose and Throat, 9

GENITO-URINARY.
An American Text-Book of Genito-Urinary and Skin Diseases, ... 2
Hyde and Montgomery—Syphilis and the Venereal Diseases, ... 8
Martin—Essentials of Minor Surgery, Bandaging, and Venereal Diseases, . . 15
Mracek and Bangs—Atlas of Syphilis and the Venereal Diseases, ... 16
Saundby—Renal and Urinary Diseases, 11
Senn—Genito-Urinary Tuberculosis, . . 12
Vecki—Sexual Impotence, ... 14

GYNECOLOGY.
American Text-Book of Gynecology, . . 2
Cragin—Essentials of Gynecology, . . 15
Garrigues—Diseases of Women, ... 6
Long—Syllabus of Gynecology, ... 9
Penrose—Diseases of Women, ... 10
Pryor—Pelvic Inflammations, ... 11
Schaeffer and Norris—Atlas of Gynecology, ... 17

MATERIA MEDICA, PHARMACOLOGY, AND THERAPEUTICS.
An American Text-Book of Applied Therapeutics, ... 1
Butler—Text-Book of Materia Medica, Therapeutics, and Pharmacology, . . 4
Cerna—Notes on the Newer Remedies, . 4
Morris—Essentials of Materia Medica and Therapeutics, ... 15
Saunders' Pocket Medical Formulary, . 11
Sayre—Essentials of Pharmacy, ... 15
Stevens—Manual of Therapeutics, . . . 13
Stoney—Materia Medica for Nurses, . . 13
Thornton—Dose-Book and Manual of Prescription-Writing, ... 13

MEDICAL JURISPRUDENCE AND TOXICOLOGY.
Chapman—Medical Jurisprudence and Toxicology, ... 5

Golebiewski and Bailey—Atlas of Diseases Caused by Accidents, ... 17
Hofmann and Peterson—Atlas of Legal Medicine, ... 16

NERVOUS AND MENTAL DISEASES, ETC.

Chapin—Compendium of Insanity, . . . 5
Church and Peterson—Nervous and Mental Diseases, ... 5
Shaw—Essentials of Nervous Diseases and Insanity, ... 15

NURSING.

Davis—Obstetric and Gynecologic Nursing, ... 6
Griffith—The Care of the Baby, ... 7
Hart—Diet in Sickness and in Health, . . 7
Meigs—Feeding in Early Infancy, . . . 10
Morten—Nurses' Dictionary, ... 10
Stoney—Materia Medica for Nurses, . . 13
Stoney—Practical Points in Nursing, . . 13
Stoney—Surgical Technic for Nurses, . 13
Watson—Handbook for Nurses, ... 14

OBSTETRICS.

An American Text-Book of Obstetrics, 2
Ashton—Essentials of Obstetrics, ... 15
Boisliniere—Obstetric Accidents, . . . 4
Dorland—Manual of Obstetrics, ... 6
Hirst—Text-Book of Obstetrics, ... 7
Norris—Syllabus of Obstetrics, ... 10
Schaeffer and Edgar—Atlas of Obstetrical Diagnosis and Treatment, ... 17

PATHOLOGY.

An American Text-Book of Pathology. 2
Durck and Hektoen—Atlas of Pathologic Histology, ... 16
Kalteyer—Essentials of Pathology, . . 15
Mallory and Wright—Pathological Technique, ... 9
Senn—Pathology and Surgical Treatment of Tumors, ... 12
Stengel—Text-Book of Pathology, . . . 12
Warren—Surgical Pathology, ... 14

PHYSIOLOGY.

An American Text-Book of Physiology, ... 2
—Essentials of Physiology, ... 15
Raymond—Manual of Physiology, . . . 11
Stewart—Manual of Physiology, . . . 13

PRACTICE OF MEDICINE.

An American Year-Book of Medicine and Surgery, ... 3
Anders—Text-Book of the Practice of Medicine, ... 4
Eichhorst—Practice of Medicine, . . . 6
Lockwood—Practice of Medicine, . . . 9
Morris—Essentials of Practice of Medicine, ... 15
Salinger and Kalteyer—Modern Medicine, ... 11
Stevens—Manual of Practice of Medicine, ... 13

SKIN AND VENEREAL.

An American Text-Book of Genito-Urinary and Skin Diseases, ... 2
Hyde and Montgomery—Syphilis and the Venereal Diseases, ... 8
Martin—Essentials of Minor Surgery, Bandaging, and Venereal Diseases, . . 15
Mracek and Stelwagon—Atlas of Diseases of the Skin, ... 16
Stelwagon—Essentials of Diseases of the Skin, ... 15

SURGERY.

An American Text-Book of Surgery, 2
An American Year-Book of Medicine and Surgery, ... 3
Beck—Fractures, ... 4
Beck—Manual of Surgical Asepsis, . . . 4
Da Costa—Manual of Surgery, ... 5
International Text-Book of Surgery, . 8
Keen—Operation Blank, ... 8
Keen—The Surgical Complications and Sequels of Typhoid Fever, ... 8
Macdonald — Surgical Diagnosis and Treatment, ... 9
Martin—Essentials of Minor Surgery, Bandaging, and Venereal Diseases, . . 15
Martin—Essentials of Surgery, ... 15
Moore—Orthopedic Surgery, ... 10
Nancrede—Principles of Surgery, . . . 10
Pye—Bandaging and Surgical Dressing, 11
Scudder—Treatment of Fractures, . . . 12
Senn—Genito-Urinary Tuberculosis, . 12
Senn—Practical Surgery, ... 12
Senn—Syllabus of Surgery, ... 12
Senn—Pathology and Surgical Treatment of Tumors, ... 12
Warren—Surgical Pathology and Therapeutics, ... 14
Zuckerkandl and Da Costa—Atlas of Operative Surgery, ... 16

URINE AND URINARY DISEASES.

Ogden—Clinical Examination of the Urine, ... 10
Saundby—Renal and Urinary Diseases, 11
Wolff—Examination of Urine, ... 15

MISCELLANEOUS.

Abbott—Hygiene of Transmissible Diseases, ... 3
Bastin—Laboratory Exercises in Botany, ... 4
Golebiewski and Bailey—Atlas of Diseases Caused by Accidents, ... 17
Gould and Pyle—Anomalies and Curiosities of Medicine, ... 7
Grafstrom—Massage, ... 7
Keating—Examination for Life Insurance, ... 8
Pyle—A Manual of Personal Hygiene, . 11
Saunders' Medical Hand-Atlases, . 16, 17
Saunders' Pocket Medical Formulary, . 11
Saunders' Question-Compends, . . . 14, 15
Stewart and Lawrence—Essentials of Medical Electricity, ... 15
Thornton—Dose-Book and Manual of Prescription-Writing, ... 13
Van Valzah and Nisbet—Diseases of the Stomach, ... 13

Nothnagel's Encyclopedia

OF

Special Pathology and Therapeutics.

IT is universally acknowledged that the Germans lead the world in Internal Medicine; and of all the German works on this subject, Nothnagel's "Special Pathology and Therapeutics" is conceded by scholars to be without question the **best System of Medicine in existence.** So necessary is this book in the study of Internal Medicine that it comes largely to this country in the original German. In view of these facts, Messrs. W. B. Saunders & Company have arranged with the publishers to issue at once **an authorized edition** of this great encyclopedia of medicine in English.

For the present a set of some ten or twelve volumes, representing the most practical part of this encyclopedia, and selected by a competent editor with especial thought of the **needs of the practical physician,** will be published. These volumes will contain the real essence of the entire work, and the purchaser will therefore obtain at less than half the cost the cream of the original. Later the special and more strictly scientific volumes will be offered from time to time.

The work will be translated by men possessing thorough knowledge of both English and German, and **each volume will be edited by a prominent specialist** on the subject to which it is devoted. It will thus be brought thoroughly up to date, and the American edition will be more than a mere translation of the German; for, in addition to the matter contained in the original, it will represent the **very latest views of the leading American specialists** in the various departments of Internal Medicine. The whole System will be under the editorial supervision of a **clinician of recognized authority,** who will select the subjects for the American edition, and will choose the editors of the different volumes.

Unlike most encyclopedias, the publication of this work **will not be extended over a number of years,** but five or six volumes will be issued during the coming year, and the remainder of the series at the same rate. Moreover, each volume will be revised to the date of its publication by the American editor. This will obviate the objection that has heretofore existed to systems published in a number of volumes, since the subscriber will receive the completed work while the earlier volumes are still fresh.

The usual method of publishers, when issuing a work of this kind, has been to compel physicians to take the entire System. This seems to us in many cases to be undesirable. Therefore, in purchasing this encyclopedia, physicians will be given the opportunity of subscribing for the entire System at one time; but any single volume or any number of volumes may be obtained by those who do not desire the complete series. This latter method, while not so profitable to the publisher, **offers to the purchaser many advantages** which will be appreciated by those who do not care to subscribe for the entire work at one time.

This American edition of Nothnagel's Encyclopedia will, without question, form **the greatest System of Medicine ever produced,** and the publishers feel confident that it will meet with general favor in the medical profession.

Milton Keynes UK
Ingram Content Group UK Ltd.
UKHW012010300124
436988UK00008B/563